Learning Simply Accounting 2009 Pro:
A Simulation Approach

Custom Edition

NELSON / EDUCATION

NELSON / EDUCATION

ISBN-13: 978-0-17-64955-6
ISBN-10: 0-17-649559-2

Consists of Selections from:

*Learning Simply Accounting by
Sage Pro 2009*
Freedman/Smith
ISBN 0-17-650218-1, © 2010

*Learning Simply Accounting by
Sage Pro 2007*
Freedman/Smith
ISBN 0-17-610533-6, © 2007

Contents

DEDICATION

This book is dedicated to all volunteers in your community who give their time and effort to help those in need. If you are a volunteer, may I offer my own thank you. We all appreciate the work you do to make your community a wonderful place to live.

ACKNOWLEDGMENTS

I would like to thank the individuals below who contributed to making this textbook a success. On behalf of the team, I hope that you find using this book a rewarding experience.

My wife **Marlene**, who reviewed the manuscript, my sons **Jeremy** and **Jason**, daughter-in-law **Julie-Ann**, grand-daughters **Jordan** and **Jessica**, for their support and encouragement while the book was in progress. I realize that I did not spend as much time with you as I would have liked.

Carol Smith, Professor at Humber College, my colleague who was the technical reviewer for this textbook, reviewed the manuscript and offered numerous suggestions, ideas and helpful criticisms to make the textbook easy to understand.

Rosemary Imola, Professor at Mohawk College, who was the keystroke reviewer, for her assistance in checking the manuscript, and the slideshows, who offered numerous suggestions and helpful criticisms to make the textbook easy to understand.

Simply Accounting by Sage staff; **Jaclyn Ng, Jim Collins,** and other members of Simply Technical Support for their ongoing technical assistance.

My own students, who always come up with new ways of looking at the same information and whose suggestions help make the textbook material more effective.

Diane van Ingen, desktop technician, who contributed many suggestions and ideas to help make this textbook visually appealing.

Rebecca Pembry-Spratley, for creating the slideshows.

Alan Cohen, for his support and encouragement.

Rod Banister, Jim Polley, Gordon Rollason and **Gail Marsden** of Thomson Nelson for their assistance on this project.

Harvey Freedman

> *Tell me and I forget.*
> *Show me how and I remember.*
> *Let me do it and I understand.*
> - Zen Proverb

CREDITS

Becky Pembry-Spratley, Project Manager
Rosemary Imola, Keystroke Tester and Reviewer (Slideshows)
Diane van Ingen, Desktop Technician

This textbook is a comprehensive introduction to *Simply Accounting 2007 Pro version B* using the hands-on approach. It takes you step by step through **analyzing**, **recording** and **processing** transactions in all Simply modules. The text includes **converting from** a manual accounting system by setting up the new Simply company data files. Month-End and Year-End processing, Project Costing, Account Reconciliation and Multi-currency features are also shown.

All Simply modules are covered in this text. They are:

1. GENERAL
2. PAYABLES
3. RECEIVABLES
4. PAYROLL
5. INVENTORY & SERVICES
6. PROJECT
7. TIME & BILLING

Software

Included with this textbook is the Simply 2007 Pro **Student Version** software for use at home. Do NOT load the software until you have read Appendix A, at the back of this textbook, for system requirements and instruction on loading the software as well as restrictions on its use.

Caution: Do not load the Simply software until you have read Appendix A at the back of this textbook.

Slideshows

On the Student Data CD that accompanies this book, you will find PowerPoint slideshows that are designed to help you understand accounting concepts that relate to specific Simply Accounting features. You will be prompted to run these slideshows at relevant points throughout the book. For instructions on how to run the slideshows, click on **About This CD** and read the information.

Other Features

The textbook also includes numerous challenge exercises to provide additional experience in using the various Simply modules. A summary of the various assignments is given later in this Preface.

What's New in Simply 2007, Appendix CD-U, in the Appendix folder of your Student Data CD will give you an overview of the new features of Simply. This information is useful for both new and experienced users of Simply Accounting.

A **Table of Contents** at the beginning of each chapter provides a detailed list of the topics in the chapter. A detailed index is also provided at the end of the textbook for your easy reference.

At the end of each chapter, a glossary appears containing **Accounting and Simply Accounting Terminology** used in the chapter. Non-accounting words are used to help you understand the material. Review questions are also given at the end of each chapter.

The first three chapters, GENERAL (Boats Company), RECEIVABLES (Santos Luggage) and PAYABLES (Tyson's Toys) will guide you in entering transactions using the software as you would in many businesses.

Chapter 2 and 3 have been split into parts A and B. Part A contains basic transactions (e.g., sales, purchases, returns, receipts, payments) that occur on a regular basis and part B contains more advanced topic transactions.

Each chapter and Challenge Exercise contains one or more transactions with the student name as a vendor or customer.

In Chapter 4 (Sarah's Kitchen Stores) you will set up a company's computer records by creating the data files, ledger accounts and other information.

In Chapter 5 (Sarah's Kitchen Stores) you will use **source documents** to record transactions in the GENERAL, PAYABLES and RECEIVABLES modules.

Chapter 6 (Shirts & Ties) is a comprehensive challenge exercise that requires you to set up a company from scratch and record transactions from source documents.

The later chapters cover the PAYROLL (Creative Wallpaper), INVENTORY & SERVICES (Printers Company Ltd.), and PROJECT (HotTubs Company) modules, RECONCILIATION & DEPOSITS (Wedding Flowers Company) journal, and Multi-currency (Saddles Company). These chapters reinforce learning by including transactions that require procedures learned in earlier chapters.

As you complete each chapter, it would be a good idea to cross-reference your entries and reports with the solutions provided to the instructor.

Appendices

Various appendices provide you with additional information that would be useful to you both in your current course and when using Simply on the job. They are provided at the back of this textbook and on your Student Data CD.

Appendix A (in textbook) Installing Simply 2007 Pro Student Version Software

The following appendices are provided on the Student Data CD. References in the textbook that specify **Appendix CD** — refer to appendices on your Student Data CD.

Appendix CD-A	Basics of Accounting
Appendix CD-B	Check & Repair Tool
Appendix CD-C	Adding a New G/L Account
Appendix CD-D	Printing a Tax (GST) Report
Appendix CD-E	Budgets – General Ledger
Appendix CD-F	Printing in Batches
Appendix CD-G	Processing in Batches
Appendix CD-H	New Business Guide
Appendix CD-I	Checklists for Task Completion
Appendix CD-J	Exporting Information
Appendix CD-K	Graphs Feature
Appendix CD-L	Data Integrity
Appendix CD-M	Post-Dated Cheques
Appendix CD-N	Restocking Fee
Appendix CD-O	Security – Passwords

Appendix CD-P	Payroll Garnishment
Appendix CD-Q	Names Fields
Appendix CD-R	Quick Reference Guide (*Print this guide for quick exercise references.*)
Appendix CD-S	Microsoft Office Documents
Appendix CD-T	Reimbursement (Payroll)
Appendix CD-U	What's New in Simply 2007
Appendix CD-V	Mini-Guide Receivables—Payables
Appendix CD-W	Printing Packing Slips
Appendix CD-X	Removing an Account from a Wrong Section
Appendix CD-Y	To Cancel a History Invoice
Appendix CD-Z	Icon Bars and Menu items
Appendix CD-AA	Setting Up a New Company File using a Template
Appendix CD-AB	Creating a Report Template
Appendix CD-AC	Adding a Salesperson's Name to an Invoice
Appendix CD-AD	Time and Billing Module
Appendix CD-AE	Setting Up Simply Custom Forms for Printing/E-mail
Appendix CD-AF	Detailed Project Budget Reports
Appendix CD-AG	No Taxes Event

GST and PST are explained in Chapter 2 and Chapter 15 to ensure that you understand the procedures for recording the GST and PST collected from Sales and the GST and PST paid on buying merchandise for resale and other goods and services.

Chapter Exercises and Challenge Exercises

Listed below is a summary of the company folders and the modules used for each chapter. The bottom chart indicates the challenge exercises provided at the end of each chapter and the modules reviewed in each exercise.

CHAPTER EXERCISES

Chapter	Folder Name	Company	GL	A/Rec	A/Pay	Payroll	Inventory	Project	Reconciliation & Deposits
1	Boats	Boats Company	Yes						
2	Luggage	Santos Luggage	Yes	Yes					..
3	Toys	Tyson's Toys	Yes		Yes				
4	Kitchen*	Sarah's Kitchens	Yes	Yes	Yes				
5	Kitchen*	Sarah's Kitchens	Yes	Yes	Yes				
6	Shirts*	Shirts & Ties	Yes	Yes	Yes				
7	Wallpaper	Creative Wallpaper	Yes	Yes	Yes	Yes			
8	Printers	Printers Company	Yes	Yes	Yes		Yes		
9	Kafa	Kafa Sweaters	Yes						
10	Kafa2	Kafa2 Sweaters	Yes						
11	HotTubs	HotTubs Company	Yes	Yes	Yes	Yes		Yes	
12	Wedding	Wedding Flowers	Yes	Yes	Yes				Yes
13	Corrections	Prizes	Yes	Yes	Yes	Yes	Yes		

CHALLENGE EXERCISES

Chapter	Folder Name	Company	G/L	A/Rec	A/Pay	Payroll	Inventory	Project	Reconciliation & Deposits
1	Movers	Movers Company	Yes						
	Readings	Readings Company	Yes						
	Driving	Driving School	Yes						
2A	Clocks	Clocks Company	Yes	Yes					
	Walkers	Walkers Company	Yes	Yes					
2B	Dresses	Brides Dresses	Yes	Yes					
	Skis	Skis	Yes	Yes					
	Sitters	House Sitters	Yes	Yes					
3A	Wheelchair	Wheelchair Company	Yes		Yes				
	Radios	Radios Company	Yes		Yes				
3B	Network	Network Company	Yes		Yes				
	China	China Company	Yes	Yes	Yes				
	Dance	Dance Studio	Yes	Yes	Yes				
	Chairs	Chairs-Prov code	Yes	Yes	Yes				
4	Balloons*	Balloons Store	Yes	Yes	Yes				
	Kojokaro	Kojokaro Company	Yes	Yes	Yes				
	Skates*	Skates Stores	Yes	Yes	Yes				
	Uniforms	R. Park Uniforms	Yes		Yes	Yes			
7	Carpets	Carpets 4Home	Yes		Yes	Yes			
8	Stain	Stain Company	Yes	Yes	Yes		Yes		
	Hair	Charlie's Hair Styling	Yes	Yes	Yes		Yes		
	Vet	Vet Services	Yes	Yes	Yes		Yes		
10	Magazines	Rama Magazines	Yes		Yes				
	Gravel	City Gravel	Yes	Yes					
12	China	China Company	Yes	Yes	Yes				Yes

* Data files to be created by student.

To Use the Text Most Effectively

Here are important tips in making the most of your Simply training:

- When you see a number and a symbol similar to **7 ➤**, it means there is something on the line or paragraph in bold for you to type or a key or keys you must press.

- It is important that you follow the instructions in the order that they are given (don't jump around). Read each section before you do the work on the computer to get an idea of what will be done. This will help you avoid errors that could be prevented by knowing information presented a little further in the book. Ask your instructor if you are not sure. Asking your fellow students may help, but the final results are your responsibility, not your classmates'.

- The instructor will have a Solutions Manual available for you to check your work. If you realize you have made an error after posting a transaction, don't panic; you can correct the error by performing one of the following actions:

1a: Use the Reverse entry icon feature to reverse the error. (shown in Chapters 1, 2, 3 and others).

1b: Record the correct entry.

2. Use the Adjust icon to reverse and correct the entry (shown in Chapters 1, 2, 3 and others).

3. Enter a correcting entry.

Your transaction listing may not match the Solutions Manual exactly; e.g., you made a mistake, but the financial statements, Income Statement and Balance Sheet must be the same as the solution.

- Always back up your data after every work session either in the classroom or at home. This can save you hours of extra work.

- Answer the **Before Moving On** questions at the end of each chapter before moving to the next chapter. This will help you understand the reasons behind the keystrokes and aid you in preparing for tests.

Your Feedback

Please send comments, suggestions or corrections to the author at:

freedmanh@rogers.com

Updates

You may access the Publisher's web site especially set up so you may download files related to this text and to previous and future releases. The Publisher's web site is:

http://www.simplyaccounting2007.nelson.com

Chapter 1

Getting Started and COMPANY Module

Photos Company

Learning Objectives

After completing this chapter you will be able to:

☐ Use the General Journal to enter and post transactions using the Double Entry method.
☐ Display General Journal entries.
☐ Advance the Session Date.
☐ Adjust a wrong Journal entry after posting.
☐ Set up, use and remove a recurring entry.
☐ Use the Additional Transaction Details feature.
☐ Display and print relevant reports.
☐ Save and back up the data file.
☐ Record backup information in a logbook.

Simply Accounting by Sage Premium 2009, which we will refer to as Simply Accounting, is sold in five different business releases: **First Step, Pro, Premium, Enterprise** and **Accountants Edition**.

FREE to you with this book, on a separate CD, is the **Simply Accounting by Sage Premium 2009, Student Version**, which we will refer to as the Student Version.

The Premium Educational Version (installed in your school lab) and the Student Version that came with this text are the same program. *Note*: The 2009 version will work with Windows XP, Windows 2000 and Windows Vista, but will not work with previous Windows versions.

> *See Appendix A at the back of the textbook for computer system requirements, restrictions and installation instructions.*

When you start Simply at school, you will see the following in the bottom right of the window:

Release B
Payroll Taxes Effective: Jan. 1, 2009

Note: This window will only display for a few seconds.

If you are using the student version, you will not see the wording: Release B.
For student version installation instructions, refer to Appendix A.

You will learn the features of the **Premium** version in this textbook. The Premium software is available as a 2-user networking software. Features such as multi-user mode and departmental accounting will be discussed, but you will not be given exercises using these features.

The first chapter, **Photos Company**, explains basic concepts to give you an idea of how Simply Accounting works using double-entry accounting. The exercises allow you to try out some of the basic techniques in recording transactions, using folders and windows, in the Simply General Ledger.

The contents of this chapter are as follows:

As you go through the text, you will come across the following icons that are accompanied by special notations. Study each one carefully.

 This icon alerts you to general information, usually relevant accounting or GAAP notation (Generally Accepted Accounting Principles). You will find the information box as a sidebar at the left of the main text.

 This icon signals caution, VERY IMPORTANT information or a reminder for you to do something that may affect processing results.

 Whenever you see this icon, run the slideshow relevant to the topic under study. It will help you to better understand concepts and procedures in the chapter.

 Whenever you see this icon, which refers to the Student Data CD, view the CD Appendix relevant to the topic under study. It will help you to better understand concepts and procedures.

 This icon will signal that you will purposely make an error which you will learn how to correct later.

 The Happy Face will alert you when you will correct an error that you purposely made earlier.

 This icon will remind you to back up your data.

 This icon will remind you to update your logbook. A logbook form is provided for you, at the back of this text, where you will log the page # and topic that you last completed.

 You will see these icons together to remind you to back up your data and update your logbook at the back of this text.

Simply Accounting 2009 Overview

Accrual Basis accounting
Generally Accepted Accounting Principles (GAAP) stipulates that revenue should be recognized and recorded when a service has been provided or a product has been delivered (for cash or on credit). Expenses should be recognized and recorded when a service has been provided or products have been delivered (for cash or on credit). This is the main premise of the **accrual** method.

Cash Basis accounting
Revenue is recognized and recorded when cash is received, and expenses are recognized and recorded when paid. This method is contrary to the accrual method and is not consistent with GAAP. The cash basis method can be used by farmers and fishermen, but is not accepted for income tax purposes.

The accrual method has been used in this book because it records revenues and expenses, when incurred, and provides appropriate reports that show profits or losses, at a specified accounting period, based on the time when actual business transactions occur and not when cash is received or paid. The accrual method is accepted for income tax purposes.

Simply Accounting is a simple, secure and integrated accounting software package designed to simplify bookkeeping functions using double entry accounting, i.e., Debit entries must equal Credit entries. You can view and/or print various financial statements and other reports whenever needed.

Subledgers, when in use, are linked to the GENERAL LEDGER (e.g., ACCOUNTS RECEIVABLE in Chapter 2 and ACCOUNTS PAYABLE in Chapter 3). This means that when a transaction is processed in any of the subledgers, the General Ledger is automatically updated. The Accounts Payable and Accounts Receivable subledgers may be linked to the INVENTORY & SERVICES subledger (Chapter 8).

Simply provides a choice of either the **Cash** method or the **Accrual** method of accounting. This text uses the **Accrual** method (see side note box).

There are some powerful features of Simply that offer many advantages over using manual bookkeeping. For example:

1. Data entry errors may be easily corrected.

2. Controls are provided to prevent data entry errors, such as addition errors or duplicate invoice numbers, transposition of numbers, etc.

3. Posting transactions is automatically performed by clicking the Post
    ⚓ Post icon, and all ledgers and journals are updated immediately.

4. Records are updated immediately.

5. Standard financial statements and reports may be printed at any time.

Company files for you to work with are supplied on the Student Data CD that accompanies this textbook. Your instructor will explain where to copy the company data files contained on the CD. Keep the Student Data CD in a safe place, in case you need to download a company file, replace a damaged data file or if you want to repeat a chapter from the beginning.

This text assumes that you are familiar with basic accounting. If you require help in this area, information on the *Basics of Accounting* can be found in Appendix CD-A, on your Student Data CD.

As you work through each section of this textbook, you will learn how to use Simply in a business setting. The purpose of the procedures and various Simply features is explained in simple terms. A thorough **knowledge** of this software will make you a valuable employee.

Run **Slideshow 1A-SIMPLY BASICS** from your Student Data CD now. It will give you a general overview of Simply Accounting Premium 2009 and the features that are available in all modules. If a CD player is not available on your workstation, consult your instructor.

Getting Started

A basic understanding of Windows is required if you wish to use Simply Accounting effectively. You can find a glossary of accounting and Simply terminology at the end of each chapter.

If the Simply software has been installed using the Typical method (most common options) on the school computer/or network, the program is located in the path: **C:\ Program Files\Simply Accounting Premium 2009**.

It is assumed that:

1. You have access to the Simply Accounting software.

2. You will be storing your data files on a storage device. This text designates the storage device as drive **C:**. If your drive is other than C: replace **C:** with the appropriate drive letter when doing your exercises.

Throughout the text, you will see capitalized wording such as RECEIVABLES, PAYABLES, INVENTORY & SERVICES, EMPLOYEES & PAYROLL, PROJECTS (DIVISIONS) BANKING and COMPANY. These refer to the module being discussed.

When you see a number followed by an arrowhead such as 1➤, 2➤, etc., it means there is something on the line or the paragraph for you to do on the keyboard or with your mouse button. Icons will alert you to special notations.

Click   Means to click the left mouse button **once**.

Double-click   You must click the left mouse button **twice** quickly (without pausing).

Words you have to type or keys you have to press are shown in **BOLD**.

Throughout the text you will see shaded references similar to: See Exercise 7-8. These references are shaded to help you quickly find them in the textbook.

Read the instructions and explanation in the exercises before executing the keystrokes on your computer. If you read ahead and understand the instructions, you may avoid making errors.

A practical storage device to back up data is a USB storage device (see picture below) which is available in varying storage capacities. It plugs into a USB port and can be easily taken in and out. Ask your teacher where the USB port is located on your computer.

VERY IMPORTANT:

Always back up your data at the end of EVERY work session, either in the classroom or at home. This can save you hours of redoing work (see side note). Answer the questions at the end of each chapter before moving on to the next chapter. This will help you understand the reasons for the various procedures. It will also aid you in preparing for tests.

A detailed index is provided at the end of the book for your easy reference.

Most schools have an anti-virus program that protects the files in the school network. If your school does not, you should be aware that your files could be corrupted if there is a virus in the system. It is imperative, therefore, that you back up your data regularly.

If you do some of your work at home, you should invest in an anti-virus program with regular updates to ensure that your files will not be damaged, and that you do not take corrupted data to school, that can infect the network system.

Exercise 1-1 – Unzipping the Master Data Files from the CD

The Master company data files you need to work through the exercises in this book are contained on the Student Data CD that accompanies this text. Each of the company data files are compressed using WinZip and are in self-extracting executable (exe) format. You need to unzip these files onto your storage device using the procedure below, which assumes that you are loading the data files to the C: drive. If you are loading the data files to a different storage device, use the procedure below, substituting the drive letter of the device for C.

> Backup files, created in Exercise 1-23, can be used to restore a data file (see Chapter 1a at the end of this chapter) if it becomes damaged or if you want to start an exercise again.

To load student data files, follow these steps:

1 ➤ Insert the **Student Data CD** into the CD-ROM drive. Windows will automatically load the **Welcome** screen. Move to step 5, or if the **Welcome** screen does not appear, or you close it and want to reopen it, go to step 2.

2 ➤ **Right-click** the start button, move and click on **Explore**.

3 ➤ Locate the CD-ROM drive in the left pane, click on SA_2009_Student (D:) .

4 ➤ In the right pane, double-click on Welcome.exe to open the Welcome screen.

5 ➤ The following Links or buttons appear on the Welcome screen:

Software Requirements for using the Simply Accounting 2009 data files on this CD.

License Agreement for using this Nelson Education CD.

About this CD refers to instructions on accessing the data files and running the PowerPoint slideshows.

Chapter Data Files refers to the individual data files in exe format. (See step 6.)

PowerPoint Slideshows refers to individual slideshows that will open as slideshows.

CD Appendix PDF files refers to the CD Appendices for additional information.

Install Adobe Reader 9. If you have an old version of Adobe Reader or you do not have Adobe Reader on your computer, click here to install this software on your computer.

Install PowerPoint Viewer if you do not have the PowerPoint program for the slideshows. Clicking this button will install the PowerPoint Viewer software on your computer at no cost.

6 ➤ Click on the **Chapter Data Files** button. This opens a new window with a list of the **exe** data files in chapter order.

e.g., 01 refers to Photos Chapter 1 data file.
01 C1-1 refers to Driving School Challenge Exercise 1-1 data file in Chapter 1.

7 ➤ Double-click on **01 Photos.exe** file and the following WinZip window will appear.

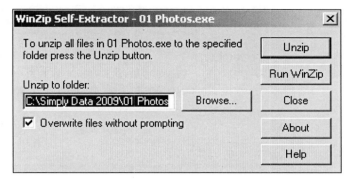

 The WinZip Self-extractor, Unzip command will create a Simply Data 2009 folder on your storage device. If you want to load the data files in a different drive/folder, change the field **C:\Simply Data 2009** to your specific location, or click **Browse** to locate the specific storage space.

If you use **Windows Explorer** or **My Computer**, you will notice that the 01 Photos folder contains a folder, with an extension of **SAJ** and a file with an extension of **SAI**. Inside the SAJ folder are 2 folders and additional files. The **mysql** folder contains the database and the **simply** folder contains the Simply files. Together these files contain information about the company, accounts, transactions, etc. When you open the data file, Exercise 1-2, step 10, you use only the **SAI** file in the window.

If you move your mouse over the SAI file, you will see information that this is a Simply Accounting Data File.

8 ➤ Click **Unzip**.

The following window indicates that the data files have been successfully unzipped and are ready for you to use.

The data folder in your storage location should have the following name:

Folder	*Company Name*	*Module used (Main)*
01 Photos	Photos Company	COMPANY

9 ➤ Click **OK**, then **Close**.

To copy other company files (e.g., 01 C1-1 Driving, Chapter 1 Challenge Case; 02 2A Luggage-A, Chapter 2A; or other company files) to your storage space (e.g., C:\Simply Data 2009), repeat the above steps.

Refer to Appendix A, at the back of the text, for instructions on installing the Student version of the Simply program.

Starting the Simply Program

 In a business setting, you may be required to enter a password before you can access a Simply data file. Passwords prevent unauthorized people from having access to your program and the company data. The exercises in this textbook do not require a password. Information on using a password can be found in Appendix CD-O, *Security—Passwords* on the Student Data CD. See your instructor for more information.

Read the instructions and explanation in each exercise before attempting to record data using the Simply program. If you ignore the instructions and explanation, you may make errors that could easily have been avoided.

Remember...
Click   means to click the left button once.
Double-click   means to click the left button twice rapidly.

Exercise 1-2 – Starting the Simply Program

DO NOT open the Simply file from the Windows Explorer or My Computer window. Use the procedure shown in this Exercise.

You need to tell the Simply program where to locate the company data files that you will be using. You will start by using the Photos Company data folder.

Your instructor will advise you how to access Simply in the classroom. If you are using your home computer, follow this procedure:

1 ➤   Click the **Start** icon. 🏁 **Start** .

2 ➤   Move the mouse to the **Programs** icon 📁 Programs ▶ , or to the
All Programs ▶ icon.

> The location of the Simply Accounting icon and/or name depends upon how your Windows program groups are set up for application software.

3 ➤   Move the mouse to 🏛 Simply Accounting Premium 2009 School Version ▶ , (if you are using the Student Version, you will see 🏛 Simply Accounting Premium 2009 Student Version ▶). (See side note box.)

Company File Check & Repair	**Company File Check & Repair**	– This link checks the data file for errors. (See Appendix CD-B, *Check & Repair Tool* on the Student Data CD.).
Microsoft Office Documents	**Microsoft Office Documents**	– This link displays various Word & Excel document files that are available to be used.
New Business Guide	**New Business Guide**	– Information can be found in Appendix CD-H, *New Business Guide* on the Student Data CD.
Simply Accounting by Sage Help	**Simply Accounting by Sage Help**	– Help features available in the program.
Simply Accounting Premium 2009	**Simply Accounting Premium 2009**	– The program that you will use.

If you are using the Student edition, you will see two additional items: Install Simply Accounting Mobile and Synchronize with Handheld Device. These two items do not work in the Student edition.

4 ➤   Click on 🌀 Simply Accounting Premium 2009 .

The Simply Accounting Start Window

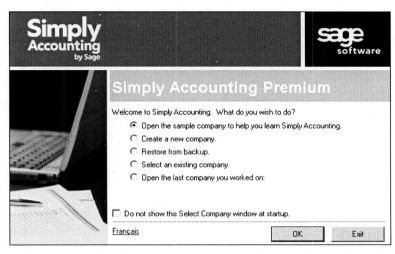

ℹ If this is the first time the software is being used you will see screen Fig.1-1a. The next time the software is being used you will see a new item added to the list. Open the last company you worked on, Fig. 1-1b.

Fig. 1-1a: Simply Accounting start window. (See side note box.)

Fig. 1-1b: Simply Accounting start window, with Open last company.

a) **Open the sample company to help you learn Simply Accounting.** Used if you want to open the sample company (Universal Construction) that was installed in the computer. You may not have access to the sample companies.

b) **Create a new company.** Used when you need to create a new company. You will use this option in Chapter 4.

c) **Restore from backup.** Used when you want to open a backup file; (e.g., to replace a damaged data file). Instructions on using this feature (Restoring a Data File from a Backup Data File) is in Chapter 1a at the end of this chapter.

d) **Select an existing company.** Used when you want to open a company that is on your storage space. (See this exercise at step 5.)

e) **Open the last company you worked on.** This option may not be applicable in a classroom setting. If the student before you was working on a different company, this choice may not be appropriate.

f) **Do not show this Select Company window at startup.** Do NOT click this selection. This option is explained in Chapter 4.

5 ➤ Click **Select an existing company**.

6 ➤ Click **OK**. You will then see the Open Company window, Fig. 1-2.

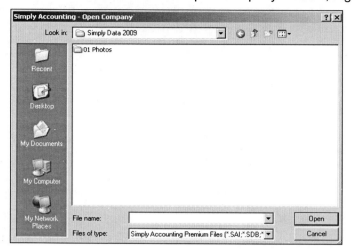

Fig. 1-2: Open Company window.

This window is the default data location. In a classroom network setting, this may not be correct. If your window does not resemble Fig. 1-2, follow the steps below (starting at step 7) to locate your drive folders.

 Remember, if your data folders are located on another drive such as **D:**, **E:** or another letter, substitute your drive letter for **C:**.

Network Procedures

On a network, a window similar to Fig. 1-3 appears.

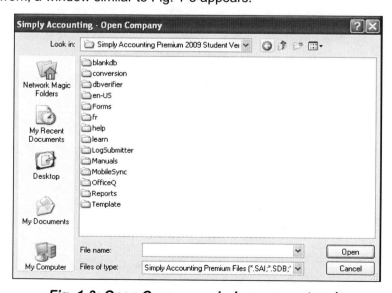

Fig. 1-3: Open Company window on a network.

7 ➤ Click the ▼ in the **Look in** box.

8 ➤ Locate and double-click the **Simply Data 2009** folder (Fig. 1-2).

9 ➤ Double-click the folder 📁 01 Photos .

10 ➤ Click the file named  (*Note*: In Fig. 1-2, you may not see the **SAI extension** in the File name box; you should see the file name: Photos.)

11 ➤ Click **Open**. Wait for the program to load. A Session Date box appears.

If you are using the
Student Version, the
program can be used for
a period of 14 months
(425 days) from the date
that you start using the
program.

The number of days
remaining will display on
the left side when you
start the program.

If you are using the Simply Student Edition at home, see the note at the left.

Fig. 1-4: New Session Date window.

Simply uses the date format as defined by Windows. The author has used the long date format: **mm/dd/yyyy** (month, day, year) format. (Simply 2009 allows the date to be displayed using an abbreviated name, i.e., Apr 10, 2014 instead of 04/10/2014).

To change the date you have three choices.

Do NOT click this field. If you click this field and OK by mistake, you enter the Photos data file. The next time you open this company, the Session Date window will NOT display and you will have to change the session date inside the data file.

To correct the mistake, and have the session date displayed as above, each time you open the data file, from the top menu bar click, **Setup, User Preferences**, **View**, and click on the 3rd item at the bottom. ☑ Show Change Session Date at Startup , click **OK** to return to the Home window.

Experienced users may click this field, but as you are learning Simply, the authors suggest that you display the session date window.

1. You may type the date in the **Date for this Session** box.
2. You may click the ▼ arrow and select the appropriate date from a range of dates. See step 12.
3. You may click the Calendar button.

The most efficient way to enter a date is by using choice 3, the Simply Calendar. It is fast and it helps you avoid making date format errors.

You will click the ▼ arrow in the next step only to understand the concept of range of dates relevant to the Session Date.

12 ➤ Click the ▼ arrow. A drop-down list of dates appears.

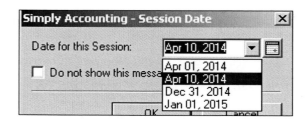

Range of Dates

The Photos Company is using a calendar fiscal year.

> Start of the fiscal year is: Jan 01, 2014
> End of the fiscal year is: Dec 31, 2014

Apr 01, 2014   This is the first day of the current month.

Apr 10, 2014   This is the last date that the Photos Company data file was used. This is known as the **session date**. In a business environment, the Session date is the current date when you are entering transactions. This date will change as you change the session date.

Dec 31, 2014   The end of Photos Company's fiscal year.

Jan 01, 2015   The start of Photos Company's next fiscal year. You must be careful NOT to select this. If you type or accept Jan 01, 2015, the start of Photos Company's next fiscal year, Simply will automatically perform year-end procedures, closing the Revenue and Expense accounts for the previous fiscal year to zero. In addition, the net profit or loss will be updated in the appropriate Equity account, e.g., Capital, Retained Earnings, etc.

You will now use the Calendar button to enter the session date. Although you can type the session date 04102014, Apr10, or select the appropriate date from the drop-down options, using the Calendar is by far the most efficient way.

13 ➤   Click the **Calendar** button. The calendar for the current month appears. To move to future months click the. To move back, click the. Try going forward and backward now.

14 ▶   Move the Calendar to April. For this exercise, you need to enter **Apr 18, 2014** as your Session Date. Click **18**. Your window should resemble the next screen:

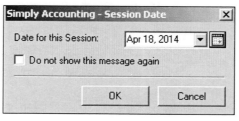

15 ➤   Click **OK**.

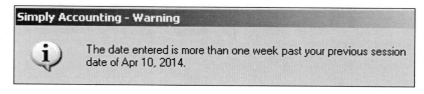

The Warning window advises you if the date you entered is more than one week (7 days) ahead of the previous session date. However, it will not advise you if you have entered a new month or if you have entered the wrong date. If you have made an error in the date, the program will give you the opportunity to change it at this point by clicking Cancel.

16 ➤ If the date is correct, click **OK** to accept the new session date.

17 ➤ Depending on the configuration at your school, you may see the following online survey window. If you do not see the survey window, move to step 19.

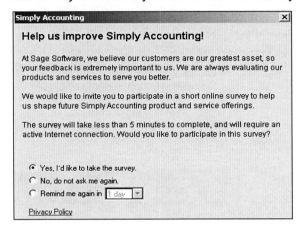

 Simply by Sage announces that you can only take the survey once. If you click the ☒ in the top corner, or click No, do not ask me again, this window will no longer appear in the future. If you click ▼ Remind me again in, you have a choice to select 1, 3, 7 or 10 days later.

18 ➤ You may select "Yes, I'd like to take the survey" or "No, do not ask me" again. Make your selection, then click **OK**.

If you were not connected to the Internet and had selected Yes, then clicked OK, you would have seen the following caution window.

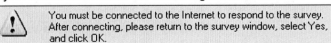

Students using the Student Edition will not see the following Welcome window.

The Welcome to the **Education Edition window shown next** will display each time you open a company data file at school. If you are using the student version, you will not see the Education Edition window.

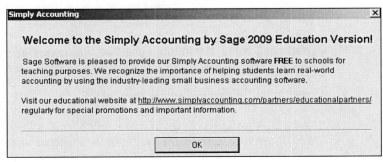

19 ➤ Click **OK**.

Students using the Student Edition will not see the Welcome window above step 19. Students using the Student Edition should jump to the information after step 19, starting with:

Your current data file...

(See side note box.)

Your current data file is for Photos Company. The Getting Started; Welcome to Simply Accounting window should look like Fig. 1-5a. The Simply **Home** window will be Fig. 1-5b. A brief explanation of the menus and icons is shown after step 22. You are welcome to experiment clicking on menu items or icons as you proceed with this overview.

Do not make any changes to any of the windows, as they may affect the data used in the practice exercises later in the chapter. To exit from this window or any window, click the ⬜X⬜ in the top-right corner. If you click ⬜X⬜ from the Home window Fig 1-5b Simply saves the work you completed and closes the file.

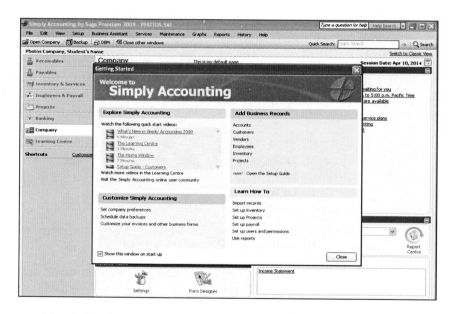

Fig. 1-5a: Getting Started; Welcome to Simply Accounting window.

The Welcome to Simply Accounting window is divided into 4 parts.

If you click on various choices, the Welcome to Simply Accounting window may disappear. You should see the 🔹**Getting Started** icon on the bottom taskbar. Click on the icon to return the Getting Started window to the foreground.

Explore Simply Accounting This section contains videos to learn about various parts of Simply. If you have used an older version of Simply (2008 or prior), you will want to review the 'What's New in Simply Accounting 2009' link, and the Learning Centre. See Also Appendix CD-C, *What's New in Simply 2009*. The other selections will be discussed in various chapters.

Add Business Records This section contains links to add items identified. This text will show you how to add the records in each chapter: Accounts in Chapter 1, Customers in Chapter 2, etc. The link to Open the Setup Guide will be discussed in Chapter 4.

Customize Simply Accounting This section contains links that you will see in various chapters. Set Company Preferences will be discussed in Chapter 4, Schedule data backups will be discussed in Chapter 4 and Customize your invoices and other business forms will be discussed in Chapter 4.

Learn How to This section contains links to Help documents. You will be shown how to set up INVENTORY in Chapter 8, PROJECTS (can also be called DIVISIONS) in Chapter 11, PAYROLL in Chapter 7, Security (Users and permissions) in Appendix CD-O, *Security – Passwords.*

20 ➤ To not see the Getting Started; Welcome to Simply Accounting window at startup and go directly to the Home window (Fig. 1-5b), click the ☑ Show this window on startup (this will remove the checkmark), then click |Close|.

Note: For other companies the ☐ Show this window on startup, has been unchecked to not display on Startup. You will go directly to the Home page.

If you have clicked the button as indicated ☐ and you want to see the Welcome to Simply Accounting window, from the menu bar on the home window, click **Setup, Getting Started Guide**.

Home Window — Enhanced View

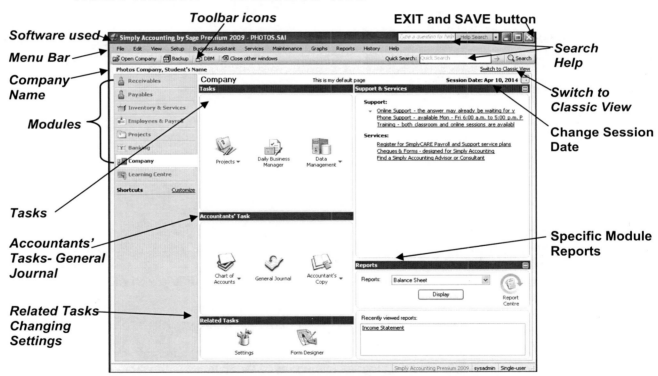

Fig. 1-5b: Simply HOME Enhanced View window.

Company Name: The internal data file company name |Photo Company, Student's Name| displays, above the module bars, near the top left side, as part of the Home window. You will be changing the "Student's Name" to your own name in Exercise 1-4. Your name will then display in the Home window and other journals.

Look at the top right side to see the location of the session date.
|Session Date: Apr 18, 2014 🗓| You will change the date using this feature in Exercise 1-8.

If you have seen previous versions of Simply (2007 and prior), you will notice a big change in the Home window.

21 ➤ On the right side, on the Support or Services line, click on the ▣ at the end of the line. The section reduces to a single line and hides the information until you need it. This works with the 3 sections on the right.

22 ➤ To expand the section that is hidden, click on the ⊞.

You can still see and use the previous version Home page, now known as the Classic View.

23 ➤ To see the **Classic View** window, click │Switch to Classic View│.

Home Window — Classic View

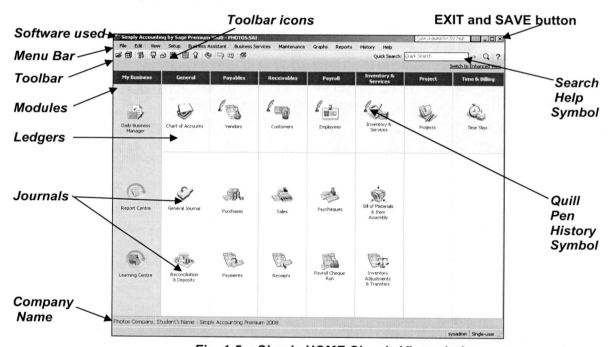

Software used ➔
Menu Bar ➔
Toolbar ➔
Modules ➔
Ledgers ➔
Journals ➔
Company Name ➔

Toolbar icons
EXIT and SAVE button
Search Help Symbol
Quill Pen History Symbol

Fig. 1-5c: Simply HOME Classic View window.

24 ➤ To return to the **Enhanced View** window, click │Switch to Enhanced View│.

When you click the X button (Exit) in the top-right corner of the Home window, Simply **saves** all entries in memory to the data file in the storage location and closes the program.

Menu Bar

Each menu item contains a drop-down list of options related to the menu heading. You can display the menu list by clicking the menu item. Try clicking each menu item now.

Toolbar

Note that there is a row with 4 icons below the Menu Bar (this text calls them **Toolbar icons**). The icons are designed to allow easy access to changing to another company data file, backing up the current data file, opening the Daily Business

Manager (shown in Chapter 2) and closing any open Simply journals or reports. When you move your mouse over a toolbar icon, an information box appears below it with a brief explanation. Position your mouse over each of the icons and read the explanation that appears.

Modules

A module is referred to, in Simply and this text, as a bar in the Home window. Each module will have different views for Tasks, Accountant's Tasks, and Related Tasks depending on the module selected. Click on each of the modules to see the differences. These will be explained in this and other chapters. The COMPANY module will be discussed in this chapter. Each module can be hidden or revealed as needed. You will see how this works in later chapters.

25 ➤ Click on the **RECEIVABLES** module and look at the Tasks area and the Customers icon.

History: This history symbol represents a module in which the history subledger information does not balance with the General Ledger. You can record Sales and Purchases to the RECEIVABLES and PAYABLES modules without having the previous balances recorded if the module has been set up. This feature would allow new users to start using the software and add previous balances when they have time.

Note: You cannot start a new fiscal year if the subsidiary ledgers do not agree with the General Ledger. This text does not record transactions until the module has been set up.

26 ➤ Click the **COMPANY** module.

Tasks

Projects: This feature can also be called Divisions, Territories or other appropriate name. This feature will allow revenues and expenses to be allocated and accumulated for projects, divisions, salesperson's territories, etc. (see Chapter 11).

Daily Business Manager: This feature allows the user to add notes for future reference and shows other Memo information, Recurring Invoices, Payments Due, Outstanding Purchase Orders, Sales Due and Sales Orders. You can also view various Business Performance ratios. You will be shown how to use this feature in Chapter 2A, Exercise 2A-7, or hide the option in Chapter 2A, Exercise 2A-11.

Data Management: You can right-click on any icon that shows the ▼ to see details of the features. This feature allows the user to Back up a data file, Restore a data file, Advanced Database Check, Consolidate Company (used when combining different businesses owned by an owner—this feature is not shown in this text) and Import and Export Records.

Accountant's Tasks

Chart of Accounts: The General Ledger (G/L) for a company. This ledger allows you to keep a complete G/L system from which you can produce financial statements. The G/L uses the following account grouping: Assets, Liabilities, Equities, Revenues and Expenses. This feature allows you to View, Add, Modify and Remove accounts. You can also add accounts from inside journals.

General Journal: This is the journal that you will use in this chapter.

You would normally use the Simply General Journal only to make entries, which cannot be made in subledgers and their associated journals. You use the Double Entry method to record these entries, which are usually banking transactions and those that relate to accrued adjustments. Transactions pertaining to sales and purchases are entered in the RECEIVABLES module (Chapter 2A, 2B) and PAYABLES module (Chapter 3A, 3B) respectively. You will learn how to record sales-related transactions in the RECEIVABLES module and purchases-related transactions in the PAYABLES module.

Some small companies, although not very many, use only the General Ledger and not any of the subledger modules. Photos Company is one of them.

Accountant's Copy: This feature allows the user to create a data file to be sent to the accountant for month or year-end entries. When the accountant sends you the updated data file, you can use the Import Entries from Accountant item. You can also Cancel the Accountant's copy.

Related Tasks

Settings This feature will allow you to change default settings in the software. This will be explained in more detail in Chapter 4.

Form Designer This feature will allow you to change default settings in various Simply forms.

Support & Services

Support & Services. Refer to the Installation instructions in Appendix A (at the back of the book) to see which support or services are not available for students.

Reports

Report Centre This feature allows the user to select a report from the Report Centre window, without having to click Reports from the menu bar, and selecting various types of reports. This feature also lets you see what the report will look like before you display it. You can also click the drop down arrow at Reports to see reports that are available in this module. Each module will have different reports available.

Recently viewed reports. This section will display the last 4 reports the user viewed. You can click any report in this section and it will display and can be printed.

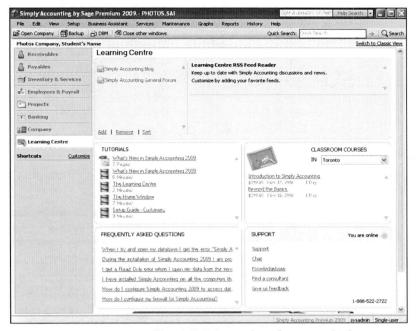

Fig. 1-5d: Learning Centre window.

The Learning Centre window is divided into 6 parts (from left to right).

Note: This window may have a different configuration than the one displayed. (i.e., that is the Tutorials may be in the top row, and Classroom Courses may be in the 2nd row on the left. Other configurations are also possible.

Tutorials This section is similar to the Videos in the Getting Started window.

Learning Centre – middle section: This section contains links to a Simply Accounting Blog and General Forum.

Learning Centre RSS Feed Reader This section displays the results of the Blog or General Forum from the middle section.

Classroom Courses This section contains information about Simply courses in various locations for a fee.

Frequently Asked Questions This section contains links to most frequently asked questions to Simply forums.

Support This section contains links to various support options in the Retail version.

The lower portion of the window may be hidden. Click the slider button to display the following.

If your company accepts credit cards to pay for invoices, you can click to receive information on a Simply Service. There are service charges for this service.

This feature allows the user to use various tutorials.

The various tasks and journals are explained in the appropriate chapters, such as Sales and Receipts, where transaction information is recorded and posted. Each of the modules must be properly configured (set up).

Using Simply HELP

Simply provides four ways to find Help within the program.

Exercise 1-3a – Using Help—Type a question for help

1 ➤ This help field, at the top right of the window, enables the user to enter questions for assistance as if they were talking to the software. Click the Help Search ▼. Select either Simply Accounting Help (default) or On Line Community. Click in the field and type your question such as: **expense**, and press **Enter**. You will see the Simply Accounting Help window. You could click on a topic in the left pane and the right pane will display the response for that topic.

2 ➤ Click on X in the top right corner to **Exit,** and return to Fig. 1-5b Home window.

Exercise 1-3b – Using Help—Search

1 ➤ In |Quick Search: Quick Search| type **expense**, and click the →| (Quick Search) button, or press **Enter**. The Search button, searches all reports and customer, vendor and other modules for instances of the information recorded.

A report with a list of 11 accounts with the word Expense in the name will appear and the Advanced Search Results Summary report will display the information next.

> **Number of Matches: 11**
> Search <All Fields> Contains expense

2 ➤ As you move your mouse over the information, a magnifying glass appears. **Double-click** on any item in the window. Simply will drill down (this will be explained in more detail in Exercise 1-16) to the information and display it. In this situation, the General Ledger, where you can change account information, will appear.

3 ➤ Click X **twice** to return to the Home window. If you can see the

|⌧ Close all other windows| icon on the tool bar, you can also click the icon and you will be returned to the Home window.

4 ➤ If you type |Quick Search: account| in the search field and click →|, or press **Enter**, you will see an Advanced Search Results report with 3 instances of the word 'account' in this file.

5 ➤ From the **Advanced Search Results** window click ⊠ in the top-right corner to return to the Home window.

Exercise 1-3c – Using Help—Database Search Tool

---

1 ➤ Click on . A Basic and Advanced tabs will display. Click the ▾ to see a list of records or transactions you can search for. This feature is not used in this text.

2 ➤ Click on the **Advanced** tab. This tab is similar to Exercise 1-17, between steps 3 and 4, Filter reports.

3 ➤ Click **Cancel**, to return to Fig. 1-5b Home window.

Exercise 1-3d – Using Help—Learning Centre

Using Learning Centre Help

1 ➤ Click the **Learning Centre** icon. Look in the **Frequently Asked Questions** list. You may have to scroll up or down to see more items.

2 ➤ Click on the **Company** icon to return to the Fig. 1-5b Home window.

The **F1** key for Help does not work in the Enhanced Home window.

Shortcuts (on left side)

You will be shown how to create a list of reports (Customize) that you may use often in Exercise 1-21a, Creating Custom Report Shortcuts. You can add or remove items in the list.

Revising Company Information

Simply allows you to make changes in the company information; e.g., the address needs to be changed if the company has moved, phone numbers may have changed, or the company may have installed additional phones. In the next exercise, you will change the company name information to include your name.

 For a quick reference guide on various exercises throughout the textbook, refer to Appendix CD-R, *Quick Reference Guide* on the Student Data CD.

Exercise 1-4 – Changing Company Information

As you and your fellow students in class start printing reports, there could be confusion as to which printout belongs to whom, because you will all have the same heading, **Photos Company, Student's Name**. You will now change the company name to include your name, so you can easily identify your own printout.

You may use the same technique shown here to change any company information.

1 ➤ In the lower Related Tasks area, click on the **Settings** icon, in the left pane click on **Information**. The Company Information window will appear.

Name:	Photos Company, Student's Name	Fiscal Start:	Jan 01, 2014
Street 1:	3000 Delrex Blvd	Fiscal End:	Dec 31, 2014
Street 2:		Earliest Transaction:	Apr 01, 2014
City:	Georgetown	Session:	Apr 18, 2014
Province:	ON ▾ Ontario	Latest Transaction:	Apr 01, 2014
Postal:	L7G 1P3		
Country:			
Phone 1:			
Phone 2:			
Fax:			
Business No.:	R321		
Industry Type:	Retail ▾		

Fig. 1-6: A portion of the Company Information window.

2 ➤ In the Name box, highlight **Student's Name** and type your **last name** (surname) and **first name** (given), then click **OK**. The company name will be changed accordingly and now will appear at the top of the modules on the left side of the Home window.

Example: **Photos Company, Oliver Megan**

You should follow the name change procedure for each new company you work on. You need to do this only once for each company.

To Display Reports

Most new companies will start by setting up the various modules, e.g., COMPANY, RECEIVABLES, PAYABLES, EMPLOYEES & PAYROLL, etc. Some new companies, however, may start with only the COMPANY module and eventually add the other modules when they determine that they have enough transactions for these modules to warrant the effort to set them up.

As mentioned earlier, the COMPANY module allows you to enter transactions into a complete General Ledger system (double entry), and allows financial statements to be displayed and/or printed at any time. Note that the other modules are not active for the Photos Company (you can tell because the History symbol 🖋 is showing with the Tasks icons inside each of the other modules).

Financial Statements for a company are generated from previously entered data, and may be displayed or printed for a range of dates or a specific day.

To start this exercise you need to be at the Photos Company Home window.

Exercise 1-5a – Displaying Reports using Recently Viewed Reports Area

Displaying the Income Statement

You can display an Income Statement for any period of time:

- one day or a few days
- a week or a few weeks
- one month or a few months
- year-to-date

1 ➤ The Recently viewed reports area is displayed with 4 reports listed. In the **Reports** field, click ▼ , select **Income Statement**, click **Display**. The report will display. Only the top portion is shown.

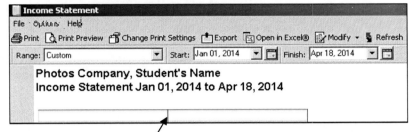

By clicking on the dividing line, you can move the columns to the left or right to change the way the columns display and/or print in statements.

2 ➤ To modify the Income Statement, click on the **Modify** icon.

Fig. 1-7: Modify Options menu.

3 ➤ Click on **Report Options**. You will see the following window.

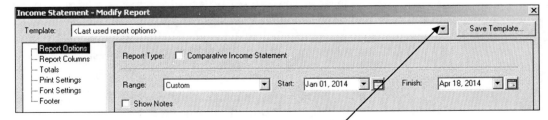

The settings on the left side are the same as those in the Modify icon drop-down area.

Comparative Income statements will be discussed and shown in Chapter 3B.

You can customize the Income Statement Print settings and/or Font settings. The same customization information is for the Balance Sheet. There is no exercise for changing Print and Font settings.

Template drop-down ▼: Click ▼ and two choices appear: `<Default report options>` `<Last used report options>`

\<Default report options\> Options used by Simply without changes.

\<Last used report options\> The options used the last time you requested the report and will be used to display the report this time.

Save Template button   You are able to save a report with any changed settings (date, terms, etc.) as a template and it can be retrieved later with the same settings.

☐ **Show Notes**   Do Not Change. You are able to add specific notes to viewed and printed statements. See Appendix CD-U, *Adding Notes/Footers to Statements* for more information.

As noted previously at Exercise 1-2, you can change the date in reports using either the ▾ or the calendar feature.

4 ➤   Range   Click ▾ and a list of various reports dates appears. Click the ▾ again to use the **Custom** selection.

5 ➤   Start   Leave the date as **Jan 01, 2014**, the start of the fiscal year.

6 ➤   Finish   Using the calendar, change the date to **April 10, 2014** (because you have not entered data in April yet).

7 ➤   Click **OK** to display an Income Statement for the period Jan 01, 2014 to Apr 10, 2014 (see side note box). **DO NOT PRINT AT THIS TIME. You will print an Income Statement in Chapters 2A and 2B.**

To view the lower part of the statement, you can use the vertical scroll bar and/or the maximize button ▢. (See side note box.) Scroll back to the top of the Income Statement.

8 ➤   New in 2009 is a management feature for the Financial Statements. You will notice the symbol ⊟ to the left of the wording ⊟ **Revenue**, ⊟ **Cost of Goods Sold** and ⊟ **Store & Admin Expenses** .

Note: This feature will hide the individual accounts and display the section total. The Revenue and Store & Admin Expense sections can be hidden for the Purchasing Manager. The Cost of Goods Sold & the Store & Admin Expense sections can be hidden for the Sales Manager and so on.

This feature will also work with the Balance Sheet.

9 ➤   To hide individual amounts, click on the ⊟ for the **Cost of Goods Sold** & the **Store & Admin Expense** sections. The Revenue section Sales accounts are still displayed. This report can be printed and distributed to managers in the Sales departments. Other reports can be distributed as needed.

To unhide statement details, repeat step 9.

Side note box:

You can view other parts of the report by scrolling down.

In the lower-left corner of the displayed statement is the wording: **Generated On**: with the current date. When the statement is printed, the wording changes to: **Printed On**: with the current date.

10 ➤ To display the previously hidden section, click on the ⊞ **(expand)** button.

11 ➤ To close the Income Statement, click the ☒ **EXIT** button and return to the Home window. The Recently viewed reports area displays the Income Statement that you just viewed.

Displaying the Balance Sheet

Exercise 1-5b – Display Balance Sheet Using the Report Menu

You can display a Balance Sheet only at a certain date, not for a range of dates. To use another method of displaying reports, follow this procedure.

1 ➤ From the Menu bar, click **Reports**, move to **Financials**, move to **Balance Sheet**, then **click**.

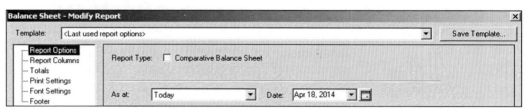

You can customize the Balance Sheet Print settings and/or Font settings.

2 ➤ Template　　　Click the ▼ and select **Default Report Options** to match the text.

3 ➤ As at　　　　Click the ▼ to see the range of dates that are available. Change to **Custom**.

4 ➤ Date　　　　Using the calendar, change the date to **Apr 10, 2014** (because you have not entered data in April yet).

5 ➤ Click **OK** to display a Balance Sheet.

> The wording **Generated on**: with the current date will appear at the bottom of all displayed reports.

> As discussed previously, the individual amounts can be hidden. If you click on the ⊟ at Photo Equipment, two accounts are hidden and only the subtotal (Net Book Value) appears.

DO NOT PRINT AT THIS TIME; you will print a Balance Sheet in Chapters 2A and 2B.
(See side note box.)

6 ➤ To close the Balance Sheet, click the ☒ **EXIT** button and return to the Home window.

Exercise 1-5c – Display the Income Statement Using the Report Centre

1 ➤ Click the **Report Centre** icon.

2 ➤ In the COMPANY module, the default is Financials. Click the ⊞ beside Income Statement to see the list of 5 statements.

3 ➤ Click on **Standard**. A sample of a similar Income Statement is displayed.

4 ➤ Click on ⬚ **Display** ⬚, the Photos Income Statement is displayed. The dates will need to change depending on your situation.

5 ➤ Start date　　　Leave the date as **Jan 01, 2014**.

6 ➤	**Finish date**	Change to **Apr 10, 2014** (because you have not entered data in April yet). Press ⌈Tab⌉ or the **Refresh** [Refresh] icon to update the information. The statement date is revised.

7 ➤	**Range**	Change to **This Calendar Year**. The Start date stays at Jan 01, 2014, and the Finish date changes to the session date Apr 18, 2014.

DO NOT PRINT AT THIS TIME. You will print in Chapters 2A and 2B. (See side note box.)

> If you need to close the 01 Photos data file before completing the chapter, refer to Exercise 1-23 to complete the backup procedure.

8 ➤		Click **X** to exit the Income Statement and return to the Report Centre. Other reports can be printed from the Report Centre. Click **Close** to return to the Home window.

Processing Transactions in the COMPANY Module

Run **Slideshow 1B-GENERAL LEDGER** from your Student Data CD. It will give you a good idea of when and how to use the COMPANY module of Simply Accounting and a review of Generally Accepted Accounting Principles (GAAP) that you need to apply when processing transactions in Simply.

In Simply, it is only in the **GENERAL Journal** that you use double entry recording (enter both debit and credit items).

To record transactions, see Exercise 1-6 that follows these steps:

1. Enter the data into a **Journal**. Each entry must have equal debits and credits; otherwise, Simply will not allow you to post the entry.

2. View the entry to make sure it is correct. Simply will allow you to make corrections if necessary.

3. When the entry is correct, click the **Posting** icon [Post], and the entry is automatically posted to the appropriate accounts in the General Ledger.

To Correct Errors

Correct Errors

A: BEFORE Posting:
Click the field(s) that require changing and change the amounts or words.

B: Reverse Entry. To Correct Errors AFTER Posting –Cancelling the entry ⌈🗙⌉
If you make an error in the journal entry and realize after you have posted it, that it is completely in error and should be cancelled, use the **Reverse entry** feature. (See Exercise 2A-18.)

The Reverse entry reverses the original entry (debits and credits) which cancels the original entry.

C: Adjust a previously posted entry. To Correct Errors AFTER Posting – by

Adjusting the entry ⌈🖊⌉ **Exercise 1-12**
If you make a minor error(s) in a journal entry and realize it after you have posted it, you can use an **Adjustment** entry to open the original entry and correct the error(s) and post the correction. This adjustment entry reverses the original entry (debits and credits) and records the correct entry. See Exercise 1-12 *Correcting an Entry*.

Correction Method A. In this exercise you will record, from a bank debit memo, the bank charges for printing new company cheques. Study the transaction:

Apr 18, 2014   **Received from the bank, new company cheques with a $31.00 bank debit memo, dated April 17, 2014 for the printing charge.**

The correct journal entry is:

Dr	Bank Charges Expense	31.00	
Cr	Cash in Bank		31.00

In order to show you how to correct errors before posting entries, you will deliberately make two errors (an account number at step 6 and an amount at step 11) and correct them before posting.

For this chapter only, GST and PST are ignored. This will allow you to focus on understanding the basics of Simply Accounting at this early stage of your learning.

Exercise 1-6 – Entering Transactions in the General Journal

To start this exercise, you need to be at the Photos Company home window.

General Journal

1 ➤   Click the **General Journal** icon.

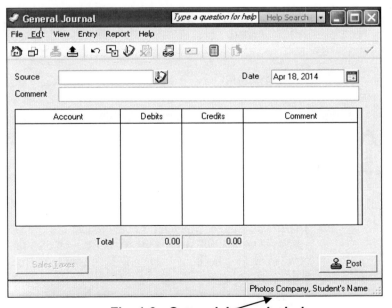

Fig. 1-8: General Journal window.

The name of the company is displayed on the bottom taskbar of the journals. This feature can be turned off and will be discussed in Chapter 4.

When you hold your mouse over each of the toolbar icons, a display below each indicates what they are used for. Try it now.

The ⎡Tab⎤ key is used to move to the next field in all journal screens.
If you want to move to a specific field, click the appropriate field or box.

Source: This field indicates where the information was taken from. It could be a bank debit or credit memo, an invoice number, a cheque number, return or adjustment numbers, a memo, etc.

2 ➤   Source

Type **Bank Debit memo** as the source, press the ⎡Tab⎤ key.

You move to the ⬇ icon. This icon will allow you to reverse and correct previously posted General Journal entries and will be shown to you in Exercise 1-12. Press ⎡Tab⎤ to move to the Date field.

3 ➤   Date

This is the date the transaction occurred. You may not always enter transactions on the day on which they occurred, depending on business volume. Although the printed cheques were received on the 18th, the bank charged (debited) our account on the 6th. The debit memo was issued on April 17; therefore, the transaction date is Apr 17, 2014. Using the calendar, change the date to **Apr 17, 2014**. ⎡Tab⎤ to move to the Comment field.

Comment: The comment line should include details of **who**, **what** and/or **why** you are making the entry. In this entry you need to record information about the printed cheques and any other important information. You may have to abbreviate the comments because the comments field allows 39 spaces only.

4 ➤   Comment

Type **Bank charges printing new cheques SN** (where SN is your initials), press ⎡Tab⎤ to move to the Account field.

Account: If you know the account number, you would type it in this field.

To see a list of General Ledger accounts, press the ⎡Enter⎤ key or double-click the Account field.

You can also search for an account number or account name description. You will search by number.

To use this feature, type the account number (as you will do at step 6) and the lower portion of window will display the accounts near the number. You could also scroll down to find the account you need. It is easier to search by Number (see step 6).

To bypass the search field and use only the lower portion of the window, you would click the **Bypass Search Field** box in the top right and the setting will take effect the next time you use the **Select Account** feature.

5 ➤   Double-click the **Account** field or press ⎡Enter⎤.

A portion of the General Ledger chart of accounts list is shown next.

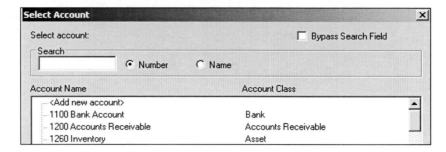

You may need to scroll down using the ▼ scroll bar to the right of the Accounts box. You will notice that the first line indicates **<Add new account>**. The <Add new account> field can be used when you cannot find an appropriate account and decide that a new account in the ledger is needed. This option is explained in Exercise 1-9b and Chapter 4.

Study the following table that shows the account numbering system in Simply:

Account Number Starts with	Type of Account	Normal Balance	To Increase Account	To Decrease Account
1	Asset	Debit	+ Debit	- Credit
2	Liability	Credit	+ Credit	- Debit
3	Equity	Credit	+ Credit	- Debit
4	Revenue	Credit	+ Credit	- Debit
5	Expense	Debit	+ Debit	- Credit

You are going to choose the wrong account and then correct the account before posting.

From a Select Account window, in the lower portion, you could also scroll down to 5320 Business Salary Expense and double-click or click Select.

6 ➤ In the **Search** field type **5** (you will notice that the lower window moves to the 5 account numbers.) Type **2** and you move further into the 5 section account numbers. You should be at the line for Office Supplies Expense. If there were other numbers (e.g., 5325) you would continue entering numbers or scroll to the account needed. Press Enter or click **Select**.

5220 Office Supplies Expense is entered in the Account field and the cursor has moved to the Debits column (0.00) for the amount.

Oops, wrong account number. This is an error that needs to be corrected.

You will now correct the account number.

7 ➤ To delete the wrong account, click **5220 Office Supplies Expense** and press the Delete key.

8 ➤ Repeat steps 5 and 6 to locate and select (double-click) **5180 Bank Charges Expense** account. The account number has been corrected.

9 ➤   In the Debits column enter the amount **31** and press 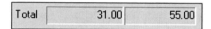. Simply puts in the missing 00 after the decimal point. If the amount was 50.25, you would need to enter 50, decimal point, 25 then ⬚. The cursor moves to the Comment column.

10 ➤   **Comment**   Use this column when you want to record additional comments for each account. Type **Printing charge new cheques**. Press ⬚ to move to the Account field.

11 ➤   Double-click the Accounts field and select **1100 Bank Account**. The amount **31.00** automatically appears in the credit column. The software calculates the net amount of the Debit and Credit entries entered and displays the amount needed to make debits and credits equal. **Bank Account** is credited because when money is deducted from the account (by debit memo or cheque) Bank Account decreases.

You will enter the wrong amount in the current field to allow you to observe what happens when you try to post an entry with unequal debits and credits.

---

12 ➤   Change the **Bank Account** amount from 31.00 to **55.00,** ⬚. This is an error which you will fix in step 15.

Notice that the totals at the bottom of the General Journal are not equal.

Total	31.00	55.00

13 ➤   Click the ⬚ **Post** button. Study the Error message box that appears:

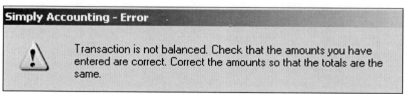

Simply Accounting - Error

⚠ Transaction is not balanced. Check that the amounts you have entered are correct. Correct the amounts so that the totals are the same.

14 ➤   Click **OK** to return to the General Journal.

You will now enter the correct amount.

---

15 ➤   Highlight **55.00,** and type **31.00,** then press ⬚. The Totals at the bottom of the Journal are now equal.

Do not post at this time.

Congratulations! You have entered a complete journal entry. Compare your window with Fig. 1-9.

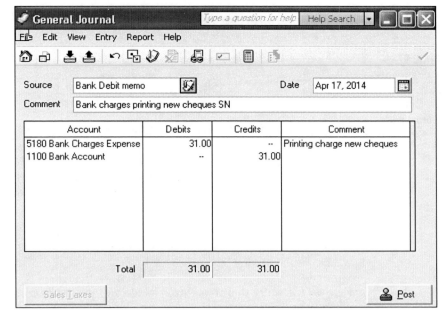

Fig. 1-9: General Journal Entry.

The Sales Taxes button
Sales Taxes is grayed
out because GST and
PST are not used in this
entry. This button will be
discussed in Chapter 3B.

⚠️ **DO NOT POST YET.** You need to verify your entry first.

Displaying the Journal Entry

Before posting, it is best to check the accuracy of your journal entry. If there is an error, it may be easily corrected before posting.

There are two ways to correct an entry before posting:

1. Highlight the wrong entry item in the General Journal window and type the correct information.

2. If the entry has quite a few errors, it is best to start over. Click the **Undo** icon. A message box will appear verifying that you want to discard the entry. Click **Yes** to discard the entry, then retype the complete entry.

Exercise 1-7 – Displaying a Journal Entry

---

1 ➤ Click **Report** on the Menu Bar.

2 ➤ Click **Display General Journal Entry Ctrl + J** (Ctrl + J is a keyboard shortcut to display the entry). You can press Ctrl + J from Fig. 1-9 without having to complete steps 1 and 2. You will notice many other shortcuts in drop-down menus.

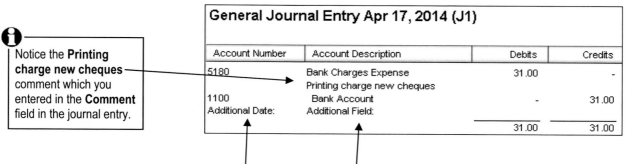

General Journal Entry Apr 17, 2014 (J1)

Account Number	Account Description	Debits	Credits
5180	Bank Charges Expense	31.00	-
	Printing charge new cheques		
1100	Bank Account	-	31.00
Additional Date:	Additional Field:		
		31.00	31.00

Notice the **Printing charge new cheques** comment which you entered in the **Comment** field in the journal entry.

Simply assigns a journal entry number, beginning with J1, to posted entries. This entry is displayed as J1. There are no previous Journal entries recorded in this data file.

The **Additional Date** and **Additional Field** information is displayed in all journal windows even if you don't enter information in these fields. The use of these fields will be explained in Exercise 1-11.

Review the entry to make sure it is correct. If it is not correct you need to close this window and correct the entry on the General Journal window before posting.

3 ➤ To exit, click the ⊠ box to return to the Journal window.

4 ➤ Click the POST button, the screen flickers and the following window appears.

Simply Accounting - Transaction Confirmation

This transaction was posted successfully.

Journal Entry: J1.

☐ Do not show this message again.

OK

This confirmation window is used to indicate that the entry was posted as Journal 1 (J1) to the General Ledger. Many students are not sure if they have posted the entry and record another entry. After you are comfortable knowing your entries are posted, you could click the "Do not show this message again" box.

If you click the "Do not show this message again" box by mistake, you can return the Transaction Confirmation window by clicking Setup, User Preferences. In the left hand window, click Transaction Confirmation, and click the right hand box, then OK.

5 ➤ Click **OK**, to accept the posting confirmation. The screen flickers, and returns to a blank journal window.

6 ➤ To exit to the Home window, click the ⊠.

GST is ignored in this chapter and will be covered later in the text.

To Advance the Session Date

The current session date is April 18 and you need to record transactions dated for the week ending April 25. You do not need to exit the program to move or advance the date. You can advance the date from the Home window.

Exercise 1-8 – To Advance the Session Date

---

1 ➤ Click the **Change** item at  icon.

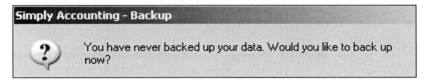

2 ➤ Using the calendar, change the date to **Apr 25, 2014** and click **OK**. You will see the following:

> **Simply Accounting – Backup**
>
> **?** You have never backed up your data. Would you like to back up now?

3 ➤ You do not need to back up at this time, so click **No**.

Recording a Compound Entry and Adding a New Account

So far, you entered a transaction where there is one Debit account and one Credit account. A compound entry uses three or more accounts.

The next transaction is a payment for a bank loan. Payments are normally recorded in the PAYABLES module. The PAYABLES module records all purchases and payments on credit, cash, cheque, credit card, or debit card. This transaction is entered in the General Journal because the bank debited the company bank account and a cheque is not being issued. You will be shown how to record payments by cheque in the PAYABLES module in Chapter 3.

Exercise 1-9a – Recording a Compound Entry

Study the following transaction:

> **Apr 21, 2014 Received debit memo, dated today, from the bank, indicating a $215.00 payment was made on the bank loan which includes Interest of $76.44. The loan was received on March 21.**

The correct compound entry is:

Dr	Bank Loan Payable	138.56	
Dr	Bank Loan Interest Expense	76.44	
Cr	Cash in Bank		215.00

A new general ledger account for Bank Loan Interest Expense will be created as part of Exercise 1-9b.

1 ➤ Click on the General Journal icon.

2 ➤   **Source**   Type **Bank Debit memo** as the source, and press `Tab`, `Tab` to move to the Date field.

3 ➤   **Date**   Using the calendar, change the date to **Apr 21, 2014**. `Tab` to move to the Comment field.

4 ➤   **Comment**   Type **Bank Loan Payment**, press `Tab` to move to the Account field.

5 ➤   **Account**   Type **2710,** Bank Loan Payable, `Tab`.

6 ➤   **Debits**   Type **138.56,** `Tab`.

7 ➤   **Comment**   **Principal repayment,** `Tab`.

Exercise 1-9b – Adding a New General Ledger Account

1 ➤   **Account**   Double-click the column or press `Enter` and click on **<Add new account>**, click `Select`.

Enter information shown in Fig 1-10a.

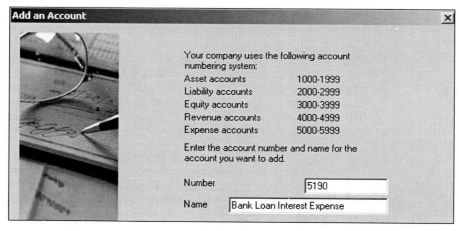

Fig 1-10a: Add an Account window.

    Number   This is the number, the owner decided, to use for the new account that is to be added. You must make sure that it fits one of the numbering sequences as noted in the window.

    Name   This is the name of the new account.

2 ➤ When the Add an Account window resembles Fig. 1-10a, click **Next >**.

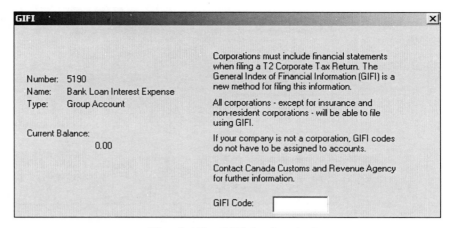

Fig. 1-10b: GIFI Code window.

Type   The default type of account code will be Group Account. It can be changed in step 5 or 6. Account Groups will be explained in more detail in Chapter 4.

Current   0.00. This is a new account for Photos Company. You cannot add a
Balance   balance to a new account in this company data file. The file is in Ready mode for the Company folder. You can create a balance for a company that is being created (History). This is discussed in Chapter 4.

If your business is a corporation, you would need to number the account number based on the GIFI codes as identified by Canada Revenue Agency (CRA). This section assumes that the business is not a corporation. If your business is a corporation, contact your accountant or Canada Revenue Agency for further information about the GIFI numbering sequences.

    3 ➤ Photos Company is not a corporation; therefore, leave the GIFI field empty. Click **Next >**.

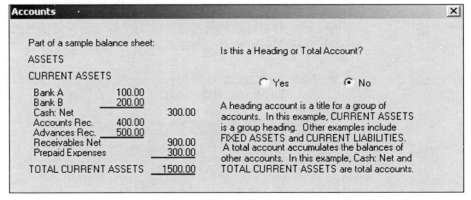

Fig. 1-10c: Accounts – Heading or Total window

If the account to be added is a Heading or a Final Total of a section, you would click the 'Yes' button. Account 5190 is an account used to accumulate Bank Loan Interest Expense and is not a Heading or a Total account. Headings and Total accounts will be discussed in more detail in Chapter 4.

    4 ➤ With a setting of **No**, click **Next>**.

        If the account being added is to be added with another account to create a subtotal, similar to Bank A and Bank B shown next, then you would click Yes. Account 5190 will not require a subtotal, similar to Prepaid Expenses.

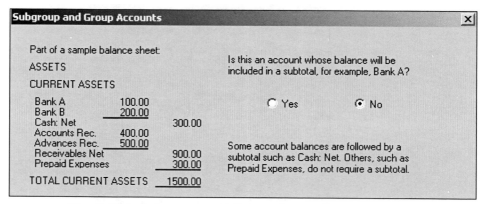

Fig. 1-10d: Subgroup and Group Accounts window.

5 ➤ With a setting of **No**, click **Next>**.

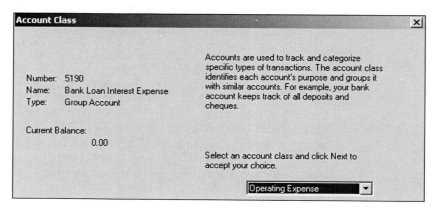

Fig. 1-10e: Account Class window.

Simply has selected Operating Expense as the Account Class. You will learn more about account classes in Chapter 4.

6 ➤ Click the ▼ and you will see various Account classes. Select the account class **Expense**, click **Next>**.

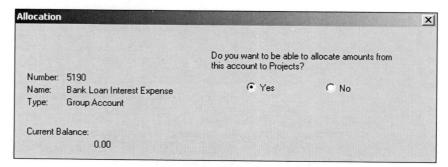

Fig. 1-10f: Allocation window.

7 ➤ If you need to allocate project revenue and expenses to this account, you would accept the Yes default selection. This business does not use the PROJECT module; therefore, change the setting to **No.** Click **Next>**.

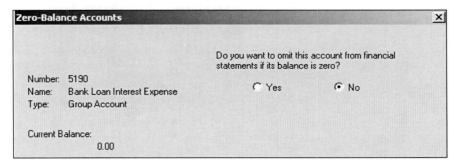

Fig. 1-10g: Zero-Balance Accounts window.

8 ➤ If you want accounts with zero balances to appear on financial statements, you would click No. If you do NOT want accounts with zero balances to appear on financial statements you would click Yes. With a setting of **No**, click **Next>**.

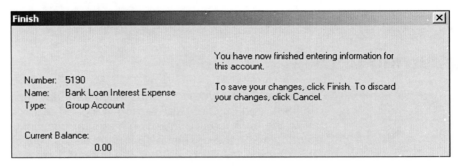

Fig. 1-10h: Finish window.

9 ➤ Click **Finish** to add the account to the General Ledger and the account column. Continue recording the entry as shown next.

10 ➤ **Account** [Tab]

11 ➤ **Debits** Type **76.44**, [Tab] to Account.

12 ➤ **Account** Type **1100** (Bank Account), [Tab].

13 ➤ **Credits** [Tab] to accept **215.00** and move to Comment.

14 ➤ **Comment** Type **Bank Loan Payment.**

DO NOT Post the transaction until you complete the next exercise.

Your General Journal window should resemble the following:

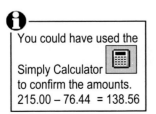

You could have used the Simply Calculator to confirm the amounts.
215.00 – 76.44 = 138.56

Source	Bank Debit memo			Date	Apr 21, 2014	
Comment	Bank Loan Payment					

Account	Debits	Credits	Comment
2710 Bank Loan Payable	138.56	--	Principal repayment
5190 Bank Loan Interest Exper	76.44	--	
1100 Bank Account	--	215.00	Bank Loan Payment

15 ➤ Don't forget to display the entry. Notice that this entry is J2 and is a compound entry.

General Journal Entry Apr 21, 2014 (J2)			
Account Number	Account Description	Debits	Credits
2710	Bank Loan Payable	138.56	-
	Principal repayment		
5190	Bank Loan Interest Expense	76.44	-
1100	Bank Account	-	215.00
	Bank Loan Payment		
Additional Date:	Additional Field:		
		215.00	215.00

Note: In Simply 2009 the Additional Date and Additional Field will be shown in journal entry display (as above) even when no information has been entered in the fields. See Exercise 1-11, step 7.

16 ➤ Click ☒ to return to the General Journal screen.

DO NOT POST YET! Continue with the next exercise.

Recurring Entries

A recurring entry refers to a transaction that may repeat many times during the year. The bank loan payment transaction is a good example. You know that you will be paying the bank loan payment on a regular basis. If you enter the above entry as a recurring entry, the next time your bank debits your account for the loan payment you can recall the entry, change the date and amounts, and it would be ready to Post. It saves time and helps you avoid errors.

Exercise 1-10 – Creating a Recurring Entry

1 ➤ To store this entry for future use, click the 3rd icon on the left side of the toolbar, **Store as recurring transaction** 🔽. The next window is where you will identify the name you wish to associate with this entry and the frequency you want Simply to remind you when it will reoccur.

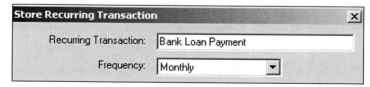

2 ➤ Notice that in the Recurring Transaction box, the comment you entered in the General Journal is automatically entered. Change the recurring transaction name to **Bank Loan Payment Monthly** ⌨Tab.

3 ➤ **Frequency** Click the ▾ to see the various choices available for how often you want this entry to appear. Leave Frequency as **Monthly**.

4 ➤ Click **OK**. The entry is now saved for future use. You will be using a different recurring entry in Exercise 1-15.

5 ➤ Post when correct.

6 ➤ You will see the J2 Transaction confirmation window. Click **OK**.

Owner Investment in Business

The owner's investment may be recorded in the General Journal as the funds were transferred, by the bank, from her personal account to the business to show the personal investment.

Exercise 1-11 – Journalizing Owner Investment in Business

Apr 24, 2014	Mrs. Chikowski, called you to advise you that she decided to invest an additional $2,000.00 in the business, as she is going to purchase a new photo machine from another photo business. She is transferring $2,000.00 from her personal bank account to the company's bank account and asked you to record the investment.

If you closed the General Journal prior to this exercise, click on the General Journal icon.

If you did not close the General Journal, you should be at a blank General Journal window.

1 ➤ **Record** the investment based on the following window.

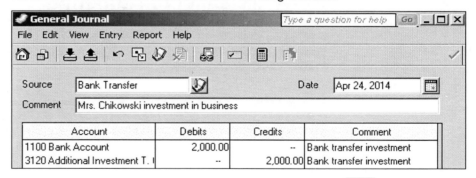

2 ➤ On the icon bar, click the **Enter Additional Information** [✔] icon and the Additional Information window appears.

This feature allows you to record additional information about the transaction, such as other dates and other information (e.g., voucher dates and voucher approvals, or entry recorded by person's name) that may be useful for the audit trail, or for future reference. This text does not use this feature in all entries.

3 ➤ **Additional Date**   Select **Apr 24, 2014** the day the transaction was recorded. [Tab].

4 ➤ **Additional Field**   Type **Mrs. Chikowski phone call message SN** (replace SN with your initials).

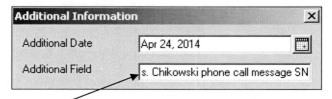

Note: the **s** refers to the word Mrs. that is partially hidden.

5 ➤ Click **OK**. Notice that the Additional Information window is gone and the General Journal window shown does not have any indication of the information just entered. This will be explained in the next 2 steps.

6 ➤ When your entry resembles the above investment window, click **Report, Display General Journal Entry**.

General Journal Entry Apr 24, 2014 (J3)

Account Number	Account Description	Debits	Credits
1100	Bank Account	2,000.00	-
	Bank transfer investment		
3120	Additional Investment T. Chiko...	-	2,000.00
	Bank transfer investment		
Additional Date: Ap...	Additional Field: Mrs. Chikowski ph...		
		2,000.00	2,000.00

7 ➤ Notice the additional information at the bottom. The additional information entered displays in the General Journal Entry window, and is retained by the system. Click ⊠ to close the entry. You will notice that the additional information is not shown in the General Journal.

8 ➤ When your entry is correct, click **Post**, and click **OK** to accept **J3**.

Correcting an Entry – Cancel or Adjusting

When you realize that an error has been made after you have posted a transaction, you can use the Reverse entry or Adjust the entry features in Simply. Simply 2009 makes this task very easy.

Exercise 1-12 – Correcting an Entry

> **Apr 25, 2014** Mrs. Chikowski advised you that she decided to increase the investment in the business to $3,000.00, when she was at the bank (April 24). She gave you the $3,000 bank transfer document.

In Exercise 1-11, you posted the following:

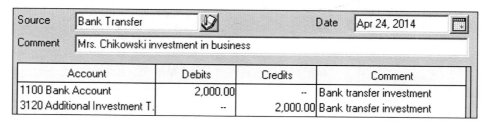

The investment was recorded for the wrong amount. Do not panic. You can reverse or correct an entry once it has been posted.

You have three ways to correct this:

1. You can manually reverse entry J3 by reversing the debits and credits. Then enter a new entry to record the entry correctly. You could make an error in the reversal and need to correct this error as well.

2. You can use the Reverse entry feature to allow Simply to reverse the debits and credits to cancel J3. Then you enter the correct entry if needed. Refer to Exercise 2A-17 and 2A-18 to see *To Correct a Receipt* or *to Cancel a Posted Invoice*.

3. You can use the Adjust a previously posted entry feature to adjust and correct J3. This will allow you to correctly record the entry. You do not need to reverse J3.

This exercise will use method 3 to adjust the J3 entry.

1 ➤ Click the **Adjust a previously posted entry** icon (it is to the right of the source field and also on the toolbar) and the following window appears.

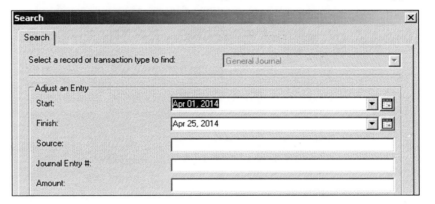

In business, you choose the dates of the entries you want to see displayed or sort by Source field description, Journal entry number or Amount.

You could leave the other fields blank and click OK to see what entries have been previously recorded.

2 ➤ Leave the other fields blank to see the entries recorded, click **OK**. Entries 1, 2 and 3 have been recorded previously and are displayed.

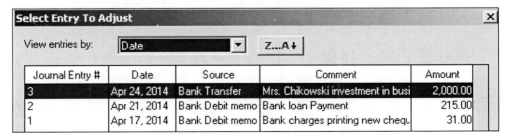

Journal Entry #	Date	Source	Comment	Amount
3	Apr 24, 2014	Bank Transfer	Mrs. Chikowski investment in busi	2,000.00
2	Apr 21, 2014	Bank Debit memo	Bank loan Payment	215.00
1	Apr 17, 2014	Bank Debit memo	Bank charges printing new chequ	31.00

3 ➤ You would click the entry that you need to reverse. **J3** should be highlighted in blue, click **Select**. Note that the previous entry with details appears and the header of the entry identifies the Source field.

General Journal - Adjusting Bank Transfer

4 ➤ Change Debits and Credits to **3000.00**. You can change any fields (source, date, comments, account names and/or amounts). Do not change the date.

5 ➤ Display the Journal entry. Note that the entry number is **J5**. J4 is the reversal entry and J5 is the correct entry.

Account Number	Account Description	Debits	Credits
1100	Bank Account	3,000.00	-
	Bank transfer investment		
3120	Additional Investment T. Chiko...	-	3,000.00
	Bank transfer investment		
Additional Date: Ap...	Additional Field: Mrs. Chikowski ph...		
		3,000.00	3,000.00

General Journal Entry Apr 24, 2014 (J5)

6 ➤ **Exit** the display window.

7 ➤ Click **Post**, click **OK** to accept confirmation number J5, click ⊠ and return to the Home window.

Displaying Corrected Entries with Reversals

When necessary, you can display entries that have been posted and subsequently corrected. The following exercise will show you how to display both the original incorrect entries and reversing entries. Later in the exercise, you will learn how to display the corrected entries only, without the incorrect entries.

This text uses displaying corrections as the default. However, your instructor may advise you to display only the correct entries without showing any of the entries you have reversed.

Exercise 1-13 – To Display Corrected Entries
---

1 ➤ At the Reports area, click ▼ and select **All Journal Entries,** click **Display**. The display shows J1, J2 and J5. We want to see what happened to the reversal and correction. Click the Modify button, select **Report Options**. Click the **Corrections** field.

Corrections: Make sure the field ☑ Corrections is checked.
Additional Information: Leave the field blank. We will concentrate on the correction and not the additional Information area.

2 ➤ Change the Start date and Finish date to **Apr 24, 2014**. This exercise will focus on the Investment correction entry. The Modify Report window should appear as shown next:

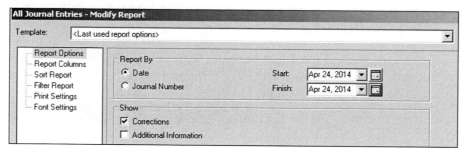

In a job situation, you would display and print all entries (with corrections) because this provides an audit trail (history) of entries that were recorded and changed. Notice that the Additional Information field is not checked.

3 ➤ Click **OK** and the following window will appear (see side note box):

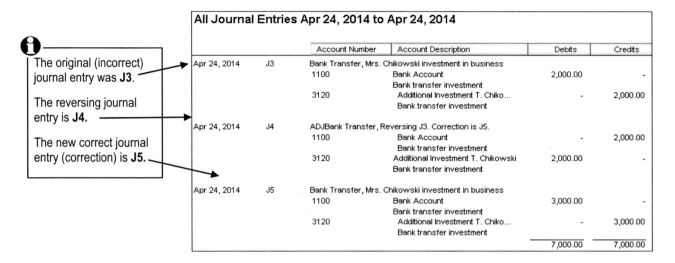

The original (incorrect) journal entry was **J3**.

The reversing journal entry is **J4**.

The new correct journal entry (correction) is **J5**.

All Journal Entries Apr 24, 2014 to Apr 24, 2014

			Account Number	Account Description	Debits	Credits
Apr 24, 2014	J3			Bank Transfer, Mrs. Chikowski investment in business		
			1100	Bank Account	2,000.00	-
				Bank transfer investment		
			3120	Additional Investment T. Chiko...	-	2,000.00
				Bank transfer investment		
Apr 24, 2014	J4			ADJBank Transfer, Reversing J3. Correction is J5.		
			1100	Bank Account	-	2,000.00
				Bank transfer investment		
			3120	Additional Investment T. Chikowski	2,000.00	-
				Bank transfer investment		
Apr 24, 2014	J5			Bank Transfer, Mrs. Chikowski investment in business		
			1100	Bank Account	3,000.00	-
				Bank transfer investment		
			3120	Additional Investment T. Chiko...	-	3,000.00
				Bank transfer investment		
					7,000.00	7,000.00

J4 shows as the reversing entry and **J5** is the corrected Journal entry. The amount **7000.00** at the bottom of the entry is the total of the debits and credits displayed. This will be explained in more detail later.

4 ➤ In order to prepare for the next steps, click the [Modify ▾] icon and select **Report Options**. The All Journal Entries- Modify Report window (seen at step 2) reappears.

To Show Corrected Entries Only

Notice that the [☑ Corrections] box is checked, which is now the default.

5 ➤ You do not want to show the original incorrect entry and the reversing entry in the report, therefore, click the [☑ Corrections] box to remove the check mark.

6 ➤ Click **OK**. Entry 3, with the error, and entry 4, the reversing entry, will not be displayed. Only the corrected entry J5 is displayed as shown below.

			Account Number	Account Description	Debits	Credits
Apr 24, 2014	J5			Bank Transfer, Mrs. Chikowski investment in business		
			1100	Bank Account	3,000.00	-
				Bank transfer investment		
			3120	Additional Investment T. Chiko...	-	3,000.00
				Bank transfer investment		
					3,000.00	3,000.00

Now, if you wish to display all entries, from a specific date only without corrections (e.g., Apr 17, 2014) follow the next step.

7 ➤ Click the **Modify** icon, select **Report Options**, and the **All Journal Entries** window reappears. Change the Start Date to **Apr 17, 2014** and make sure the ✓ has been removed from Corrections. Click **OK**.

All Journal Entries Apr 17, 2014 to Apr 24, 2014					
		Account Number	Account Description	Debits	Credits
Apr 17, 2014	J1		Bank Debit memo, Bank charges printing new cheques SN		
		5180	Bank Charges Expense	31.00	-
			Printing charge new cheques		
		1100	Bank Account	-	31.00
Apr 21, 2014	J2		Bank Debit memo, Bank loan Payment		
		2710	Bank Loan Payable	138.56	-
			Principal repayment		
		5190	Bank Loan Interest Expense	76.44	-
		1100	Bank Account	-	215.00
			Bank loan payment		
Apr 24, 2014	J5		Bank Transfer, Mrs. Chikowski investment in business		
		1100	Bank Account	3,000.00	-
			Bank transfer investment		
		3120	Additional Investment T. Chiko...	-	3,000.00
			Bank transfer investment		
				3,246.00	3,246.00

Entry 3, with the error, and entry 4, the reversing entry, will not be displayed. Only the correct entries are displayed.

8 ➤ **Exit** the display window.

To Remove a Recurring Transaction Entry

Exercise 1-14 – Removing a Recurring Transaction Entry

You previously created a recurring transaction entry for Bank Loan Payment Monthly. This exercise will show you how to delete a recurring transaction entry, but you will not actually remove it.

1 ➤ Click the **General Journal** icon.

2 ➤ Click the 4th icon on the left ⬆ (Recall recurring transaction) and the following window appears.

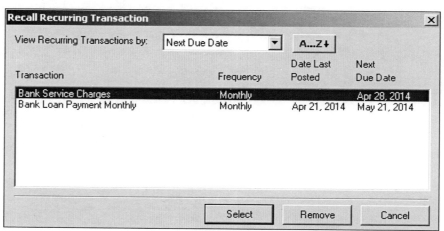

3 ➤ Click the ▼ and a drop-down list of report options is displayed. Leave the choice as **Next Due Date**. Click the **A...Z↓** and the report will be sorted automatically in descending or ascending order.

4 ➤ Return the display to ascending as shown in step 3.

5 ➤ Click the **Bank Loan Payment Monthly** listing, then click the **Remove** button and a warning message box appears.

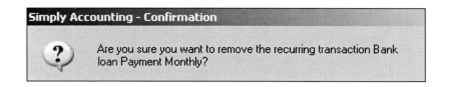

6 ➤ Click **No,** as you do not want to remove this item. This exercise is only to show you how you could remove a recurring entry. Click **Cancel** and you are returned to the General Journal window.

7 ➤ If the Home window is showing, you can click the 🗙 **Close All Other Windows** icon to close the General Journal window and any other Simply windows and return to the Home window. If you cannot see the 🗙 icon, click ☒ to return to the Home window.

8 ➤ Advance the date to **Apr 30** and click **No** on the Simply Accounting – Backup window as you do not need to back up now.

Using a Recurring Transaction

Bank charges are levied each month and, as shown in Exercise 1-14, in the Recall Recurring Transaction window, an April 28 bank charges recurring transaction was set up for future use on April 28. You will also use a recurring entry in Chapter 3.

Exercise 1-15 – Using a Recurring Transaction

Apr 30, 2014	You received a Bank Statement with a Debit memo dated April 29, 2014 from the bank advising that they have deducted $22.46 from your bank account for service charges.

To use the Bank Charges recurring entry, complete the following steps:

1 ➤ Click on the **General Journal** icon.

2 ➤ From the **General Journal** window, click the **Recall Recurring Transaction** icon, 4th icon on the left, and the following window appears.

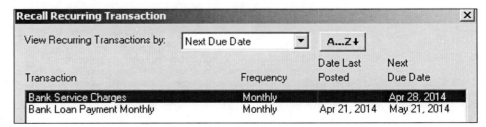

3 ➤ **Bank Service Charges**, should be highlighted in blue, click Select and the General Journal window appears with the recurring transaction information.

4 ➤ **Date** Change the date to **Apr 29, 2014**. This is the date the money was removed from the bank account.

5 ➤ Change the **date** and the **amount** as shown in the journal below.

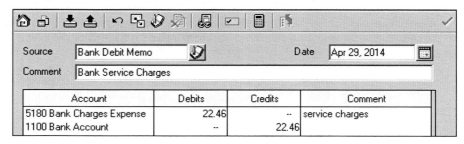

6 ➤ Click the **Enter Additional Information** [✓] icon.

This feature allows you to record additional information about the transaction, such as other dates and other information (e.g., voucher dates and voucher approvals, or entry recorded by person's name) that may be useful for the audit trail, or for future reference. This text does not use this feature in all entries.

7 ➤ **Additional Date**   Change the date to **Apr 29, 2014** the day the service charges were taken from the account.

8 ➤ **Additional Field**   Type **Recorded by SN** (replace SN with your initials).

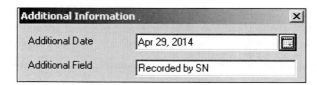

9 ➤ Click **OK**.

10 ➤ When your entry resembles the above window, click **Report, Display General Journal Entry**.

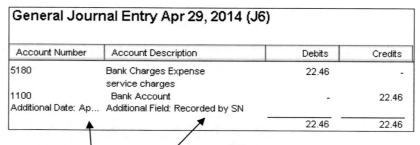

11 ➤ Notice the additional information. Click ⊠ to close the entry.

12 ➤ When your entry is correct, click **Post**.

You will see the Confirmation message shown next:

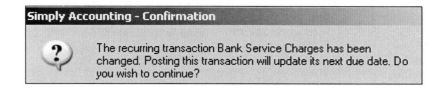

You have recorded the bank charges for the period ending April 29. The recurring Due date (28th) is from the initial creation date. If the date or other information needs to change, the recurring entry could be resaved with the new information. Many businesses set up several recurring entries to help save time; you change only fields that need changing, and post.

13 ➤ Click **Yes**, J6 posting confirmation window appears. Click **OK**. The entry will be available for next month. (See the Next Due Date window in step 14.)

14 ➤ Click the 🔼 **Recall recurring transaction**. (See side note box and Next Due Date field.)

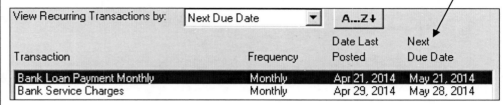

View Recurring Transactions by:	Next Due Date ▼	A...Z↓		
Transaction		Frequency	Date Last Posted	Next Due Date
Bank Loan Payment Monthly		Monthly	Apr 21, 2014	May 21, 2014
Bank Service Charges		Monthly	Apr 29, 2014	May 28, 2014

15 ➤ Click **Cancel** and ⓧ to return to the Home window.

Drill Down (Trace Back)

From an Income Statement, Balance Sheet or other reports, you can drill down (trace back) one level at a time to review a transaction in order to see the relevant information (including amounts) in the report.

This drill down feature works in all modules.

Exercise 1-16 – Drill Down (Trace Back)

Your manager has asked you to review the transactions you entered earlier, using the Income Statement. The following instructions will show you various techniques in tracing back transactions.

1 ➤ Display the **Balance Sheet** for Photos Company for **Apr 29, 2014** (see Exercise 1-5b).

2 ➤ As you move your cursor over the accounts, the cursor changes to a magnifying glass.

3 ➤ Move down to the **Equity section**, **Additional Investment – T. Chikowski** account and double-click.

The General Ledger Report for account 3120 displays for the same time period.

General Ledger Report Apr 01, 2014 to Apr 29, 2014
Sorted by: Transaction Number

Date	Comment	Source #	JE#	Debits	Credits	Balance
3120	**Additional Investment T. Chikowski**					- Cr
Apr 24, 2014	Mrs. Chikowski investment in business	Bank Transfer	J5	-	3,000.00	3,000.00 Cr

If you hide the error and reversing entry (J3 and J4) from the Journal Entries display as shown in Exercise 1-13, they will still display in the General Ledger report if the Show Corrections box is ✓.

This report is sorted by Transaction Number (default). As shown in Exercise 1-17 (Display and Print the General Journal), the report can be sorted by date. Using the Drill down feature, this report does not display the Adjusting entries (J3 and J4).

4 ➤ Position the cursor on **J5**, or the amount, or the Source field information, and double-click. The General Journal entry that created the entry is displayed. (See side note box.) If you want to see the Journal entry window, double-click on J5 and you are taken to the journal window. Click ⊠ to return to the step 3 window.

If you want to see the original and reversing entries, on the Modify icon, click on Report Options and click on ☑ Corrections. Click OK to see the original, reversing and correcting entry.

In the CUSTOMERS and VENDORS modules, Chapters 2A & 2B and 3A & 3B, when the journal entry is displayed, you will be able to see the aged report for that firm if you click the Customer or Vendor name.

5 ➤ Click the ⊠ in the right corner of the open windows to return to the Balance Sheet.

6 ➤ Click ⊠ to return to the Home window.

To Display and Print the General Journal

It is a good idea at this point to print a report of entries you have recorded from Session Date Apr 17 to Apr 29. The printed copy provides proof of what has been recorded in the company file.

Exercise 1-17 – To Display and Print the General Journal

The Reports area, will display only: All Journal entries. Use the following procedure to display and print only General Journal entries from the COMPANY module.

Although you might know that there are no transactions between April 1 to 17, you should use the beginning of the month for the Start Date to ensure that your system does not have entries posted before the entries you processed.

You should be at the Home window to start this exercise.

1 ➤ Click the **Report Centre** icon, in the left pane, click on **Accounts**, click on **General Journal Entries**. If you were sure of the setting to change, you could click on 'Modify this report' to change a setting. You will do this in step 2. Click **Display**.

2 ➤ To change a setting, click on **Modify icon**, **Report Options**. The Start Date should be **Apr 01, 2014** (the first day of the month and the End Date should be **Apr 30, 2014** (current Session date).

When you choose the ✓ show **Additional Information,** the **Additional Date** and **Additional Field** will display in all entries regardless if you used the field or not.

In the future, if you do not want the **Additional Date** and **Additional Field** to appear in Journal windows or printouts, make sure the field is unchecked.

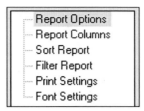

3 ➤ Make sure the boxes are ✓ to have this information shown in the report. (See side note box.)

There are a number of reports that can be customized to the user's requirements. See left panel shown next.

- Report Options
- Report Columns
- Sort Report
- Filter Report
- Print Settings
- Font Settings

There is no exercise in this text to use these features. If you customize any of the reports, you must return to the original default choice; otherwise, future displays and/or reports will be different as compared to the text.

Report Options Shown previously.

Report Columns Customize column settings for this report. This feature will allow you to change the width of the columns and columns to be displayed/printed in reports. In the left pane, click on **Report Columns**, click on **Custom report column settings** button.

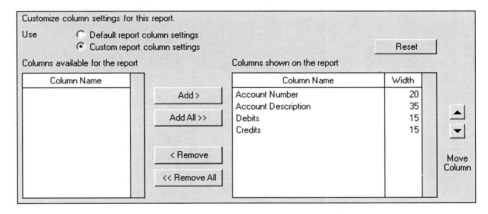

Sort Report — Custom sort order

Click **Sort Report**, and **Custom sort order**. This feature allows you to sort columns (fields) in reports.

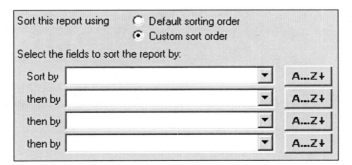

Click **Filter Report**, and click **Use your filter specification**.

This feature allows you to prepare reports in modules with various columns equal to the data requested; e.g., Customers with balances over $1,000.00.

> Filter the data to specify what to include in the report. Only the records you selected on the previous screen will be filtered.
>
> If any of the three fields on a filter is blank, then that filter will be skipped.
>
> ☑ Use your filter specification
>
> Only include data if:
>
> | Field | Matching criteria | Value | |
> |---|---|---|---|
> | ▼ | ▼ | | ⊙ And ○ Or |
> | ▼ | ▼ | | ⊙ And ○ Or |
> | ▼ | ▼ | | ⊙ And ○ Or |
> | ▼ | ▼ | | |

Print Settings — **Custom page orientation** and **Custom margins**

Click **Printer Settings,** click **Custom page orientation**.

This feature allows you to set Portrait or Landscape and to Customize the margins as the default print setting.

> Customize print settings for this report.
>
> Page Orientation
>
> Use ○ The report printer's current setting
>
>   ⊙ Custom page orientation
>
>   ⊙ Portrait
>   ○ Landscape
>
> Margins (inches)
>
> Use ○ The company's current report settings
>
>   ⊙ Custom margins
>
>   Top: 0.00
>   Left: 0.00

Font Settings — **Custom font settings**

4 ➤ Click **Font Settings,** click **Custom font settings**.

This feature allows you to change report fonts and colours, sizes, Bold, Italicize and Align information left, centre or right.

> Customize font settings for this report.
>
> Use ○ The company's current report settings.
>   ⊙ Custom font settings
>
> | | | | | |
> |---|---|---|---|---|
> | Report Header: | ▼ | Arial ▼ | 12 ▼ | B I ≣ ≣ ≣ |
> | Report Title: | ▼ | Arial ▼ | 12 ▼ | B I ≣ ≣ ≣ |
> | Column Titles: | ▼ | Arial ▼ | 8 ▼ | B I |
> | Section Headings and Totals: | ▼ | Arial ▼ | 8 ▼ | B I |
> | Detail Lines: | ▼ | Arial ▼ | 8 ▼ | B I |
> | Positive Amounts: | ▼ | | | |
> | Negative Amounts: | ▼ | -1234.56 ▼ | | |
> | Report Footers: | ▼ | Arial ▼ | 8 ▼ | B I ≣ ≣ ≣ Default |

5 ➤ Click **OK** to display the Journal Entries.

You may experiment with any of the customizations, but you must return to the default settings choice; otherwise, future displays and/or reports will be different as compared to the text.

General Journal Apr 01, 2014 to Apr 30, 2014

		Account Number	Account Description	Debits	Credits
Apr 17, 2014	J1		Bank Debit Memo, Bank charges printing new cheques SN		
		5180	Bank Charges Expense	31.00	-
			Printing charge new cheques		
		1100	Bank Account	-	31.00
Additional Date:		Additional Field:			
Apr 21, 2014	J2		Bank Debit memo, Bank Loan Payment		
		2710	Bank Loan Payable	138.56	-
			Principal repayment		
		5190	Bank Loan Interest Expense	76.44	-
		1100	Bank Account	-	215.00
			Bank Loan Payment		
Additional Date:		Additional Field:			
Apr 24, 2014	J3		Bank Transfer, Mrs. Chikowski investment in business		
		1100	Bank Account	2,000.00	-
			Bank transfer investment		
		3120	Additional Investment T. Chiko...	-	2,000.00
			Bank transfer investment		
Additional Date: Apr 24, 2014		Additional Field: Mrs. Chikowski phone call message SN			
Apr 24, 2014	J4		ADJBank Transfer, Reversing J3. Correction is J5.		
		1100	Bank Account	-	2,000.00
			Bank transfer investment		
		3120	Additional Investment T. Chikowski	2,000.00	-
			Bank transfer investment		
Additional Date: Apr 24, 2014		Additional Field: Mrs. Chikowski phone call message SN			
Apr 24, 2014	J5		Bank Transfer, Mrs. Chikowski investment in business		
		1100	Bank Account	3,000.00	-
			Bank transfer investment		
		3120	Additional Investment T. Chiko...	-	3,000.00
			Bank transfer investment		
Additional Date: Apr 24, 2014		Additional Field: Mrs. Chikowski phone call message SN			
Apr 29, 2014	J6		Bank Debit Memo, Bank Service Charges		
		5180	Bank Charges Expense	22.46	-
			service charges		
		1100	Bank Account	-	22.46
Additional Date: Apr 29, 2014		Additional Field: Recorded by SN			
				7,268.46	7,268.46

Fig. 1-11: General Journal Transactions (no hidden entries).

> The total amount, i.e., 7,268.46, is the sum of journal entries 1 to 6, and verifies the equality of debit and credits only. The total does not indicate the accuracy of the values recorded.

The total amount at the bottom (7,268.46) which is the sum of journal entries 1 through 6 does not have to equal your numbers if you have made more entries. (See side note box.)

To ensure you have processed your entries correctly, you must compare your entries to each entry in the solution set. (You cannot rely on the debit and credit column totals.)

You can use the [🔍 Print Preview] icon on the toolbar to view the report before printing to make sure it is what you want. If you see ... on some lines, click [X] to return to the General Journal Display. You can click the top report header and move the columns to display the missing information. If you expand the columns, watch for the right column (dotted line) that indicates a page break.

6 ➤ To print this report, you can click Print in the Print Preview window, or return to the General Journal Display and click the 🖨 Print icon. Wait for the Print dialog box to disappear before moving on.

7 ➤ **Exit** to the Home window.

Display and Print the General Ledger Report

The General Ledger report displays the transactions posted to each General Ledger account.

The report could be printed by Transaction Number (the default) or by Date. The date feature would be useful if entries were recorded on a random date basis. The date report would place all entries with the same date together, regardless of the date when they were recorded. There is no exercise for the date feature. The report can also be printed with each account on a separate page (see step 3).

Exercise 1-18 – To Display/Print the General Ledger Report

To print all entries in the General Ledger:

> You can also view and print from the menu bar, click Reports, Financials, General Ledger.

1 ➤ In the Reports Area, click 🔽, select **General Ledger**, click **Display**. (See side box.)

2 ➤ The report displays with the default of Apr 01, 2014 to Apr 30, 2014 and the default of printing with Transaction Number and Show transaction comment.

3 ➤ A feature in Simply is the ability to print each account on a separate page. This feature is demonstrated, but not completed in order to save paper in a classroom setting.

From the General Ledger Report window, click the **File** menu, and click on the Separate Each Account on a New Page when Printed item. You are returned to the General Ledger Report window and can see the ...... page separators.

4 ➤ Click the **File** menu and you will see a ✓ beside ✔ Separate Each Account on a New Page when Printed .

Click ✔ Separate Each Account on a New Page when Printed again to remove the ✓ check mark and you are returned to the General Ledger Report window with only 1 page separator lower in the report.

5 ➤ Click the 🖨 Print icon to print the report without printing on separate pages.

To display the report with journal line comments, instead of transaction comments, or if you wanted to print only 1 general ledger account, follow these steps.

6 ➤ Click on the **Modify** button, click on **Report Options**. To print only 1 account (e.g., 1100 Bank Account) in the middle pane, scroll up to **1100 Bank Account** and **click**. The other accounts turn white. If you also wanted to print account 3120 additional Investment T. Chikowski, **scroll down** to 3120 and press **CTRL** and click on **3120**. It turns blue like 1100. You could also change the lower setting to **Show line comment**.

7 ➤ Click **OK**. Only 2 accounts are displayed. Compare the Comments column in this report, with the Comments printed in the report in step 5. It is not possible to print the G/L report with both Comments in a report.

8 ➤ **Exit** from the display window.

If you wanted to see the report with the Corrections displayed, you would click the Modify button, select Show corrections, and OK. Many businesses will prefer to see the GL report without the corrections showing. Management may want to concentrate on the correct entries.

Exercise 1-19 – Printing Financial Statements

1 ➤ Refer to Exercise 1-5, and **print**:

- Income Statement for period Jan 01, 2014 to Apr 30, 2014. Net Income = $10,650.10.
- Balance Sheet as at Apr 30, 2014. Total Assets: $62,148.54.

Exercise 1-20 – Printing the Recurring Transactions Report

1 ➤ Click the **Report Centre** icon, in the left pane, click on **Recurring Transactions**. Select **General,** at the bottom under the right pane, click **Display**.

The report as shown next indicates the Module type.

Recurring Transactions

Type	Description	Frequency	Last Processed	Due Date
General	Bank Loan Payment Monthly	Monthly	Apr 21, 2014	May 21, 2014
General	Bank Service Charges	Monthly	Apr 29, 2014	May 28, 2014

2 ➤ Click X and **Close** to exit to the Home window.

Exercise 1-21a – Creating Custom Report Shortcuts

Look at the Recently viewed reports: area on the right side under Reports. This area displays the last 4 reports that are viewed in all modules. In future chapters, the section may no longer display the Income Statement and Balance Sheet links.

This exercise will create shortcuts (a maximum of 10 reports or reports and blank separators) under the Shortcuts area on the left side of the Home window for the Income Statement and Balance Sheet that are used often. Other reports can be added as you will see in this exercise.

Shortcuts   Customize

1 ➤ From the Home window, in the Shortcuts area, click on **Customize**. The Customize Shortcuts window appears.

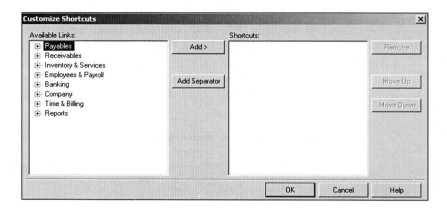

2 ➤ Click the ⊞ beside **Reports**, click the ⊞ at **Financials**, click the ⊞ at **Income Statement,** click on **Standard**.

3 ➤ Click **Add>**. The Standard item moves to the right side of the Shortcuts display window.

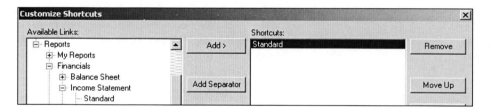

4 ➤ Click **OK**. In the Shortcuts pane you will see.

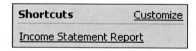

5 ➤ Repeat the procedure to add a Standard Balance Sheet Report, and a Gross Margin - Standard report (under Income Statement) to display the following:

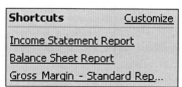

Exercise 1-21b – To Remove a Report Shortcut

---

1 ➤ In the Shortcuts area, click on **Customize**. The Customize Shortcuts window appears.

2 ➤ In the right side pane, click on **Gross Margin – Standard**.

3 ➤ Click the Remove button, and the item is removed.

Exercise 1-21c – To Add a Blank Space between Reports

This exercise will add a blank space between reports. Note you can have only 10 reports or a combination of reports and blank separator spaces equaling 10.

1 ➤   In the Shortcuts right pane window, click on the first **Standard** Item.

2 ➤   Click on the **Add Separator** button, and the window changes to:

3 ➤   Click **OK** and the Shortcuts area changes to:

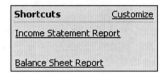

4 ➤   To remove the expander ..., click **Customize**, click on the blank line with **...** Click on the Remove button. Click **OK**.

The left side now displays.

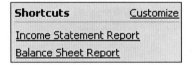

You can add reports from any of the modules shown in the left-hand pane.

Saving Your Work

If there is a power outage during your work session, you can lose what you have done before the power went out. To avoid this, you can save your work periodically during the work session.

The saving techniques in the next exercise may also be used for copying and backing up purposes. The main difference between the copy and backup functions is that when you copy the company file to another storage device, the copy has the same file size as the original; when you use the backup function in Simply, the file is compressed in a CAB file and your data file gets smaller (similar to a zip file).

Exercise 1-22 – Saving Your Work

To start this exercise, you need to be at the Photos Company Home window.

1 ➤   Click the **File** selection on the Main Menu. Study the different methods of saving:

    Save As   Saves a copy of the current company data under a different
                file name on your hard drive, zip or other storage device. You
                have an option of changing the location and company name
                from the default file name of NEW.SAI.

DO NOT USE THIS FEATURE in your exercises in this book, because all future saves will be made to the new location and company name. If you leave the default settings, all future saves will be made to that same folder, but with a name **New**. When you open the file, the name on the top menu bar will be *New*.

If you use this feature outside of class, change the file name from *New* to a more descriptive name such as:

G:\Simply 2009 Backup\Backup_01_Photos_Sep_08_2009a_SN

G:\Simply 2009 Backup is the drive and folder where you will keep the backup copies of your work. Refer to **Exercise 1-23, step 3**.

Sept_08_2009a refers to the actual date that the student is working on the material and not the data file date and will help in identifying the saved file. If you were making a second backup on the same day, you would change 2009a to 2009b. Record in your logbook (see Exercise 1-24) the page you get to in the text.

Save a Copy

This feature is similar to the Save As choice. You can save the current company data under a different file name and location, and at the same time you will continue to work in the original storage location with the original company data file.

For the copy file, you should change the company name to a descriptive name such as:

Backup_01_Photos_Sep_08_2009a_SN
(The actual date you are making the backup.)

Be sure your storage device has enough space available. Use a USB storage device as discussed in the "Getting Started" section on page 1-5.

Backup

There are a number of options to backup. You can click this Backup option, or click on the [Backup] icon on the tool bar, or you can click ▼ on Data Management in the Tasks area and select Backup. In the next exercise you will back up using the Data Management option. Backing up will compress (make your data file smaller) for saving on your USB storage device.

Restore

Restore a data file from a previous saved file. You can also restore a data file by clicking ▼ on Data Management in the Tasks area and select Restore. See Restoring a Data File at the end of this chapter (Chapter 1a).

Exit

Save work and exit Simply. You can also Exit and Save by clicking on the X in the Home window on the top.

The computer stores the entries in the RAM memory of the computer. When you request a display of a Financial Statement, Ledger account or click X to exit, the program will add the entries in memory to the current balance of the accounts, and will update the files on your storage location.

This tool bar option is the same as **File, Backup** on the menu bar, or the Backup option in the Data Management icon. See the next exercise.

2 ➤ Click anywhere on the Home page to exit the menu list for File.

Why Back Up?

You have just spent a considerable amount of time recording entries and learning about the Simply Accounting software. What would you do if your hard drive crashed or you lost your storage device? It is always safe to have your backup stored in a different location from your original data.

If you need to restore your data files, see Restoring a Data File in Chapter 1a (at the end of this chapter).

Here are other recommendations:

- Use a USB storage device for storage of backups. Keep the protective tab for the computer end. This may reduce the possibility of damage from accidental spilling of pop, coffee, etc.

- Keep your storage device(s) at room temperature. Do not leave them in an automobile where they can be subjected to extreme hot or cold temperatures.

- Do not take your storage device out of the drive before you have completed the Exit or backup procedure. If you remove the device during the procedure you may lose some of the work you have just completed!

Backup Procedures

You will need to become familiar with the mechanics of backing up. There are a number of ways to back up your data.

As noted previously, Simply Accounting has provided a number of ways to back up your company's working data from your hard drive.

In the next exercise, you will use the Data Management option to back up. As noted it will condense (compress) your data and back up the information to a USB storage device that your computer supports.

You can back up many company folders to the USB device.

(See side note box.)

Exercise 1-23 – Backing Up Your Data

1 ➤ Click the ▼ at **Data management**, select **Backup** and a window similar to the following will appear.

This exercise assumes that you are using a USB storage device for storage of the backup files.

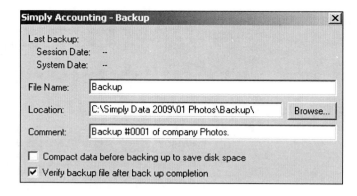

Last backup:

> **Session Date:** The date is blank as you have not backed up previously. The window would indicate the Session date that was used on a previous backup.

> **System Date:** The date is blank as you have not backed up previously. The window would indicate the computer system date that was used on a previous backup.

2 ➤ File Name: Change the File Name to: **Backup_01_Photos_Sep_08_2009a_SN**. This will identify the backup with a company name and date the backup was created. We are assuming an actual working date of Sep 08, 2009. The **01** refers to the chapter number of the data file and the 2009a refers to the first backup of the data file. If you were creating a second backup for the same day and chapter, you would use the next letter 2009b, then 2009c for the third backup if needed. This will allow you to have a backup for different saving points in the chapter in case you want to redo an Exercise that you have completed or your data file became corrupt. The **SN** (Student's Name) would be your initials as identification in case your instructor requires you to submit a backup file.

3 ➤ Location: Change the location to: **G:\Simply 2009 Backup**. All backup files will be located in this folder.

Newer computers have DVD and CD-ROM drives and the drive letter available for the USB device may not be G. If your storage device's drive letter is different, substitute the appropriate drive letter for G. Use a backup file name that includes the company name and use the actual date the backup was created (in this example, September 08, 2009).

4 ➤ Comment Do NOT change the Comment field. This identifies this backup as the first backup of the Company file named Photos. In future backups, Simply will update the backup by increasing the number accordingly; i.e., 0002, 0003, etc.

ⓘ
> The location name may be truncated (reduced) (e.g., Simply~1\Photos\Backup) depending on your computer configuration.

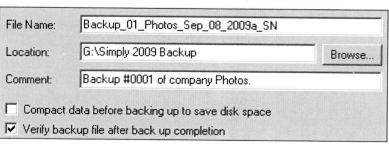

Fragmented means that portions of this file or many data files are not together on the drive. Fragmentation can slow down the performance of the computer.

There is no exercise for this feature.

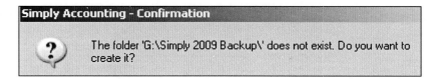 DO NOT CHANGE. You would ✓ this box if your drive and/or data file was fragmented and you wanted Simply to defrag the file before Backing up. This procedure is not necessary in the classroom. (See side note box.)

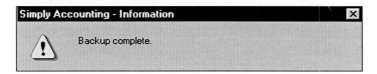 Leave this feature ✓. Verification of the backup file is important. If it was not verified, data corruption could occur during the backup and you would not know until you needed to use the backup. With the ✓, if data corruption occurred during the backup, the verification would display a warning message.

5 ➤ Click **OK** and the following Confirmation window appears:

Simply Accounting - Confirmation

? The folder 'G:\Simply 2009 Backup\' does not exist. Do you want to create it?

6 ➤ Click **Yes**. The backup may take a few minutes to complete.

7 ➤ When successful, a Backup complete window appears as shown next.

Simply Accounting - Information ✕

⚠ Backup complete.

8 ➤ Click **OK** and you are returned to the Home window.

9 ➤ **Exit** Simply by clicking the **X** box in the top-right corner of the Home window.

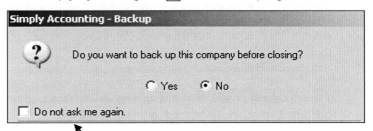

10 ➤ Change the selection to **No** as you have already backed up. It is also a reminder to back up if you forget.

☐ Do not ask me again. Do not select this. If you select this choice the Backup window will not display when you close Simply for this company. You can reset this choice and this will be discussed in Chapter 4.

11 ➤ Click **OK** to close the company.

When you click the EXIT $\boxed{\text{X}}$ box in the top-right corner of the Home window, Simply saves all entries in memory to the data file in the storage device and closes the company and the program.

Go to the G: drive, or the drive letter of where you put your file, then double-click the **Simply 2009 Backup** folder. You should see the file:

Backup_01_Photos_Sep_08_2009a_SN1.CAB

This means a Photos backup CAB file was created with the creation date September 8, 2009. Simply added the **1** in 2009a_SN1 to indicate this is the first backup file in a series. There is no second backup (series) file for Photos.

You should back up your work on a USB drive or any storage device on a regular basis to reduce the chance of losing data.

From this point onward, back up whenever you see the icon at the left, before you leave the classroom or when you are moving to another exercise and you want to save the file at that point.

If there are any error messages during the Backup process, complete the Backup procedure again. If the same error messages or others appear, there may be some damage to the storage device. Write the error message(s) on paper and have your instructor look at the storage device and messages.

Using a Logbook or Diary

A logbook may be used to maintain a list of the work you have finished, and what backup drive you used on a specific date. This will be useful in determining where to start on your next work session. If you have a drive failure or you lose your backup drive, you can refer to your logbook to find out which drive and file name you used last.

Exercise 1-24 – Maintaining a Logbook

A logbook form is provided at the back of this book.

1 ➤ Enter the information from the backup that you completed in the previous exercise in the logbook. See the next example.

Date	Backup	Data Information Where you get to each class	Name of File in Storage Location
Sept 8	1	Finished Ex. 1-13, page 1-44	01_Photos_Sep_08-2009a
Sept 8	2	Finished Ex. 1-23, page 1-59	01_Photos_Sep_08-2009b
Sept 19	1	Finished Ex. 2A-14, page 2A-103	02_Luggage_Sep_18_2009a
Sept 26	2	Chapter 2A finished, page 2A-126	02_Luggage_Sep_25_2009b

It is recommended that you copy the backup file from the USB drive to your own computer as another form of backup away from the main computer. This will reduce the amount of work you have to redo if your storage location data is damaged or lost.

 Back up your data and update your logbook (located at the back of this textbook) now. **Remember, if it is important, back it up**.

Backing Up in an Office Environment

Most companies store their working data files on the hard drive of the computer and would back up daily to a hard drive of another computer, USB device, CD-ROM, DVD or other storage devices. The important thing is to ensure that the backup is not on the same storage device as the working data file and that the backup is kept at a different location. This way, if anything happens to one storage device, there is still a means to retrieve the company data.

 It is very important to record in a daily log the backup number and important information about the day or session. Information such as last cheque, last sales invoice, last purchase invoice recorded, etc., should also be recorded in the log. This way, if the working data file becomes damaged, you will have a record of what was entered on each of the backup disks.

Here is one backup procedure:

1. Use a set of 7 folders on an external storage device. Label each folder for every working day of the week: **Sunday, Monday, Tuesday, Wednesday, Thursday, Friday, Saturday**. It is assumed that many businesses record accounting information 7 days a week.

2. Prepare another set of 5 folders labelled **Week 1** to **Week 5**.

3. Prepare another set of 12 folders labelled for each month of the year: **January, February, March**, etc.

4. At the end of each day, back up your data into the appropriate backup folder; e.g., on Monday copy your data into the Monday backup folder, etc.

5. At the end of the week, copy the Saturday data file to a folder labelled Week 1, etc. to Week 5 (some months have 5 Saturdays).

6. At the end of each month, another backup should be made on the appropriate folder and dated.

The backup storage device should be stored off-site.

In a classroom situation, while you are learning to use the software, making a backup of your data at the end of every work session will be sufficient.

Do not take your storage device out of the drive before the light on your backup storage device goes off, because the backup procedure would not have been completed. If you remove the storage device, you may lose some of the work you have just completed.

Update your logbook regularly, identifying the page you last worked on, and which backup destination drive is being used on a specific date.

Summary

Some of the benefits of computerized bookkeeping, compared to manual bookkeeping, are:

1. Data entry errors may be easily corrected.

2. Controls are provided to prevent data entry errors, such as addition errors or duplicate invoice numbers, transposition of numbers, etc.

3. Posting transactions is automatically performed by clicking the Post icon, and all ledgers and journals are updated immediately.

4. Standard financial statements and reports may be printed any time.

When starting Simply, you are required to enter a date, which is the work session date. For each transaction you enter, you must enter the actual **Transaction** date, which could be either the same date as the Session date or earlier.

Simply is an integrated accounting system. The system contains **modules** that are similar to ledgers and subledgers in a manual system. The modules in Simply are:

- RECEIVABLES subledger with Sales and Receipts journals.

- PAYABLES   subledger with Purchases and Payments journals.

- INVENTORY & SERVICES subledger with Build, Adjust and Transfer journals.

- EMPLOYEES & PAYROLL subledger with Payroll Cheque and Pay Remittance journals. To automatically calculate payroll taxes, businesses must purchase a Payroll ID code to activate Automatic payroll calculations.

- PROJECT module with Sales, Purchases, Paycheques and General Journal.

- BANKING ledger with Receipt, Deposits, Transfer funds and Bank Reconciliation journals.

- COMPANY ledger with General Journal.

- In previous versions, module TIME SLIPS (formerly called TIME & BILLING) is now located in the RECEIVABLES AND EMPLOYEES & PAYROLL modules.

To save your work and exit from Simply, click the X in the top-right corner.

Budgets: Simply Accounting has a feature to record and display budget amounts. Information on Budget input and display can be found in Appendix folder CD-E, *Budgets — General Ledger* on the Student Data CD. See your instructor for more information.

This chapter (Photos Company) uses only the GENERAL module and does not have a subledger section for each customer or vendor.

In Chapters 2A & 2B, using the Santos Luggage company files, sales are recorded in the RECEIVABLES subledger. Individual customer detail is available and includes items sold.

In Chapters 3A & 3B, Tyson's Toys, all purchases of merchandise for resale, services, e.g., rent paid, telephone bill, owner's withdrawals and goods for business use, are recorded in the PAYABLES subledger module. Individual Vendor transaction detail is available and includes details of items or services purchased.

The General journal would be used only for bank service charges, and adjustments that do not relate to specific customers or suppliers (vendors).

To View Corrections

To view corrections that need to be made to the text, please go to:

http://www.simplyaccounting2009.nelson.com

On the right side, click on Student Resources.

On the right side, click on Corrections.

Corrections to the text, if any, will be listed.

Before Moving On . . .

Read the following questions and make sure you know the answers to them; otherwise, read the corresponding part in the chapter before moving on:

1. What is the best way to open the Simply Accounting program and data files?

2. Describe Toolbar icons.

3. The firm's year-end (fiscal year) is on December 31, 2014. You received on January 22 a bank debit memo dated January 20, 2014, for service charges on the bank account:

    What would be your **Session date**? _____ Your **Transaction date**? _____

4. What important information does the **Source** field indicate?

5. What is the **Comment field** (box) used to record?

6. What is the **Comment column** used to record?

7. Describe two ways to display a list of accounts when entering a General Journal entry.

8. An Income Statement may be displayed/printed for only 1 day, a month at a time, or a time period which can be several months or parts of a month (e.g., January 1 to February 17). Explain why.

9. Why would you use the **Drill Down** feature in Simply?

10. Describe an effective backup routine in an office environment.

11. A logbook/diary, as discussed in this chapter, is used for what purpose?

12. How or where can you get help in Simply Accounting?

Challenge Exercise 01 C1-1, Driving School

(General Ledger Review)

1 ➤ Refer to Exercise 1-1 to unzip the **01 C1-1 Driving.exe** file.

2 ➤ Open the **01 C1-1 Driving** file.

The Driving school is a single-owner business, operated by Tanya Gauci. You should record the following transactions in the General Journal (double-entry accounting). You will learn how to record some of these entries more efficiently in the RECEIVABLES and PAYABLES module in Chapters 2 & 3. The fiscal year is Jan 1 to Dec 31. Use appropriate additional Info and comment fields in 3 transactions.

Note: This assignment does not involve GST or PST, similar to Photos Company.

This business uses the **Track Additional Transaction Details** feature where necessary.

3 ➤ **Record** and **Post** the following transactions in the General Journal for the month of January using the Double-Entry method.

Jan 2   Purchased $80.00 worth of office supplies from Kanwal Supplies and issued cheque #652. Note that these supplies are assumed to be used up by the end of the month.

Jan 2   Issued $80.00 invoice #324 to YOUR name (your name in the comment line) for 2 hours of lessons before your driving test.

Jan 3   Issued $600.00 cheque #653 to Uptown Mall for rent of a store in the mall.

Jan 4   Received cheque #113 from YOUR name (your name in the comment line) for invoice #324.

Jan 5   Issued $50.00 invoice #325 and received cheque #748 from Vito Campize for one-hour driving lesson ($40.00) and rule book test ($10.00) for his daughter Toula.

Jan 6   Issued $320.00 cheque #654 to Capilano Advertising for advertisements in flyers being delivered to homes in the area today.

Jan 8   A new client, Naomi Regalea, recommended by Marta Grez, took a 3-hour driving lesson. Received her $120.00 cheque #522 for invoice #326.

Jan 9   Issued $120.00 cheque #655 to Morton Medina (driving teacher) for wages.

Jan 11 Purchased 2 driving lesson DVDs at $75.00 each for use in the Beginners "In Class" course approved by the government. They will be used in the course starting tomorrow and once used they cannot be returned. Cheque #656 issued to Major Film Labs.

Jan 11 Beginners "In Class" course started today. Received cash $50.00 (2 clients) and cheques $200.00 (8 clients). Deposited $250.00 in the bank today.

Jan 12 Issued $110.00 cheque #657 to Amrit Devon (In Class teacher) for wages.

Jan 12 Record the $308.00 Bank Debit memo for a payment on the bank loan. This amount includes interest of $32.40.

4 ➤ **Print** the following:
    a) General Journal Entries for the period, Jan 02 to Jan 12, **with additional information**
    b) Income Statement for the period Jan 02 to Jan 12
    c) Balance Sheet as at Jan 12
    d) General Ledger for all accounts to Jan 12

Challenge Exercise 01 C1-2, Astrology Readings

(General Ledger Review)

1 ➤ Refer to Exercise 1-1 to unzip the **01 C1-2 Readings.exe** file.

2 ➤ Open the **01 C1-2 Readings** file.

The business is a sole proprietorship, owned by Harriet Patel. You should record the following transactions in the General Journal (double-entry accounting). You will learn how to record some of these entries more efficiently in the RECEIVABLES and PAYABLES module in Chapters 2 & 3. The fiscal year is Jan 1 to Dec 31.

Note: This assignment does not involve GST or PST, which is similar to Photos Company.

3 ➤ **Record** and **Post** the following transactions in the General Journal for the month of January using the Double-Entry method:

Jan 4   Paid $500.00 rent for the month to Eastwood Mall Inc. Cheque #131 issued to the attention of the manager, Mrs. Hilk.

Jan 4   Manager advised the rent has increased to $520.00 on new lease. Reverse and correct the previous entry to the correct amount. Cheque #132 issued.

Jan 4   Paid $50.00 to YourTown Newspaper for an advertisement in today's paper. Invoice #7622. Cheque #133 issued.

Jan 5   Issued invoice #231 for astrology reading (Your sign) to YOUR name (your name in the comment line). Received your cheque #788 in the amount of $130.00.

Jan 6   Issued invoice #232 for astrology reading for Sylvia Ciuciura (Leo). Received cash in the amount of $130.00.

Jan 7   Paid $20.00 for special computer paper, for astrology printouts, from Grand Supplies on invoice #8964. Cheque #134 issued. Charge to expense because it will be used by the end of the month.

Jan 9   Received $43.00 telephone bill for regular service from Metro Phones. Cheque #135 issued.

Jan 9   Issued invoice #233 for astrology reading for Ying Xiang (Scorpio). Received her cheque #465 in the amount of $120.00.

Jan 26   Received invoice #356. Issued $100.00 cheque #136 to Jeremy Design Studio, for graphic design work on new advertising brochure.

Jan 31   Issued invoice #234 for astrology reading for John Harwood (Scorpio). Received his cheque #611 in the amount of $125.00.

4 ➤ **Print** the following:

   a) General Journal Entries for Jan 1 to 31, **with corrections**
   b) Income Statement for Jan 1 to 31
   c) Balance Sheet as at Jan 31
   d) General Ledger at Jan 31

Challenge Exercise 01 C1-3, Movers

(General Ledger Review)

1 ➤ Refer to Exercise 1-1 to unzip the **01 C1-3 Movers.exe** file.

2 ➤ Open the **01 C1-3 Movers** file.

The business is a single-owner business, owned by Henry Kelly. You should record the following transactions in the General Journal (double-entry accounting). You will learn how to record some of these entries more efficiently in the RECEIVABLES and PAYABLES module in Chapters 2 & 3. The fiscal year is Jan 1 to Dec 31.

Note: The store was closed from January 1 to January 3 and the transactions start at Jan 4.

Note: This assignment does not involve GST or PST, which is similar to Photos Company.

3 ➤ **Record** and **Post** the following transactions in the General Journal for the month of January using the Double-Entry method.

Jan 4   Paid $700.00 rent for the month to Trudeau Realty; cheque #178 issued.

Jan 7   Purchased and received $500.00 of bubble wrap to be sold (use Purchases), from John Currie Wraps Ltd., invoice #28643. Terms Net 30.

Jan 11   Sold $140.00 of moving boxes and $65.00 of bubble wrap to YOUR name (your name in the comment line) on invoice #385. Received your cheque #232 in the amount of $205.00.

Jan 16   Received cheque #28426, for a $4,923.00 payment from a customer, Canadian Insurance Co., for invoice #360, dated December 14.

Jan 18   Paid $412.00 to Direct Advertising Co. for an advertisement in today's paper. Invoice #10-38962. Next cheque #179.

Jan 25   Sold $1,100.00 worth of boxes and $250.00 of bubble wrap to Gilmore Stores on invoice #386. Net 30 days.

Jan 26   Received $83.00 telephone bill #9901 from Metro Phones for regular service. Issued cheque #180.

Jan 30   Issued cheque #181 to Mrs. G. Sohi, $440.00, as an employee, for her work in the office.

Jan 30   Use the Recurring entry to record bank service charges for the month. This month's charges are the same amount as in the recurring entry.

Note: Remember, the store is closed January 31.

4 ➤ **Print** the following:

   a)   General Journal Entries for the monthly activity with no corrections
   b)   Income Statement for the monthly activity
   c)   Balance Sheet as at Jan 30

Accounting and Simply Accounting Terminology

Account: A form in which transactions are recorded individually. Each account has a name (e.g., Cash, Accounts Receivable, etc.) and is identified with a number (e.g., 1010 to represent Cash, 1200 to represent Accounts Receivable, etc.) An account will have a left side (Debit) and a right side (Credit). Accounts are contained in a ledger.

Backup: A copy of your data on another medium such as a USB storage device, CD-ROM or DVD drive using a computer operating system such as Windows or specialized software (e.g., CD-Creator). If the original storage device is lost or damaged, you can restore the data from the backup copy.

Backup: A storage device that contains a backup copy of the current working data files. If files are copied onto another device, the receiving device is called a **Destination** or **Target** device.

Balance Sheet: A financial report that shows a business's assets (what they own), liabilities (what they owe) and equity (owners' or shareholders' investment) at a certain date.

Company Data: Transaction entries and general ledger files referring to one particular company, which are stored in one directory/folder separate from data belonging to other companies.

Default: A preset value; e.g., the default date format is month, day, year, unless the user changes it. A default date is also the last date the program was used.

Drive Letter: **C:** in a standalone hard drive computer system or D or any letter after C: for a USB or other storage device, CD-ROM or DVD drive. The letter indicates that you are at the root directory of the current drive, or any letter after C in a network system, indicating that you are at the root directory of your current drive.

Folders: A separate location, in Windows, where you can keep various reports or data files. May also be called directories or subdirectories.

GAAP: **G**enerally **A**ccepted **A**ccounting **P**rinciples are guidelines used by ethical practitioners in the Accounting field.

Icon: A symbol, normally a graphic image that represents a menu item within Windows.

Import: To bring data into a file from another file or program; e.g., importing data from an Excel worksheet into Simply.

Income Statement: A financial report that shows revenues (earnings) less expenses (costs) resulting in net profit/loss for a period.

Integrated Accounting Software: A type of accounting software in which the subledgers are linked to the General Ledger. When entries are posted in the subledgers, the General Ledger is updated.

Journal Entry: The process of recording an accounting transaction, which may consist of one or more debit entries (DR) and one or more credit (CR) entries. Total Debits must equal total Credits.

Logbook: A dated record of activities, which will contain information on the material covered (the last page of text read or work completed), and the storage file name used for backup.

Master CD-ROM: The Student Data CD supplied with the textbook that contains the data files. These files are copied to the student's computer storage space (School server, home computer, etc.).

Module: Referring to a part of a software program designed for a specific function. A module may be separate from the other parts of the program (as in a modularized accounting software), or it may be linked with other modules (as in integrated accounting packages such as Simply Accounting).

Network: Two or more computers connected directly or through a server, and able to share data files and peripheral equipment; e.g., printers or scanners.

Path: Also referred to as pathname; includes the drive and the folder/directory name directing the system to specific files. For example, if you have a set of company files on drive C in a folder called PHOTOS, the path or pathname would be **C:\\01 PHOTOS\\PHOTOS**. When indicating a path, one must be careful of the spelling, spacing between names, filename extensions and backslashes.

Post: To transfer the information recorded in a journal transaction to the appropriate subledger and/or general ledger, thus updating the company data.

Range of Dates: A time period, generally between two dates, in which data may be entered. The transaction date must be on or between the two dates.

Session Date: In Simply, it is the actual working date when you are using the computer. In this text, the simulated date is advanced on a regular basis for classroom use.

Standalone: A computer system that is working on its own and not connected to a network.

Relevant Appendices

The following appendices are available on the Student Data CD.

Appendix 2009 CD-A	**Basics of Accounting**
Appendix 2009 CD-C	**What's New in Simply 2009**
Appendix 2009 CD-E	**Budgets – General Ledger**
Appendix 2009 CD-H	**New Business Guide**
Appendix 2009 CD-O	**Security – Passwords**
Appendix 2009 CD-R	**Quick Reference Guide**
Appendix 2009 CD-U	**Adding Notes/Footers to Statements**

Restoring a Data File from a Backup Data File

You would want to restore a data file when:
a) the data file is corrupt;
b) you have made one or more mistakes in recording transactions and want to start over again from a previous backup (before the mistake(s) were made), instead of correcting the mistakes.

The following procedure will allow you to restore a previous backup data file and continue recording transactions.

Check your logbook to ensure that you have chosen the correct backup data file stored on a storage device.

In this example, it is assumed that you are using a backup of the file named **Photos** (for Photos Company) in the G: drive. The file was created in Chapter 1, Exercise 1-23.

File Name:	Backup_01_Photos_Sep_08_2009a_SN
Location:	G:\Simply 2009 Backup Browse...
Comment:	Backup #0001 of company Photos.

☐ Compact data before backing up to save disk space
☑ Verify backup file after back up completion

Use My Computer or Windows Explorer to look at the G: drive, and you will see a folder **Simply 2009 Backup** with a file Backup_01_Photos_Sep_08_2009a_SN1.CAB inside the folder. Depending on the configuration of your computer you may not see the .CAB.

Exercise 1a-1: Restoring a Data File from a Backup

1 ➤ Start Simply in the normal way and you will see a portion of the window similar to the following:

Simply Accounting Premium

Welcome to Simply Accounting. What do you wish to do?
- ○ Open the sample company to help you learn Simply Accounting.
- ○ Create a new company.
- ⊙ Restore from backup.
- ○ Select an existing company.
- ○ Open the last company you worked on:
  C:\Simply Data 2009\01 Photos\Photos.SAI

2 ➤ Click **Restore from backup**.

3 ➤ Click **OK**.

Restore from Backup window

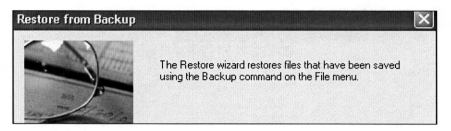

Make sure the storage device that you are using to restore files is in the G: drive (assumed USB drive).

4 ➤ Click **Next>**.

Select Backup File window- part 1

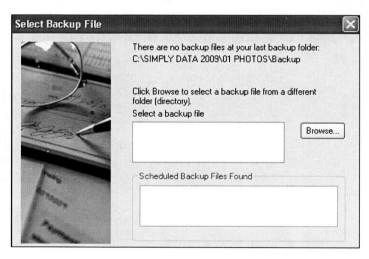

Simply assumes that the backup file is located on:

C:\Simply Data 2009\01 Photos\Backup drive and folder.

5 ➤ Your backup file is not on the C: drive, therefore, click on the **Browse** button to locate the files.

6 ➤ Locate the **G**: drive, and double-click on the **Simply 2009 Backup** folder.

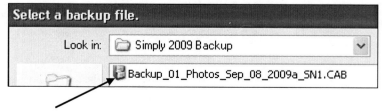

7 ➤ The icon in the lower field may be different on your computer. Double-click on **Backup_01_Photos_Sep_08_2009a_SN1.CAB**. Depending on the configuration of your computer you may not see the .CAB.

Select Backup File window – part 2

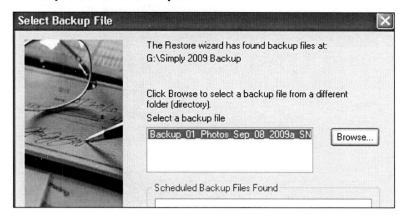

Scheduled Backup Files

There are no scheduled backups created in the textbook data files. See Chapter 4, Exercise 4-3 for a discussion on this topic.

8 ➤ Click **Next>**.

Confirm Backup file window

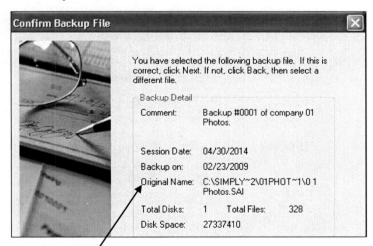

Session Date: This is the session date of the data file. To make sure you are restoring the correct file, confirm the date with your log book.

Backup on: 02/23/2009. This is the actual date the backup was created by the author. Your date will be the actual date you backed up.

Original Name: Depending on the configuration of your computer, this field is the path where the original file was created. It should read: C:\Simply Data 2009\01Photos\Photos.SAI.

Total Disks: Each company data file contains a folder with an extension of SAJ. The MySQL data-base and company data files (accounts, transactions) are contained in the SAJ folder. A file with an extension of SAI is used by Simply to open the SAJ files.

9 ➤ This window contains information about the backup data file being restored. The information will be different depending on when and where you stored your backup. Click **Next>**.

New File Name window

10 ➤ **Enter** the name of the folder and data file name you want to use. It is best to restore to the same folder and file name where you normally have your data. Using **Browse** to find the folder rather than typing in the name would be a faster and more accurate way.

11 ➤ Click **Next>**.

Confirmation window

12 ➤ This window confirms your choice of folder and data file. Click **Yes** when the information is correct.

Finish Restoring from Backup window

13 ➤ Click **Finish** to complete the restoration process. The Session Date of your restored file will appear in the Session Date window.

14 ➤ If this is the correct session date you want to work with, click **OK**.

If you click OK, you will be at the Home window of the file you are going to use. It is best to print a Journal entry report to confirm the entries that you had previously posted and where you want to start from.

If you click Cancel you will return to step 1 of this procedure. You will need to find the backup storage device that contains the appropriate file that you want to restore. Refer to your logbook.

Chapter 2A

RECEIVABLES Module—Part A

Santos Luggage

Learning Objectives
After completing this chapter you will be able to:

☐ Process sales quotes, orders, invoices and sales returns.
☐ Add new customers and make changes to existing customers' data files.
☐ Process receipts from customers in full or partial payment of invoices with or without cash discounts and record cash/and or ATM (bank card) or credit card sales.
☐ Process deposits from customers for sales orders.
☐ Reverse and correct errors in invoices and cheques.
☐ Use Daily Business Manager and other Simply special features.
☐ Display and print various Receivable reports and journals.

Note: After finishing Chapter 2A and Chapter 8, you can complete selected transactions from Chapter 2A, using the Perpetual INVENTORY module. See Challenge Exercise 08 C8-4 Luggage-PI.

The contents of this chapter are as follows:

RECEIVABLES Module Overview

This chapter Parts A and B, using **Santos Luggage**, will guide you through recording transactions that affect the amount of money owed to the company, involving Accounts Receivable subledgers and the General Ledger.

Below are two main types of transactions recorded in the RECEIVABLES module with the corresponding journals:

1. Sales of merchandise or services   - Sales Quotes
   (Sales Journal)   - Sales Orders
                                        - Sales Invoices on credit (on account)
                                        - Sales Invoices paid by Cash/Cheque
                                        - Sales Invoices paid by Credit Card (Part B)

2. Receipts from customers   - Partial payment
   (Receipts Journal)   - Full payment with or without cash discounts
                                        - Deposits against a future invoice (Part B)

Slideshow 2A – RECEIVABLES Part A will help you understand how the RECEIVABLES module works. It will also give you a review of the GAAPs applicable to accounts receivable transactions. Run it now.

Company Profile – Santos Luggage

Santos Luggage has been selling luggage and accessories, for over 10 years, to various stores (wholesalers) and has an outlet store at the back of the warehouse to sell slightly damaged items and samples to retail customers. The business has an acceptable level of receivables outstanding based on selling to large stores with cash discounts for prompt payment.

Santos Luggage uses the Periodic Inventory method for calculating ending inventory. The Perpetual Inventory method will be demonstrated in Chapter 8. A perpetual inventory Challenge Exercise, 08 C8-4 using Santos Luggage part A, is available after completing Chapter 8.

Assume that you are a part-time bookkeeper and work at Santos Luggage on a variable time schedule. Some days you work an hour; some days you work for three hours, and other days you work the whole day.

The owner, Mrs. Santos, has decided at this time not to use the Track Additional Transaction Details feature of the software.

Opening the RECEIVABLES Module

In a job situation, it is most likely that you would work on an accounting system that has already been set up. Santos Luggage's RECEIVABLES module is ready to use. In this chapter, you will access the RECEIVABLES module of Santos Luggage and enter transactions related to sales and receipts of payment from customers.

Exercise 2A-1 – Opening the RECEIVABLES Module

> Review Exercise 1-2 if you need help to open a data file.

1 ➤ Refer to Exercise 1-1 to unzip the **02 2A Luggage-A.exe** file.

2 ➤ Start **Simply Accounting**.

3 ➤ At the **Select Company** window, click **Select an existing company** button, and **OK**.

4 ➤ At the Simply Accounting - **Open Company** window, in the **Look in**: box, locate your student location drive and folder, **Simply Data 2009**. **Double-click** on the **Simply Data 2009** folder.

5 ➤ Double-click the ⌈📁 02 2A Luggage-A⌋ folder. You will see a ⌈📁 Luggage-A.SAJ⌋ folder and a ⌈📑 Luggage-A.SAI⌋ file in the window. The image at the left of Luggage may be different depending on the configuration of your computer and the SAI may be in lower case.

6 ➤ Click on ⌈📑 Luggage-A.SAI⌋. The lower **File name** box will change to: Luggage-A.SAI. (.SAI may not display or will be in lower case.)

7 ➤ Click **Open** to open the **Luggage-A.SAI** file.

8 ➤ The Session date will be **Feb 29, 2016**. This is the date when the file was last used. Click **OK**.

Study the Santos Luggage Home window: **EXIT and SAVE button**

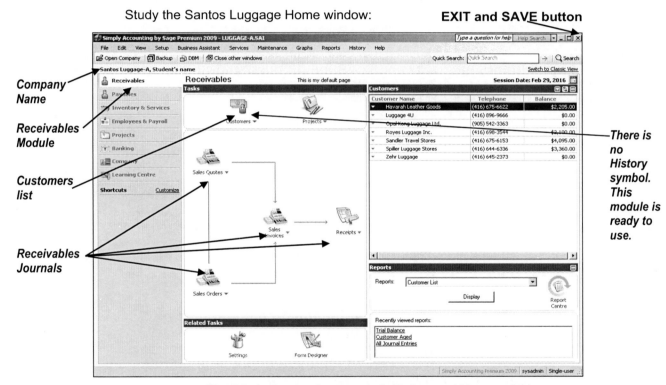

Fig. 2A-1: Santos Luggage-A, Enhanced Home window.

The History symbol appears for some icons in the **PAYABLES, INVENTORY & SERVICES** and **EMPLOYEES & PAYROLL** modules. This means that these modules have not been set up for use and cannot be used to record entries.

Notice that on the right side, in the Customer's window, the name of the customer, telephone number and current balance are displayed. You can click on each of the column headings to sort the column in ascending or descending order. If you right click the column, you will see 2 check boxes for Telephone or Balance. Clicking the check mark will hide the column. You can bring back the hidden column by right clicking a column that is not hidden and clicking the column that is hidden and it will display.

9 ➤ On the left, click on the following modules: **PAYABLES, INVENTORY & SERVICES, EMPLOYEES AND PAYROLL**, **BANKING** and **COMPANY**.

10 ➤ Click the **RECEIVABLES** module on the left.

Notice that the History symbol does not appear for **RECEIVABLES, BANKING**, and **COMPANY** modules. This signifies that these modules are set up and ready for recording entries. (See side note box.)

11 ➤   Remember to change the company name to include your name; e.g., **Santos Luggage, Oliver Megan**.

12 ➤   Display the Trial Balance to make sure it agrees with the values shown in Fig. 2A-2. From the Menu bar, click **Reports**, **Financials**, **Trial Balance**, leave the date at Feb 29, 2016, then **OK**.

13 ➤   Study the Santos Luggage Trial Balance next. (First, see side note box.)

The majority of the transactions in this chapter will affect Balance Sheet accounts:
1020 Bank Chequing
    Account,
1030 Visa Credit Card
    Bank Account,
1200 Accounts
    Receivable,
2630 GST Charged on
    Sales,
2650 PST Payable; and
    Income Statement
    accounts
4100 to 4200 Sales
    accounts.
The above accounts are shaded in Fig. 2A-2. When you have confirmed that the Trial Balance is correct, exit to the Home window.

Santos Luggage, Student's Name
Trial Balance As At Feb 29, 2016

		Debits	Credits
1020	Bank Chequing Account	19,436.86	-
1030	Visa Credit Card Bank Account	0.00	-
1200	Accounts Receivable	11,760.00	-
1300	Inventory	23,680.00	-
1320	Prepaid Supplies	712.00	-
1420	Office/Warehouse Furniture/Equip...	25,163.00	
1425	Accum. Amort Office/Ware Furn/E...	-	4,100.00
2200	Accounts Payable	-	11,255.00
2630	GST Charged on Sales	-	1,120.00
2640	GST Paid On Purchases	525.00	-
2650	PST Payable	-	0.00
3100	Capital, Maria Santos	-	63,683.68
3160	Additional Investment	-	0.00
3180	Drawings, Maria Santos	2,200.00	-
4100	Sales	-	40,125.00
4150	Sales-Discounts	320.00	-
4200	Sales-Returns & Allowances	355.00	-
5010	Beginning Inventory	21,000.00	-
5040	Purchases	28,000.00	-
5050	Purchase Returns	-	1,000.00
5080	Purchase Discounts	-	335.00
5090	Ending Inventory	-	23,680.00
5310	Wages Expense	8,000.00	-
5320	Advertising Expense	432.00	-
5330	Bank Charges & Interest	95.00	-
5340	Credit Card Charges	34.30	-
5350	Rent Expense	800.00	-
5370	Bad Debt Expense	0.00	-
5410	Office/Warehouse Supplies Expense	216.00	-
5450	Rent Expense Warehouse	2,000.00	-
5460	Utility Expense	263.89	-
5550	Telephone Expense	305.63	-
		145,298.68	145,298.68

Fig. 2A-2: Santos Luggage-A Trial Balance.

14 ➤   Click $\boxed{X}$ to return to the Home window.

To Display and Print the Customer Aged Report

To find out the status of your company receivables, you can display and/or print the Customer Aged Report. Simply Accounting groups receivables calculated from the date of the invoice to the current Session Date, and provides a list of accounts that are **Current**, **31 to 60** days overdue, **61 to 90** days overdue, and **91+** days overdue.

Simply provides two options: **Summary** and **Detail**. Your choice depends on the purpose for which you need the reports. At this point, if you wish to acquaint yourself with the company customers, their purchasing pattern, their balances, and what accounts are overdue, you would then select **Detail**. You will display/print both report options in this exercise.

When displaying this report, it is important the Session Date is correct; otherwise, the aging will not be accurate.

Depending on the type of printer that is connected to the computer or network, you may see two dotted lines. One dotted line on the right side of 61 to 90 and another on the right of 91+. This means the report will print on 2 pages. This will be adjusted in step 3.

61 to 90	91+

Exercise 2A-2 – Displaying/Printing Customer Aged Report

The default Detail report does not display Terms. In this exercise, you will display a **Detail** Customer Aged Report and modify it to display terms. Later you will display a **Summary** report. Observe the type of information each report provides, so you can determine which type you will need in the future.

1 ➤ On the left, click on **RECEIVABLES**, at the right in **Reports**, click ▼, select **Customer Aged Detail**, click **Display**. You will see the Customer Aged Detail window. Notice that the display shows a dotted line on the right side of 91+. This means the report will print on 1 page. (See side note box.)

2 ➤ Click the **Modify** icon, click on **Report Options**. Click **Include Terms**. All customers should be in blue, meaning they have been selected. Click **OK**. The report will display with the right side showing 2 columns (dotted lines) and a portion will print on the second page.

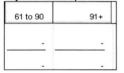

Columns shown on the report	
Column Name	Width
Source	19
Date	14
Terms	15
Transaction Type	17
Total Balance Owing	14
Current	14
31 to 60	14
61 to 90	11
91+	11

3 ➤ To reduce the size of the columns, double-click on the divider line (this is new in 2009) at **Source**, **Date**, **Transaction Type**, **Total**, **Current**, **31-60**, **61 to 90** and **91+**. You may have to move some of the divider line columns manually to the left, until the page divider line disappears, to save printed paper. See Fig. 2A-3. This will happen with a number of reports.

(See side box with revised column widths used in the 2A-3 report.) Note, your computer monitor widths may be different. It is best to change the widths using the method described in step 3.

4 ➤ At the top left, at **As at:**, click ▼ and you will see a number of choices. Select **Today**. The Date should be **Feb 29, 2016**. (See side note box.)

Do **NOT** Print now. To print this report with an earlier date, change the **Date** accordingly. This is useful when the session date was advanced and you want to produce a report for a previous period. Do not change the Feb 29, 2016 date.

If you are able to change the printer to display/print in landscape mode, click File. Printer Setup, (on some computers you click Properties) and click the appropriate boxes on your system. You will have to ask your faculty member on which of the appropriate items to click to print in Landscape mode. This text assumes you are printing in portrait mode (default).

You should now see the Customer Aged Detail report. Note the information it provides. (See side note box beside Fig. 2A-3.)

The arrow is pointing at **Total deposits/prepaid order:** this refers to all customers.

If there are no deposits paid by customers, deposits/prepaid order will display blanks (-).

Customer Aged Detail As at Feb 29, 2016

Source	Date	Terms	Transaction Type	Total	Current	31 to 60	61 to 90	91+
Havarah Leather Goods								
2253	Feb 26, 2016	2%/10, Net 30	Invoice	2,205.00	2,205.00	-	-	-
Total outstanding:				2,205.00	2,205.00	-	-	-
Royes Luggage Inc.								
2212	Jan 31, 2016	2%/10, Net 30	Invoice	945.00	945.00			
2256	Feb 27, 2016	2%/10, Net 30	Invoice	1,155.00	1,155.00			
Total outstanding:				2,100.00	2,100.00	-	-	-
Sandler Travel Stores								
2197	Jan 26, 2016	2%/10, Net 30	Invoice	4,095.00	-	4,095.00		-
Total outstanding:				4,095.00	-	4,095.00	-	-
Spiller Luggage Stores								
2230	Feb 20, 2016	2%/10, Net 30	Invoice	3,360.00	3,360.00	-	-	-
Total outstanding:				3,360.00	3,360.00	-	-	-
Total unpaid invoices:				11,760.00	7,665.00	4,095.00	-	-
Total deposits/prepaid order:				-	-		-	-
Total outstanding:				11,760.00	7,665.00	4,095.00	-	-

Fig. 2A-3: Customer Aged Detail Report (reduced column sizes).

DO NOT PRINT NOW. You will print this report at the end of the chapter.

5 ➤ To save these column settings and have the same report style available for another time, click the **Modify** icon, click **Report Options**, at the top, click Save Template button. In the Save Template as: type, Receivable Aged Detail on 1 page , click **Save** and **OK**. This template displays.

You will see Fig 2A-3, with a header change identifying your saved report.

Customer Aged Detail As at Feb 29, 2016 - Receivable Aged Detail on 1 page

You can repeat these steps for other module reports as well.

6 ➤ To exit your template, click X, and you will see the Fig 2A-3 report.

7 ➤ To display the Summary report click the Modify icon, click **Report Options**, at Report Type, click **Summary** (the customers should be blue); the date should be **Feb 29, 2016**; click **OK**. (See side note box.)

Do **NOT** print now. To display/print this report with an earlier date, you would change the **As at: Date** accordingly. This would be useful if the session date was advanced and you want to produce a report for a previous period. For now, do not change the Feb 29, 2016 date.

The Customer Aged Summary report displays. This report does not need to have the column sizes reduced.

Customer Aged Summary As at Feb 29, 2016

Name	△	Total	Current	31 to 60	61 to 90	91+
Havarah Leather Goods		2,205.00	2,205.00	-	-	-
Royes Luggage Inc.		2,100.00	2,100.00	-	-	-
Sandler Travel Stores		4,095.00	-	4,095.00	-	-
Spiller Luggage Stores		3,360.00	3,360.00	-	-	-
Total outstanding:		11,760.00	7,665.00	4,095.00	-	-

Fig. 2A-4: Customer Aged Summary window.

You will notice that the **Detail** report shows the individual invoices owed by each customer, and that the **Summary** report shows only the total owed by each customer. You will print the Detail report at the end of the chapter.

8 ➤ **Exit** the Summary window, **exit** the Customer Aged Detail default window and return to the Home window.

9 ➤ To see your saved template report, at **Reports**, click ▼, select **Customer Aged Detail**, click **Display**. The Customer Aged Detail window will display with the right column displaying to print on 2 pages as shown before. Click the **Modify** icon, click **Report Options**. To the left of the **Save Template** button, click ▼ , and select Receivable Aged Detail on 1 page . Click **OK**.

10 ➤ Click **X** to **exit** your detail window and click **X** to **exit** to the Home window.

The RECEIVABLES Journals

The following types of transactions are entered in the three Sales journals:

Sales Quotes	a form sent to a customer indicating the price of products or services as requested by the customer.
Sales Orders	a confirmation of a commitment to purchase by a customer. A sales order can be issued without a previously issued sales quote. The product will be delivered at a later date, at which time a sales invoice will be issued.
Sales Invoices Pay Later	a sale on account (credit), which may or may not be issued without a sales Quote and/or a Sales Order.
Sales Invoices Paid by	a sale fully paid by cash, bank card, cheque or credit card.
Sales Invoices Adjustment	an entry to record a return of goods or an adjustment to the sales price, also called a Credit Memo.

The following types of transactions are recorded in the **Receipts Journal**:

Receipts   Payments (receipts) from customers on invoices, which may or may not be previously recorded.

Receipts can be:

1. Full payment of sales invoice on credit (Invoice-Pay Later) with or without cash discounts.

2. Partial payment of sales invoice on credit (Invoice-Pay Later) with or without partial cash discounts.

3. Deposits against a future sales invoice (Part B).

The Sales Journals

A customer may request a quote from a vendor (the selling company) to confirm/ guarantee sales prices. The vendor prepares a **sales quote,** which is recorded in the Sales Quote Journal. The sales quote is printed and sent to the customer. When you record the sales quote, neither the customer subledger nor any ledger account is updated with an accounting entry, as no sale has been made at this point. Although a sale is not made at this time, a record of the sales quote is useful for sales staff for follow-up purposes. Copies of printed quotes need to be kept because Simply does not provide a printed report of outstanding quotes.

When the customer confirms that the quote has been accepted, the quote can be converted into a **sales order**. At this point, the customer subledger and ledger accounts are still not updated with an accounting entry. The sales order is recorded in the company's **Sales Order Listing** and can be printed as a **Pending Sales Order** report. It is best to record the sales order to avoid the shipment getting missed in case there may be a delay in the delivery, or if the customer does not send a Purchase Order form. The Sales Order can also be displayed in the Daily Business Manager detail. See Exercise 2A-7.

When a sales quote is converted into a sales order, the information on the **sales quote** is automatically entered into the **sales order** window. Likewise, sales order information is entered into the **sales invoice** window upon conversion.

When the goods/services are delivered, the sales order is converted into a **sales invoice**. At this time, an accounting entry is made and the sales transaction is posted to the corresponding ledger accounts and customer subledgers. (See side note box.)

Sales Quote ⟶ Sales Order ⟶ Sales Invoice

In the Sales Journal, the following options are available for **Paid by:**

Option	Used For	Linked with account
Pay Later	on credit	Accounts Receivable
Cash	when paid in cash	Bank account
Cheque	when paid by cheque	Bank account
Bank Debit Cd	when paid by ATM (debit card)	Bank Debit Card
Visa Credit	when paid by credit card	Bank Credit Card account

When you record entries in the Sales Journals, you enter only one part of the entry. The program knows you are in the RECEIVABLES module and will debit or credit the appropriate account (Receivable or other account shown above) and appropriate taxes, as required.

For example, If you had recorded in Chapter 1, in the General Journal, a credit sale (invoice #239) transaction for a $70.00 Laptop Back Pak to J. Tang, you would have entered the following using a Double Entry recording.

Debit   1020 Accounts Receivable   70.00
Credit   4100   Sales   70.00

The entry in the General Journal would have looked similar to the following:

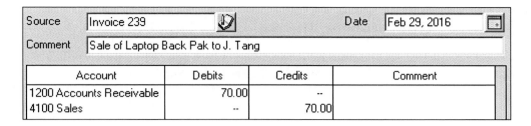

Source	Invoice 239			Date	Feb 29, 2016	
Comment	Sale of Laptop Back Pak to J. Tang					

Account	Debits	Credits	Comment
1200 Accounts Receivable	70.00	--	
4100 Sales	--	70.00	

To properly enter this type of transaction in the RECEIVABLE module, you need to enter the quantity, **credit** amount (base price) and account, which in this case is the 4100 Sales account, as shown next.

Quantity	Order	Back Order	Unit	Description	Base Price	Disc. %	Price	Amount	Tax	Acct
1			each	Laptop Back Pak	70.00		70.00	70.00	G	4100 Sales

In the RECEIVABLE module, Simply will automatically debit the 1200 Accounts Receivable Account. *Note*: You cannot enter a credit sale transaction in the General Journal (or any transaction affecting 1200 Accounts Receivable (control account)), once you have activated (added customer history) and are using the RECEIVABLES module.

Exercise 2A-3 – Deleting Columns (Customizing) & Resizing the Sales Journal

Sales Invoices ▼

1 ➤ Right click on the **Sales Invoice** icon. Notice the selections. Select **Create Invoice**. The Sales Invoice Journal will appear.

Study the basic format of the Sales Journal - Sales Invoice as shown next.

ⓘ

Column arrows indicate columns not needed at this time. To be removed in Exercise 2A-3.

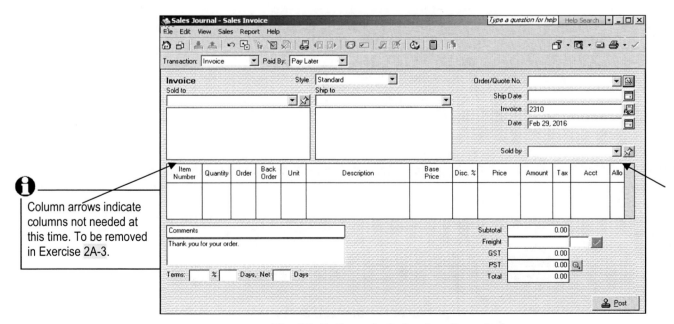

Fig. 2A-5: Sample Sales Invoice window.

Customizing the Sales Journal Window

The **Item Number** column is not used when the company records sales or purchases of merchandise using the **periodic** inventory system. The other system, **perpetual** inventory, discussed in Chapter 8, requires detailed records of goods (merchandise) being sold or purchased and will use the **Item Number** column.

Santos Luggage in this chapter uses the **periodic** inventory system. You need to customize the Sales Journal window to include only columns for information you will enter in the Sales Journal.

Exercise 2A-3 will show you how to hide the **Item Number** and **Allo** (Allocation) columns (see arrows in Fig. 2A-5) to customize the Sales Journal window for Santos Luggage. You may use the same procedure to hide any other column that you do not wish to appear on your sales journal. For example; a **service** company would not use **Ship Date**, **Order**, **Back Order**, and **Unit**. A service company would hide these columns to streamline invoices.

Follow the steps below to hide the **Item Number** and **Allo** columns.

2 ➤   Click the **Customize Journal** icon ⬚ and the Customize Journals window will appear, click on **Columns**. Form settings styles will be shown after step 8.

3 ➤   Click the **Item Number** box. A ✓ will appear and the **Account** name will fade.

4 ➤   You will also not need the Allocations field. Click the **Allocations** box and a ✓ will appear. (See side note box.)

5 ➤   On the left side of the window, click on the ⊞ at **Sales Orders**, then **Columns**. (The author has completed steps 3 and 4 for you, as well as for the Retail and Professional styles.) You could also in the left pane select Quotes, then click **Columns.** The author has completed steps 2 and 3 to not display the Item Number and Allocations columns.

6 ➤   Click **OK** when you are finished. The column area will now display as follows: (See step 7 to change the column widths.)

> ℹ️ Notice that the **Item** and **Allo** columns no longer display on the customized window.

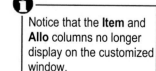

Quantity	Order	Back Order	Unit	Description	Base Price	Disc. %	Price	Amount	Tax	Acct	

Fig. 2A-6a: Customized Sales Journal window (before sizing).

7 ➤   In order to show more information in the Description and Acct fields, type the information as shown in Fig. 2A-6b. Place your mouse over a column heading dividing line between 2 columns (e.g., Description), then use the windows ⬌

icon to drag the column left or right to resize the columns to the approximate size as shown. This information will be deleted in step 8, but the column widths will remain the same size.

Quantity	Order	Back Order	Unit	Description	Base Price	Disc. %	Price	Amount	Tax	Acct
-100			each	Suitcase w/w regular size	23.00		23.00	-2,300.00	GP	4200 Sales- Returns & Allowan

Fig. 2A-6b: Customized Sales Journal window (after sizing).

8 ➤ When you have the columns to this approximate size, click the  and you will see the following.

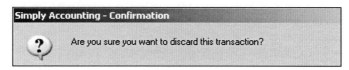

Simply Accounting - Confirmation

Are you sure you want to discard this transaction?

9 ➤ Select **Yes** to return to a blank invoice. The column sizes remain as you have set them up.

Sales Invoice Styles

1 ➤ Click the ▾ beside **Style** and you will see that there are 3 invoice template styles available.

Style Standard ▾
Professional
Retail
Standard

The headings that will appear on a Standard Invoice window are:

Quantity	Order	Back Order	Unit	Description	Base Price	Disc. %	Price	Amount	Tax	Acct

2 ➤ Click on **Retail**. You will see that the Order and Back Order columns are not displayed.

Quantity	Unit	Description	Base Price	Disc. %	Price	Amount	Tax	Acct

The **Retail** template could be used in a business that does not use Sales Quotes or Orders.

3 ➤ Click on **Professional.** You will see that the Order and Back Order columns from the Standard template and Item, Quantity, Unit, Base Price, Disc % and Price columns are not displayed from the Retail template.

Description	Amount	Tax	Acct

The **Professional** template could be used in a business that sells services (Accounting, real estate, legal, etc., and does not sell and list items or units).

In this text we will use the **Standard** style, and have modified the columns to not display Item and Allocation.

4 ➤ Select the **Standard** style invoice.

5 ➤ **Exit** to the Home window.

Entering Transactions in the RECEIVABLES Module

A common question asked is, "When should transactions be entered?" The answer depends on the volume of transactions. Smaller volumes (10 to 20 transactions a week) may be entered weekly; anything more than 10 a day should probably be done on a daily basis.

Another factor is the type of transaction. In general, you would like your accounting records to be up to date, especially when it concerns customers; therefore, sales quotes, orders, invoices, receipts and adjustments (including sales returns and discounts) must be entered with the original date of the transaction in order to record cash discounts and full payment dates properly. If the invoice date is not recorded properly, the aging of invoices will not be accurate.

Recording a Sales Quote

One thing to remember about a Sales Quote is that a sales transaction has not taken place; therefore, a quote does not affect the company accounts. The quote is a record of an inquiry — with no commitment on the part of the customer to buy.

When a company sells items to a business that will resell the items to others, the buying company does not pay PST on these goods. This is referred to as buying **PST-Exempt**. The business receives a PST tax-exemption number from the government and must inform the seller of this number. The seller does not charge PST to these exempt businesses.

Exercise 2A-4 – Recording a Sales Quote

---

1 ➤   Change the Session date to **Mar 01, 2016**.

Sales Quotes ▼

There are 4 different ways to create a Quote. The same choices apply to Sales Orders, Sales Invoices or Receipts.

a) Right click on the Sales Quote icon, select Create Quote.
b) At the Sales Quote icon, click the ▼, notice the 3 choices, select Create Quote.
c) Click the Sales Quote icon to go directly to the Sales Quote window.
d) At the Sales Invoice icon, click the ▼, notice the 3 choices, select Create Invoice, at Transaction, click the ▼, select Quote.

This text will use method c) to Create Sales Quotes, Sales Orders and Sales Invoices.

2 ➤   Click the **Sales Quotes** icon. The Sales Quote Journal will appear.

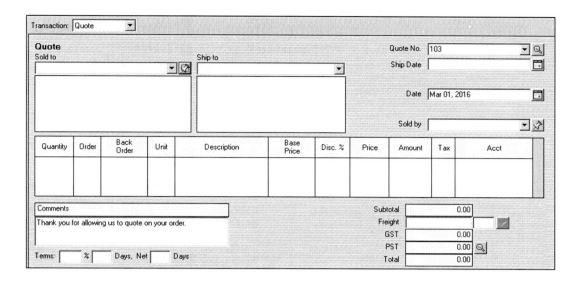

Study this transaction:

Mar 01, 2016 Luggage 4U has requested a quote for the following items that are to be picked up by their van on March 3. Their purchasing manager was very specific that the goods must be received by March 3 or the order will not be accepted. Their delivery van driver will pick up the quote before 2:30 p.m. today. Your manager has asked you to complete the Sales Quote, as the items requested are in stock and have been put aside for this customer:

     5 Laptop Back Paks at $70.00 each
     8 Suitcase w/w (with wheels) large size at $62.00 each
     9 Suitcase w/w regular size at $56.00 each

     Add GST at 5% on all items. Luggage 4U purchases the goods PST-exempt. Terms are 2/10, net 30.

ℹ

You can also press the first letter of the company name. Simply will display the customer list with the names beginning with this letter.

Click the yellow stick pin 🖈 to enter sales information for the same customer on the next invoice. You do not have to choose the customer again until you need to enter information for a new customer.

To record the quote, complete the following steps:

3 ➤ Sold to   Click the ▾ arrow to display the list of customers to choose from. Notice that the customers are displayed in alphabetical order and require no customer numbers. You may have to move ▲ or ▾ to see more customers. Click to select **Luggage 4U**. (Also see side note.)

The address details for Luggage 4U are automatically shown in the Sold To and Ship To fields.

4 ➤ Press the ⃞Tab key once to move to the yellow stick pin, (see side note box) and ⃞Tab again to move to the **Ship To** field. When you choose a customer in step 4, the Ship to field changes to: `<Mailing Address>` ▾.

If you click the ⏷ the field can be changed to Ship-to Address. The shipping address could be inserted here if the goods are being ordered by a Head Office and the goods are to be shipped to one of the stores. This feature will be demonstrated in Exercise 2A-20. Leave the choice as Mailing Address.

5 ➤ Ship To

Pressing the [Tab] key moves the cursor to each line of the address. If there were no changes in this field you could use the mouse to click the next field, **Quote No**.

6 ➤ Quote No.

The number **103** is displayed, which is the number of the next quote in Santos Luggage company's records. [Tab] once to move to the Select Order or Quote button [🔍]. (This will be explained in Exercise 2A-6.) You will learn how to insert the automatic numbering in Chapter 4. [Tab] again to move to the Ship Date field.

7 ➤ Ship Date

This is the date agreed upon that the goods will be shipped to the customer. Use the calendar icon and change the date to **Mar 3, 2016**. [Tab] to move to the **Date** field.

8 ➤ Date

This is the date the quote is given to the customer. The date should be **Mar 01, 2016**.This date is important because quotes, with sale items, may expire within a set number of days from the quote date. [Tab] [Tab] to move to the **Sold By** field.

9 ➤ Sold by

You will not use this field in these exercises. See Appendix CD-AC, *Adding a Salesperson's Name to an Invoice*, for information on the steps you would need to complete to have this field available. Not all companies would make use of this field. [Tab] [Tab] to move to the **Order** field.

Quantity

This column is skipped and will be used when goods are shipped to the customer.

10 ➤ Order

Type **5**, [Tab].

Back Order

The Back Order column is skipped on a Sales Quote or a Sales Order. It is used when a sales invoice is being produced and some of the goods ordered by the customer (part of the order) is not available. The goods will be shipped when stock arrives.

11 ➤ Unit

Type **each**, [Tab].

12 ➤ Description

Type **Laptop Back Paks** [Tab].

13 ➤ Base Price

This field represents the price before any sale discounts are given to a customer. Type **70.00** [Tab].

Disc %

This field would be a sale discount percentage and does not represent a discount for paying an invoice within the discount terms. This field will be explained in Exercise 2B-33. [Tab].

14 ➤ Price

This field represents the price after any sale discounts from the Disc % column. [Tab].

ℹ️

GST refers to the **Goods and Services Tax** applied by the federal government to goods and services sold.

GST rate of 5% is used in this text and reflected in the solutions. This rate, however, may have changed since publication date. When on the job, be sure to use the appropriate GST and PST rates.

PST refers to the **Provincial Sales Tax** applied by provincial governments to goods and services sold, except for PST-exempt goods or services.

For additional information on GST and PST, refer to Chapter 15, *Taxes*.

The codes **G**, **GP** and **P** are created by the company and may be different for each company. A company may make up any two-letter combination and wording for a tax code.

15 ➤ Amount   This field represents the calculated amount from fields **Order** times **Price**. `Tab` to accept 350.00.

16 ➤ Tax   Press `Enter`. A list of Tax Codes and information is displayed (see below).

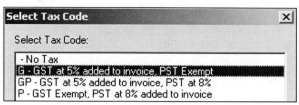

No tax   This includes items that are GST-exempt (No GST charged), GST Non-Taxable (No GST charged) and GST taxable (GST with a rate of 0%).

G   Price of goods **plus G**ST. The **G**ST is not included in the selling price and must be added to the selling price of the items; e.g., Selling price of $200.00 plus 5% GST of the price ($10.00). The **G** code would be used when the customer is buying the goods PST-exempt.

GP   This code is used for a **retail sale**. It combines both taxes: price of goods **plus G**ST and **P**ST. The GST and PST are not included in the selling price and must be added to the selling price of the items; e.g., Selling price of $200.00 plus 5% GST of the price ($10.00) plus 8% PST of the price ($16.00). Taxes total $26.00.

P   This code applies on a sale where **P**ST only is charged (GST is Exempt). An example of this is when you buy or sell insurance. Only PST at 8% (Provincial Sales Tax) is charged. The **P** code will be used in Chapter 3.

---

17 ➤ Select **G**. (You may also type g or G.) This means the selling price does not include GST, and the customer is buying the goods PST-exempt.

18 ➤ Acct   Press `Enter`. The G/L chart of accounts should be displayed. You may have to scroll using `▼` or `▲` to see more accounts. Simply is looking for an account to credit. Select account **4100 Sales** by double-clicking on it. You can also type **4** and the selection window changes to accounts beginning with 4. If needed, you could then type **2** and the account window would change to accounts beginning with 42.

19 ➤ Enter the next two items on the quote. The tax code and the sales account will be the same for all items (w/w means, *with wheels*).

     8   Suitcase w/w large size at $62.00 each
     9   Suitcase w/w regular size in red colour at $56.00 each

Note the **Description** field when you type "Suitcase w/w regular size **in red colour**." Simply will word wrap the required information to the next line(s) if the information does not fit on one line. You can use the ⬌ icon and drag left or right to resize the column as required. (See side note box.)

20 ➤ Remove the words: **in red colour**.

> By moving the ⬌ to the right, you can expand the column if you want the column wider. Do not change the column width for this exercise.

Comments box. This field displays a variety of messages you want customers to see on quotes, orders and invoices. Note the default for quotes. You will be shown how to enter other comments in Chapter 4.

The **Terms** boxes should display **2.00%, 10 days, Net 30 days**, the terms previously agreed upon by the customer. If the terms are different from the default, click the appropriate box, and change as required.

Freight	Santos Luggage does not charge for delivery; therefore, this field is not used.

21 ➤ Shipped by   On the **icon** bar, click  the **Track Shipments** icon.

22 ➤   Click the ▼ arrow to display a list of shippers. Select **Your Vehicle** (the customer's vehicle).

Tracking Number	This will be blank because there is no need to track the shipment, since it is being picked up by the customer's vehicle. The software can track shipments; however, this text does not provide an exercise for tracking shipments on the Internet. Click **OK**.
	You will notice that the Shipping information does not display in the window. It prints on the printed Quote.

When you have completed entering the above information, the window display should look as follows:

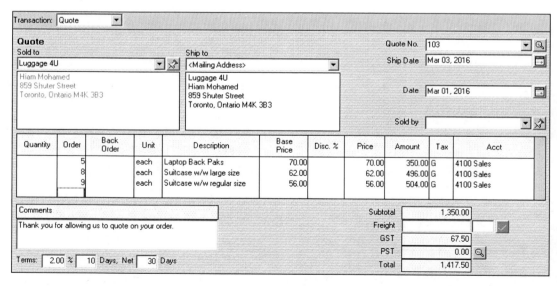

If your business uses pre-printed forms bearing the company name and/or logo and other relevant information, you would click the 🖨 from the Quote window. The information being printed on the Pre-printed form will look similar to Fig. 2A-7.

23 ➤   To display the Quote using the Custom Simply Form document, click on 🔲. You should see the following error message.

Simply Accounting - Error

⚠ To use Print Preview, you must select a Simply form. To do this, click the Reports & Forms button on the toolbar. Then, on the page for the form you want to preview, select Custom Forms and change the Form Type to Custom Simply Form.

The settings for the Simply Custom Forms have not been selected.

24 ➤ Click **OK** to return to the Quote window.

Do not record; continue with Exercise 2A-5.

Santos Luggage-A, Student's Name
635 Semple Avenue
Toronto, Ontario M9L 1V5   103

                                                                   Mar 01, 2016

                                                                   1 of 1

Luggage 4U   Luggage 4U
Hiam Mohamed   Hiam Mohamed
859 Shuter Street   859 Shuter Street
Toronto, Ontario M4K 3B3   Toronto, Ontario M4K 3B3

5	each	Laptop Back Paks	G	70.00	350.00
8	each	Suitcase w/w large size	G	62.00	496.00
9	each	Suitcase w/w regular size	G	56.00	504.00

                    Subtotal   1,350.00
                    G- GST at 5% added to invoice PST exempt   67.50
                    GST

                    PST Exempt: #89-8A

                    Terms: 2%/10, Net 30

Santos Luggage-A, Student's Name GST: #V8956325
Shipped by Your Vehicle.
Thank you for allowing us to quote on your order.   1,417.50

Pre-printed forms will normally have the company name and address printed on the form. The information shown in Fig. 2A-7 indicates the company name printed by Simply. If you are required to print the forms in the lab/classroom, the name printed by Simply will allow you to identify your printouts in class.

Fig. 2A-7: Sales Quote information printed on pre-printed forms (see side box).

Revising the Sales Quote Form

You can use Windows features such as Cut (selects text inside one column at a time), Copy and Paste from the Edit menu of the Sales Journal window (see side note box). You can cut, copy and paste text from one Simply window to another, or from a Simply window to another program (e.g., word processing). It will save time in typing information.

Using the Edit menu you can Insert or Remove a line in the Sales Quote, Sales Order or Sales Invoice.

In the following exercise you will use the Insert and Remove feature for the information in a row within a Quote.

Edit Notes...
To Cut, Copy and Paste: Select (highlight) the text with the left mouse button. Choose **Edit** from the top menu of the window and then select either Cut (to remove) or Copy. The text is temporarily copied to the Windows clipboard, and can be retrieved using the Paste feature. Reposition the cursor, click **Edit**, then **Paste** to place the text at the new cursor location.

Exercise 2A-5 – Revising the Sales Quote Form

The manager has asked you to move the regular size suitcase to the middle line of the invoice before you record the quote.

1 ➤ Click **8** in the Order field, then click **Edit, Insert Line**. A blank line appears as the second line of the invoice. The new line can be entered at the top, or between any items on the invoice. If you are not replacing any item, you could enter the item(s) you want as the second sales item.

2 ➤ **Retype** or cut and paste appropriate information, for the regular suitcases as the 2nd item.

3 ➤ Click **9** in the bottom item, click the **Edit Remove line** function, from the menu bar, to remove the bottom sales item, or you could press the **Delete** key to remove the sales information from each of the columns for the regular size suitcase. (See side note boxes.)

More Edit Notes...

To Move a Whole Column to a New Position: Click and hold down the left mouse button positioned on a column heading. Drag the column to a new position, then release the mouse button.

Restoring the Original Column Width and Positions: There is no selection to restore the window back after a column is moved. If you use the View menu, Restore feature it will return the window to the original default column size.

The Quote information area should now resemble Fig. 2A-8.

Quantity	Order	Back Order	Unit	Description	Base Price	Disc. %	Price	Amount	Tax	Acct
	5		each	Laptop Back Paks	70.00		70.00	350.00	G	4100 Sales
	9		each	Suitcase w/w regular size	56.00		56.00	504.00	G	4100 Sales
	8		each	Suitcase w/w large size	62.00		62.00	496.00	G	4100 Sales

Fig. 2A-8: Revised Quote information area.

4 ➤ Make corrections to any fields, if necessary.

5 ➤ To display the Sales Journal entry created by this quote, click **Report**, then **Display Sales Journal Entry**.

The window should display:

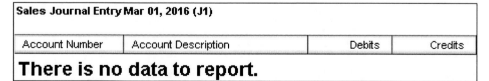

Account Number	Account Description	Debits	Credits

There is no data to report.

See the Mini-guide at the end of Chapter 2B, before the Glossary. This form will help you identify when entries are recorded in the RECEIVABLES module of Simply and which journal they are recorded in. You can find the document on the Student CD as Appendix CD-V, *Mini-Guides Receivables—Payables*.

6 ➤ **Exit** from the Sales Journal Entry window.

7 ➤ Click the [🖳 Record] button. Notice that the confirmation window says Transaction recorded successfully, but it does not indicate a Journal entry #.

There is no entry made in the company records, because a sale has not taken place. At this point, the customer has requested a formal price quote and will decide whether to buy the goods at the quoted price. Santos Luggage must now wait for the customer to make a decision.

8 ➤ Click **OK** and **Exit** from the Sales Journal-Quote window to the Home window.

Converting a Sales Quote into a Sales Order

When you record a Sales Quote, it is recorded in the Sales Quote database and it will remain there until it is converted into a Sales Order or it is deleted. When converting a Sales Quote into a Sales Order, the details are automatically forwarded to the Sales Order, but may be revised.

Remember that a **Sales Order** does NOT affect the company books because no goods were shipped. The order, when recorded, goes to a Sales Order listing.

Exercise 2A-6 – Converting a Sales Quote into a Sales Order

The Purchasing Manager of Luggage 4U confirmed, by fax, to your Sales Manager the approval of Quote #103. To change the sales quote into a sales order, complete the following steps:

Sales Orders ▼

ℹ️ The sales quote is recorded in the Sales Quote database of the program and cannot be printed as a report. You will be able to see a list of Quotes as shown in Exercise 2A-6. The Sales Quote does NOT get posted to the General Ledger.

1 ➤ Advance the Session date to **Mar 02, 2016**.

2 ➤ At **Sales Orders**, click the ▼ to display the 3 choices. Click the **Create Order** item, or click the **Sales Order** icon. The Sales Order Journal will appear.

3 ➤ Order No. Click the **Order No.** finder 🔍 icon. (See side note box.)

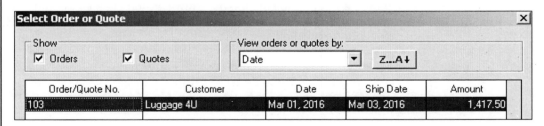

Order/Quote No.	Customer	Date	Ship Date	Amount
103	Luggage 4U	Mar 01, 2016	Mar 03, 2016	1,417.50

This window will display details about previously recorded customer quotes and orders for all customers. Quote **103** is the only outstanding quote at this time.

4 ➤ View orders or quotes by: Click the ▼ and you will see the different columns the report can be sorted by. Note the report can also be sorted in ascending or descending order.

5 ➤ Click **Select** or double-click **103** to accept the Quote.

The Sales Order window fills with the details from the Sales Quote.

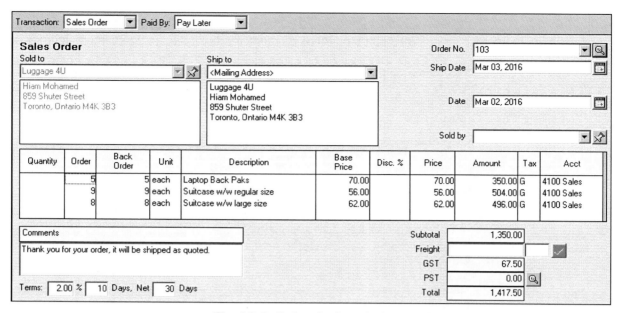

Fig. 2A-9: Sales Order window – filled in.

Back Order The B ack Order column shows **5**, **9 & 8** respectively, the quantity ordered. This means that 5, 9 and 8 of the specified items are backordered (not yet shipped since this is only a Sales Order form). The goods are due to be shipped to the customer on March 3, 2016. Do NOT change values in this column. Simply will keep track of the amounts.

All other details of the order are the same as entered in the quote. At this point, the quote could be revised. For example, the buyer might decide to increase or decrease the quantity. The price could also be changed if the final selling price was lower. Remember that a quote is a commitment by the seller to provide a product or service at the agreed upon price for the period of the quote (usually shown in **Ship Date**). If there is a price hike after the sales quote is issued and before the Ship Date, the buyer is protected from price increases. However, a price lower than the price quoted is to the advantage of the buyer, so it can be changed without consulting the buyer. For now, do not change any fields.

6 ➤ To display the Sales Journal entry created by this Sales Order, click **Report**, **Display Sales Journal Entry**. The window should display:

Sales Journal Entry Mar 02, 2016 (J1)

Account Number	Account Description	Debits	Credits

There is no data to report.

Similar to the Sales Journal Entry window for the sales quote, an entry to the company books has not been created, because a sale has not yet taken place.

7 ➤ **Exit** from this window by clicking the ⊠ button.

8 ➤ Make corrections to the sales order, if necessary.

9 ➤ Click the 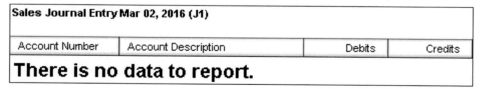 button. This records the sales order in the Pending Sales Order listing and does NOT post to the General ledger.

Study the message that appears when you click the Record button:

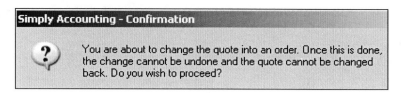

Simply Accounting – Confirmation

? You are about to change the quote into an order. Once this is done, the change cannot be undone and the quote cannot be changed back. Do you wish to proceed?

10 ➤ Click **Yes** to proceed. The Confirmation window says the Transaction was recorded successfully, but it does not indicate a Journal Entry #, as a sale has not taken place. Click **OK**.

11 ➤ **Exit** from the Sales Order window.

Daily Business Manager

The Daily Business Manager (DBM) [DBM] is located **on the icon tool bar**. The Daily Business Manager is a business tool that can be displayed when you start Simply (the default setting), and/or when you advance the session date, or when you need to display the window. This window is very helpful for managing customer receivables in a business setting. You will see that outstanding Sales Orders are displayed in this window.

Exercise 2A-7 – Using the Daily Business Manager (DBM)

1 ➤ Change the Session date to **Mar 3, 2016**.

2 ➤ Click [DBM] the **Daily Business Manager** icon and the DBM will appear as shown next.

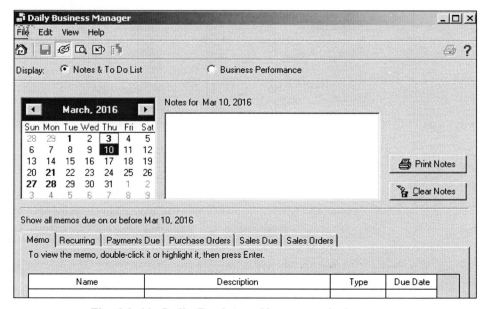

Fig. 2A-10: Daily Business Manager window.

The lower window will list reminders about tasks you need to do, for the next 7 days, relating to the various tabs shown (Memo, Recurring, Payments Due, etc.).

The **Reminder** date Mar 10, 2016 for all tabs is calculated from the **Session** date, Mar 03, 2016. *Note:* Sales Quotes will not display.

3 ➤ Click each of the tabs in the lower-half of the window.

Memo	Lists general information that has been placed in the customer file. This will be explained later in this chapter.

Recurring	Lists all recurring entries that are due within the next 7 days. Santos Luggage has not used recurring entries.

Payments Due	Shows all invoices that must be paid on or before Mar 10, 2016. This would include invoices for which discounts are available, if paid within the terms agreed upon (e.g., 2/10, net 30) when purchased. There are no items listed: Santos Luggage does not use the PAYABLES module.

Purchase Orders	Shows all purchase orders that are due to be shipped to your company on or before Mar 10, 2016. Santos Luggage does not use the PAYABLES module.

Sandler Travel Stores' invoice was due to be paid on Feb 25, 2016 and is now 6 days overdue. Someone from your company will have to contact this customer to follow up the outstanding invoice.

| Sales Due | This tab lists overdue sales invoices and sales invoices that are due to be paid within the next 7 days.

If you double-click on an invoice, you will be taken to the Receipts Journal. **Exit** from the Receipts Journal window to discard the receipt. (See side note box.) |
|---|---|

Sales Orders	The display shows the Outstanding Order #103 for Luggage 4U. If you double-click any column, you will be taken to a filled-in Sales Invoice. It is assumed that you want to record a sale. **Exit** from the Sales Invoice window to discard the invoice.

By studying the information in the various tabs, you may find items that may need to be followed up.

You can also use the Daily Business Manager to manage your daily tasks. The window to the right of the calendar will display messages that can be used to remind you to call customers, back up data files, prepare special reports for management, etc. However, those messages will not appear automatically. You will need to make notes for yourself.

Exercises 2A-8 and 2A-9 illustrate how you can use the Daily Business Manager to view outstanding invoices, orders, and memo notes to assist employees, and provide graphical analysis for management.

To use the **Notes** feature, follow the steps in the next exercise.

Exercise 2A-8 – Using the Notes Feature of the DBM

1 ➤ In the calendar on the left side of your screen, click **8** (Mar 08, 2016).

2 ➤ Click in the **Notes for Mar 08, 2016** box near the top. Type **Prepare draft newspaper advertisement for local paper.**

3 ➤ In the calendar on the left, click **March 10**. Type **Finalize newspaper advertisement for local paper**.

4 ➤ Click **March 8**. The previous message you typed is displayed.

Exercise 2A-9 – Using the Business Performance Feature of the DBM

---

1 ➤ **Display** Click the 🔘 **Business Performance** item.

There are three Business Performance Measurements (ratios) shown in the top portion. A graphical representation of the measurements is shown in the lower portion. There are no entries made to this point; therefore, the graphs are a straight line.

2 ➤ Click the **Daily Business Manager Options** 🔳 icon. Click the **Business Performance** tab.

3 ➤ Management may like to see different measurements graphically. To set up a new measurement in the left window, click **Sales (Past 7 Days)**, click **Select >**, then **OK**. It is now moved to the right side pane. In Exercise 2B-25, you will return to this Business Performance window to see the graphical display.

4 ➤ To exit, click **X** to return to the Home window.

Exercise 2A-10 – To Display the DBM

---

1 ➤ In the menu bar, click **Setup, User preferences, View** in the left-side pane, and at Daily Business Manager, click **At Start Up**, to display the ✓. Notice the other choice is after Changing the Session Date, which would be appropriate in a business setting. Click **OK**. The module is displayed the next time you start up (open) the company file.

From this point on, it is assumed that the DBM will not display each time you open the company. See Exercise 2A-11. Your faculty member may ask you to display the DBM each time you open the file.

Exercise 2A-11 – To Hide the DBM

As noted in Exercise 2A-10, we do not want the DBM to appear each time we open the company file.

1 ➤ From the Home window, click **Setup**, **User Preferences**, **View**, at Daily Business Manager, click **At Start Up** to remove the ✓. Click **OK**. The DBM will be hidden next time you open the file.

🛈 To View the Pending Sales Orders Report

This report can also be viewed in **Detail** on two pages, before changing column widths. This report also lists the description and quantity of items that are backordered. The item column in the Detail report refers to **Perpetual** inventory data and will not contain any information for Santos Luggage.

You need to view and/or print the Pending Sales Orders Report regularly to ensure that no sales order is missed.

Exercise 2A-12 – To View the Pending Sales Orders Report

---

1 ➤ From the **Home** window, click **Report Centre**, the left pane should be **Receivables**, click **Pending Sales Orders Summary by Customer**, click the blue **Modify this report**. Change the **Date** to **Mar 10, 2016, OK**. This report will assist management in displaying all outstanding (pending) sales orders due within 1 week from the current Mar 03, 2016 session date. (See side note box.)

Orders with shipping dates due later than the date specified (Mar 10, 2016) will not display.

Pending Sales Orders Summary by Customer As at Mar 10, 2016			
Sales Order Number	Sales Order Date	Ship Date	Original Order Amount
Luggage 4U			
103	Mar 02, 2016	Mar 03, 2016	1,417.50
			1,417.50
			1,417.50

2 ➤ Exit to the Home window.

IMPORTANT: BACK UP your data after every work session and update your logbook.

Producing a Sales Invoice from a Sales Order

It is common practice to print multi-copy sales invoices and/or sales orders for distribution to the customer and various departments in the company as illustrated in Fig. 2A-11.

Santos Luggage
635 Semple Avenue
Toronto, Ontario M9L 1V5
Phone: (416)698-3333 ✦ Fax (416)698-3345

INVOICE
2310

Date: Mar 03, 2016

SOLD TO
Luggage 4U
Hiam Mohamed
859 Shuter Street
Toronto, Ontario M4K 3B3

SHIP TO
Luggage 4U
Hiam Mohamed
859 Shuter Street
Toronto, Ontario M4K 3B3

Re: Order No. 103

Business No.: V8956325

SHIP	ORDER	B/O	UNIT	DESCRIPTION	TAX	PRICE	AMOUNT
5	5			Laptop Back Paks	G	70.00	$ 350.00
9	9			Suitcase w/w regular size	G	56.00	504.00
8	8			Suitcase w/w large size	G	62.00	496.00
				Subtotal			1,350.00
				G- GST at 5% added to invoice PST exempt GST			67.50
				PST Exempt: #89-8A			
				Terms: 2%/10, Net 30.			

Shipped by Your Vehicle.
Thank you for your order

TOTAL $ 1,417.50

Copy 1 Customer
Copy 2 Accounting
Copy 3 Sales
Copy 4 Packing Slip

Fig. 2A-11: Sales Invoice Form and Distribution Schedule.

Exercise 2A-13 – To Produce a Sales Invoice from a Sales Order

---

Sales Invoices ▾

All goods ordered by Luggage 4U on Sales Order #103 are ready to be shipped. To record the sale, complete the following steps:

1 ➤ Right click the **Sales Invoices** icon, click **Create Invoice**. The Sales Journal-Sales Invoice window appears.

Transaction:	Invoice ▾	Paid By:	Pay Later ▾		

Invoice		Style	Standard ▾	Order/Quote No.	▾ 🔍
Sold to	▾ 🖉	Ship to	▾	Ship Date	🔲
				Invoice	2310
				Date	Mar 03, 2016 🔲
				Sold by	▾ 🖉

Quantity	Order	Back Order	Unit	Description	Base Price	Disc. %	Price	Amount	Tax	Acct

Comments		Subtotal	0.00
Thank you for your order.		Freight	
		GST	0.00
		PST	0.00 🔍
Terms: __ % __ Days, Net __ Days		Total	0.00

       Transaction: Do not change the default from Invoice.

2 ➤ **Order/Quote No.** Click the **Order No.** finder 🔍 icon.

As in Exercise 2A-6, this window will display details about previously recorded customer quotes and orders for all customers. Order 103 is the only outstanding order.

3 ➤ Click **Select** or double-click to accept Order #103. The Sales Invoice window fills with the details from Sales Order #103 recorded previously.

4 ➤ **Paid by:**   Click the ▾ arrow and 5 choices appear:

- *Pay Later*   for a sale on credit.
- *Cash*   used when cash is received as payment.
- *Cheque*   used when a cheque is received as payment.
- *Bank Debit Cd* used if a Bank Debit card is received as payment.
- *Visa Credit*   used if the Visa Credit Card is used as payment. This is the credit card that Santos Luggage accepts.

Because it is on account (on credit), select **Pay Later**, `Tab`.

The full order is ready to ship. You can complete the invoice in one of two ways:

a.   If you clicked in the **Quantity** column you would enter the quantity of each item shipped, `Tab` and continue entering the quantity shipped. Note that the Back Order column changes to blank because there are no goods backordered.

b.   If you click the ⬛ (Fill backordered quantities) icon Simply will fill in the Quantity columns for you. This would be used when all the items ordered are filled and there are no back orders.

5 ➤   Click the ⬛ icon and the middle portion window will change to the following. The quantity field has been filled in and the Back Order field is blank, as the goods are being shipped.

Quantity	Order	Back Order	Unit	Description	Base Price	Disc. %	Price	Amount	Tax	Acct
5	5		each	Laptop Back Paks	70.00		70.00	350.00	G	4100 Sales
9	9		each	Suitcase w/w regular size	56.00		56.00	504.00	G	4100 Sales
8	8		each	Suitcase w/w large size	62.00		62.00	496.00	G	4100 Sales

6 ➤   Display the Sales Journal entry created by this invoice.

Sales Journal Entry Mar 03, 2016 (J1)

Account Number	Account Description	Debits	Credits
1200	Accounts Receivable	1,417.50	-
2630	GST Charged on Sales	-	67.50
4100	Sales	-	1,350.00
Additional Date:	Additional Field:		
		1,417.50	1,417.50

J1 (Journal Entry #1) indicates that this is the first Simply journal entry in the Santos Luggage Company records.

Notice the automatic debit to 1200 Accounts Receivable account made by Simply. Also notice the automatic credit to the GST CHARGED ON SALES calculated by Simply, based on the GST code or rate previously entered. The automatic linking to the debit and credit General Ledger accounts will be explained in Chapter 4.

7 ➤   **Exit** from the entry window.

In this text, you will not need to print Invoices or Packing Slips.

8 ➤   Click the ⬇ on the right beside the Printer icon. You will see:

✔ Print Invoice	Ctrl+P
Print Packing Slip	Ctrl+Shift+P
Print Invoice and Packing Slip	Ctrl+Shift+K

The current default is to print an Invoice. This can be changed. You will see this in Chapter 4. Do NOT print the Invoice to save paper. Click in the invoice to exit this window.

> See Appendix CD-W, *Printing Packing Slips* for more information on printing and what will print on the Pre-printed packing slip form (lists the quantity and description of items to be shipped). You do not need to print the Packing Slip in this exercise.

In this text, we will not need to print Invoices or Packing Slips.

9 ➤   Click the **Post** button to post the invoice.

The next information box informs you that the complete sales order has been filled (no back order), and that the sales order will be removed from the Sales Order Listing.

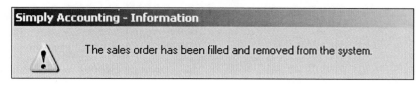

10 ➤ Click **OK**. The Posting Confirmation window displays that Journal entry J1 was posted successfully. Click **OK**.

11 ➤ **Exit** from the Sales Invoice window to the Home window.

Journalizing Sales Returns

Sometimes customers return goods that are damaged, goods that were delivered but not ordered, or goods delivered in excess of what was ordered. This type of transaction is referred to as a **Sales Return** and is recorded as a negative Sales Invoice.

	They are a CUSTOMER to you
Sale to your customer	Dr Accounts Receivable Cr GST on Sales Cr Sales
Sales Returns from your customer (Issue a Credit Note to the customer)	Dr Sales Returns/Allow Dr GST on Sales Cr Accounts Receivable

Sales Returns are journalized in the Sales Journal as a decrease to Sales (in the Sales section of the Income Statement). The **GST Charged on Sales** must also be reduced accordingly (in the Balance Sheet). Follow the steps in the next exercise.

Exercise 2A-14 – Journalizing a Sales Return

Mar 3, 2016	Havarah Leather Goods returned 2 Laptop Back Paks, as they had ordered too many. Santos Luggage does not charge a Restocking Fee. The Back Paks were originally purchased on invoice #2253 at 70.00, plus GST. We sent Havarah Leather Goods our credit memo #124 dated today in the amount of $147.00, and referenced it to invoice #2253Rt.

1 ➤ Right-click the **Sales Invoice** icon, select **Create Invoice**.

2 ➤ **Sold To**   Select **Havarah Leather Goods**, [Tab]. Click in the **Invoice** field.

3 ➤ **Invoice**   Many firms enter the invoice number with a return code (Rt) or other codes as shown below. This cross-references the return with the original sales invoice.

Type **2253Rt CM124**. When displaying the customer detail the invoice number will show first in the column. [Tab] [Tab] to Date.

Other invoice codes used to identify action taken are:

Ad	Adjustment	**Al**	Allowance Granted	**Co**	Correction
Dp	Deposit	**NS**	NSF	**Rt**	Returned goods
Rv	Reversal	**TS**	Transfer	**Wo**	Write-off

4 ➤ **Date**   **Mar 3, 2016** is the date the goods were received by our firm. [Tab]. You should not backdate the return to the original date of the sale (Feb 26, 2016). You want your records to reflect dates when transactions actually happened. Click in the **Quantity** field.

5 ➤ **Quantity**   Type **-2** (negative) (2 items returned), [Tab].

6 ➤ **Unit**   Type **each**, [Tab].

7 ➤ **Description**   Type **Laptop Back Paks Not needed**, [Tab].

8 ➤ **Base Price**   Type **70.00** (the original selling price). [Tab] [Tab] [Tab] to Amount as there is no % discount.

9 ➤ **Amount**   [Tab] to accept **-140.00**. The minus sign before the invoice amount will make this entry a **Debit** to the account selected and a **Credit** to Accounts Receivable.

10 ➤ **Tax**   [Tab]. The **G** code is still valid for a sales return.

11 ➤ **Acct**   The default **4100 Sales** revenue account cannot be used because this is not a sale. It is a return of some or part of a sale. Many companies use a separate account to keep a record of returns.

Press [Enter]. The G/L accounts should be displayed.

Select account **4200 Sales - Returns & Allowances**. [Tab] to accept. Click in the **Comments** field.

12 ➤ **Comments**   The default comment code is not appropriate for a return. Change the comment by highlighting the current comment and typing **Return accepted, not needed**, [Tab]. You could leave the comment space blank, but it is best to enter a note for future reference.

13 ➤ **Terms**   Leave the 2.00%. Change the terms to **5 days** and **Net 25 days**. Goods were sold on the 26th, and returns were accepted on the 3rd. There are 5 days remaining in the discount period.

The Information about Mrs. Santos approving the return will not print on the customer return invoice.

14 ➤ Click the **Enter Additional information** ☑ icon and type the information shown. (See side note box.)

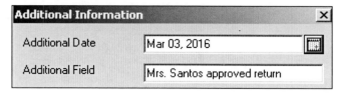

Additional Information   ✕

| Additional Date | Mar 03, 2016 | 🔲 |
| Additional Field | Mrs. Santos approved return | |

15 ➤ Click **OK**.

16 ➤ View the Sales Journal Entry as shown next.

Sales Journal Entry Mar 03, 2016 (J2)

Account Number	Account Description	Debits	Credits
2630	GST Charged on Sales	7.00	-
4200	Sales- Returns & Allowances	140.00	-
1200	Accounts Receivable	-	147.00
Additional Date: Ma...	Additional Field: Mrs. Santos appro...		
		147.00	147.00

17 ➤ **Exit** from viewing the Sales Journal entry.

The invoice window display should appear as follows:

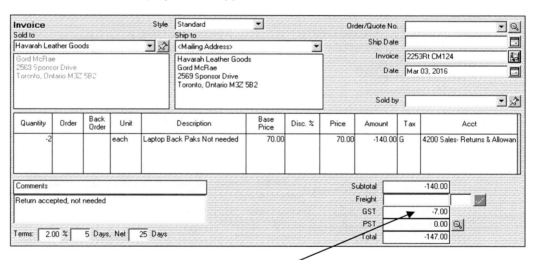

Notice that GST originally charged on this invoice has been reduced by the amount corresponding to the return. Negative **-7.00** is 5% of the $140.00 returned goods.

18 ➤ **Post** when correct, click **OK** for the J2 confirmation window and **Exit** to the Home window.

19 ➤ **Recently Viewed Reports Area**   Display the **Havarah Leather Goods Customer Aged Detail** report at **March 3, 2016**, without terms. Click on **Customer Aged**, the report displays. Click the **Modify** icon, **Report Options**, select **Havarah Leather Goods**, **Detail** button should be selected, click on **Include terms** button to remove the ✓, click **OK**. Notice the **2253Rt** reference, and the amount is shown with a minus.

Customer Aged Detail As at Mar 03, 2016				
Source	Date	Transaction Type	Total	Current
Havarah Leather Goods				
2253	Feb 26, 2016	Invoice	2,205.00	2,205.00
2253Rt CM124	Mar 03, 2016	Invoice	-147.00	-147.00
Total outstanding:			2,058.00	2,058.00

20 ➤   Exit the Aged Detail window and return to the Home window.

 Remember to back up your data and update your logbook at the end of every work session.

The Receipts Journal

The Receipts Journal is used to record all types of payments from customers:

- Payment without discount
- Payment with discount(s)
- Deposits (see part B)

Most companies, that have a large volume of sales invoices, have a procedure to record receipts of payments. Upon receipt of the customer's cheque, it is usually stamped on the back with a notation "For Deposit Only" or "For Deposit to the Account of (company)." This prevents unauthorized persons from using the cheque for any other purpose. The date of receipt is also stamped on the back of the cheque, which is used in the journal entry as the date of the transaction.

The date of receipt may be backdated one or two days to accommodate a sales discount. This would apply when a customer's cheque was mailed on the tenth day from the invoice date. There may also be a delay in mail delivery or a cheque received on a Monday when the due date was on a Saturday or Sunday.

The receipts are usually deposited daily to update customer balances owing. A record of each receipt is detailed in the bank deposit book.

Journalizing a Receipt with Cash Discount

Cheques for payment of an invoice are usually accompanied by an advice, a detachable form that provides the details of the payment.

Fig. 2A-12 illustrates a cheque received for this transaction, accompanied by an advice. The date and security stamps on the back of the cheque are also shown. You will use the details shown on the cheque and the advice to journalize the payment.

	ROYES LUGGAGE INC. 256 Ochos Blvd. Toronto, Ontario M4K 3V3	**438** DATE ___02 03 2016___ DD MM YYYY	← *Cheque*

PAY One thousand one hundred thirty three 00/100 - - - - Dollars	$1,133.00

To The Order Of	Santos Luggage 635 Semple Avenue Toronto, Ontario M9L 1V5

Bank of The Atlantic   ROYES LUGGAGE INC.
19 Swell Avenue
Toronto, Ontario M4C 2A1   *J.A. Royes*
_____

⊓■438⊓ |:055661⊓006| :   24⊓181-8⊓■

DETACH BEFORE CASHING
ROYES LUGGAGE INC.   438   ← *Advice*

DATE	DESCRIPTION	AMOUNT
Mar 02, 2016	Full Payment of Invoice #2256	$ 1,133.00

FOR DEPOSIT ONLY   ←*Back*

RECEIVED   Mar 3, 2016   ←*Transaction
Date*

← *Fig. 2A-12: A Payment Cheque with Advice.*

Exercise 2A-15 – To Record a Receipt with Discount

Study the following transaction:

**Mar 03, 2016   Received from Royes Luggage Inc. cheque #438 for $1,133.00
in full payment of invoice #2256.**

Receipts ▼

There are 3 different ways to create Receipts:

1 ➤ A)   At the **Receipts** icon, click the ▼, notice the 3 choices. Select **Create Receipt**. In the **From** field, click ▼ and select the customer. The screen fills with the outstanding invoices. Click **X** to return to the Home window.

   B)   Click the **Receipts** icon, to go directly to the Receipts Journal window. In the **From** field click ▼ and select the customer. The screen fills with the outstanding invoices. Click **X** to return to the Home window.

   C)   In the **Customers** area, click the ▼ or **right click on the customer from whom we received the cheque**, select **Receive Payments**. The screen fills with the outstanding invoices. Click **X** to return to the Home window.

2 ➤   Using step 1, method **C**, click the ▼ at **Royes Luggage Inc.**, select **Receive Payments**. The Receipts Journal will display the name and address of the customer as shown:

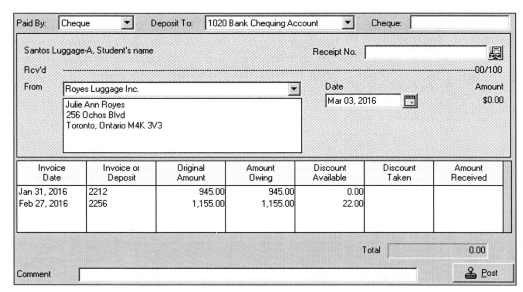

Fig. 2A-13: Receipts Journal window.

The menu bar items are the same as the Sales Journal, except for **Receipt**.

Receipt   Menu with choices for **Enter Deposits** and **Include Fully Paid Invoices/deposits** in the top detail section of the Receipts window. You can adjust a previously posted receipt or look up (view) a receipt.

The details of all outstanding invoices for a specific customer are listed in the lower section, including the original Invoice Date. Royes Luggage Inc. has two invoices that have not been paid in full. They are paying only invoice 2256 at this time.

The terms for this client are 2/10, net 30, (i.e., a discount of 2% if the invoice is paid within 10 days, or the full amount due in 30 days). The discount is calculated on the invoice amount **before** taxes (GST and PST not included). This customer purchased goods PST-exempt. GST is not affected by discounts taken.

Invoice #2256 amounts to $1,100.00 for various luggage goods, plus GST of $55.00 totaling $1,155.00. The 2% discount is calculated on the luggage sold at $1,100.00, which equals $22.00. To summarize:

Invoice #2256	
Luggage Sold	$1,100.00
GST	55.00
Total	$1,155.00
Discount	
.02 x $1,100.00 =	$22.00
Cheque received	
1,155.00 less 22.00 =	$1,133.00

3 ➤   Paid By: Click the ▼ and 4 choices are available. Select **Cheque**, and Tab to the next field.

4 ➤ Deposit To: Click the . Simply Accounting allows the receipt to be deposited to one of many bank accounts. This would be useful if the business has Canadian, U.S. and other currency bank accounts; e.g., Euro, Mexican peso, etc. and accounts for depositing credit card receipts.

Santos Luggage uses two bank accounts:

1020 Bank Chequing Account is used for normal receipts from customers.
1030 Visa Credit Card Bank Account is used to deposit credit card receipts at a different bank.

5 ➤ Select **1020 Bank Chequing Account** and ⌗Tab⌗ to Cheque.

6 ➤ Cheque This field will show the cheque number received from the customer.

The cheque number will not appear in the Journal Entries All or Journal Entries Receipts entries. It will appear in the Reconciliation & Deposits Journal only.

Change the window to the following:

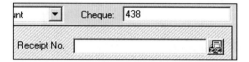

You will see an error message about the **Receipt No.** field in step 15. It will be corrected in step 16.

7 ➤ Receipt No. Leave blank. This field can also be used for a receipt number if the firm records cheques received with a sequence number.

8 ➤ Date The date should be Mar 03, 2016, the date the cheque was received. (This company is not using the additional information fields.) Change the date to **Mar 09, 2016**.

The **Disc. Available** column should be **0.00** for both, indicating that the discount period has passed for both invoices. Simply will calculate the discount available within the days allowed by the terms of the invoice.

9 ➤ Change the date back to **Mar 03, 2016** and the correct discount of 22.00 shows in the **Disc. Available** column. ⌗Tab⌗.

If the customer's cheque amount is less than the amount showing in the **Amount Owing** column and the discount amount shown is **0.00**, you should change the date back a few days (e.g., March 01) to see if the cheque reflects a discount taken by the customer.

Ask your manager what to do if a cheque is received a day or two late and misses the discount period. In most cases the manager will allow the discount.

10 ➤ Invoice Date The cursor jumps to this field. *Note*: The payment is being made for invoice #2256 dated Jan 31, 2016. Use the ↓ key on the keyboard to move down to invoice 2256 dated Feb 27, 2016 that is being paid. You can also use your mouse to position the cursor on 2256. [Tab].

Invoice or Deposit	This field indicates the invoice number or deposit number issued.
Original Amount	This field indicates the original amount of each invoice.
Amount Owing	This field indicates the balance remaining on each invoice if partial payments have been received.
Discount Available	This field indicates the amount of any cash discounts available based on the terms agreed upon. This client's terms are 2/10, net 30. Most firms calculate the cash discount amount on the invoice price ($1,100.00) before taxes. The correct discount is $22.00.

11 ➤ **Discount Taken** — The cursor jumps to this field. If the **Discount Available** field is blank, it indicates that no discount is available for this invoice. You can override the **Discount Taken** field by typing in an amount. [Tab] to accept the discount of 22.00. (See side note box.)

12 ➤ **Amount Received** — The field now shows 1,133.00, the amount of the outstanding invoice after the discount has been taken off, and is also the amount of the cheque received. [Tab] to accept the receipt of 1,133.00 against this outstanding invoice.

Total — This field (grayed out) shows the total of the Amount Received column. It should agree with the cheque received.

When a customer/ vendor takes a 2% discount for paying an invoice within terms of 2/10, net 30, GST regulations consider it a finance charge and not a reduction to the GST portion.

If the cursor was on the invoice 2212 line and you pressed the [Tab] key twice by mistake to move to the Amount Received column, the amount of 945.00 appears in the Amount Received field. Press the *Delete* key to remove the amount.

13 ➤ Display the Receipts Journal Entry. Click **Report**, then **Display Receipts Journal Entry**. The entry should appear as follows:

Receipts Journal Entry Mar 03, 2016 (J3)

Account Number	Account Description	Debits	Credits
1020	Bank Chequing Account	1,133.00	-
4150	Sales -Discounts	22.00	-
1200	Accounts Receivable	-	1,155.00
Additional Date:	Additional Field:		
		1,155.00	1,155.00

The G/L account numbers did not need to be entered. All payments received will automatically be debited to the **Deposit To:** bank account identified in step 4, and credited to ACCOUNTS RECEIVABLE.

All merchandise cash discounts will be debited to SALES DISCOUNTS.

14 ➤ When finished viewing, **exit** from the entry window. (See side note box.)

To change any of the amounts, click the incorrect field and enter the correct information. Remember to view the entry to make sure you have made the changes properly.

15 ➤ Click the [=] (e-mail icon at the top-right corner of the window) and a message box appears. This is related to Step 7 earlier.

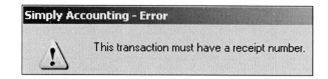

Simply requires a Receipt Number in the Receipt No. field to post the transaction.

Most companies like Santos Luggage do not use receipt numbers, but record the **cheque number** in the **Receipt No.** field for easy verification (Audit trail). Using this method, they can see the cheque number in the journal entry as shown at step 24 and still be able to use the Reconciliation & Deposit Journal at a later time.

16 ➤ Click **OK** to return to the Receipts Journal.

17 ➤ **Complete your window** as shown next:

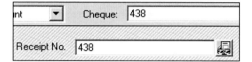

This will now correct the error message seen at step 15.

All companies in this text use this method of recording cheque numbers in both fields.

18 ➤ Click the [e-mail icon] (e-mail icon) again and the following message appears.

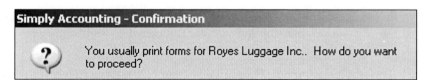

19 ➤ This is to advise you that you normally print forms for Royes Luggage Inc.

There is no Exercise to e-mail the receipt. Click **Cancel** to return to the Receipt Journal window.

20 ➤ **Post** when correct, click **OK** to accept the confirmation for J3. In future exercises, when the instruction is to Post, it also means to accept the confirmation.

21 ➤ **Exit** from the Receipts Journal.

22 ➤ **View** the Receipts Journal Entry. At **Reports**, click ▼, select **Receipts Journal Entries**, click **Display**. (See side note box.)

If there were other receipt entries and you wanted to display certain ones, click the **Modify** icon, **Report Options**, change the dates as required, or click Journal Number and change the information as required.

Receipts Journal Feb 28, 2016 to Mar 03, 2016

		Account Number	Account Description	Debits	Credits
Mar 03, 2016	J3	438, Royes Luggage Inc.			
		1020	Bank Chequing Account	1,133.00	-
		4150	Sales -Discounts	22.00	-
		1200	Accounts Receivable	-	1,155.00
				1,155.00	1,155.00

The 438 cheque number is shown in the posted entry.

23 ➤ **Exit** from the Receipts Journal window.

24 ➤ View the Customer Aged Detail report only for Royes Luggage Inc. In the Customers area at **Royes Luggage Inc.**, click ▼ select **Display Customer Aged Detail Report**. The Detail report displays only Royes Luggage Inc.

Notice how the Payment and Discount appear, with a – minus sign, and the Discount wording in the Transaction Type column in Fig. 2A-14.

Customer Aged Detail As at Mar 03, 2016

Source	Date	Transaction Type	Total	Current	31 to 60	61 to 90
Royes Luggage Inc.						
2212	Jan 31, 2016	Invoice	945.00	-	945.00	-
2256	Feb 27, 2016	Invoice	1,155.00	1,155.00	-	-
438	Mar 03, 2016	Discount	-22.00	-22.00	-	-
438	Mar 03, 2016	Payment	-1,133.00	-1,133.00	-	-
Total outstanding:			945.00	-	945.00	-

Fig. 2A-14: Customer Aged Detail.

If you customize (filter) any report, the changes will affect all future reports and your report total may not agree with the General ledger control account; Accounts Receivable.

Cheque number **438** is shown on both the **Discount** and **Payment** lines. (See side note box.)

25 ➤ **Exit** from the Customer Aged Detail report. Notice that in the Customer Area on the Home page, the Balance for Royes Luggage now displays as 945.00.

Journalizing a Partial Receipt with No Discount

When a customer pays the full amount of an invoice within the discount period, the discount as per the terms of sale is allowed. However, if the customer pays only part of the invoice amount, discount on the partial payment is normally not allowed.

The procedure to journalize this transaction is similar to that in Exercise 2A-15. Enter the exact amount of the payment. Simply will deduct the partial payment from the invoice without discount and will show the remaining amount outstanding.

Exercise 2A-16 – To Journalize a Partial Receipt without a Discount

You are going to enter the wrong amount for the cheque and then correct the error after posting. You will later also make an error in an invoice and correct it after posting.

Study this transaction and complete the following steps.

> **Mar 03, 2016**　　**Received cheque #159, in the amount of $2,000.00, from Sandler Travel Stores as a partial payment on their outstanding invoice #2197 from January 26, 2016.**

1 ➤　　Using the ▾ in the Customers area, click on **Receive Payments** for Sandler Travel Stores.

2 ➤　Cheque　　Type **159** for the customer's cheque number, [Tab] to accept. The cursor moves to the From area.

3 ➤　Receipt No.　　Type **159,** [Tab] [Tab].

4 ➤　Date　　[Tab] [Tab] to accept Mar 03, 2016.

5 ➤　Invoice Date　　At Jan 26, 2016, for Invoice **2197,** [Tab].

　　Disc. Available. There is no discount available, because it is more than 10 days since the invoice date of Jan 26, 2016.

6 ➤　Disc. Taken　　[Tab] to leave the field blank. (See side note box.)

A firm may allow a discount under special circumstances, even when the discount period has passed. If a customer asks for a discount or if you receive a payment showing an unauthorized discount, consult your manager.

To practise correcting an error after posting a transaction, you will deliberately make an error and then correct it later.

Amount Received　　Type **2200.00** (This amount is not correct. You will correct it in the next exercise.) [Tab] to show a receipt of $2,200.00 against invoice #2197.

7 ➤　　**View** the entry.

Receipts Journal Entry Mar 03, 2016 (J4)

Account Number	Account Description	Debits	Credits
1020	Bank Chequing Account	2,200.00	-
1200	Accounts Receivable	-	2,200.00
Additional Date:	Additional Field:		
		2,200.00	2,200.00

8 ➤　　**Exit** to the Receipts Journal and **Post** J4 with the error.

You will be at a blank Receipt window.

9 ➤　From　　Select **Sandler Travel Stores**. You will see that the **Amount Owing** column is reduced by the partial payment.

Invoice Date	Invoice or Deposit	Original Amount	Amount Owing
Jan 26, 2016	2197	4,095.00	1,895.00

You have just realized that you have made an error in the amount, as the Amount Owing should have been $2,095.00. Complete the next exercise to reverse and correct the error in posting.

Exercise 2A-17 – To Correct a Receipt Error

You will now correct the error that you deliberately made in the last exercise. You have two choices.

1. You can use the 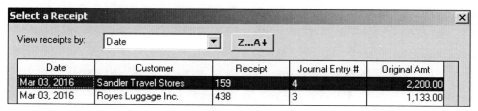 **Adjust Receipt** icon as shown in this exercise. This would be useful if the amount or invoice(s) to be paid or customer would be changing.

2. You could use the **Reverse Receipt entry** icon to reverse and cancel the entry. This method would be useful if you posted the error to the wrong customer or you wanted to cancel the entry with the error and start the entry again. Refer to Chapter 13, To Reverse a Cash Receipt.

1 ➤   **Receipt No.**   Click the **Lookup a Receipt** icon.

2 ➤   Click **OK**. The **Select a Receipt** window appears.

Select a Receipt				
View receipts by: Date ▼ Z...A+				
Date	Customer	Receipt	Journal Entry #	Original Amt
Mar 03, 2016	Sandler Travel Stores	159	4	2,200.00
Mar 03, 2016	Royes Luggage Inc.	438	3	1,133.00

3 ➤   Select **Sandler Travel Stores**.

4 ➤   The **Receipts Journal - Receipt Lookup** window appears and the **Paid By:**, **Deposit To:**, **Cheque:**, **Receipt No.**, **From** and **Date** fields are grayed out.

5 ➤   Click the **Adjust Receipt** icon. The top header changes to **Receipts Journal - Adjusting Receipt 159** and only the lower portion of the **From** field is grayed out. The customer cannot be changed, because we are reversing an entry to their account.

6 ➤   Click the **Amount Received** column and change the amount to **2000.00**, [Tab].

   If you display the entry, it will display as J6. **Exit** the entry.

7 ➤   **Post** when correct.

8 ➤   **Exit** from the Receipts Journal.

9 ➤   **Display** the Customer Aged Detail report for **Sandler Travel Stores**.

Customer Aged Detail As at Mar 03, 2016						
Source	Date	Transaction Type	Total	Current	31 to 60	61 to 90
Sandler Travel Stores						
2197	Jan 26, 2016	Invoice	4,095.00	-	4,095.00	-
159	Mar 03, 2016	Payment	-2,000.00	-	-2,000.00	-
Total outstanding:			2,095.00	-	2,095.00	-

Note that only the correct posting of -2,000.00 displays.

10 ➤   **Exit** from the Customer Aged Detail.

11 ➤   Display the **Receipts Journal Entries** as shown in Exercise 2A-15.

The default display is to NOT show corrections (e.g., J4 and J5). To see the Corrections, click **Modify, Report Options,** click **Corrections** to have a ✓, click **OK**. You will notice that J5 is the reversing entry for J4 (the error) and J6 is the correct entry.

12 ➤   **Exit** from the Receipts Journal window and return to the Home window.

Remember to back up your data and update your logbook at the end of your work session.

To Cancel an Invoice After Posting

There may be situations where you need to cancel an invoice. You posted a sale to the wrong customer, or a customer decides they don't want/need the product just purchased. This would be different from a sales return. The customer did not take the merchandise out of the store, so it is technically not a sales return.

1 ➤   Advance the date to **Mar 04, 2016**.

2 ➤   **Record** and **Post** the following transaction.

Mar 04, 2016	**A clerk from Havarah Leather Goods is being sent to pick up 2 Laptop Back Paks.** **Record and Post the sale (invoice #2311) in the regular way at $70.00 each, plus GST. Terms 2/10,n30. Invoice total $147.00.**

Exercise 2A-18 – To Cancel a Posted Invoice

---

1 ➤   In this exercise, you will cancel the invoice, based on the information below.

Mar 04, 2016	**As the Havarah Leather Goods clerk is preparing to leave the store, he receives a cell-phone message that he is to change the order to 3 extra large Laptop Back Paks. Your store does not carry this particular item and your supplier does not stock this item. The clerk confirms with his boss that the order for 2 Laptop Back Paks is to be cancelled. They will go elsewhere.**

2 ➤   Click the **Lookup an Invoice** icon [icon] and the Invoice Lookup window appears.

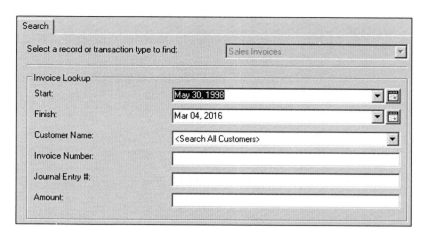

A range of dates and/or customers, invoice numbers or Journal entry numbers may be selected at this point. In this exercise you will view all posted invoices.

3 ➤   Click **OK**. The *Select An Invoice* window is displayed listing the invoices you have entered in this chapter. *Note*: Only a partial window is shown.

Date	Customer	Invoice #	Journal Entry #	Original Amt
Mar 04, 2016	Havarah Leather Goods	2311	7	147.00
Mar 03, 2016	Havarah Leather Goods	2253Rt CM124	2	-147.00
Mar 03, 2016	Luggage 4U	2310	1	1,417.50

4 ➤   **Select** invoice **2311**. The invoice details are inserted into the Sales Journal-Invoice Lookup window for *review only*.

5 ➤   You want to cancel invoice 2311; therefore, click the ▣ **Reverse Invoice** entry icon. (See side note box.)

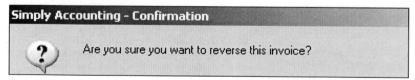

6 ➤   Click **Yes**.

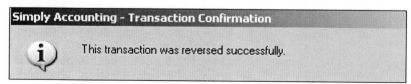

7 ➤   Click **OK**. The window returns to a blank invoice. The reversing entry has been posted; therefore, the original entry has been reversed.

8 ➤   **Exit** the invoice and return to the Home window.

9 ➤   Display the **Sales Journal Entries** for Mar 04, 2016 (change the Start date) with Corrections ✓. Click **Modify**, **Report Options**, click **Corrections**, change the **Start Date** to **Mar 04, 2016**, **OK**.

> The icon ▣ remains the same, but the wording in each Journal window will change.
>
> If you reverse a receipt the same icon is named "Reverse Receipt".

Sales Journal Mar 04, 2016 to Mar 04, 2016

		Account Number	Account Description	Debits	Credits
Mar 04, 2016	J7	2311, Havarah Leather Goods			
		1200	Accounts Receivable	147.00	-
		2630	GST Charged on Sales	-	7.00
		4100	Sales	-	140.00
Mar 04, 2016	J8	ADJ2311, Reversing J7. Correction is J8.			
		2630	GST Charged on Sales	7.00	-
		4100	Sales	140.00	-
		1200	Accounts Receivable	-	147.00
				294.00	294.00

Journal entry 8 has cancelled Sales journal entry 7. The above information will not display in the Customer Aged Detail report as there was no sale.

This procedure can also be used to cancel Sales Quotes, Sales Orders, Receipts, Purchase Quotes, Purchase Orders, Purchase Invoices, and Payments.

10 ➤ Exit the Sales Journal window and **X** to return to the Home window.

The Customers Ledger

When you set up a customer account in the RECEIVABLES module, you are creating a ledger for that customer. When you enter sales or payment transactions referring to the particular customer in the RECEIVABLES module, the corresponding customer's ledger will be updated.

Exercise 2A-19 – Viewing a Customer Ledger

In this exercise, you will familiarize yourself with the Customers window and view a customer ledger. You would need to view a customer's ledger when you receive an inquiry about the customer's account.

1 ➤ Advance Session date to **Mar 05, 2016**.

2 ➤ In the **Tasks** area, at **Customers** icon, click ▼ to see the 4 choices. Select **View Customers**. As discussed in previous Exercises, you can also click the Customers icon to go directly to the Customers window. Study Fig. 2A-15.

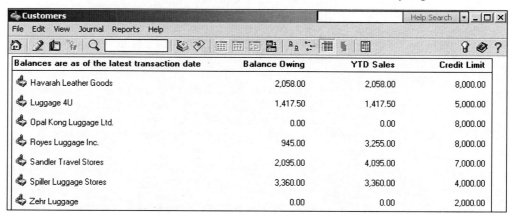

Balances are as of the latest transaction date	Balance Owing	YTD Sales	Credit Limit
Havarah Leather Goods	2,058.00	2,058.00	8,000.00
Luggage 4U	1,417.50	1,417.50	5,000.00
Opal Kong Luggage Ltd.	0.00	0.00	8,000.00
Royes Luggage Inc.	945.00	3,255.00	8,000.00
Sandler Travel Stores	2,095.00	4,095.00	7,000.00
Spiller Luggage Stores	3,360.00	3,360.00	4,000.00
Zehr Luggage	0.00	0.00	2,000.00

Fig. 2A-15: Customers Summary Information.

This window shows summary information about the customer, including the credit limit the customer is allowed.

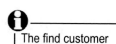

The find customer feature. Click the magnifying glass on the left, and the **Find Customer Search** window appears. You would use this if you want to find a specific customer in a long list of similar names (e.g., Smith, Singh, etc.).

The FIND icon is a quick way to locate an item from a long list. Simply provides this facility in various fields in most windows. Use it. It can save you time!

You will see that the Customers window has the following menu bar choices: (Also see side note box.)

File	Menu with choices for opening a customer, creating a new customer or removing a current customer (only if balance is nil and prior invoices have been cleared).
Edit	Menu item allows you to search for a customer record.
View	Menu choice for displaying customer information (changing the size of the icons for the display). **Icon** displays 2 customers on a line, **Small icon** displays 3 customers on a line, or **Name** displays customer detail information as shown in Fig. 2A-15. If you maximize the window, depending on the monitor, resolution and icon you are using, you may see 2, 3 or 4 customer names on a line, and Restore Window to default setting.
Journal	Menu choice of either the **Sales** or **Receipts** Journal for data entry. (Icons are also provided on the toolbar for this.)
Reports	A drop-down menu listing reports available for display.
Help	The Simply Help menu.

3 ➤ Return to the **Home** window.

Adding a New Customer Record

Simply allows you to create two basic types of customers and add new customers in two different ways:

1. **Regular Customer** – You create individual ledgers for customers who buy from the company more than once during the accounting period. The ledger would include the customer's name, address and other details of the company. You can enter a new customer:

   a) using the Customers icon.
   b) using the Sales Invoice Journal.

   In Exercise 2A-20, you will create a ledger for a new regular customer using method b.

2. **One-time Customer** – There are two options available when you need to record a sale to a customer who is not likely to buy again. These options are available when you use the Sales Invoice icon, and select Create Invoice. When you enter a name of a customer that is not in the Customers List you have two choices.

   a) **<One-time customer>** (see Exercise 2B-27) with customer information *not retained* in the customer list.

   Simply allows you to record the details of the individual sale including the customer's name and address (in the lower box), but Simply will not create a ledger for the customer. You can view the record of the sale (Journal entry) at a later time, as it will be in the list of transactions.

When you record a sale using this option, Simply will allow you to enter a cash sale only (cash, cheque, bank card or credit card). Payment from the customer for the sales amount is journalized at the same time as the sale.

b) Type the customer's name and use the **Continue** button (see Exercise 2B-28) with customer information *retained* for the new customer in the Journal Entry report but not in the customer list. Simply will not create a ledger for the customer.

Exercise 2A-20 – Creating a Regular Customer Ledger & Invoice in the Sales Invoice Window

Study this transaction:

Mar 05, 2016 You have made a sale to a new customer. The details are: A-Your Name Luggage Rack; Contact: Your Name; 256 Trillium Way, Oakville, Ontario, L6J 2H8; telephone 905-699-8000, extension 2563; fax number 905-699-8010; credit limit $3,000.00 and PST Exempt number X125-585-B.

The goods ordered and shipped on this first order are:

6 Carry on bags – small @ $21.00 each, plus GST
3 Suitcase w/w large   @ $62.00 each, plus GST
4 Power adapters   @ $10.50 each, plus GST

The goods **are to be picked up by their own delivery truck and delivered** to the Hamilton store, operated by Jackie Welland, as follows: **939 Fennel Avenue West, Hamilton, Ontario, L9N 3T1.**

Note: You will be recording the Hamilton Store information in the Customer Ledger Address tab.

Your Name Luggage Rack is a good example of a regular customer, as they are likely to buy from you again. Since there is no existing ledger for this new customer, you need to create a Customer Ledger, and then record the sale.

Sales Invoices ▾

1 ➤ Click the **Sales Invoices** icon, at **Sold To:** type, **A-Your Name Luggage Rack**, ⎡Tab⎤. The following window will display.

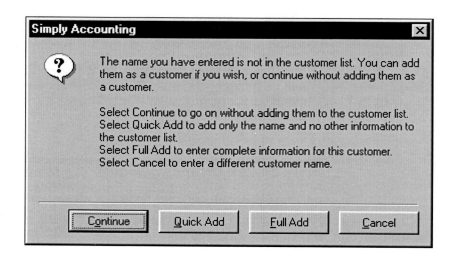

This is where you would identify the customer type by clicking the appropriate button:

 You would select this when you type the name of the one-time customer in the **Sold To** field. It allows you to continue recording the sale without adding the customer to the customers list. Remember, however, that if you select this option, you can enter only a cash or credit card sale.

 This feature will add the customer to the Customers Ledger but will omit details about the customer (address, phone number, terms, credit limit, etc.), `Tab` . The cursor will move to the **Ship to:** field. Type the customer address and complete the invoice. You can use this feature with a quote or order. You will need to go back to the customer account and add the details later.

Full Add This feature will add the customer to the Customers Ledger and will open the Receivables Ledger window to record details about the customer. When the details have been entered, you are returned to the previous window. You can then produce the invoice. *Note:* The address information will be automatically entered from the Customer Ledger information. You can use this feature with a quote or order.

Cancel To cancel the current operation. Simply will then allow you to enter a different customer name.

2 ➤ Select **Full Add**. The Receivables Ledger window will open with the name of the customer displayed. The Receivables Ledger window opens.

Address tab

3 ➤ Enter the information for Your Name Luggage Rack, as shown next:

In this window, you can add a new customer's details on various tabs. You can also click the Edit icon to amend details on the tabs for a customer.

Customer:	A-Your Name Luggage Rack		

Address | Ship-to Address | Options | Taxes | Statistics | Memo | Import/Export | Additional Info

Contact:	Your Name	Phone 1:	(905) 699-8000 2563
Street 1:	256 Trillium Way	Phone 2:	
Street 2:		Fax:	(905) 699-8010
City:	Oakville	E-mail:	
Province:	Ontario	Web Site:	
Postal Code:	L6J 2H8	Salesperson:	
Country:		Customer Since:	Mar 05, 2016

Customer
Type **A-Your Name Luggage Rack**, Tab . The A- is used to place your name at the beginning of the customer list regardless of the first letter of your name.

Contact
Your name as the contact person for this company.

Postal Code
When you type **L6J2H8** or l6j2h8 and press Tab , the postal code will format automatically.

Enter the phone/fax numbers without dashes. Simply will automatically format them with a dash and brackets as you press Tab .

Phone
Type **9056998000** (without dashes) and Tab .

To add the extension number **2563** to the phone number, click at the end of the phone number, press the space bar and type the extension number (up to 10 numbers), Tab Tab . If you type the number and extension as 90569980002563 and then press Tab , the number and extension will not format.

Fax
Type **9056998010** (without dashes) and press Tab .

E-mail:
Leave blank. This text does not show sending E-mail.

Web Site:
Leave blank. This text does not show accessing a customer's web site.

Salesperson:
As discussed earlier, this field is not used in the chapter. See Appendix CD-AC, *Adding a Salesperson's Name to an Invoice.*

Customer Since:
This feature lets clerks see, at a glance, when the customer started buying goods from Santos Luggage.

Note: Santos Luggage has not updated previous customers. It is assumed that they have been customers for many years.

Ship-to Address

4 ➤ Click the **Ship-to Address** tab. This window information would be used when you are sending the invoice to the mailing address of a company (usually the Head Office) and always send the goods to a different store location.

The address information is grayed out as it is assumed that this is the default mailing address and shipping address for all invoices.

5 ➤ Click the **Add New** button, Type the Address Name information as shown next. Each customer can have up to 100 different shipping addresses. You can also add shipping addresses from the invoice. Shown later in this Exercise, Journalizing the Sale, step 2.

6 ➤ Click **OK**. You are returned to the Receivables ledger.

7 ➤ Enter the information shown next. Ignore Phone and other information.

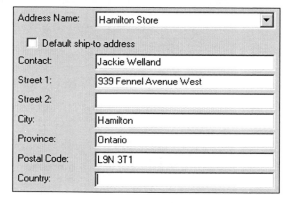

Options

8 ➤ Click the **Options** tab, and **complete** the information as shown.

Revenue Account	This will make **4100 SALES** the default account which will display in the Sales Quotes, Orders or Invoice window for this particular customer. Note this default will be for the first line of each invoice only.
Price List	(See side note box.)
Conduct Business in	This field indicates the ability to have screen displays and printouts in French for the customer. Santos Luggage has not had requests to conduct business in French.
Standard Discount	This field would indicate the discount that would apply to each item the customer buys. This is not to be confused with a cash discount for paying early (within term time limits). This discount is for good customers who buy a lot of goods and deserve a reduction to the selling price. If an amount is entered here, it will appear in the Disc. % column for the customer. Santos Luggage will not be using this field, in part A. See Exercise 2B-33 after step 8, 2nd information area for a discussion on the Quantity or Trade Discount.
Early Payment Terms	When customers are given time to pay for the goods or services they purchase, it is called purchasing goods on credit. The time is normally 30 days.
	Some customers are allowed special terms of 2/10, net 30. This means that if the customer pays the balance owing within 10 days they can deduct 2% of the cost of the goods bought as a cash discount; otherwise, the balance is to be paid within 30 days. These terms with discount are what are referred to as **Early Payment Terms. 2/10 net 30** is the default.
	A-Your Name Luggage Rack is a new customer, and as a general practice, your company allows payment terms of 2/10 net 30 days to new customers to provide an incentive to pay early.
	Do NOT change from the default.
Produce Statements for this Customer	Do NOT change. A ✓ in the box will allow you to print a summary statement to be sent to a customer. You will learn how to produce a customer statement in Exercise 2B-37.
Forms for this Customer	There are two choices: **E-mail** and **Print**. Leave the choice as **Print**.
Synchronize with Microsoft® Outlook®	When this box is ✓, the customer's e-mail address will be placed in the Microsoft® Outlook® Mailing address list. Do NOT change. There is no exercise for this feature.

> The **Price List** field would be used with the **Perpetual Inventory** module for special pricing for customers who buy a lot of goods or services. Simply 2009 supports 1,000 different price lists. This is discussed in Chapter 8.

Taxes

9 ➤ Click the **Taxes** tab and complete the information as shown.

Indicate which taxes this customer is exempt from by entering Yes for Tax Exempt.

Tax	Tax Exempt	Tax ID
GST	No	
PST	Yes	X125-585-B

Choose the tax code that includes the taxes that you normally charge this customer:

G - GST at 5% added to invoice, PST Exempt

Tax Exempt	On the line with PST, click **No** in the field. It will change to **Yes**. This customer is exempt from PST.
Tax ID	**X125-585-B**. This would be the PST Tax Exempt Identification number given to the customer by the provincial government.
	In the lower box, click the ▼ and a list of Tax codes appears.
	Select **G - GST added to Invoice at 5%, PST Exempt**. The G code will appear on the first line of the sales invoice.

Statistics

10 ➤ Click the **Statistics** tab and complete the information as shown.

Credit Limit: 3,000.00 This is the customer's credit limit.

Many companies give each customer a maximum credit balance. When the customer's balance is larger than its preset limit, a warning message box will appear when you try to post a new sale to the customer's account. Although a customer may have exceeded its limit, sales to that customer can still be processed in Simply, but you would first consult your manager on how to properly handle this situation. Management may require a payment from the customer to reduce the Accounts Receivable before any additional sales could be made, or your manager may approve the extended credit limit based on financial records of the customer.

You should check the sale and payment history of customers on a regular basis to ensure that each customer is making payments within the agreed terms.

Memo

The open space allows you to make notes about the customer. Click in the open box and the status bar informs you that you have up to 255 characters to make your note.

11 ➤ Click the **Memo** tab and complete the information as shown.

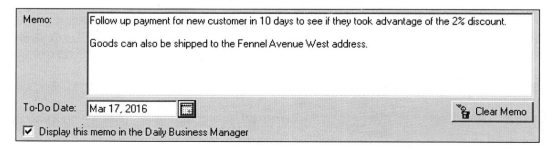

Memo:	Follow up payment for new customer in 10 days to see if they took advantage of the 2% discount. Goods can also be shipped to the Fennel Avenue West address.
To-Do Date:	Mar 17, 2016 📅 🗑 Clear Memo
☑ Display this memo in the Daily Business Manager	

You will see this message in Exercise 2B-25, step 2.

To-Do Date: This is the date (10 days from the date of the sale, plus two days for late mail delivery) that you want to be reminded to deal with the information in the box.

Display this memo in the Daily Business Manager   Click the box to enter a ✓ in this field. This ✓ will allow the above messages to appear in the Daily Business Manager display.

Import/Export

12 ➤   Click the **Import/Export** tab.

Address	Ship-to Address	Options	Taxes	Statistics	Memo	Import/Export	Additional Info

☐ This customer has Simply Accounting and can import invoices and quotes

☐ This customer uses my item numbers on orders

Match the customer's item number to my item number or an account number for importing orders:

Customer's Item No.	My Item No.	My Account

This customer has...   Leave this box blank. You would ✓ this box if you know the customer uses *Simply Accounting,* and can import your quotes and invoice information. The text does not have an exercise for importing or exporting information to another company. This feature is not used often.

This customer uses my item numbers...   You would click in the box to insert a ✓ only if your company uses the perpetual inventory method in recording sales and you know the customer uses the item numbers of your goods when ordering from your company.

Additional Info

13 ➤   Click the **Additional Info** tab. The fields in this window allow you to add additional information that will display when the customer is selected in a transaction. Complete the information as shown.

		Display this information when the customer is selected in a transaction
Field1 :	Remind new customer of 2% discount in 10 days	☑
Field2 :	when buying goods	☑

See the Appendix CD-Q, *Names Fields* on the Student Data CD for more information.

14 ➤   Click **💾 Save and Close** . The customer account is created and you are returned to a Sales Invoice window.

15 ➤   The Sales Invoice window, with the name and address you entered, with the **G** tax code and the **4100** default **Sales** account indicated is displayed. `Tab`.

16 ➤   The Additional Info note window for fields 1 and 2 will appear in front or behind the Sales Invoice window. If the Info window is partially hidden, click on the box, and then click **Close**. You can also click Close later.

Journalizing the Sale

Now that you have completed the new customer file, follow these steps to journalize the sale to this customer:

Transaction	Do not change the default **Invoice**.
Paid by	Do not change the default **Pay Later**.
1 ➤ **Ship to**	The goods are being shipped to the Hamilton store. Click the ▼ and select **Hamilton Store**. The address field changes. `Tab`
Order/Quote No.	This field will be blank, as no previous sales quotes or orders were received from this customer.
Ship Date	This date field can be left blank as the goods were not ordered on a Sales Quote or Sales Order, and the goods are being shipped the same day as the invoice date.
Invoice	The next invoice number is **2312**.
Date	**Mar 05, 2016** This is the date the goods are shipped to the customer.

A-Your Name Luggage Rack ordered the following items:

6 Carry on bags - small   @ $21.00 each, plus GST
3 Suitcase w/w large   @ $62.00 each, plus GST
4 Power adapters   @ $10.50 each, plus GST

The goods are to be picked up by their own delivery truck and delivered to the Hamilton store.

2 ➤ **Quantity**	Type **6,** `Tab`. (These are the units being sold and shipped.)
Order	This column is skipped. The goods are ordered and shipped.
Back Order	This column is skipped. There are no goods backordered on this invoice.
3 ➤ **Unit**	Type **each,** `Tab`.
4 ➤ **Description**	Type **Carry on bags - small,** `Tab`.
5 ➤ **Base Price**	Type **21.00,** `Tab` `Tab` `Tab` to Amount.
6 ➤ **Amount**	This field represents the calculated amount from fields **Quantity** times **Price**. `Tab` to accept **126.00**.

7 ➤ Tax   The default code **G** (GST with PST exempt) is entered as you set this up earlier. This is correct. Tab to accept.

GST is not included in the selling price of each item. (See Exercise 2A-4, for a discussion of the tax codes.)

8 ➤ Acct   4100 is shown as the default General Ledger account number as you set this up earlier. If you want to change the account number, press Enter. The G/L chart of accounts available should be displayed. You may have to move ▲ or ▼ to see more accounts. Select or type account **4100** Sales and Tab to accept 4100.

9 ➤ Enter the remaining sales information from step 1.

The default tax code **G** and G/L account **4100** is used only for the first item. You will have to type or select the tax code and account number for each of the additional items.

Subtotal   This field is the subtotal of the goods being sold without taxes.

Comment   This field would display a variety of messages you want the customers to see on quotes, orders and invoices. The default for all invoices is shown. You will learn how to enter this type of information in Chapter 4.

Terms   Should show **2.00%, 10 days, Net 30 days**, the terms you set up earlier. If the terms are different, you can click on these fields and enter the correct terms.

Freight   Your company does not charge for delivery and, therefore, does not use this field.

10 ➤ Track Shipments   Click the 🗗 **Track Shipments i**con. Click ▼ and a drop-down list of shipping companies is displayed. Select **Your Vehicle**, Tab. The shipped information will not display in the Invoice window, but will print on the invoice.

11 ➤ Tracking Number   This will be blank because there is no need to track the shipment if it is being picked up by the customer's vehicle. Click **OK**.

12 ➤ When you have completed recording the above information, the window display should look like Fig 2A-16.

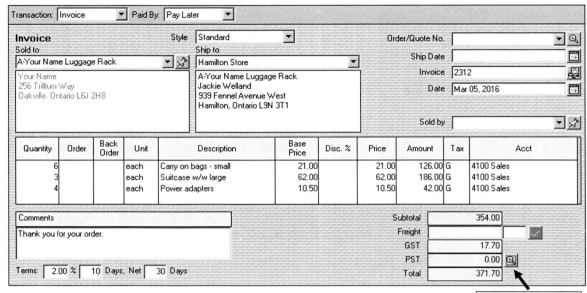

Fig. 2A-16: A-Your Name Luggage Rack Invoice.

Tax Summary icon

When an invoice is created to record cash register summary tapes, there may be a few cents difference in the GST and/or PST amounts. As stated in the **Tax Summary** window, the amount field can be changed. If in doubt, use the Simply calculator and make the changes, if necessary.

13 ➤ To see information about the taxes, click the **Tax Summary** icon 🔍 and the summary displays as shown next. This would be a summary of the GST and PST fields to the left. (See side note box.)

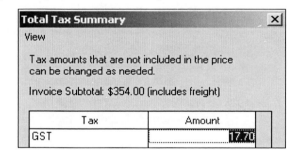

14 ➤ Click **OK**.

15 ➤ Display the Sales Journal entry created by this invoice. The window should display as follows:

Sales Journal Entry Mar 05, 2016 (J9)

Account Number	Account Description	Debits	Credits
1200	Accounts Receivable	371.70	-
2630	GST Charged on Sales	-	17.70
4100	Sales	-	354.00
Additional Date:	Additional Field:		
		371.70	371.70

Recording this invoice allows the preparation of a journal entry, given that a sale has taken place. Notice the automatic debit to the Accounts Receivable account made by Simply. Notice that the automatic credit to the GST Charged on Sales, calculated by Simply, is based on the GST code or rate entered.

16 ➤ **Exit** from this window by clicking the **X** button.

17 ➤ Make corrections to any fields that have errors in them. Click the **Post** icon. The entry will be posted to the customer's account in the RECEIVABLES module and will also be posted to the General Ledger.

18 ➤ **Exit** to the Home window.

19 ➤ If the Additional Info window is displayed **close** it now.

Additional Transactions

1 ➤ Advance the Session date to **Mar 07, 2016**.

Process the following transactions:

Mar 06, 2016	**Sold to Zehr Luggage (PST Exempt) Terms 2/10, net 30, 10 Suitcases w/w large size at $62.00 each, 4 Suitcases w/w regular size @ $56.00, plus GST on all items. Invoice 2313, $886.20.**

Mar 06, 2016	**You made a sale to a new customer, Hanlan's Luggage Store, contact: Liam Hanlan, 2318 Avondale Drive, Oakville, Ontario, L6H 5A1; telephone 905-399-5000, Revenue Account 4100, Terms No %, 0 days, Net amount 0 days, PST Exempt number X1A2-658, GST code G. Credit limit $3,000.00, and they paid by business cheque #739. You will record this as a sale and then record the receipt separately. You will see how to combine this into one transaction in Chapter 2B.**
	The goods ordered and shipped on this first order are:
	6 Carry on bags – small @ $21.00 each, $126.00 plus GST

When a business has a lot of customers and they cannot see all of them in the Customers area, you can scroll down the listing and/or expand the area. In the Reports area, click the ▣ minimize icon. The Reports area is minimized. *Note:* This will only work for the current session. To expand the Reports area, click the ▣ expand icon.

Mar 07, 2016	**Zehr Luggage returned 3 Suitcases w/w large as the zippers do not work properly. The suitcases will need to be returned to the manufacturer. Record the Sales Return. You do not need to record a return to the manufacturer. Purchases Returns will be shown in Chapter 3A, Toys.**
	Issued Credit Memo #125, with reference to original sales invoice. Terms amended to 9 days, net 29 days.
	–3 Suitcases w/w large @ $62.00, plus GST (net return –$195.30).

Remember to back up your data and update your logbook at the end of your work session.

Printing Reports When Needed

The following reports may be printed for management's information and for filing for the audit trail.

- Journal Entries may be printed in one of two ways (see Exercise 1-17).

    a) **Journal Entries All** will print all journal entries from all modules (with or without corrections). All transactions, in the time-period requested, are numbered in this journal in sequential order (even if entered in a subledger; i.e., RECEIVABLES or PAYABLES module).

    b) **Journal Entries General** will print journal entries entered in the COMPANY module only.

    1 ➤ To save time and paper, **print** only the following:

    a) Journal entries, All (with corrections)   Mar 01 to Mar 07
    b) Income Statement for period   Jan 01 to Mar 07
    c) Balance Sheet at   Mar 07
    d) Customer Aged Detail report at   Mar 07
    e) General Ledger   Mar 01 to Mar 07

Your instructor may request printouts of the Sales and/or Cash Receipts Journals. See Exercise 2B-38.

> *Refer to the second last page of Chapter 2B for the complete list of Accounting and Simply Accounting Terminology for the Receivables chapter.*

Relevant Appendices, Part A

The following appendices are available on the Student Data CD.

Appendix 2009 CD-Q   **Names Fields**

Appendix 2009 CD-V   **Mini-Guide Receivables—Payables**

Appendix 2009 CD-AC   **Adding a Salesperson's Name to an Invoice**

Note: After finishing Chapter 2A and Chapter 8, you can complete selected transactions from Chapter 2A, using the Perpetual Inventory module. See Challenge Exercise 08 C8-4 Luggage-PI.

Summary, Part A

Here is a summary of the transactions entered in this chapter:

Transaction:	Journal/Ledger:	Remarks:
Sales Quotes	*Sales Quotes*	Creates a quote that may be printed and sent to a customer. Simply records it in the Sales Quote database, but does not post to the General Ledger.
Sales Order	*Sales Orders*	Creates a sales order record when an order is received from a customer. May be created by converting an existing sales quote. Simply records in the Sales Order Listing, but does not post to the General Ledger.
Sale on Account	*Sales Invoices*	Records SALES amounts only. User selects the appropriate GST code. Simply automatically debits Accounts Receivable and credits the appropriate tax accounts.
Sales Adjustment	*Sales Invoices*	Use Adjustment icon.
Receipt	*Receipts*	Select the invoice(s) paid.
Receipt with Discount	*Receipts*	Apply the receipt against the original invoice less the discount amount calculated on the sales amount before taxes.
Return on Account/ Credit Memo	*Sales*	Enter the memo as a minus amount with GST.
New Customer	*Customers*	Remember to select an appropriate Revenue account and appropriate tax code for each customer.
Cancel an Invoice	*Sales*	Use the **Reverse Invoice** icon to reverse the original invoice. Can also be seen in Chapter 13.
Revise a Cash Receipt	*Receipts*	Use **Lookup** to find the original receipt and adjust the amounts as required. Can also be seen in Chapter 13.

Before Moving On..., Part A

Read the following questions and make sure you know the answers to them; otherwise, review the corresponding section in the chapter before moving on.

1. What types of transactions are journalized in the RECEIVABLES module?

2. What is the main difference in journalizing transactions between the RECEIVABLES module and the COMPANY module?

3. What occurs when you post journal transactions in the RECEIVABLES module?

4. Why would a business need to use more than one bank account?

5. Explain the concept of aging in customer accounts.

6. Name at least two uses of the Customer Aged Detail report.

7. What is the difference between a sales quote and a sales order?

8. The default Revenue account is used for what purpose?

9. What is a cheque payment advice?

Challenge Exercise 02 C2A-1 Clocks

RECEIVABLES and COMPANY Modules

Clocks is a business that sells various type of clocks (e.g., table, desk, grandfather, etc.) and is open 7 days a week.

You do *NOT* need to print Sales invoices or receipts. Terms are varied for different customers. GST is 5%, and PST is exempt for wholesale customers only.

1 ➤ Refer to Exercise 1-1 to unzip the **02 C2A-1 Clocks.exe** file.

2 ➤ Open the **02 C2A-1 Clocks** file, and enter the following Accounts Receivable transactions for May:

May 1   Sold 10 model #256 desk clocks at $30.00 each, plus GST, to Carney's Clocks. Invoice #212 issued with terms 2/10, net 30.

May 1   Issued Sales Quote #136 to **Your Name** (Your actual name must appear). Terms net 5 days. Other information: 623 Autumn Breeze Way, Mississauga, Ontario, L5B 9P2. Phone and fax numbers may be left blank. Credit limit $2,500.00 for a grandfather clock at $2,000.00, plus PST & GST. Free delivery and setup of the clock. Your Name will return from a business trip on Friday, May 4 and will advise about the quote on the clock. Ship date Tuesday, May 8.

May 4   **Your Name** accepted quote #136 and ordered the grandfather clock. The order was increased to include 2 travel alarm clocks at $35.00 each, plus taxes.

May 5   Issued invoice #213 for sale of one antique style desk clock model #128 for $140.00, plus taxes, to Carlton Shippers. Cheque #258 received.

May 8   The grandfather and travel alarm clocks on Order #136 were delivered to **Your Name** and the grandfather clock was installed. Invoice #214 was left at the home.

May 9   Issued sales order #137 to wholesale customer, Sandy's Clock Town, for 10 desk clocks model #899 at $62.50 each, plus GST. The clocks are scheduled to be shipped May 14. Terms are net 2/10, net 30 days.

May 10   Your Name returned one of the travel alarm clocks as it does not work. Your Name does not want a replacement. Credit his account.

May 11   Received cheque #847 from Carney's Clocks to pay for outstanding invoice #212.

May 13   Received cheque #148, as payment from Your Name re invoice #214.

May 14   Issued invoice #215 to Sandy's Clock Town for 9 desk clocks from their order. One clock is back ordered and will be shipped on May 23. If you see a confirmation window, click **NO**.

3 ➤ When you have recorded the above entries, **print** the following reports:
    a. Customer Aged Detail Report as at May 14
    b. Journal Entries All, for May 1 to 14
    c. Sales Journal for May 1 to 14
    d. Cash Receipts Journal for May 1 to 14
    e. Income Statement for Jan 1 to May 14
    f. Pending Sales Order report with an As at date of May 14.

Challenge Exercise 02 C2A-2, Dog Walkers

RECEIVABLES and COMPANY Modules

Dog Walkers is a business that looks after pets during the day, evening or when the owners are away for a period of time. The business takes the dogs for walks and play in parks.

You do *NOT* need to print Sales invoices or receipts.

Note: All invoices are left at the residence or business at the end of each week (5 day walking) or at the end of the walking period if the period is less than a week. Terms are varied for different customers. GST is 5%, and PST is exempt for all customers.

1 ➤ Refer to Exercise 1-1 to unzip the **02 C2A-2 Walkers.exe** file.

2 ➤ Open the **02 C2A-2 Walkers** file, and enter the following Accounts Receivable transactions for May.

May 1   Issued Sales Quote #362 to Ms. Sadia Kalirai for 3 walking services at $20.00 plus GST per day for her dog "Ranger", while they are out of town starting on Friday, May 4. Terms net 3 days.

May 2   Left invoice #782 for 4-day walking services for Ms. Rachel Tran's dog, Duffer, at $20.00 plus GST per day with terms of net 3 days.

May 2   Ms. Sadia Kalirai accepted quote #362 for Ranger.

May 5   Received cheque #829 from Ms. Rachel Tran for invoice #782.

May 6   Issued and left invoice #783 for $63.00 (3 day service at $20.00 per day plus GST) at Ms. Sadia Kalirai's home.

May 7   Issued sales order #363 to a new business client, Your Name Transport (Your Name must appear), to take their 2 security dogs for walks in the park during the day when they are not able to. The first Sales order is for a minimum of 10 days for the month. Use May 31 as the Ship Date. The dogs are to go on longer walks and play sessions and the charge will be $40.00 plus GST per visit. Other information: 889 Ancaster Avenue, Stoney Creek, Ontario, L8E 6Z9, phone and fax numbers may be left blank. Terms are 2% 10 days net 20 days. (Special terms arranged for business clients.) Credit limit $500.00.

May 8   Received $41.00 Bank Debit memo re service charges on the Bank account.

May 8   Received cheque #529 from Ms. Kalirai for invoice #783.

May 11   Issued invoice #784 against sales order #363 to Your Name Transport for 3 days walking for the dogs.

May 21   Received cheque #8961 from Your Name Transport for invoice #784.

May 21   Issued invoice #785 to Manpreet Foss for 2 day walking services at $20.00 per day, plus GST with terms of net 3 days. Mr. Foss left cheque #603 on the kitchen table for us.

3 ➤ When you have recorded the above entries, **print** the following:
      a. Customer Aged Detail Report as at May 21
      b. Journal Entries All, for May 1 to 21
      c. Journal Entries-General, for May 1 to 21
      d. Sales Journal for May 1 to 21
      e. Pending Sales Order report at May 31
      f. Income Statement for Jan 1 to May 21

RECEIVABLES Module—Part B

Santos Luggage

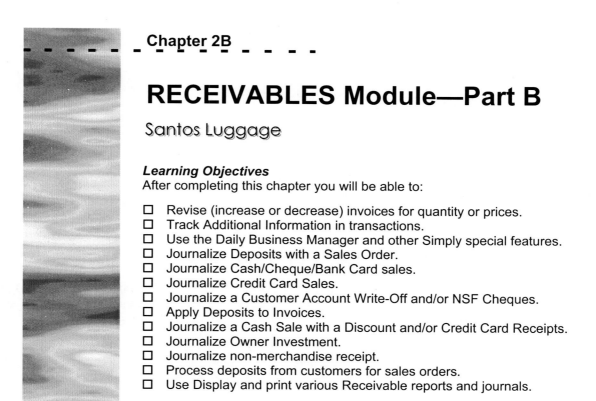

Learning Objectives

After completing this chapter you will be able to:

- ☐ Revise (increase or decrease) invoices for quantity or prices.
- ☐ Track Additional Information in transactions.
- ☐ Use the Daily Business Manager and other Simply special features.
- ☐ Journalize Deposits with a Sales Order.
- ☐ Journalize Cash/Cheque/Bank Card sales.
- ☐ Journalize Credit Card Sales.
- ☐ Journalize a Customer Account Write-Off and/or NSF Cheques.
- ☐ Apply Deposits to Invoices.
- ☐ Journalize a Cash Sale with a Discount and/or Credit Card Receipts.
- ☐ Journalize Owner Investment.
- ☐ Journalize non-merchandise receipt.
- ☐ Process deposits from customers for sales orders.
- ☐ Use Display and print various Receivable reports and journals.

This chapter is a continuation of Chapter 2A. You should download the 02 Luggage 2B data file for use with this chapter.

The contents of this chapter are as follows:

Opening the RECEIVABLES Module, Part B

In this chapter (2B), you will access the RECEIVABLES module of Santos Luggage and enter transactions related to sales, receipts of payment from customers, and other Receivable transactions, starting from March 8.

The 02 2B Luggage-B exe file contains the ending balances of the General Ledger accounts and Customers files from Chapter 2A of this text (see Trial Balance shown on next page). These balances will be the starting point of the B file and journal entries will start at J1.

Exercise 2B-21 – Opening the 02 2B Luggage-B data file

Review Exercise 1-2 if you need help to open a data file.

1 ➤ Refer to Exercise 1-1 to unzip the **02 2B Luggage-B.exe** file.

2 ➤ Start **Simply Accounting**.

3 ➤ At the Select Company window, click **Select an existing company** button, and **OK**.

4 ➤ At the Simply Accounting - **Open Company window**, in the **Look in**: box, locate your student location drive and the **02 2B Luggage-B** folder.

    02 2B Luggage-B

5 ➤ **Double-click** the 02 2B Luggage-B folder and the Luggage-B.SAI will appear in the box. (The image at the left of Luggage may be different depending on the configuration of your computer and the SAI may be in lower case.)

6 ➤ Click the Luggage-B.SAI icon. The **File name** box will change to Luggage-B.SAI (.SAI may not display).

7 ➤ Click **Open** to open the **Luggage-B.SAI** file.

8 ➤ The Session date will be Mar 07, 2016. Click **OK**.

```
Santos Luggage, Student's Name
Trial Balance As At Mar 07, 2016
                                         Debits        Credits
1020   Bank Chequing Account           22,702.16          -
1030   Visa Credit Card Bank Account       0.00          -
1200   Accounts Receivable            10,938.10          -
1300   Inventory                      23,680.00          -
1320   Prepaid Supplies                  712.00          -
1420   Office/Warehouse Furniture/Equip...  25,163.00
1425   Accum. Amort Office/Ware Furn/E...      -      4,100.00
2200   Accounts Payable                     -     11,255.00
2630   GST Charged on Sales                 -      1,237.40
2640   GST Paid On Purchases            525.00          -
2650   PST Payable                          -          0.00
3100   Capital, Maria Santos                -     63,683.68
3160   Additional Investment                -          0.00
3180   Drawings, Maria Santos          2,200.00          -
4100   Sales                                -     42,799.00
4150   Sales-Discounts                   342.00          -
4200   Sales-Returns & Allowances        681.00          -
5010   Beginning Inventory            21,000.00          -
5040   Purchases                      28,000.00          -
5050   Purchase Returns                     -      1,000.00
5080   Purchase Discounts                   -        335.00
5090   Ending Inventory                     -     23,680.00
5310   Wages Expense                   8,000.00          -
5320   Advertising Expense               432.00          -
5330   Bank Charges & Interest            95.00          -
5340   Credit Card Charges                34.30          -
5350   Rent Expense                      800.00          -
5370   Bad Debt Expense                    0.00          -
5410   Office/Warehouse Supplies Expense   216.00        -
5450   Rent Expense Warehouse          2,000.00          -
5460   Utility Expense                   263.89          -
5550   Telephone Expense                 305.63          -
                                      148,090.08    148,090.08
```

Exercise 2B-22 – To Set Up a Default Revenue Account for a Customer

In Exercise 2A-4, step 18 you had to locate and select the Revenue account for Luggage 4U. In Exercise 2A-20, step 8 you set up a default revenue account for Your Name Luggage Rack. (All customers except Luggage 4U have a default Revenue account.)

1 ➤ Return to the Customer's Receivable Ledger window of Luggage 4U and add the default **Revenue Account 4100,** ⌨Tab . All regular customers will then have a default revenue account. This will help avoid errors and will make inputting information faster.

2 ➤ Click **Save and Close** to return to Home window.

Slideshow 2B – RECEIVABLES Part B demonstrates the use of Simply's special features and more transaction processing techniques. Run it now.

Using Simply's Special Features

Simply has some special features that maximize efficiency in your everyday tasks and optimize the use of a computerized accounting software. You learned earlier how to use the Daily Business Manager. Below are special features relevant to tasks involving sales and customers.

The Lookup Feature

The **Invoice Lookup** feature shown in the next exercise can be used when management wants to view previously posted invoices in order to verify details. This is especially useful if the paper copy of the invoice(s) cannot be located, or to locate a previously posted invoice that you wish to correct.

Exercise 2B-23a – To Process a Transaction with an Increase in Quantity

In this exercise you will record a transaction while the customer, Mr. Tran, is still in the store and the order is being prepared. After the invoice is **Posted**, the customer decided to increase the quantity for the carry on bags. You could prepare a new invoice for the additional items, but the customer wants all the items on one invoice.

You will be shown how to correct the posted invoice in the exercise that follows.

1 ➤   Advance the Session date to **Mar 08, 2016**.

2 ➤   **Record** and **Post** the following transaction.

On future invoices, if **Shipped by** details are not provided, do not enter any information. Also assume **Mailing address** and **Ship to** address are the same if not specified.

Mar 08, 2016   **Sold 15 Carry on bags – small at $21.00 each and 3 Power adapters at $10.50 each, plus GST, to a new customer, Tran's Luggage Warehouse, contact person is Huong Tran, 875 Burke Avenue, Markham, Ontario L2S 2Y9. Phone number and fax number 905-768-3620, the default Revenue account is 4100, price list is Regular, terms are 2/10, net 30, PST exempt number 87-B98-5, tax code is G, credit limit is $1,500.00. Invoice #2315 for $363.83 including $17.33 GST.**

To Correct a Posted Invoice

You will now correct the invoice that you just posted.

Exercise 2B-23b – To Correct a Posted Invoice (Lookup Feature)

It is assumed that you are still in the Sales Journal-Invoice window.

1 ➤ Invoice   Click the 🖳 **Invoice Lookup** icon and the Invoice Lookup window appears.

2 ➤ Click **OK**, and the Select Invoice Window appears.

3 ➤ Select **Invoice 2315** and click **Select**. The Sales Journal-Invoice Lookup window appears with the original 2315 invoice. (See side note box.)

4 ➤ Click the 🖳 **Adjust Invoice** icon. (The icon is identical to the Adjust Receipt icon used previously.) The **⬛ Sales Journal - Adjusting Invoice 2315** banner appears at the top.

5 ➤ Change the 15 Carry on bags - small to **18**, **Tab**. The Invoice total changes to $429.98, which includes $20.48 GST. Mr. Tran is pleased that you could make the change for him.

6 ➤ Post this transaction and **Exit** to the Home window.

7 ➤ Advance the date to **Mar 11, 2016**.

If other invoices were posted, you could use the ◀🗐 🗐▶ **Look up previous** or **Look up next** icons to move forward or backward in the list of invoices.

To Track Additional Transaction Details

This feature is the same as the feature you used in Chapter 1, Exercise 1-11. You will be able to add additional information about transactions when required.

Exercise 2B-24 – Using the Additional Transaction Details

Mrs. Santos has decided to have the **Additional Date and Information** fields available and used when appropriate. You have been asked to use this feature.

Mar 09, 2016	**Received cheque #1256 dated Mar 07, 2016 in the amount of $2,018.80 (after a net $39.20 discount after the return) from Havarah Leather Goods on invoice 2253. Use additional transaction detail information as noted in this exercise.**

1 ➤ Click the **Receipts** icon. **Record** this transaction using the **Mar 09, 2016** date as the transaction date (the actual date the cheque was deposited — this will match up to the bank statement). Don't forget to input cheque #1256 into the cheque number and receipt fields.

The cheque was mailed by the customer on the 10th day of the discount period and should be given the discount. In steps 3 and 5, at the Disc. Taken field, you will type the Discount taken amount to override the blank amount shown.

Invoice Date	Invoice or Deposit	Original Amount	Amount Owing	Discount Available	Discount Taken	Amount Received
Feb 26, 2016	2253	2,205.00	2,205.00	0.00		
	2253Rt CM124	-147.00	-147.00	-2.80		

Note the Invoice Date column. Simply 2009 does not display the date of the return or other credits.

Change the date to Mar 07, 2016 and the **Discount Available** field changes to 42.00 with the return discount -2.80 as a negative. Goods were returned, therefore, no discount is allowed on the returned goods. (See side note box.)

Invoice Date	Invoice or Deposit	Original Amount	Amount Owing	Discount Available	Discount Taken	Amount Received
Feb 26, 2016	2253	2,205.00	2,205.00	42.00		
	2253Rt CM124	-147.00	-147.00	-2.80		

Change the date back to Mar 09, 2016. You will note that the **Discount Available** field is back to 0.00, [Tab] .

If it is longer than 3 days, you need to speak to a manager to approve the discount.

2 ➤ **Invoice/Deposit** At invoice 2253, [Tab] .

3 ➤ **Discount Taken** Type **42.00** to allow the discount, [Tab] . Management will usually allow a 2 or 3 day grace period as there could be mail delivery problems or holidays affecting the delivery. (See side note box.)

4 ➤ **Amount Received** [Tab] to accept 2,163.00. The cursor moves to the 2253Rt CM124 Discount Taken line.

Original Purchase	$ 2,100.00	Discount available	$ 42.00
Less Return	$ (140.00)	Return Discount lost	$ (2.80)
Net Sale	$ 1,960.00 x 2% = $39.20	Net Discount	$ 39.20

5 ➤ **Disc Taken** At **-2.80**, [Tab] to allow the negative discount on the return.

6 ➤ **Amount Received** [Tab] to accept -144.20. The lower portion should resemble the following.

Invoice Date	Invoice or Deposit	Original Amount	Amount Owing	Discount Available	Discount Taken	Amount Received
Feb 26, 2016	2253	2,205.00	2,205.00	42.00	42.00	2,163.00
	2253Rt CM124	-147.00	-147.00	-2.80	-2.80	-144.20
					Total	2,018.80

7 ➤ Click the **Additional Information** icon [✓] and record the information to show that a cheque dated on the 8th was received and deposited on the 9th. Click **OK**.

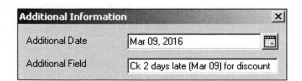

Additional Information	✕
Additional Date	Mar 09, 2016
Additional Field	Ck 2 days late (Mar 09) for discount

The journal entry window should look like the following:

Receipts Journal Entry Mar 09, 2016 (J4)

Account Number	Account Description	Debits	Credits
1020	Bank Chequing Account	2,018.80	-
4150	Sales -Discounts	39.20	-
1200	Accounts Receivable	-	2,058.00
Additional Date: Ma...	Additional Field: Ck 2 days late (M...		
		2,058.00	2,058.00

8 ➤ **Exit** the journal window, **Post** this transaction and **Exit** to the Home window.

9 ➤ **Record** and **post** the following two transactions:

Mar 09, 2016   Sold to Havarah Leather Goods, 10 Briefcases narrow at $70.00 each, 3 Briefcases large at $105.00 each, 3 Carry on bags - small at $21.00 each, 15 Suitcases w/w large at $62.00 each, plus GST. Terms are 2/10, net 30. GST in the amount of $100.40 is added to the goods purchased to give a final invoice total of $2,108.40.

Mar 10, 2016   Sold to Royes Luggage Inc., 10 Laptop Back Paks at $70.00 each, 10 Locks one size at $3.50 each, and 14 Suitcases w/w small at $49.00, each plus GST. Terms are 2/10, net 30. GST in the amount of $71.05 is added to the goods sold to give a final invoice total of $1,492.05.

---

10 ➤ When finished processing the transactions, **Exit** from the Sales Journal and return to the Home window.

Exercise 2B-25 – Using the Daily Business Manager (DBM)

1 ➤ Advance the Session date to **Mar 17, 2016**.

2 ➤ In Exercise 2A-20 at step 11 you identified Mar 17 as the date to display the memo note in the Daily Business Manager. To see the note in the Related Tasks Area, click the **Daily Business Manager** icon on the tool bar. If the Memo tab information is not displayed in the lower window, click the **Memo** tab. The clerk would advise management about the memo note for further action.

3 ➤ **Display**   In Exercise 2A-9, you were shown how to display the Business Performance window. Select **Business Performance**. You can now see that the straight line (in Exercise 2A-9) has changed with the entries you have recorded.

4 ➤ **Display**   Click **Sales (Past 7 Days)** to see another change. This information can be very helpful for management when planning staff work schedules.

5 ➤ Return to the Home window.

Journalizing a Deposit

Assume a special order of **clothes and laptop suitcases** for March 29 (a future date) of $6,000.00, plus GST of $300.00 for a total of $6,300.00. The customer pays a deposit of $3,500.00 to ensure that the goods are delivered on time. This is similar to paying a fraction of the total price to lay away a special dress or suit. The seller will take the dress/suit off the rack or special order the goods, but would want assurances that you will come back. The deposit is usually applied toward the final price.

When you record a deposit of $3,500.00 before a sale is completed, it is entered as a **credit** in the customer RECEIVABLES Ledger. Since there is no sale, it is, in essence, a negative receivable and the money is owed to the customer until the corresponding service is rendered or goods are delivered.

Exercise 2B-26 will show you how to record a deposit as you record a Sales order.

Remember: A deposit cannot be recorded on a Sales Quote.

A deposit transaction is not a sale but rather a deposit on a future sale.
Simply would record the following entry as an example:

Dr BANK ACCOUNT	**$3,500.00**	
Cr ACCOUNTS RECEIVABLE		**$3,500.00**

This, in effect, gives the customer a **credit** balance of $3,500.00.

When the goods or services are delivered, the sale is recorded with a **debit** invoice ($6,300.00) in the customer RECEIVABLES Ledger.

When the remaining outstanding balance ($2,800.00) on the invoice is received, the $2,800.00 receipt and the $3,500.00 prepayment are applied to the total invoice of $6,300.00, to clear the invoice from the outstanding list. (The invoice would then be fully paid.)

Exercise 2B-26 – Journalizing a Deposit with a Sales Order

You will now journalize the $3,500.00 deposit as you record the Sales Order.

Study the transaction:

Mar 15, 2016 Opal Kong Luggage Ltd. has placed a special order for 30 Clothes and Laptop suitcases w/w with embossed Price Company logos (approved by the CEO of the Price Company). The cost will be $200.00 each, plus GST. Total order including GST is $6,300.00. Estimated shipping date is Mar 29, 2016. We have received Opal Kong Luggage Ltd.'s cheque #433 for a $3,500.00 deposit (or prepayment) on this special order.

Due to the company's logo on the goods, the goods are not returnable unless defective.

To Record the Sales Order

1 ➤ Create an Order using the **Sales Order** icon.

2 ➤ **Transaction**   Do not change, from Sales Order.

3 ➤ **Sold To**   Select **Opal Kong Luggage Ltd.**, `Tab`.

Before you continue, look at the Ship Date and Date fields. There is no field between them.

4 ➤ **Paid By**   Select **Cheque**. You will now see the fields

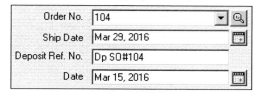

between the Ship Date and Date fields. You will also see `Deposit Paid [      ]` in the lower section. You will use these fields in step 5 and 10 of this exercise. `Tab` `Tab`.

         Deposit To   Do not **change**.

5 ➤ **Cheque**   Type **433**. `Tab`.

Complete the information as shown.

Order No.	104
Ship Date	Mar 29, 2016
Deposit Ref. No.	Dp SO#104
Date	Mar 15, 2016

         Order No.   You have to type order number **104.** Simply creates the Quote numbers, but cannot create the Order numbers.

         Deposit Ref No.   **Dp SO#104** refers to Deposit Special Order #104. Some companies will use the number of the cheque received and others may use a deposit reference number, which is different than the cheque number received. `Tab`.

6 ➤ **Date**   Select **Mar 15, 2016** the day the cheque is received. `Tab` `Tab` `Tab` to Order.

7 ➤ Complete the information as follows.

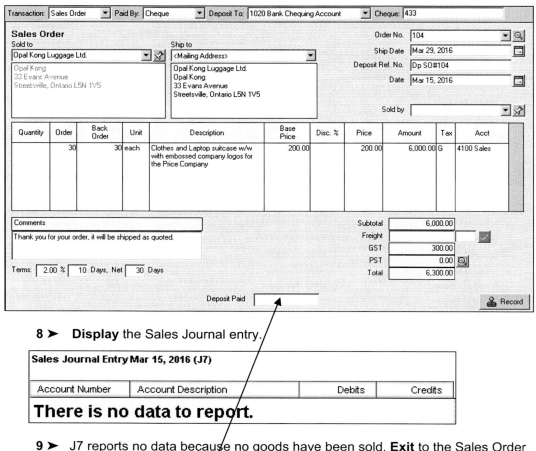

8 ➤ **Display** the Sales Journal entry.

Sales Journal Entry Mar 15, 2016 (J7)			
Account Number	Account Description	Debits	Credits
There is no data to report.			

9 ➤ J7 reports no data because no goods have been sold. **Exit** to the Sales Order window.

10 ➤ Enter the information in the lower part of the window as shown.

Deposit Paid	3,500.00

Notice that the Sales Order Total (6,300.00) has not changed. The order is still for the full amount.

11 ➤ **Display** the Sales Journal entry; it should look like the following. The entry records the money received on the Sales Order.

Sales Journal Entry Mar 15, 2016 (J7)			
Account Number	Account Description	Debits	Credits
1020	Bank Chequing Account	3,500.00	-
1200	Accounts Receivable	-	3,500.00
Additional Date:	Additional Field:		
		3,500.00	3,500.00

12 ➤ **Exit** from the entry and **Record** the transaction.

13 ➤ **Exit** to the Home window.

14 ➤ Display the **Customer Aged Detail Report** for Opal Kong for **Mar 17, 2016** (see Exercise 2A-2: Displaying/Printing Customer Aged Report).

Customer Aged Detail As at Mar 17, 2016				
Source	Date	Transaction Type	Total	Current
Opal Kong Luggage Ltd.				
Dp SO#104	Mar 15, 2016	Prepaid Order	-3,500.00	-3,500.00
Total outstanding:			-3,500.00	-3,500.00
Total unpaid invoices:			-	-
Total deposits/prepaid order:			-3,500.00	-3,500.00

The Opal Kong report shows a deposit (Prepaid Order) of **-3,500.00** in two places.

15 ➤ **Exit** from the Aged Detail Report and return to the Home window.

Journalizing Cash/Cheque/Bank Card Sales

This type of sale can be recorded in the Sales Journal as a One-time customer, because you do not expect to have repeat sales with the customer. This option is appropriate because there is no need to keep detailed computer records for a One-time customer. However, the sales record is useful for the audit trail or for inquiries of goods sold, etc.

When you use this option, Simply automatically allows you to enter only a sale paid by cash, cheque, credit or bank debit card. This means that nothing (name or amounts) will be posted to the ACCOUNTS RECEIVABLE account in the G/L. The One-time Customer transaction will appear in the journal and ledger printouts similar to:

Mar 15, 2016	J8	456, 2318, <One-time customer>

The sales invoice will, however, record the name/address of the customer in the lower box and can be viewed at a later time.

The next exercise shows you how to enter the name of the customer in the lower **Sold to** field to enter a cash sales transaction with a One-time customer, which allows you to have the One-time customer wording (instead of name) as shown above to appear in journal entries.

Exercise 2B-27 – Journalizing a Retail Sale (by cheque)

> Mar 15, 2016 **Mrs. Arlene Hirsch has purchased from the outlet store, at the back of the warehouse, 2 Suitcases w/w large at $80.00, 2 Carry on bags - small at $28.00, and 2 Locks at $4.50 each, plus GST and PST. (The Outlet store selling prices, although seconds and samples, are higher than goods sold to chain stores but lower than regular retail prices.) Cheque #456 for $254.25 was accepted, as Mrs. Hirsch is a friend of one of our staff.**

1 ➤ Create an invoice using the **Sales Invoices** icon.

Transaction Do not change the default Invoice.

2 ➤ **Paid by** Select **Cheque**, Tab .

3 ➤ **Deposit to**   DO NOT CHANGE, `Tab` to accept 1020 Bank Account.

4 ➤ **Cheque**   Type **456**. `Tab`.

5 ➤ **Sold to**   Click the ▼ and select **<One-time customer>**. `Tab` `Tab`.

For audit trail information and verification purposes you should type in the name of the customer (as shown) and address information. The manager, however, decided you do not need the cash customer's address. Mrs. Hirsch is a friend of one of the employees. Enter the information as shown next.

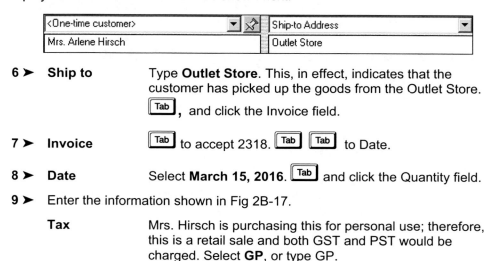

6 ➤ **Ship to**   Type **Outlet Store**. This, in effect, indicates that the customer has picked up the goods from the Outlet Store. `Tab`, and click the Invoice field.

7 ➤ **Invoice**   `Tab` to accept 2318. `Tab` `Tab` to Date.

8 ➤ **Date**   Select **March 15, 2016**. `Tab` and click the Quantity field.

9 ➤ Enter the information shown in Fig 2B-17.

   Tax   Mrs. Hirsch is purchasing this for personal use; therefore, this is a retail sale and both GST and PST would be charged. Select **GP**, or type GP.

The Sales Invoice window should appear as follows: (See side note box.)

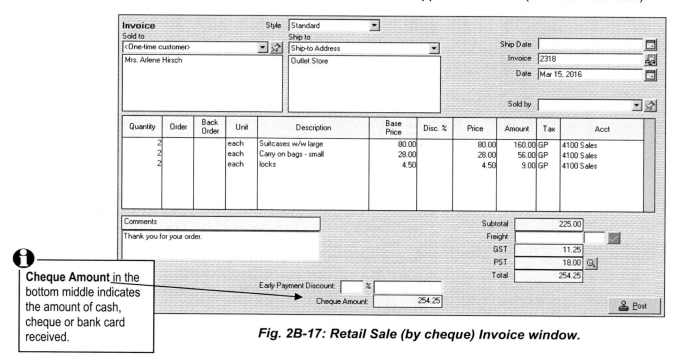

Cheque Amount in the bottom middle indicates the amount of cash, cheque or bank card received.

Fig. 2B-17: Retail Sale (by cheque) Invoice window.

The Early Payment Discount field would be used for a customer who received terms of 2/10, net 30 days who buys today and pays today. Mrs. Hirsch does not receive this discount.

10 ➤ **View** the Sales Journal Entry. The window should appear as follows:

Sales Journal Entry Mar 15, 2016 (J8)			
Account Number	Account Description	Debits	Credits
1020	Bank Chequing Account	254.25	-
2630	GST Charged on Sales	-	11.25
2650	PST Payable	-	18.00
4100	Sales	-	225.00
Additional Date:	Additional Field:		
		254.25	254.25

11 ➤ **Exit** from the display window.

12 ➤ **Post** when correct and **Exit** to the Home window.

Journalizing a Credit Card Sale

Credit Card sales are, in essence, **cash** sales. However, journalizing them is a bit different from a sale where the customer pays cash or uses an ATM (debit) card. When a customer pays with a credit card, the vendor's credit card company charges the vendor a fee for the privilege of accepting the credit card. This is called a **discount charge**. The credit card discount rate varies depending on the dollar volume of sales processed by the vendor.

When journalizing this type of sale, the sale amount is reduced by the amount of the credit card company's discount fee, and the discount fee is entered as a separate item.

Depending on the arrangement with the credit card company, your bank may credit your account for this type of sale, or you may be required to deposit credit card receipts at your bank.

Exercise 2B-28 – Journalizing a Credit Card Sale

Santos Luggage has arranged to have credit card receipts credited automatically to their bank account.

The credit card discount fee for Santos Luggage is 3.5% of the sales amount (including taxes) and is entered in a separate account; e.g., 5340 Credit Card Charges.

Mar 17, 2016 **Another sale from the Outlet store. Mr. Jerry Tyson, of Tyson's Toys, used his business credit card to purchase 1 Briefcase wide for $135.00, plus GST and PST. The invoice total was $152.55, including all taxes.**

1 ➤ Create an invoice using the **Sales Invoice** icon.

    Transaction   Do not change Invoice.

2 ➤ **Paid by**   Select **Visa Credit**. Santos Luggage accepts the Visa Credit Card. `Tab`.

3 ➤ **Sold to**   **Mr. Jerry Tyson**, `Tab`, click `Continue`. This is similar to selecting <One-time Customer>, but as noted previously, the customer's name will appear in the printouts, similar to 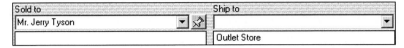. This is the author's recommended way to record this type of transaction, as the customer's name will display and print in the journals and G/L. To ensure privacy, do not type credit card numbers on screen. They should be recorded on paper only. Type **Outlet Store** as shown. `Tab`.

Sold to	Ship to
Mr. Jerry Tyson	
	Outlet Store

Invoice Accept **2319**.

Date Accept **Mar 17, 2016**.

4 ➤ Enter the information shown next:

Quantity	Order	Back Order	Unit	Description	Base Price	Disc. %	Price	Amount	Tax	Acct
1			each	Briefcase wide	135.00		135.00	135.00	GP	4100 Sales

Tax Mr. Tyson is purchasing this for personal use, therefore, this is a retail sale and both GST and PST would be charged.

Disc % There is no discount on this sale.

The screen display should display the following:

Transaction: Invoice	Paid By: Visa Credit	Tell me more about processing credit card payments

Invoice Style Standard Order/Quote No.

Sold to: Mr. Jerry Tyson Ship to: Outlet Store

Ship Date
Invoice 2319
Date Mar 17, 2016
Sold by

Quantity	Order	Back Order	Unit	Description	Base Price	Disc. %	Price	Amount	Tax	Acct
1			each	Briefcase wide	135.00		135.00	135.00	GP	4100 Sales

Comments: Thank you for your order.

Subtotal	135.00
Freight	
GST	6.75
PST	10.80
Total	152.55

Early Payment Discount: %
Visa Credit Amt 152.55

Post

Fig. 2B-18: Sales Journal – Sales Invoice for credit card sale *(see side note box)*.

Because you selected **Visa Credit** in the **Paid By** box on the sales invoice when you journalized the transaction, Simply automatically deducted the $5.34 discount fee (invoice total of $152.55 * 3.5%) and posted it to **5340 Credit Card Charges**. The remainder $147.21 is debited to **1020 Bank Account**.

The **Total** and **Visa Credit Amount** of $152.55 on the sales invoice remain the same.

5 ➤ Display the Sales Journal entry.

Sales Journal Entry Mar 17, 2016 (J9)

Account Number	Account Description	Debits	Credits
1030	Visa Credit Card Bank Account	147.21	-
5340	Credit Card Charges	5.34	-
2630	GST Charged on Sales	-	6.75
2650	PST Payable	-	10.80
4100	Sales	-	135.00
Additional Date:	Additional Field:		
		152.55	152.55

6 ➤ **Exit** from the display window.

7 ➤ **Post** when correct and **Exit** to the Home window. You will see the Simply Accounting Sign UP for Sage Payment Solutions information. This feature requires the user to pay a user fee for this service. This feature will not be discussed in this text. Click **Do Not Show Me again**, to exit to the Home window.

8 ➤ Advance the Session date to **Mar 18, 2016**.

Journalizing a Customer Account Write-off

A write-off may be either a reduction by the full amount or by a partial amount from a specific invoice or the balance in the customer ledger. When all attempts to collect the amount from the customer have failed due to bankruptcy, business closing, etc., the account balance of the customer would be written off.

If there is a dispute over the goods or services supplied, a partial or full write-off on the specific invoice may be made. In the next exercise, a portion of an invoice will be written off after you received notification from the customer's lawyer that the company declared bankruptcy and the cheque received, a partial payment of an invoice, will be the final amount paid.

Mar 18, 2016 **Received cheque #3431 for $840.00 and a letter from Spiller Luggage Stores' lawyer advising our company that Spiller Luggage had a severe uninsured fire at their store, and they have declared bankruptcy. The cheque received is the final amount to be received.**

Maria Santos, the owner, reviewed the letter and advised you to write off the $2,520.00 difference to the following accounts: BAD DEBT EXPENSE $2,400.00
                                  GST ON SALES $ 120.00

Mrs. Santos advised you to record a notation in the client memo file that $2,520.00 has been written off.

To record the write-off properly, you should do it in three steps:

1. Update the customer memo notes if required.
2. Record the write-off.
3. Record the receipt.

Mrs. Santos has asked you to first enter a note in the customer's file, then record the write-off and record the receipt.

Exercise 2B-29 – Record a Note in a Customer's File

Record a Note in a Customer's File

Refer to Exercise 2A-20, which specifically describes the memo tab in the customer's Receivables Ledger file.

1 ➤ Click the ▼ at **Spiller Luggage Stores** in the Customers area, click **View Customer Record**.

2 ➤ Click the **Memo** tab, and enter the following information.

> Mar 18, 2016 Received $840 cheque from customer's lawyer regarding business bankruptcy. Wrote off the account balance per memo from Mrs. Santos.

    To-Do Date   Leave blank. No need to have this information reported later.

3 ➤ Click Save and Close, return to the Home window.

Exercise 2B-30a – Journalizing a Partial Write-off

Follow this procedure to write off the $2,520.00 difference for invoice #2230 using a negative invoice.

1 ➤ In the Customers area, click the ▼ at **Spiller Luggage Stores**, click **Create Invoice**.

    Transaction   Do not change from **Invoice**.

    Paid by   Do not change from **Pay Later**. (You must use **Pay Later** to match the write-off to the previous sale.)

2 ➤ **Invoice**   Type **2230Wo**, Tab Tab. Simply does not allow the entry of an invoice number twice, so adding **Wo** (code for **write-off**) to the original invoice number allows you to reference the write-off to the original sales invoice.

3 ➤ **Date**   Tab to accept Mar 18, 2016 (18th is the date the decision was made to write off the amount). Tab. Click on **Description**.

4 ➤ **Description**   Type **Write-off partial invoice balance.** Tab. Click on **Amount**.

5 ➤ **Amount**   Type **-2400.00**. The minus sign before the amount will make this entry a Debit to the account selected. Tab to accept.

6 ➤ **Tax**   Tab to select code **G**.

7 ➤ **Acct**   Press Enter. Select account **5370** for Bad Debts Expense, Tab. (See side note box.)

8 ➤ **Comments**   Type **Write-off approved by Mrs. Santos.** Tab.

9 ➤ **Terms**   Remove **2, 10, 30**. There is no discount on a write-off.

> ⓘ
> Alternatively, some companies estimate hard-to-collect accounts and set up an **Allowance for Doubtful Accounts or Allowance for Bad Debts**. The allowance is adjusted at year-end (or more frequently) to **Bad Debts Expense**. Actual Accounts Receivable write-offs reduce **Allowance for Doubtful Accounts**.

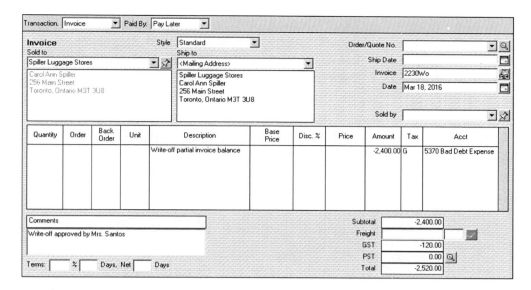

10 ➤ Display the Sales Journal Entry.

Sales Journal Entry Mar 18, 2016 (J10)

Account Number	Account Description	Debits	Credits
2630	GST Charged on Sales	120.00	-
5370	Bad Debt Expense	2,400.00	-
1200	Accounts Receivable	-	2,520.00
Additional Date:	Additional Field:		
		2,520.00	2,520.00

11 ➤ **Exit** from the display window.

12 ➤ **Post** after verifying accuracy and **Exit** to the Home window.

Exercise 2B-30b – Journalizing the Receipt

1 ➤ In the Customers area, click the ⏷ at **Spiller Luggage Stores**, click **Receive Payments**.

2 ➤ **Cheque**   Type **3431**, ⎡Tab⎤.

      From   Spiller Luggage Stores is filled in.

3 ➤ **Receipt No.**   Click in the No. field, type **3431**, ⎡Tab⎤ ⎡Tab⎤.

4 ➤ **Date**   ⎡Tab⎤ ⎡Tab⎤ to accept **Mar 18, 2016**.

5 ➤ **Invoice Date**   ⎡Tab⎤ to accept Feb 20, 2016.

6 ➤ **Disc. Taken**   ⎡Tab⎤ there is no discount.

7 ➤ **Amount Received**   ⎡Tab⎤ to accept the original 2230 invoice $3,360.00.

8 ➤ **Disc. Taken**   ⎡Tab⎤ there is no discount.

If your invoice 2230Wo line has a **-48.00 Disc. Available** amount showing, it means that you did not remove the 2% terms in the previous exercise. Use the ⬚Delete⬚ or ⬚Backspace⬚ key to remove **-48.00**.

9 ➤ Amount Received   ⬚Tab⬚ to accept the write-off of **–2,520.00**. The lower portion to the Receipts window will look similar to the following:

Invoice Date	Invoice or Deposit	Original Amount	Amount Owing	Discount Available	Discount Taken	Amount Received
Feb 20, 2016	2230	3,360.00	3,360.00	0.00		3,360.00
	2230Wo	-2,520.00	-2,520.00	0.00		-2,520.00
					Total	840.00

The **Total** box 840.00 at bottom will indicate the amount of the cheque received, which is the net amount of invoice 2230 ($3,360.00), less the write-off allowed (-2,520.00).

10 ➤ Display the Receipts Journal entry.

Receipts Journal Entry Mar 18, 2016 (J11)

Account Number	Account Description	Debits	Credits
1020	Bank Chequing Account	840.00	-
1200	Accounts Receivable	-	840.00
Additional Date:	Additional Field:		
		840.00	840.00

11 ➤ Exit from the display window.

12 ➤ Post when correct and **Exit** to the Home window.

13 ➤ Display the Customer Aged Detail Report, using the ▾ in the Customers area for Spiller Luggage Stores at March 18.

The screen should look as follows:

Customer Aged Detail As at Mar 18, 2016

Source	Date	Transaction Type	Total	Current	31 to 60
Spiller Luggage Stores					
2230	Feb 20, 2016	Invoice	3,360.00	3,360.00	-
3431	Mar 18, 2016	Payment	-3,360.00	-3,360.00	-
2230Wo	Mar 18, 2016	Invoice	-2,520.00	-2,520.00	-
3431	Mar 18, 2016	Payment	2,520.00	2,520.00	-
Total outstanding:			-	-	-

The lower portion of the report has hyphens (-) to indicate no dollar values.

Notice that cheque **3431** has been applied to both the **invoice 2230** and **invoice 2230Wo**. For future reference, the negative invoice 2230Wo is shown to be applied to original invoice 2230.

14 ➤ The following procedure works with the RECEIVABLES AND PAYABLES modules and assumes that you want to display details of the original invoice(s). Double-click on any item on the invoice **2230Wo** line. The original invoice that created the $ values is displayed with a **PAID** image. This will assist you in verifying if payment was received on an invoice.

15 ➤ **Exit** the Invoice Lookup, and **Exit** the Aged Detail report.

Additional Transaction

1 ➤ **Record** the sale shown in the information box, using the Customers area.

The Additional Info note box for **A-Your Name Luggage Rack** (normally appears in the top left corner of the window) appears to remind you to discuss the 2% discount in 10 days with the customer. **Close** the Additional Info box.

Mar 18, 2016	**Sold to the Oakville branch of A-Your Name Luggage Rack the following: 4 Suitcases w/w large @ $62.00 each, plus GST Total Invoice including GST of $12.40, is $260.40. Credit terms 2%/10 n30.**

---

2 ➤ **Post** when correct.

Journalizing a Customer's NSF Cheque

When a customer's cheque is returned by the bank as **NSF** (**N**ot **S**ufficient **F**unds), it means the customer did not have enough money in their account to cover the cheque that they had sent to you for payment. In a real sense they still owe you money for the invoice that you now show as paid in your records.

To correct this situation, enter in the Sales Journal an increase (Debit) to **Accounts Receivable** in the amount of the NSF cheque plus bank charges, if any, and a decrease (Credit) to **Bank Account** (or Cash) for the same amount as the debit. To keep track of the fact that the entry is due to an NSF cheque, you can use the same invoice number as the original invoice with the code NS or NSF; e.g., Invoice #12345NSF.

DO NOT use the Reverse Entry icon. You do not want to reverse the original sale. The sale has taken place, only the payment is not valid.

Exercise 2B-31 – Journalizing an NSF Customer Cheque

---

1 ➤ Advance the Session date to **Mar 25, 2016**.

Study this transaction:

Mar 23, 2016	**You were notified by a bank debit memo, from your bank, that Mrs. Arlene Hirsch's cheque #456 in the amount of $254.25 was returned NSF (Not Sufficient Funds).**
	You called Mrs. Hirsch and she explained that she has changed banks, as she moved recently and inadvertently used the wrong cheque. She promised that she will send you a replacement cheque from her new home at *993 Ashdown Crescent, Toronto M3H 2K8*, new phone number *905-585-6366*.

Some banks charge an NSF service fee for processing the returned cheques. If your company is charged a fee, the amount will be added to the amount the customer owes your firm (original account receivable plus the service fee). (See following note box for an entry if a service fee was charged.) Fortunately, your bank does not charge a fee for this kind of service; therefore, you will not charge Mrs. Hirsch a service fee for this transaction.

If the bank charged a fee to process an NSF cheque, the entry would be similar to:

      1200 Accounts Receivable   269.25*
      1020   Bank Chequing Account   269.25
            * ($254.25 + $15.00 Admin Fee)

When you recorded the cheque on Mar 15, 2016 from Mrs. Hirsch, you journalized the entry as an **Invoice Paid by Cheque** for a **One-time customer** in the Sales Journal, and made the following entry:

Sales Journal Entry Mar 15, 2016 (J8)

Account Number	Account Description	Debits	Credits
1020	Bank Chequing Account	254.25	-
2630	GST Charged on Sales	-	11.25
2650	PST Payable	-	18.00
4100	Sales	-	225.00
Additional Date:	Additional Field:		
		254.25	254.25

The bank, by the debit memo, has reduced our bank account balance by $254.25 (the amount of the NSF cheque); therefore, Mrs. Hirsch now owes the company the same amount. We need to set up Mrs. Hirsch as a customer and show this amount as being outstanding until her replacement cheque is recorded.

When you record the NSF cheque, you will record the following entry:

1200	Accounts Receivable	254.25	
1020	Bank Chequing Account		254.25

2 ➤   Using the **Sales Invoices** journal icon, create an Invoice as follows.

3 ➤   **Sold to**   Type **Mrs. Arlene Hirsch** ⌷Tab⌷ .

4 ➤   Select **Full Add** and set up **Mrs. Hirsch** as a customer with the **address information** provided; customer since **Mar 15, 2016**. Leave Revenue Account field blank, terms will be **0%** discount, and **Net amount due within 4 days**. Use **No** Tax code. Credit Limit **0.00**.

There is no sale when you record an NSF cheque. The sale took place on March 15, and you are now recording the fact that the customer owes you the money originally received.

She will have a **0.00** credit limit, and the memo note could be:

Replacement cheque for NSF cheque required from customer
NSF cheque #456 received in Outlet Store. Friend of employee (put in your name).

To-Do date   Select **Mar 29, 2016,** as a reminder to verify that the cheque was received.

Display this Memo	Click this field to place a ✓ in the box.

Click the Save and Close button when done.

5 ➤ Invoice   Type **2318NS Cheque 456** and Tab   Tab . Remember that Simply prevents the entry of an invoice number twice, so adding NS (for Not Sufficient Funds) to the invoice number will allow you to enter the original invoice number twice. This will also indicate to you later that this entry is a re-entry of a previous sale due to an NSF cheque. The 456 represents the cheque number that was received NSF. 456 is recorded for tracing purposes, if required.

6 ➤ Date   Select **Mar 23, 2016**, Tab . Click on Description.

7 ➤ Description   Type **NSF cheque #456**, Tab . Click on Amount.

8 ➤ Amount   Type **254.25**, Tab   Tab to Acct. This will leave a blank Tax field. This is the same as double-clicking and selecting - No Tax.

9 ➤ Acct   Press Enter . Select **1020 Bank Chequing Account**. This results in a credit to the Bank Account.

10 ➤ **Remove** the Comments box information, Tab . The lower section should look like the following:

Quantity	Order	Back Order	Unit	Description	Base Price	Disc. %	Price	Amount	Tax	Acct
				NSF cheque #456				254.25		1020 Bank Chequing Account

Comments				
	Subtotal	254.25		
	Freight			
	GST	0.00		
	PST	0.00		
Terms: % Days, Net 4 Days	Total	254.25		

Fig. 2B-19: NSF Sales Invoice.

An alternate method to record a returned cheque is to reverse the payment transaction (see Chapter 13, *Correcting Transaction Errors after Posting*).

The invoice method shown in this exercise is preferred by many businesses because it allows you to send an invoice to the customer advising them that they owe you the money.

11 ➤ Display the Sales Journal Entry. The window should appear as follows:

Sales Journal Entry Mar 23, 2016 (J13)

Account Number	Account Description	Debits	Credits
1200	Accounts Receivable	254.25	-
1020	Bank Chequing Account	-	254.25
Additional Date:	Additional Field:		
		254.25	254.25

Notice that there is no amount posted to the Sales account. The sale was recorded on March 15, 2016. The credit to the Bank Account shows that the payment from Mrs. Hirsch was NSF. This entry reverses the bank deposit entry of March 15, and debits (increases) the customer's Accounts Receivable account.

12 ➤ **Exit** the Sales Journal Entry window and **Post** the entry.

You will receive the following warning message. (The credit limit was set to 0.00.) (See side note box.)

> Advisor: This sale will cause the customer to exceed the credit limit. Are you
> sure you want to process this transaction?

13 ➤ Click **Yes**. You entered a 0.00 credit limit for this customer.

14 ➤ **Exit** from the Sales Journal. Return to the Home window.

Another Transaction

1 ➤ **Journalize** and **post** the following transaction: Return to the Home window.

**Mar 24, 2016 Cheque #186 from Sandler Travel Stores in the amount of
$2,095.00 for Jan 26, 2016 invoice #2197 received and deposited
to the bank.**

Applying an Invoice to a Deposit

On March 15, 2016 Opal Kong Luggage Ltd. placed a $6,300.00 sales order with a
deposit of $3,500.00. The customer ledger shows a **-3,500.00** balance.

When the goods are shipped, you would convert the sales order into a sales
invoice for $6,300.00.

The $6,300.00 sales invoice less the deposit of $3,500.00 you recorded earlier,
will leave a receivable balance owing of $2,800.00.

Exercise 2B-32 – Applying an Invoice to a Deposit

Here is the full transaction description:

**Mar 25, 2016 The special order of 30 Clothes and Laptop suitcase with
embossed company logos for Opal Kong Luggage Ltd. was
received this morning from your supplier. The cases were
checked and then sent to Opal Kong. The $6,300.00 price is per
sales order #104.**

---

1 ➤ Change Sales Order #104 to an invoice #2321 (see Caution information
below). **Record** and **Post** the invoice as the order has been filled. The Sales
Invoice window lower portion should display as shown next.

Simply may have changed the **Paid By** field to **Cheque** (last used selection when
the Sales Order was created). Change it to **Pay Later**.

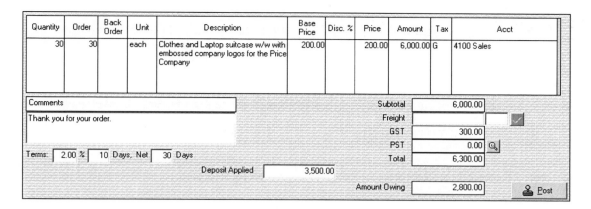

Quantity	Order	Back Order	Unit	Description	Base Price	Disc. %	Price	Amount	Tax	Acct
30	30		each	Clothes and Laptop suitcase w/w with embossed company logos for the Price Company	200.00		200.00	6,000.00	G	4100 Sales

Comments		
Thank you for your order.		

Subtotal	6,000.00
Freight	
GST	300.00
PST	0.00
Total	6,300.00

Terms: 2.00 % 10 Days, Net 30 Days

Deposit Applied 3,500.00

Amount Owing 2,800.00   Post

The Deposit Paid wording has changed to **Deposit Applied**.

The **Total** field shows the invoice amount as the correct $6,300.00. See Step 2 Journal entry.

The **Amount Owing** field now shows the balance owing (after reduction of the deposit). You will also see it reduced in Step 4, when you display the Aged Detail report. However, the printed invoice does not show the reduced balance.

2 ➤ Display the Sales Journal entry; it will look similar to the following:

Sales Journal Entry Mar 25, 2016 (J15)

Account Number	Account Description	Debits	Credits
1200	Accounts Receivable	6,300.00	-
2630	GST Charged on Sales	-	300.00
4100	Sales	-	6,000.00
Additional Date:	Additional Field:		
		6,300.00	6,300.00

3 ➤ **Exit** the entry, **Post** the sale. The information box Sales Order has been filled and removed from the system displays. Click **OK**.

4 ➤ **Exit** to the Home window. Display a Customer Aged Detail report at March 25, for Opal Kong Luggage Ltd., and note how Simply displays the deposit and sale. The report should display as follows:

Customer Aged Detail As at Mar 25, 2016

Source	Date	Transaction Type	Total	Current
Opal Kong Luggage Ltd.				
Dp SO#104	Mar 15, 2016	Prepaid Order	-3,500.00	-3,500.00
2321	Mar 25, 2016	Applied	3,500.00	3,500.00
2321	Mar 25, 2016	Invoice	6,300.00	6,300.00
2321	Mar 25, 2016	Payment	-3,500.00	-3,500.00
Total unpaid invoices:			2,800.00	2,800.00
Total deposits/prepaid order:			-	-

Dp SO#104 and **Prepaid Order**   This is the deposit received when Opal placed her order on the 15th.

Applied	The **Prepaid** amount is transferred from the Sales Order record to the invoice, when you changed the sales order into a sales invoice, shown at line 4 (in the Aging report) as a payment.
Invoice	This is the regular **$6,300.00** Invoice recorded previously.
Payment	This is from the **Applied** amount discussed above.

You will note that the amount **Unpaid by Opal** in this transaction is **2,800.00** ($6,300.00 sale less the $3,500.00 deposit).

5 ➤   **Exit** from the display and return to the Home window.

Journalizing a Cash Sale with a Discount

You learned earlier how to journalize a payment for a sale on credit with a discount. In this exercise, you will learn how to journalize a cash sale with a discount; e.g., a senior's discount. This procedure would also apply if the business was giving a discount to a firm for buying a lot of merchandise or services.

Exercise 2B-33 – Journalizing a Cash Sale with a Discount (Senior)

---

1 ➤   Advance the Session date to **Mar 29, 2016**.

Santos Luggage has had a number of inquiries from senior citizens who want to buy various luggage articles, and would appreciate a senior's discount, similar to what other businesses allow. Mrs. Santos has decided that it would be appropriate to offer a 10% discount to senior citizens (this is not the same as a cash discount for paying early on credit sales). Mrs. Santos has decided that she did not need to track this type of discount and does not need a new ledger account for senior's discount. See the information after step 11 for alternate ways to track this type of discount by setting up a new General Ledger account; e.g., SENIOR'S DISCOUNT.

These sales will be recorded in the Sales Journal by typing the customer's name and using the **Continue** button because the business wants a record of the customer's name in the entry, similar to other entries made from the Outlet Centre. See Exercise 2B-28 **Sold To** area.

Mar 29, 2016   Mr. Ronald Peddle, a senior citizen, provided you with a
senior's card and purchased 2 Suitcases w/w large at
$80.00 each, before a 10% senior's discount. PST and GST
would be added to the price after the discount as follows:

Suitcases w/w large, 2 @ $80.00	$160.00	
Senior's discount less 10%	$ (16.00)	
Net Sales amount before taxes		$144.00
GST 5% on $144.00		$ 7.20
PST 8% on $144.00		$ 11.52
Amount to be paid		$162.72

Mr. Peddle paid the bill in full with his cheque #749.

You will record the sale with the regular selling price and also show the discount on the invoice. However, only the $72.00 net amount for each suitcase (total $144.00) is posted to the Sales account. Follow these steps:

2 ➤ Create an invoice using the **Sales Invoices** icon.

    Transaction Do not change from Invoice.

3 ➤ Paid By Select **Cheque**, `Tab` to Deposit To.

4 ➤ Deposit To Do not change the default 1020 BANK, `Tab` to Cheque.

5 ➤ Cheque Type **749**, `Tab`.

6 ➤ Sold to Type **Mr. Ronald Peddle**, `Tab`, click **Continue**, then `Tab` `Tab` to move to the address area and type **2569 Plaster Lane**, `Tab`, type **Mississauga, ON**, `Tab`, type **L5N 3K7**, `Tab`. Click the **Ship to** field.

7 ➤ Ship to If you click the ▼ there will not be an address listed. A cash sale customer would not require a Ship-to-Address. `Tab` to move to the lower box. Type **Outlet Store**, `Tab`. Click on **Quantity**.

8 ➤ Quantity Complete the information as shown next.

Quantity	Order	Back Order	Unit	Description	Base Price	Disc. %	Price	Amount	Tax	Acct
2			each	Suitcase w/w large with senior's discount	80.00	10.00	72.00	144.00	GP	4100 Sales

Other Information:

    Tax **GP** (Retail Sale) (5% GST and 8% PST will be removed from 10% of the original Sales price).

Early Payment Discount:	%	
Cheque Amount		162.72

 Do not type an amount in the Early Payment Discount field. This field is linked to the Sales Discount account for paying within 2% 10 days discount terms and is not applicable to Senior's Discounts.

 Some firms would also use the Disc % column to give discounts to businesses that buy a lot of goods or services. This is usually called **Quantity** or **Trade discount**. If so, then the original sales price is shown, with the appropriate discount for the customer in the Disc % column. The Price column would show the reduced price for each item on the invoice.

Quantity	Order	Back Order	Unit	Description	Base Price	Disc. %	Price	Amount	Tax	Acct
5			each	Suitcase w/w large	80.00	15.00	68.00	340.00	GP	4100 Sales

The Sales Invoice window for the senior's discount should look like the following:

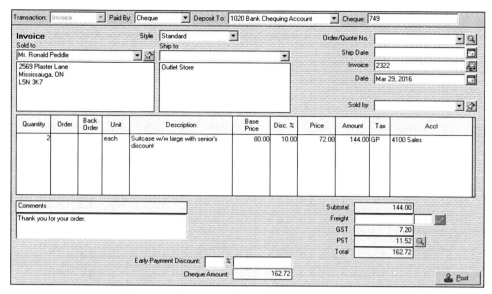

Fig. 2B-20: Sales Invoice window – Senior's Discount.

9 ➤ **Display** the Sales Journal Entry. It should resemble the following:

Sales Journal Entry Mar 29, 2016 (J16)

Account Number	Account Description	Debits	Credits
1020	Bank Chequing Account	162.72	-
2630	GST Charged on Sales	-	7.20
2650	PST Payable	-	11.52
4100	Sales	-	144.00
Additional Date:	Additional Field:		
		162.72	162.72

10 ➤ **Exit** from the display window and **post** the entry when correct.

11 ➤ **Exit** to the Home window. (See the Information note box that follows.)

Some firms want to keep track of the dollar value of discounts given to seniors and would create a new G/L account **Senior's Discount**. If so, the invoice window would be similar to that shown below.

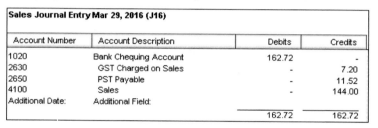

Quantity	Order	Back Order	Unit	Description	Base Price	Disc. %	Price	Amount	Tax	Acct
2			each	Suitcase w/w large	80.00		80.00	160.00	GP	4100 Sales
2			each	Senior's Discount	-8.00		-8.00	-16.00	GP	4170 Senior's Discount

The journal entry would be similar to:

Sales Journal Entry Mar 29, 2016 (J16)

Account Number	Account Description	Debits	Credits
1200	Accounts Receivable	151.20	-
4170	Senior's Discount	16.00	-
2630	GST Charged on Sales	-	7.20
4100	Sales	-	160.00
Additional Date:	Additional Field:		
		167.20	167.20

Journalizing Credit Card Receipts

A credit card received as a payment on any ACCOUNTS RECEIVABLE amount owing may be recorded directly to a specific credit card account which may be linked to one of the bank accounts. In your company's Chart of Accounts, 1030 Visa Credit Card Bank Account is linked to the Visa Credit Card. If you record a payment using a credit card from Visa, it updates the 1030 Visa Credit Card Bank Account.

Exercise 2B-34 – Journalizing a Credit Card Receipt

Study the following transaction:

> **Mar 29, 2016 Mrs. Hirsch came in to pay her account. She decided to pay her account (NSF cheque) using her Visa card. Process her payment using the credit card.**

1 ➤   Using Mrs. Arlene Hirsch from the Customers Area, use **Receive Payments**.

2 ➤   **Paid By**   Select **Visa Credit,** $\boxed{\text{Tab}}$ to From.

   From   Mrs. Arlene Hirsch is selected.

3 ➤   **Receipt No.**   This is a credit card receipt which does not have a cheque or invoice number. You do NOT want to record the Authorization code from the credit card company on this document because of privacy concerns. Click the field, type **Visa**. $\boxed{\text{Tab}}$ $\boxed{\text{Tab}}$ to Date.

4 ➤   **Date** $\boxed{\text{Tab}}$ to accept. $\boxed{\text{Tab}}$ to Invoice Date.

5 ➤   **Invoice Date** $\boxed{\text{Tab}}$ $\boxed{\text{Tab}}$ to Amount Received.

   Discount Taken There is no discount on this invoice.(NSF cheque).

6 ➤   **Amount Received** $\boxed{\text{Tab}}$ to accept 254.25

7 ➤   **Comment**   Type **Paid by Visa Credit Card**.

The Receipt window should look like the following:

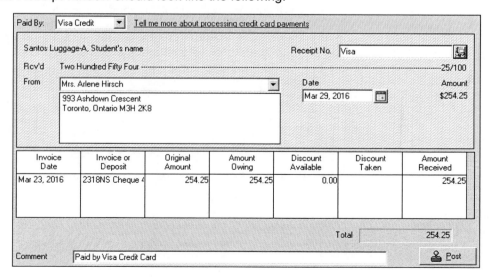

8 ➤   **Display** the Receipts Journal entry. It should resemble the following:

Receipts Journal Entry Mar 29, 2016 (J17)

Account Number	Account Description	Debits	Credits
1030	Visa Credit Card Bank Account	245.35	-
5340	Credit Card Charges	8.90	-
1200	Accounts Receivable	-	254.25
Additional Date:	Additional Field:		
		254.25	254.25

9 ➤ **Exit** from the display window and **Post** the entry when correct.

10 ➤ **Exit** to the Home window.

11 ➤ Advance Session date to **Mar 31, 2016**.

Owner Investment in Business

The owner's investment may be recorded by either of the following methods:

1. Recording a General Journal entry to show the personal investment where funds have been transferred by the bank.

2. Setting up a customer ledger with the owner's name and recording a sales invoice (using the Capital account or Additional Investment by Owner account) paid by cheque whenever the owner invests more money in the business.

Method #1 is the preferred method.

Exercise 2B-35 – Journalizing Owner Investment in Business

Mar 31, 2016 **Mrs. Santos has decided to invest an additional $6,000.00 in the business, as she is going to purchase a large number of suitcases from a company that is going out of business. She, therefore, transferred $6,000.00 from her personal bank account to the company's bank account. She brought the bank transfer form as a source document for the business.**

The General Journal method will be used to record the investment.

1 ➤ Click on the **COMPANY** module and click on the **General Journal** icon. **Record** and **Post** the investment based on the following window.

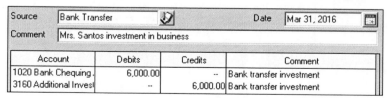

Account	Debits	Credits	Comment
1020 Bank Chequing	6,000.00	--	Bank transfer investment
3160 Additional Invest	--	6,000.00	Bank transfer investment

2 ➤ **View** the General Journal entry. The window should appear as follows:

General Journal Entry Mar 31, 2016 (J18)

Account Number	Account Description	Debits	Credits
1020	Bank Chequing Account	6,000.00	-
	Bank transfer investment		
3160	Additional Investment	-	6,000.00
	Bank transfer investment		
Additional Date:	Additional Field:		
		6,000.00	6,000.00

3 ➤   **Exit** from viewing the General Journal entry.

4 ➤   **Post** when correct and **Exit** to the Home page.

Additional Transactions

Process the following two transactions:

Mar 31, 2016	**Mrs. Santos visited the Royes Luggage Inc. store yesterday evening, and discussed the problems (conditions of goods received) with their manager. Mrs. Santos and the manager agreed that there is a problem with the goods. Mrs. Santos will give a Sales price allowance for the goods on invoice #2212, in the amount of $100.00 plus GST. Mrs. Santos received Royes Luggage Inc.'s cheque #496 in the amount of $840.00 as payment for this invoice less the allowance. There are no discount terms on this allowance as it is more than 10 days from the purchase date.**
	1. Record the allowance. **2. Record the cheque received.**

Mar 31, 2016	**Sold to Luggage 4U, to be picked up today, 5 Suitcases w/w large @$62.00 plus GST, and 4 Power Adapters @ $10.50 each plus GST. Issued invoice #2323 for $369.60 including 17.60 GST, terms 2/10 net 30 days.**

Recording a Receipt for a Non-Merchandise item

There will be situations when the business receives a cheque(s) for goods that are not being resold (e.g., sale of your old equipment, rebate cheque, etc.).

This next exercise shows you how to enter the rebate information as a cash transaction (refer to Exercise 2B-27), as an invoice is normally created for the cheque received. The name of the firm issuing the cheque will appear in journal entries.

Exercise 2B-36 – Journalizing a Non-Merchandise Cheque

Mar 31, 2016	**Mrs. Santos handed you a $10.20 mail-in-rebate cheque #2897561 that she forgot was in her briefcase. The rebate cheque is for a case of computer paper the business purchased last month from the Office Supply Store.**
	You would not create a customer ledger for the Office Supply Store as they are a vendor in the PAYABLE module.

1 ➤   Create an invoice using the **Sales Invoice**s icon.

      Transaction   Do NOT change the default Invoice.

2 ➤ **Paid by**   Select **Cheque**, [Tab].

3 ➤ **Deposit to**   Do NOT change, [Tab] to accept 1020 Bank Chequing Account.

4 ➤ **Cheque**   Type **2897561** [Tab].

5 ➤ **Sold to**   Enter the information shown next.

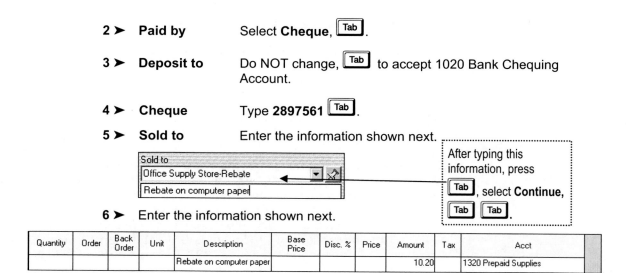

6 ➤ Enter the information shown next.

Quantity	Order	Back Order	Unit	Description	Base Price	Disc. %	Price	Amount	Tax	Acct
				Rebate on computer paper				10.20		1320 Prepaid Supplies

Tax   You will not be able to recover tax (GST or PST) on a rebate. Leave the field blank.

Acct   Select **1320 Prepaid Supplies**, as this is the account that was charged when the computer paper was purchased.

7 ➤ **Comments**   **Remove** the comments. They are not needed for a rebate. The complete Invoice window is shown next.

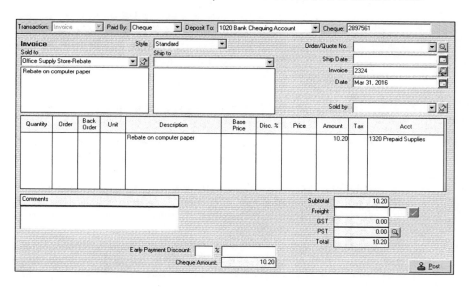

8 ➤ **View** the Sales Journal Entry. The window should appear as follows:

Sales Journal Entry Mar 31, 2016 (J22)

Account Number	Account Description	Debits	Credits
1020	Bank Chequing Account	10.20	-
1320	Prepaid Supplies	-	10.20
Additional Date:	Additional Field:		
		10.20	10.20

9 ➤ **Exit** from the display window.

10 ➤ **Post** when correct and **Exit** to the Home window.

The following would appear in the Reports, Journal Entries - All display.

> 2897561, 2324, Office Supply Store-Rebate

Printing Customer Statements

Many businesses send their customers a statement, which is a record of the transactions recorded in their account. This will give customers a chance to check their own records and investigate any invoices that do not agree. It is also a very effective reminder to customers of any overdue amounts. Statements may be printed or e-mailed for all customers or for individual customers at any time during the month.

If a firm prints statements for mailing, they can use the built in Simply Custom forms or they can purchase pre-printed forms from a printing company, which can include the company logo and will have shaded column headings for Simply to print the information that is shown in Fig. 2B-21. A brochure of various forms available is included in the software manufacturer's package. You can order the forms through Simply, or you would take the brochure to a commercial printer to have forms customized for your company. You can also e-mail a version of the statement to the customer if you have their e-mail address.

Remember that statements may be printed at any time (whenever there is a customer account inquiry, to collect an overdue account, etc.), not only at the end of the month. To reduce paper use, your instructor may request you to print only one statement (on plain paper) for an individual customer to allow you to see what will print on preprinted forms.

Exercise 2B-37 – Printing Customer Statements

For practice, you will print one customer statement on blank paper. Be sure your printer is ready.

1 ➤ From the Home window, in the **Customers** area, at **Royes Luggage Inc.**, click on ▼ and click on **View Customer Record**.

2 ➤ Click the **Options** tab.

3 ➤ Make sure the **Produce Statements for this Customer** box is (✓). Statements for customers may be printed only if this box is (✓).

4 ➤ **Exit** from the Receivables Ledger window.

There are two options for printing statements:

1. In the Tasks area click on the ▼ at **Customer's** icon, click on **View Customers**. From the menu bar, click **Reports, Customer Statements** and you will see the Customer Statements window displayed. Select **Royes Luggage Inc.** the customer who will receive the statement. With a setting of **Print**, click **OK** and the statement prints.

   Return to the Home window to see another way to print this statement.

2. From the Home window, click **Reports, Receivables, Customer Statements** and you are at the Customer Statements window.

5 ➤ Using either method, make sure the ⦿ Print button, in the top-right corner, is selected. Select **Royes Luggage Inc.**, then **OK**. The statement should print.

Your printout on plain paper should resemble Fig. 2B-21. This information will be printed on the pre-printed form, or similar information can be e-mailed to your customer.

Santos Luggage-B, Student's Name
635 Semple Avenue
Toronto, Ontario M9L 1V5

Mar 31, 2016

Royes Luggage Inc.   Royes Luggage Inc.
Julie Ann Royes
256 Ochos Blvd.
Toronto, Ontario M4K 3V3   Mar 31, 2016

Jan 31, 2016	2212	Invoice	945.00			
Mar 31, 2016	496	Payment	-945.00			
				0.00	2212	0.00
Feb 27, 2016	2256	Invoice	1,155.00			
Mar 03, 2016	438	Discount	-22.00			
Mar 03, 2016	438	Payment	-1,133.00			
				0.00	2256	0.00
Mar 10, 2016	2317	Invoice		1,492.05	2317	1,492.05
Mar 31, 2016	2212AI	Invoice	-105.00			
Mar 31, 2016	496	Payment	105.00			
				0.00	2212AI	0.00

Current	31-60	Over 60		
1,492.05	0.00	0.00	1,492.05	1,492.05

Fig. 2B-21: Customer Statement information printed on pre-printed forms.

Notice how Simply displays information for sales (Invoices) and receipts (Payment and Discount). Information for invoice #2212 is shown in two places (2212AI) as the report lists invoices by date order.

Be sure to back up your data and update your logbook at the end of every work session.

Printing Period-End Reports

The following reports may be printed for management's information and for filing for the audit trail.

- Journal Entries may be printed in one of two ways (see Exercise 1-17).

  a) **Journal Entries All** will print all journal entries from all modules (with or without corrections). All transactions, in the time-period requested, are numbered in this journal in sequential order (even if entered in a subledger; i.e., RECEIVABLES or PAYABLES module).

  b) **General Journal Entries** will print journal entries entered in the COMPANY module only.

- The General Ledger — complete general ledger listing of transactions for the month.

- The Receivable Sales Journal for the month.

- The Receivable Receipts Journal for the month.

- The Balance Sheet as at March 31.

- The Income Statement for the year to March 31.

- The Customer Aged Detail report.

- The Aged Overdue Receivables Detail.

- The GST Report — all transactions in the month with GST are shown in this report (see Appendix CD-D for more information).

1 ➤ To save time and paper, **print** only the following:

a) All Journal entries, with corrections Mar 07 to Mar 31
b) General Journal entries   Mar 07 to Mar 31
c) Income Statement for period   Jan 01 to Mar 31
d) Income Statement for period   Mar 07 to Mar 31 for Sales Manager. Hide details of Cost of Goods Sold and Office/Warehouse Expenses.
e) Balance Sheet at   Mar 31
f) Customer Aged Detail report at   Mar 31
g) General Ledger   Mar 07 to Mar 31

Your instructor may request printouts of the Sales and/or Cash Receipts Journals.

2 ➤ Compare the amount in the ACCOUNTS RECEIVABLE account on the Balance Sheet with the Customer Aged Detail total balance. They should be the same!

3 ➤ Compare your printouts with the RECEIVABLE data files for Santos Luggage provided on the Solutions Disk with your instructor.

As you were going through the lessons earlier, you learned how to print some of the reports above. Instructions for reports that you have not printed earlier follow.

Exercise 2B-38 – To Print Period-End Reports

To Print a Gross Margin Income Statement

The **Gross Margin Income Statement** can also be called the **Gross Profit Income Statement** and is an income statement that breaks down Expenses into two categories; **Cost of Goods Sold** (takes into account items that refer to goods purchased for resale) and **Expenses** (referred to as purchases of goods/services not for resale).

1 ➤ Click **Report Centre**, click **Financials**, click the **+** at Income Statement, select **Gross Margin – Standard**, click **Modify this Report**.

2 ➤ The Start and Finish dates should be **Jan. 01, 2016** and **March 31, 2016**. You can change the dates to display the report for different dates. Click **OK** to display the Income Statement.

3 ➤ Click the **Print** icon to print the report. Note the change in wording for various lines; Net Sales and Total Revenue to: TOTAL REVENUE and TOTAL OPERATING REVENUE. A GROSS MARGIN line has been added and the information below the Total Expenses line. Refer to your accounting textbook for discussion of these changes as this text does not explain the various changes.

4 ➤ **Exit** from the display window.

To Print the Sales Journal

1 ➤ Click **Report Centre**, move to **Receivables, Sales Journal Entries.** Click **Modify this Report.** The **Start date** should be **Mar 07, 2016** (the day the file was started). If required, click Modify, Report Options, to add or remove the ✓ at Corrections. Click **OK** to display the sales journal entries.

2 ➤ Click the **Print** icon to print the report.

3 ➤ **Exit** from the display window.

To Print the Receipts Journal

1 ➤ Click **Report Centre,** move to **Receivables, Receipt Journal Entries.** Click **Modify this Report**. The **Start date** should be **Mar 07, 2016** (the day the file was started). If required, click Modify, Report Options, to add or remove the ✓ at Corrections.

2 ➤ Click the **Print** icon to print the report.

3 ➤ **Exit** from the display window.

View/Print Graphs

Simply also has a Graph feature that allows you to view and/or print your data in graph format.

 Additional information on using the graph feature (pie and bar charts) can be found in Appendix CD-K, *Graphs Feature* on the Student Data CD.

Exercise 2B-39 – Viewing/Printing Graphs

To View Graphs

1 ➤ From the Home page, click **Graphs** from the menu bar.

2 ➤ Click Receivables **by Customer**, **Select All**, **OK**. A pie chart will display.

The Generated on date will correspond to the date you display the graph.

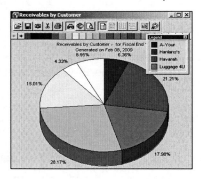

3 ➤ At this point, you may print the graph by clicking the **Print** button. The Legend will not print with the graph.

4 ➤ **Exit** from the graph display.

Summary, Part B

Here is a summary of the transactions entered in Chapter 2B.

Transaction:	Journal/Ledger	Remarks:
Deposit	*Receipts*	Enter a deposit when you receive a partial payment with the Sales Order.
Cash Sale	*Sales*	Select **Transaction Invoice** and **Paid by: Cash/Cheque** with Payments; **One-time Customer,** or type the **customer's name** in the Sold to field and click **Continue**, for an automatic cash/cheque sale.

Credit Card Sale	*Sales*	Select **Transaction Invoice**, and choose the Credit Card Company in the **Paid by** drop-down box.
Write-off	*Sales*	Enter write-off as a minus amount with GST.
NSF cheque	*Sales*	Enter a revised invoice or new invoice for the original cheque (plus bank charges) with ***no*** taxes. Select the **Cash in Bank** account *(not* Sales).
Post-dated cheques	*Receipts*	The post-dated entry (debit Bank, credit Accounts Receivable) will not appear in reports until the date the cheque is deposited. More information is found in the Appendix folder CD-M *Post-Dated Cheques* on the Student Data CD.
Revise an Invoice		Use **Lookup** to find the original invoice and adjust with the corrected amounts. Can also be seen in Chapter 13.

Review **Slideshows 2A** and **2B**.

Before Moving On..., Part B

Read the following questions and make sure you know the answers to them; otherwise, review the corresponding section in the chapter before moving on.

1. What is a deposit? In what circumstances would a business require a deposit? Where do you record the deposit?

2. Which of the following business events does not need a negative amount to record the transaction?

   a) A retail sale invoice for a pair of sunglasses was issued for $172.89 ($153.00 plus taxes) and should have been issued for the correct amount of $152.55 ($135.00 plus taxes).
   b) Write off a customer balance due to the bankruptcy of the customer.
   c) Record a sale with PST and GST to a customer.
   d) Return of an unopened DVD movie by a customer.
   e) None of the other choices.

3. How would you record a senior's discount?

4. Give the journal entry (or entries) for a $210.00 NSF cheque for which the bank has added bank charges of $15.00 (no GST) to your company bank statement. Indicate the Simply module in which the entry is made.

5. What is a customer account write-off? In what circumstances would a business write off a customer account?

6. A customer wants to pay an outstanding invoice $315.00 (which includes $15.00 of GST) with a credit card. Which Journal would you use to record it and what entry is made in the accounting records assuming the bank charges 3% for processing credit cards?

7. Your manager would like you to prepare a Gross Margin Income Statement. What is it?

8. How do you record a Quantity discount for a good customer?

Challenge Exercise 02 C2B-1, Brides

RECEIVABLES and COMPANY Modules

1 ➤ Refer to Exercise 1-1 to unzip the **02 C2B-1 Brides.exe** file.

2 ➤ Open the **02 C2B-1 Brides** file and enter Receivable transactions for May for a company that sells bridal gowns, other dresses, and accessories. GST is 5%. Retail customers are charged 8% PST. Brides Company does not print Sales invoices or receipts.

Note: All sales are personally picked up; therefore, leave 'Shipped by' field blank.

May 3   Issued Sales Order #30 to Marlene's Bridal Fashions for 4 pink bridesmaid dresses. Each dress will sell for $410.00, plus GST. Accept default terms 2/10, net 30. Total order $1,722.00. Delivery date will be May 27.

May 3   Received cheque #689 ($3,090.00 net of $60.00 discount) as payment in full from Bev's Bridal Shop re outstanding invoice #381.

May 5   Retail sale to credit card customer Navneet Banwait of 1 bridal gown for $1,200.00 and 4 accessories at $30.00 each (all items plus GST and PST). Credit card authorization #D1962 for $1,491.60.

May 6   Sold 3 bridal gowns to Brenda's Dresses at $800.00 each, plus GST. Terms 2/10, net 30 days. Invoice total $2,520.00.

May 9   Sold 3 bridal gowns at $800.00 each and 10 accessories at $25.00 each, plus GST, to new customer, **Your Actual Name Dresses**, contact **Your Actual Name**, 967 Spadina Street, Markville, Ontario, L3X 2Z9. Phone and fax number are 905-826-3820. Credit limit will be $5,000.00 with terms of 2/10, net 30 days, PST tax code ID is L38-126. Invoice total $2,782.50.

May 14 **Your Actual Name Dresses** returned 10 accessories, as the customers did not like the style. Return accepted, and credit note referring to invoice #784 sent to customer.

May 19 Sold a dress at $250.00, plus PST and GST, to Mrs. Petra Kurek, a senior citizen, for an engagement party. Mrs. Kurek qualifies for the 10% senior's discount. Use any of the methods discussed in the chapter. Cheque #556 received.

May 19 **Your Actual Name Dresses** cheque #613 as payment in full was received.

May 24 The bank advised that Mrs. Kurek's cheque #556 for $254.25 was returned "Account Closed." Mrs. Kurek was contacted and she will be sending a certified cheque to cover the error.

May 24 A new customer, Saira Heggie (any address information is acceptable), ordered a $900.00, plus GST and PST, cream wedding dress to be delivered by June 12. Sales Order #31 was issued and a $300.00 cheque #134 was received as a deposit. Leave discount terms blank.

May 25 The pink bridesmaid dresses ordered on sales order #30 arrived and were picked up by Marlene's Bridal Fashions. Invoice amount per the May 3 order.

May 31 The owner, Mrs. Mehta, gave you a bank transfer for $4,000.00 which is for her additional investment in the business.

> If an Additional Investment account does not exist in the Chart of Accounts, use the Capital Account for the investment.

3 ➤ When you have recorded the above entries, print the following:

    a.   Customer Aged Detail Report as at May 31
    b.   Journal Entries All, for the monthly activity
    c.   Journal Entries-General, for the monthly activity
    d.   Sales Journal for May
    e.   Cash Receipts Journal for May
    f.   Income Statement for May 1 to May 31

Challenge Exercise 02 C2B-2, Skis

RECEIVABLES and COMPANY Modules

1 ➤ Refer to Exercise 1-1 to unzip the **02 C2B-2 Skis.exe** file.

2 ➤ Open the **02 C2B-2 Skis** file and enter Receivable and General Ledger transactions for March for a company that sells skis and related sporting equipment. GST is 5%. Retail customers are charged 8% PST.

Note: All sales are personally picked up; therefore leave 'Shipped by' field blank.

Mar 2　Retail sale of 1 pair of Blanchard skis and bindings $550.00 plus taxes to Miss Devon Cutronia. Received her Universal credit card for payment.

Mar 3　Issued Sales Order #212 to Jordan's Sports Equipment for 10 Jock SnowBoards at $500.00 each plus GST. Snowboards shipping date will be March 31, terms 2/10, net 30 days. (Note special price for long-time customer.)

Mar 5　Owner Hong Duaog invested an additional $5,000 in the business. Received a bank transfer showing the money was put in the bank account today.

Mar 5　Sold to Mr. Lopez a package containing 1 pair of used skis, bindings, and poles for $300.00 plus taxes. Mr. Lopez produced a senior card from a competitor and the manager allowed a 10% senior's discount. Cheque #326 received.

Mar 6　As a new customer, **Your actual Last (Family) name Skiing Lodge** (add any address and PST tax code, ID S39-454) ordered and received 3 Jock SnowBoards at $510.00 and 3 ski goggles (glasses) at $60.00 each. All items plus GST. Credit limit $7,000 and terms 2/10, net 30.

Mar 9　**Your actual Last (Family) name Skiing Lodge** returned 1 Jock SnowBoard ($510.00 plus GST) because it has a tiny crack in the middle. The board has not been used and the manager approved a credit to the account.

Mar 16　Sold one set of ski poles to Mr. Obi for $56.00 plus taxes. Received his cheque #985 in full payment. This customer is moving at the end of April to Edmonton.

Mar 16　Received cheque #638 from **Your actual Last (Family) name Skiing Lodge** as payment on the goods ordered on the 6th and the return on the 9th.

Mar 23　Bank advised that Mr. Obi's cheque #985 was returned NSF. Sent registered letter to Mr. Obi. The mailing address was on the cheque.

Mar 26　Received a $13.10 bank debit memo for bank service charges to Mar. 23.

Mar 31　Only 8 snowboards ordered by Jordan's Sports Equipment on the 3rd arrived. The other 2 Jock SnowBoards are to be delivered within 5 days. Called Jordan's and they agreed to receive the 8 boards we received. Issued next sales invoice for this order, and the company picked up the boards.

3 ➤ When you have recorded the above entries, print the following:

    a.　Customer Aged Detail report as at Mar 31
    b.　Journal Entries All, for the monthly activity
    c.　Journal Entries-General, for the monthly activity
    d.　Income Statement for the year-to-date activity, for the Sales Manager. Hide appropriate information.
    e.　Sales Journal

Challenge Exercise 02 C2B-3, House Sitters

RECEIVABLES and COMPANY Modules

House Sitters is a business that looks after your house or apartment while you are away. The business waters plants, looks after pets, makes sure the furnace, water heater and air conditioning are working, and brings in the mail and newspapers, etc.

House Sitters Company does *NOT* print Sales invoices or receipts.

Note: All invoices are left at the residence or business on the day the client returns. Terms are varied for different customers. GST is 5%, and PST is exempt for all customers.

1 ➤ Refer to Exercise 1-1 to unzip the **02 C2B-3 Sitters.exe** file.

2 ➤ For this review assignment open the **02 C2B-3 Sitters** file, and enter the following Accounts Receivable transactions for May.

May 1   Completed 4-day sitting for Hagos Aulakh at $30.00 plus GST per day. Invoice #177, in the amount of $126.00 with terms of net 5 days.

May 3   Received $94.50, cheque #752, as payment from Winston Chun re outstanding invoice #170.

May 6   Left $94.50 invoice #178, at Mr. & Mrs. Thomas Royes' home for service for three days at $30.00 plus GST per day. Terms net 5 days.

May 6   Received $126.00, cheque #829 from Mr. Hagos Aulakh for invoice #177.

May 9   Received $94.50, cheque #256 from Mr. & Mrs. Thomas Royes as payment for invoice #178.

May 10 Completed 2-day sitting for Mrs. Manpreet Foss at $30.00 plus GST per day. Invoice #179, in the amount of $63.00 with terms of net 3 days, left in the house.

May 12 Mrs. Foss came to the office and paid invoice #179 in full with $63.00 cash.

May 18 A new business client, **Your Actual Name Ceramics**, requested us to check her store 3 times a day at $30.00 plus GST per visit. She will be out of town May 19 and 20 for a family function. Other information: 889 Ancaster Avenue, Stoney Creek, Ontario A0A 3C3, phone and fax numbers may be left blank. Terms are 2%, 10 days, net 30. (Special terms arranged for business clients.) Credit limit $200.00.

May 20 Left invoice #180 for $189.00 in the office at the back of **Your Actual Name Ceramics** store.

May 28 Received **Your Actual Name Ceramics** cheque #158 in the amount of $185.40 as payment in full for invoice #180 with $3.60 discount taken.

May 31 Completed 2-day sitting for Hagos Aulakh at $30.00 plus GST per day. Invoice #181 issued for $63.00 with terms net 5 days.

3 ➤ When you have recorded the above entries, **print** the following:
- a. Customer Aged Detail Report as at May 31
- b. Journal Entries All, for May 1 to 31
- c. Sales Journal for May 1 to 31
- d. Cash Receipts Journal for May 1 to 31
- e. Income Statement for Jan 1 to May 31

Mini-guide for Transactions in Chapter 2

Mini-guide for transactions in Simply Accounting Premium 2009***
Not all types of transactions listed here.

***Study Suggestion - Add additional transactions from your chapters.

Receivable Events	Entry	Module	Journal	Comments	You fill in the Text Ref
Customer asks for price quote	No entry	RECEIVABLE	Sales, Orders & Quotes	No sale, customer asking for prices	
Customer confirms quote & places order for later delivery	No entry	RECEIVABLE	Sales, Orders & Quotes	No sale, price confirmed for future delivery	
Sale of Merchandise	A/Rec	RECEIVABLE	Sales, Orders & Quotes	may be preceded by sales quote	
	Sales			may be preceded by sales order	
	GST collected on Sales			may be a sale without prior quote or order	
Sales Rtn of Merchandise	Sales Rtns & Allowances	RECEIVABLE	Sales, Orders & Quotes	Add "Rt" to invoice number	
	GST collected on Sales			If credit memo listed, then add "CMxxx"	
	A/Rec				
Receipt (no discount)	Cash	RECEIVABLE	Receipts	-can be partial or full receipt	
	A/Rec			-can be after a return	
Receipt, with discount	Cash	RECEIVABLE	Receipts	-full receipt	
	Sales Discount			-can be after a return	
	A/Rec				

* Note: Refer to the CD-V *Mini-guide* on the Student Data CD.

Accounting and Simply Accounting Terminology

Advice: A detachable form on a cheque that provides the business receiving the cheque with details of the payment.

Aging: A process of sorting Accounts Receivable transactions in predefined categories: 30, 60, or 90 days based on the current session date; e.g., an invoice dated 26 days before the session date would appear in the "30 day" column in the Accounts Receivable Customer Aged report.

Backordered: Goods or merchandise ordered by a customer, but currently not in stock. The sales order will be filled at a later date when stock is available.

Cash Sale: Sale for which cash is received. In many businesses these sales are recorded in a cash register and are summarized daily.

Codes: Abbreviations of words to indicate action taken. The code Rv indicates a reversal; the code Rt indicates a return item. (See Exercise 2A-14.)

Credit memo: A memo similar to an invoice sent to customers to advise them that the amount owed to your company has been reduced as a result of a return of goods or price reductions.

Debit memo: A memo similar to an invoice sent to customers to advise them that the amount owed to your company has increased, usually as a result of errors in the original invoice, price changes that were overlooked in the original invoice, or extra charges for NSF cheques.

Deposit: 1) A sum of money paid in advance by customers for a guarantee that goods will be reserved for them. 2) Required of a new customer who has not yet established a good credit rating. 3) From a regular customer who has had trouble making payments on previous orders. May also be referred to as **Prepayment**.

Gross Margin Income Statement: Is an Income Statement that breaks down the Expenses into two categories; **Cost of Goods Sold** and **Expenses**. The Gross Margin Income Statement can also be called the **Gross Profit Income Statement**.

GST: **G**oods and **S**ervices **T**ax. *See notes below and Chapter 15 *Taxes*.

Invoice: A bill sent or given to a customer for goods or services sold.

Merchandise: Goods that were purchased or manufactured by a company for the purpose of resale.

NSF: **N**ot-**S**ufficient **F**unds: A bank advice that a cheque received from a customer and deposited in your bank account was returned because the customer did not have enough money in their bank account to cover the cheque. You would ask the customer to issue a new cheque.

Prepayment: See *Deposit*.

PST: **P**rovincial **S**ales **T**ax. Companies selling to the public have to collect PST, except from companies involved in wholesale distribution and which have an exemption licence.

Sales Order: A form issued to a customer to confirm that the goods or services listed on the Sales Quote are acceptable and will be shipped as indicated on the Sales Order form.

Sales Quote: A form requested by a customer advising them of selling price(s) for goods (merchandise) or services.

Sales Returns: Goods returned by customers for a number of reasons; e.g., wrong goods delivered, damaged goods received, etc.

Terms (of Sale): The time allowed for a customer to pay an invoice; e.g., **net 30 days** to pay the full amount within 30 days or **2%/10, net 30.** This means that a 2% discount will be given if paid within 10 days; if not, the full amount is due within 30 days.

Write-off: Journal entry to reduce an outstanding balance from a customer's account, when the amount is no longer collectable for any reason; e.g., the customer is bankrupt or refuses to pay the amount. *Note:* A part or the full amount of the outstanding amount may be written off.

GST/PST Summary

Price *plus* GST and PST (Simply Tax code GP) means the goods are being purchased for personal use. This is considered a retail sale and both taxes (GST and PST) are charged. For an item valued at $200.00, add 5% GST ($200.00 x 5% = $10.00) and add 8% PST ($200.00 x 8% = $16.00), total invoice price = $226.00.

Price *plus* GST (Simply Tax code G) means the GST must be added to the invoice price amount; e.g., for an item valued at $200.00, add 5% GST ($200.00 x 5% = $10.00) total invoice amount = $210.00.

Relevant Appendices, Part B

The following appendices are available on the Student Data CD.

Appendix 2009 CD-D	**Printing a Tax (GST) Report**
Appendix 2009 CD-F	**Printing in Batches**
Appendix 2009 CD-G	**Processing in Batches**
Appendix 2009 CD-K	**Graphs Feature**
Appendix 2009 CD-M	**Post-Dated Cheques**
Appendix 2009 CD-U	**Adding Notes/Footer to Statements**
Appendix 2009 CD-V	**Mini-Guide Receivables—Payables**

Chapter 3A

PAYABLES Module—Part A

Tyson's Toys

Learning Objectives

After completing this chapter you will be able to:

☐ Record purchase orders, invoices and returns.
☐ Add new vendors and make changes to existing vendors.
☐ Record payments to vendors in full or partial payment of invoices with or without cash discounts.
☐ Record payments to other suppliers.
☐ Display and print various payable reports (vendor balances outstanding, etc.) and journals.

Note: After finishing Chapter 3A and Chapter 8, you can complete selected transactions from Chapter 3A, using the Perpetual INVENTORY & SERVICES module. See Challenge Exercise 08 C8-5 Toys-PI.

The contents of this chapter are as follows:

The PAYABLES Module Overview

The PAYABLES module consists of the Vendors Ledger, the Purchase Quotes (Tyson's Toys does not use the Purchase Quotes Journal), Purchase Orders, Purchase Invoices and the Payments Journals. The Vendors Ledger is the same as the Accounts Payable (A/P) subledger in a manual accounting system.

Purchase Quotes and Purchase Orders are recorded (not posted) in the database. Purchase Invoices and Payments Journal transactions are posted to the individual vendor ledger accounts and to the linked accounts in the General Ledger.

The following transactions are normally recorded in the **Purchase** journals:

- Purchase quotes, purchase orders, and/or purchase invoices on credit from vendors (suppliers).

- Prepayments with a purchase order.

- Purchases on company credit card.

The following are recorded in the **Payments** journal:

- Payments to vendors (suppliers):
  - partial payment of an invoice.
  - full payment of an invoice with discount.
  - full payment, no discount.
  - cash purchase paid with a cheque, credit card or ATM card.

- Payments for expenses: all other payments such as rent, electricity, water bills, owner drawings, tax payments (GST/PST) to the government, etc.

At any time, reports (e.g., Aged Vendor reports, etc.) can be produced that show the balances that are payable to vendors. Remember, the total of all payable balances to vendors must match the balance of the ACCOUNTS PAYABLE account in the General Ledger.

In working with the PAYABLES module, you must be very careful in determining the difference between purchases of **goods for resale** (also referred to as merchandise) and purchases of **services or goods not for resale**.

Slideshow 3A – PAYABLES Part A is designed to help you understand how the PAYABLES module works and the GAAP related to it. Notice the similarities (and differences) between the RECEIVABLES and PAYABLES modules. Run the slideshow now.

Company Profile – Tyson's Toys

Jerry Tyson and his wife, Helen, owners of Tyson's Toys, sell wooden toys for children from a store in the local mall. Helen works in the store and also travels to toy conventions in search of new toys to sell in their store and to promote their business.

Only the COMPANY and PAYABLES modules, for the month of April, are used in the following exercises in this chapter Parts A and B.

Jerry normally waits until the last day of the invoice terms to pay for goods purchased on credit. Helen has been trying to get him to pay the outstanding invoices so that he can take advantage of the 2% discount. However, he has been focusing on selling the toys rather than good money management. With your help he can manage the business more effectively.

In Part A, Tyson's Toys uses the data folder **03 3A Toys-A**. Cost of ending inventory is calculated monthly using the **Periodic** method.

The business does not use the Track Additional Details feature to record information.

Study Tyson's Trial Balance.

Tyson's Toys-A, Student's Name
Trial Balance As At Mar 31, 2016

		Debits	Credits
1010	Bank Account	11,425.00	-
1020	Bank Account US funds	580.60	-
1200	Accounts Receivable	12,899.00	-
1310	Toys and parts Inventory	6,907.29	-
1330	Prepaid Office Supplies, etc.	625.00	-
1340	Prepaid Insurance	0.00	-
1510	Store Equipment	25,138.45	-
1515	Accum. Amort. Store Equipment	-	12,136.00
1520	Office Furniture/Equipment	2,812.60	-
1525	Accum. Amort. Office/Furniture/Equi	-	1,605.00
2200	Accounts Payable	-	9,924.09
2210	Visa Credit Card Payable	-	0.00
2550	GST Charged On Sales	-	1,738.25
2560	GST Paid On Purchases	650.14	-
2580	PST Payable	-	65.08
2610	Bank Loan Payable	-	14,310.86
3100	Capital Jerry Tyson	-	11,924.65
3120	Drawings Jerry Tyson	3,500.00	-
3200	Capital Helen Tyson	-	11,924.65
3210	Drawings Helen Tyson	3,500.00	-
4100	Sales	-	34,126.00
4150	Sales - Discount	212.30	-
4200	Sales - Returns & Allowances	604.00	-
5010	Beginning Inventory	5,421.49	-
5040	Purchases	18,408.80	-
5050	Purchases Returns	-	300.00
5080	Purchase Discounts	-	289.80
5090	Ending Inventory	-	6,907.29
5310	Rent Expense	6,000.00	-
5340	Advertising Expense	516.00	-
5345	Bank Loan Interest	301.00	-
5350	Bank Charges	135.00	-
5355	Credit Card Charges	0.00	-
5360	Insurance Expense	303.00	-
5370	Auto Lease Expense	1,200.00	-
5440	Office/Store Supplies Expense	750.00	-
5450	Telephone Expense	912.00	-
5460	Utility Expense	1,250.00	-
5470	Bad Debts Expense	0.00	-
5480	Delivery Expense	1,200.00	-
		105,251.67	105,251.67

Fig. 3A-1: Trial Balance, Tyson's Toys-A.

Session Date

In Chapter 2 (A and B) you entered transactions for Santos Luggage at various times and advanced the Session Date as needed. Tyson's Toys has adopted a policy of entering its Accounts Payable transactions on a daily basis, unless you, the clerk, are not available.

Advance the Session Date as noted in the instructions for each exercise.

Starting Simply for Payables

Exercise 3A-1 – Opening the PAYABLES Module

1 ➤ Refer to Exercise 1-1 to unzip the **03 3A Toys-A.exe** file.

2 ➤ Start **Simply Accounting**.

3 ➤ At the Select Company window, click **Select an existing company** button and **OK**.

4 ➤ At the **Simply Accounting - Open Company** window, in the **Look in** box, locate your student location drive, and the Toys folder ▢ 03 3A Toys-A .

5 ➤ Double-click the ▢ 03 3A Toys-A folder and the ▢ Toys-A.SAI will appear in the box below. (The image at the left of Toys may be different depending on the configuration of your computer and the SDB may be in lower case sdb.)

🛈

Review Exercise 1-2 if you need help to open a data file.

6 ➤ Click the ▢ Toys-A.SAI icon. The **File name** box will change to Toys-A.SAI.

7 ➤ Click **Open** to open the Toys-A file.

8 ➤ The **Session Date** window will be **Mar 31, 2016**. Click **OK**.

Study the Toys Home window. The other modules are hidden.

The Vendor ledger does not have the **History** (quill pen) symbol. This indicates that this ledger with journals is ready to use.

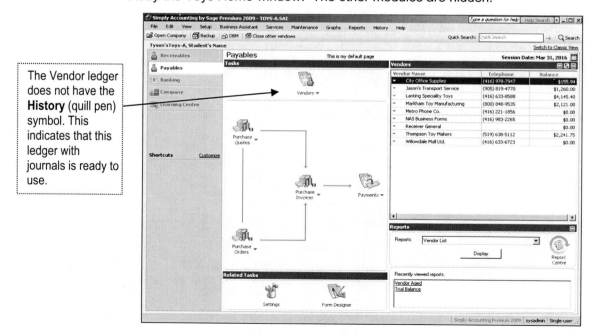

Fig. 3A-2: Toys-A Home window.

9 ➤ Remember to revise your company information to add ***your name*** to the company information in order to have your name printed on your printouts. Refer to Exercise 1-4 if you need help. **This is the last reminder. It is assumed you will add your name to each of the company records from here on.**

To Display the Vendor Aged Report

As in the RECEIVABLES module, you can find out the status of the company payables by displaying and/or printing the Vendor Aged Report. Similarly, Simply groups payables calculated from the date of the invoice to the current Session Date. It provides a list of accounts that are **Current**, **31 to 60** days overdue, **61 to 90** days overdue, and **91+** days overdue.

Also, as in the RECEIVABLES module, Simply provides two options: **Summary** and **Detail**. Your choice depends on the purpose for which you need the reports. At this point, if you wish to acquaint yourself with the balances owing to vendors, and which vendor invoices are overdue, you would select **Detail**. In the next exercise you will display the Detail Vendor Aged report.

When printing this report, it is important that the **Session Date** is correct; otherwise, the aging will not be accurate.

Exercise 3A-2 – Displaying the Detail Vendor Aged Report

---

1 ➤ From the menu bar click **Reports**, **Payables**, **Vendor Aged**, **Detail** should be selected. If necessary, **Select All** to highlight all Vendors in blue, click **OK**.

Compare the window display to Fig. 3A-3. Notice that the screen shows columns that are based on the age of the invoices. As in the RECEIVABLES module, the aging schedule can be changed. This is covered in Chapter 4. Notice that the Detail Report has the session date (As at date) on which the aging of invoices is based.

← As at date

Vendor Aged Detail As at Mar 31, 2016

Source	Date	Transaction Type	Total	Current	31 to 60	61 to 90	91+
City Office Supplies							
1235	Mar 02, 2016	Invoice	155.94	155.94	-	-	-
Total outstanding:			155.94	155.94	-	-	-
Jason's Transport Service							
6691	Mar 01, 2016	Invoice	1,260.00	1,260.00	-	-	-
Total outstanding:			1,260.00	1,260.00	-	-	-
Lanting Speciality Toys							
6198	Feb 22, 2016	Invoice	982.80	-	982.80	-	-
6211	Feb 25, 2016	Invoice	3,162.60	-	3,162.60	-	-
Total outstanding:			4,145.40	-	4,145.40	-	-
Markham Toy Manufacturing							
1622	Mar 22, 2016	Invoice	1,073.10	1,073.10	-	-	-
1638	Mar 30, 2016	Invoice	1,047.90	1,047.90	-	-	-
Total outstanding:			2,121.00	2,121.00	-	-	-
Thompson Toy Makers							
886	Mar 15, 2016	Invoice	2,241.75	2,241.75	-	-	-
Total outstanding:			2,241.75	2,241.75	-	-	-
Total unpaid invoices:			9,924.09	5,778.69	4,145.40	-	-
Total prepayments/prepaid order:			-	-	-	-	-
Total outstanding:			9,924.09	5,778.69	4,145.40	-	-

Fig. 3A-3: Tyson's Vendor Aged Detail window.

As in the RECEIVABLES module, the aged report will show the total for each vendor when there are two or more invoices listed.

2 ➤   Exit from the display window.

To Display and Print the Income Statement

As part of your task in getting acquainted with the company, you would display and/or print the Income Statement.

Exercise 3A-3 – To Display/Print Income Statement & Balance Sheet

---

1 ➤   Display and **print** the **Year-to-date Income Statement** with start and end dates of **Jan 01, 2016** and **Mar 31, 2016**. Keep this printout because you will be using it to compare with the Income Statement printed at Exercise 3B-33. Do Not Hide any amounts.

2 ➤   Display and **print** the **Balance Sheet at Mar 31, 2016**. Keep this printout because you will be using it to calculate the GST amounts in Exercise 3B-30. Do Not Hide any amounts.

Vendor Invoices Guidelines and Procedures

Tyson's Toys follow common accounting procedures in processing transactions in the PAYABLES module.

When journalizing vendor invoices in the Purchases Journal, you must know to which G/L account the purchase should be charged. The following guidelines are used by Tyson's Toys:

*   Toys and parts purchased, to be sold to customers (stores and retail), are charged to **PURCHASES**.

*   Other payables (rent, advertising, utilities: water, gas, electricity, etc.) are charged to the appropriate expense account.

*   Any goods or services paid for in advance (e.g., office supplies, insurance, etc.) are charged to a **PREPAID ASSET** account.

When a purchase invoice is received, the invoice is usually stamped on the back with the date of receipt and an approval stamp (see Fig. 3A-11).

The purchase invoice is then sent to a department manager or other supervisor who is authorized to approve payment and will assign a G/L account number to the amount(s) purchased. It is then signed or initialed, dated, and sent to the accounting department for recording and issuing of the cheque. The owner, Jerry Tyson, would then review the relevant documents and sign the cheque(s) for payment.

Companies that buy items for resale do not pay PST on the goods. This is called buying **PST-Exempt**. The business receives a PST tax-exemption number from the government and must inform the seller of this number. Remember that the seller does not charge PST to PST-exempt companies.

The PAYABLES Journals

The PAYABLES Module has four journals: **Purchase Quotes, Purchase Orders, Purchase Invoices** and **Payments Journals**. The following options are available in the Purchase Journals when entering transactions:

Purchase Quotes   used to record a form received from a vendor indicating the price of products or services that they will sell the product or service to you. Tyson's Toys does not use this Journal.

Purchase Orders (PO)   used to record a confirmation of a commitment to purchase. You would normally send a copy of the purchase order to a vendor. You may record a purchase order although there is no purchase quote recorded earlier.

The following options are available in the Home page in the Purchase Journal – Purchase Invoices when entering transactions:

Create Invoice   used to enter a purchase on account (credit). A purchase quote and/or a purchase order may or may not have been issued earlier. When a purchase invoice is posted, an accounting entry is recorded affecting both General Ledger and Payables subsidiary ledger accounts.

Find Invoice   look up a posted invoice.

Adjust Invoice   using a negative invoice, this is used to record a return of goods or an adjustment to the purchase price, also called a **Debit Memo**. Similar to the Create Invoice option above, when an Adjustment invoice is posted, an accounting entry is recorded affecting both General Ledger and Payables subsidiary ledger accounts.

When entering the Purchase Journal – Purchase Invoice window, the following option is available.

Invoice-Paid by (Chapter 3, Part B)   You can also record a purchase with Paid by: Cash, Cheque or Visa Credit card.

The following options are available in the Payments Journal icon when entering transactions:

Pay Purchase Invoices   used to record payments to vendors for invoices previously recorded using the Purchase Invoice-Pay Later option.

Pay Credit Card Bills   used to record payments where a credit card is used for invoices previously recorded. Tyson's Toys does not use this feature.

Pay Expenses   used to record payments for invoices or debit/credit memos that have not been recorded previously; e.g., rent, drawings, purchase paid by cash, cheque, credit card or bank card. Previously known as: Make Other Payment.

Pay Remittances (Chapter 3, Part B)   used to record payments for payroll deductions (e.g., CPP, EI, and Income Tax.

When entering the Payments Journal window, you can record a payment with the following options. Note: they are spelled differently than above.

Type   Pay Purchase Invoices, Pay Credit Card Bill, Make Other Payment (Pay Expenses from home window) and Pay Remittance.

Paid by (Chapter 3, Part B)   You can also record a payment by: Cash, Cheque or Visa Credit card.

The Purchase Orders Journal

This journal is intended to look like a future invoice, and is used to record purchase quotes. Purchase orders and purchase invoices windows are similar. Similar windows were seen in sales quotes, sales orders and sales invoices in the RECEIVABLES module.

Similar to the Sales Journal, when you record entries in the Purchases Journal, you enter only one part of the entry. The program knows you are in the PAYABLES module and will automatically debit or credit the Accounts Payable account and appropriate taxes.

Customizing the Purchase Orders Journal

As with the Sales Journals, you may also customize the Purchase Journals. Tyson's Toys uses the **Periodic Inventory** method, and does not need the **Item** and **Allo** columns. In this exercise, you will customize the Purchase Orders journal by removing the Item and Allo columns. You were shown how to do this in Exercise 2A-3.

Exercise 3A-4 – Customizing the Purchase Orders Journal

---

1 ➤ Advance the Session date to **Apr 01, 2016**.

2 ➤ As in the RECEIVABLE module, you can click the ▼ to see the choices available. Click the **Purchase Orders** icon and the Purchase Order window displays.

3 ➤ Click the **Customize** icon, click on **Columns**. Make sure a ✓ appears in the **Item Number** (the Account field is grayed out) and **Allocations** fields do not display these columns.

4 ➤ Click **OK** when you are finished.

5 ➤ Type the following into the columns shown. Resize the columns as shown in Exercise 2A-3.

Quantity	Order	Back Order	Unit	Description	Price	Tax	GST	PST	Amount	Acct
				Cheques Special Order						1330 Prepaid Office Supplies

Fig. 3A-4: Customized Purchases Journal window (after sizing).

6 ➤ When you have the columns to this approximate size, click the ↰ and you will see the following.

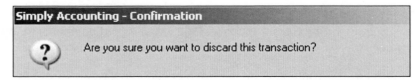

7 ➤ Select **Yes** to return to the Purchase Order window.

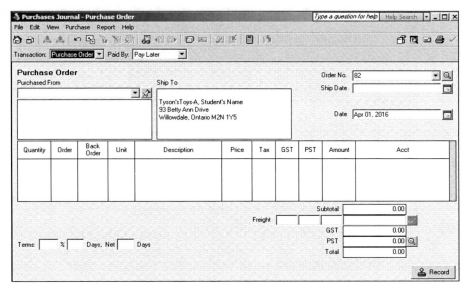

Fig. 3A-5: The Purchase Order Journal window.

Toolbar Icons

The toolbar icons are similar to the icons seen in the RECEIVABLES module Fig. 2A-5, Sample Sales Invoice window.

Entering Purchase Orders

> When a purchase quote is converted into a purchase order, the information on the purchase quote is automatically entered into the Purchase Order window. Likewise, purchase order information is entered into the Purchase Invoice window upon conversion.

A purchase order is a commitment by a purchaser to buy goods, merchandise or services, etc., at the agreed-upon price, terms and date. The goods are to be delivered, or services provided, within the stated time period.

In the PAYABLES module you can:

1. enter a Purchase Quote;

2. convert it into a Purchase Order (PO); then

3. convert the PO into a purchase invoice.

(See side note box.)

Purchase Quote ⟶ Purchase Order ⟶ Purchase Invoice
Purchase Order ⟶ Purchase Invoice
Purchase Invoice

Similar to the RECEIVABLES module, the purchase quote and the purchase order do not affect the subledgers; they are simply recorded in a Purchase Quote or Purchase Order Listing.

Tyson's Toys records purchase orders; it does not record purchase quotes. Although there are no serious consequences if you do not record purchase quotes, it is important to record purchase orders in order to make sure that all ordered goods or services are provided by the vendor(s). Remember, PURCHASES are goods for resale; if you do not receive your shipments from your vendors, you might not have anything to sell!

Exercise 3A-5 – Entering a Purchase Order

Apr 01, 2016	**Jerry Tyson issued purchase order #82 to Markham Toy Manufacturing for 35 Trucks small for $14.32 each, plus GST with PST exempt. The trucks will be delivered on Apr 5. Credit terms are 2/10, net 30.**

Some firms may use a numbering sequence for purchase orders that reflects the date; e.g., 100401 (for PO#100 for Apr 1). Mr. Tyson has decided to use a numerical sequence. The next PO is #82.

When entering a purchase transaction, from a Purchase invoice, in the Purchases Journal, Simply will automatically **credit** the Vendor account and ACCOUNTS PAYABLE in the G/L with the total invoice amount (including taxes).

1 ➤ Transaction   Click the ▼ arrow and note that the choices are similar to the Receivables Journal, select **Purchase Order**. `Tab`.

2 ➤ Paid By   Click the ▼ arrow and note the four choices available. If you use the Cash, Cheque or Visa Credit Card option, the software assumes you are making a prepayment (a payment in advance to a vendor) on the Purchase Order. (See side box.) Leave the choice as **Pay Later**. `Tab` to Purchased From.

ℹ️

Simply records money **paid** on a future order in the PAYABLES module (Chapter 3B) as a **Prepayment**. In the RECEIVABLES module (Chapter 2B), Simply records money **received** on a future order as a **Deposit**.

3 ➤ Purchased From   Select **Markham Toy Manufacturing**.

Note that the address for Tyson's Toys is recorded in the **Ship To** box. If the goods are to be shipped to a different address, you will need to type the information in the box, as no field is available to list different Addresses as is available in the RECEIVABLES module.

Notice that the **Tax** and **Acct** fields have already been filled in, based on the Vendor Options tab, Expense account identified. You can change the tax and account fields when necessary.

Order No.   82 will be the next Purchase Order number. Do Not Change.

4 ➤ Ship Date   Click the **calendar** and choose **Apr 05**, `Tab`.

5 ➤ Date   `Tab` to accept **Apr 01, 2016**, `Tab` `Tab` to Order.

Quantity   This field is skipped because we have not received the goods that were ordered.

6 ➤ Order   Type **35**, `Tab`.

7 ➤ Back Order   These are items that have not been received from a purchase order. `Tab` to accept 35.

8 ➤ Unit   Type **each**, `Tab`.

9 ➤ Description   Type **Trucks small**, `Tab`.

10 ➤ Price   Type **14.32**, `Tab`.

11 ➤ **Tax**   Press [Enter] or double-click. You will see tax codes like those used in Santos Luggage, Chapter 2. Select **G**. [Tab].

12 ➤ **GST**   The GST amount should be 25.06 which is 5% of 501.20 (35 pieces x 14.32 = 501.20) in the Amount column, [Tab].

         PST   This field is skipped because the goods are purchased PST-Exempt.

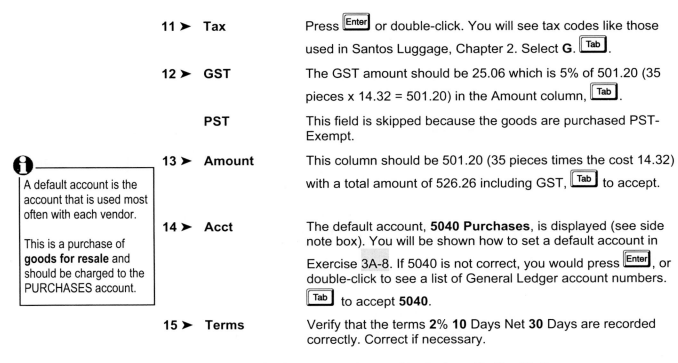

A default account is the account that is used most often with each vendor.

This is a purchase of **goods for resale** and should be charged to the PURCHASES account.

13 ➤ **Amount**   This column should be 501.20 (35 pieces times the cost 14.32) with a total amount of 526.26 including GST, [Tab] to accept.

14 ➤ **Acct**   The default account, **5040 Purchases**, is displayed (see side note box). You will be shown how to set a default account in Exercise 3A-8. If 5040 is not correct, you would press [Enter], or double-click to see a list of General Ledger account numbers. [Tab] to accept **5040**.

15 ➤ **Terms**   Verify that the terms **2% 10** Days Net **30** Days are recorded correctly. Correct if necessary.

The purchase order is now complete and is displayed in Fig. 3A-6.

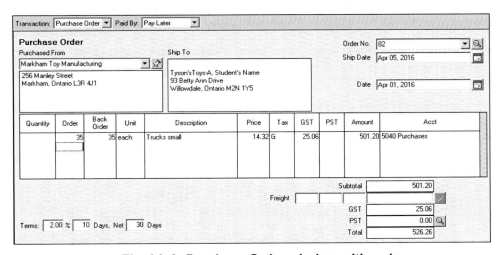

Fig. 3A-6: Purchase Order window with order.

16 ➤ Display the **Purchases Journal Entry**. It should be as shown in Fig 3A-7:

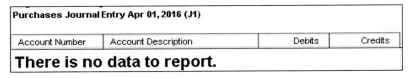

Purchases Journal Entry Apr 01, 2016 (J1)			
Account Number	Account Description	Debits	Credits
There is no data to report.			

Fig. 3A-7: Purchases Journal Entry window.

There is no journal entry created with a PO, because the goods have not been purchased. When the goods arrive, the PO is converted into a purchase invoice and a journal entry is then created and posted.

17 ➤ **Exit** from the Purchases Journal Entry window.

The Reports and Forms Options have been set at Pre-printed. You do not need to print the Purchase Order.

18 ➤ After verifying that the PO is correct, click the **Record** button.

19 ➤ Click **OK** to exit the Transaction Confirmation window. **Exit** the Purchase Order window to return to the Home window.

Exercise 3A-6 – Revising a Purchase Order

> **Apr 01, 2016** Jerry Tyson reviewed purchase order #82 to Markham Toy Manufacturing and decided to increase the order to 40 Trucks small for $14.32 each, plus GST, with PST exempt. The other information did not change.

1 ➤ Click **Purchase Orders** icon, click 🔍 **Find Order** icon. The Select Order or Quote window appears with **Quote 82** highlighted. Click **Select** and the window changes to the PO with 35 items backordered.

To correct or cancel a Purchase Quote, Purchase Order or Purchase Invoice after recording, you would repeat this procedure which is also appropriate for a Quote or Invoice. You may refer to Chapter 13, *Corrections*.

2 ➤ Click the 🖫 **Adjust Purchase Order** icon.
The header changes to: **Adjusting Purchase Order 82**.

3 ➤ **Order** Change the quantity to **40**, Tab, and the Subtotal amount changes to 572.80 and the total changes to 601.44. Mr. Tyson is pleased with the change.

4 ➤ After verifying that the PO is correct, click the **Record** button.

5 ➤ Click **OK** to exit the Transaction Confirmation window, and **exit** to the Home window. (See side note box.)

Pending Purchase Order Report

It is good practice to view/print the Pending Purchase Order report to ensure that all goods you have ordered are either received or have been scheduled for shipping by the vendor(s).

Exercise 3A-7 – To View/Print Outstanding Purchase Orders

---

1 ➤ To display the Pending PO report, click **Report Centre,** from the Payables tab, select **Pending Purchase Orders Summary by Vendor,** click **Display**. The report will display that there is no data to report. Simply defaults to the last time the report was used Apr 01, 2016. Click the **Modify** button, **Report Options** and change the Date to: **Apr 08, 2016** (a week in the future; all items should be in blue (if not, click Select All), click **OK**.

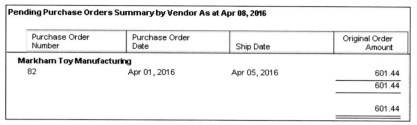

Fig. 3A-8: Purchase Order Summary window.

This report displays the outstanding Purchase Orders and the dates the goods are expected to be shipped.

2 ➤ **Exit** from the Pending Purchase Order window and return to the Home window.

The Vendors Subledger

Before you can enter transactions for a vendor, you need to create a Vendors Subledger account for that vendor. The procedure is very similar to creating a customer subledger in the RECEIVABLES module.

Exercise 3A-8 – To Enter a New Vendor

---

1 ➤ Advance the Session date to **Apr 05, 2016**.

Study this transaction:

Apr 05, 2016 **Mr. Tyson issued PO #83 to a new vendor A-Your Name Toy Parts, contact Your Name, 956 West Credit Avenue, Mississauga, Ontario, L6X 3K9. Phone number 905-820-3865 extension 2056, Fax 905-820-3865. Ordered 100 Truck wheels (to be sold as parts) at 99 cents plus GST, PST exempt, per wheel, terms 2/10, net 30. Total Purchase Order is $103.95 and the wheels are to be shipped on Apr 15.**

Notice that in the PAYABLES module, there is no **Continue** button.

You can enter a one-time vendor while entering a Purchase Invoice transaction. As in the RECEIVABLES module, the purchase from a one-time vendor must be paid at the same time as the date of purchase in cash, cheque, credit card or ATM card.

If you select **<one-time vendor>** the window changes to a Purchase Invoice.

Before you can enter a transaction for Your Name Toy Parts, you need to enter a new Vendor account in the Vendors (Accounts Payable) subledger.

2 ➤ From the Home window click on **Purchase Orders** ▼ and select **Create Order**.

3 ➤ Transaction Do not change from **Purchase Order**, Tab Tab.

4 ➤ Purchased Type **A-Your Name Toy Parts**, Tab. Type **A-** in front of
From your name. (See side note box—there is no Continue button.)

5 ➤ Similar to the RECEIVABLES module, you can create a new vendor in the Payables ledger as you enter transactions. Click **Full Add**.

Address

6 ➤ **Enter** the appropriate information as shown in Fig. 3A-9.

Enter the phone/fax numbers without dashes. Simply will automatically format them with a dash and brackets as you press ⌷Tab⌷. Refer to Exercise 2A-20 to record the extension number.

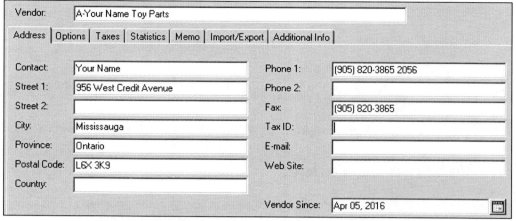

Fig. 3A-9: Payables Ledger window – Address tab.

Tax ID	This field would be used for subcontractor tax numbers required by Canada Revenue Agency for T5018 forms. Tyson's Toys does not use subcontractors for selling toys.
E-mail	Not used in this case.
Web Site	Not used in this case.
Vendor Since	As noted in Receivables, this field lets the user know how long they have been using that particular vendor. It is assumed that previous vendors have been used for a long time.

Options

7 ➤ Click the **Options** tab, and enter information as shown:

Expense Account	**5040 Purchases**. This becomes the default for this vendor and will show in all purchase orders or invoices for this vendor. It can be changed if necessary.

Conduct Business in	As discussed in Chapter 2, there is the ability to have screen displays and printouts in French for the customer. Tyson's Toys has not had any requests to conduct business in French.
Early Payment Terms	Type as shown. This is the discount for paying within the terms time period.
Calculate Discounts before Tax	Click the box. A ✓ will appear, Tab .
Include this Vendor when Printing T5018 Slips	DO NOT CHANGE. This box would be ✓ to include this vendor when printing the T5018 slips. Leave blank as Tyson's Toys does not use subcontractors and does not need T5018 forms.
Print Contact on Cheques	DO NOT CHANGE. You would click this box to print the contents of the "Contact" field on the cheques printed for this vendor. Mr. Tyson does not want to print the contact name on cheques produced by the program; therefore, you may leave the box blank.
Purchase orders for this Vendor	DO NOT CHANGE. You have a choice of sending a purchase order by e-mail or printing and mailing the purchase order. Leave choice as **Print**.
E-mail Confirmation of Purchase Invoices and Quotes	DO NOT CHANGE. This box would be ✓ if the vendor was able to e-mail you their quotes and/or invoices. Leave blank, as this text does not have an exercise to receive e-mail.
Synchronize with Microsoft® Outlook®	DO NOT CHANGE. As discussed in Chapter 2A, when this box is ✓, the vendor's e-mail address will be placed in the Microsoft® Outlook® Mailing address list. There is no exercise for this feature.

Taxes

8 ➤ Click the **Taxes** tab. This tab will indicate the appropriate taxes that are applied to purchases from this vendor.

9 ➤ Enter the information as shown. Select Tax code **G** because PST is exempt as we are buying goods for resale. Leave PST No, as we may buy goods in the future that are not PST exempt.

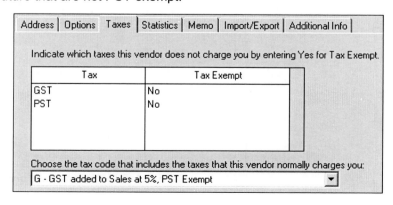

Statistics

10 ➤ Click the **Statistics** tab. DO NOT CHANGE. This tab will show the value of purchases and payments with each vendor.

Memo

11 ➤ Click the **Memo** tab. DO NOT CHANGE. This tab will allow you to keep information about the vendor and have the information shown in the Daily Business Manager.

Import/Export

12 ➤ Click the **Import/Export** tab. DO NOT CHANGE. This tab is similar to the Import/Export tab in RECEIVABLES. It refers to importing quotes and invoices from your vendors with your firm's item numbers.

Additional Info

13 ➤ Click the **Additional Info** tab. DO NOT CHANGE. This tab could show additional information about the vendor. Refer to the Appendix CD-Q, *Names Fields* on the Student Data CD for more information.

14 ➤ Click Save and Close button to save this vendor in the Payables Ledger and return to a Purchase Order window.

15 ➤ You can now enter purchase order **#83** information for Your Name Toy Parts.

100 Truck wheels at 99 cents plus GST per wheel, terms 2/10, net 30. Total Purchase Order is $103.95 and the wheels are to be shipped on Apr 15.

16 ➤ **Record** the Purchase order when correct. **Exit** to the Home window.

You can also create a new vendor as follows:

a) From the Home window, click the **Vendors** ▼ arrow, select **View Vendors**. The Vendors window (Fig. 3A-10) displays icons and information for all vendor accounts.

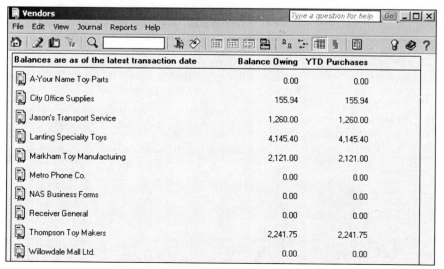

Fig. 3A-10: Vendors window.

The new toolbar icons at the top of the Vendors window mean the following:

Purchases: Displays a blank Purchases Journal for entry of purchase invoices. If a vendor icon is highlighted and this icon is clicked, the vendor address details are automatically inserted in the blank Purchases Journal.

Payments: Displays a blank Payments Journal for entry of a payment to a vendor. If a vendor icon is highlighted and this icon is clicked, the vendor address details are automatically inserted in the blank Payments Journal.

b) From the **Vendors** window, click the **Create** icon ![icon] , and the Payables Ledger window appears similar to Fig. 3A-9, with a red asterisk beside Vendor* and a red *Required Field to the right.

c) **Enter** the appropriate vendor information.

d) **Exit** the Vendors window and return to the Home window.

Purchase with No Purchase Order (PO)

Simply will also allow you to enter a purchase in the Purchases Journal without a Purchase Quote or a Purchase Order.

Study the sample Vendor Invoice:

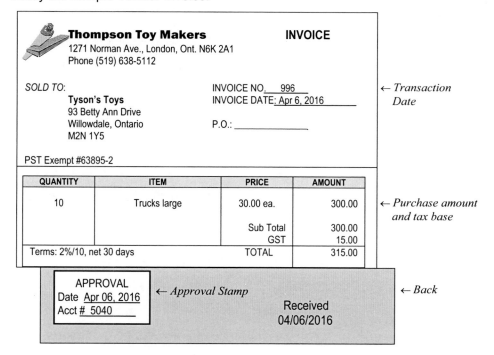

Fig. 3A-11: Vendor Invoice.

Exercise 3A-9 – Recording a Purchase with NO Purchase Order (PO)

Remember that a **purchase** refers to buying goods for resale. Buying services and goods that are not for resale are recorded as **expenses or prepayments**.

1 ➤ Advance the Session date to **Apr 06, 2016**.

The vendor invoice in Fig. 3A-11 is a credit purchase of toy trucks for sale and should be charged to the Purchases account in the G/L.

There are three ways to create a Purchase invoice.

a) Click the ▼ at Purchase Invoices icon, view the choices, select Create Invoice, at Purchased From: select your vendor. The window fills with the vendor name and address.

b) Click on Purchase Invoices icon to open the Purchase Invoice Journal, at Purchased From: select your vendor. The window fills with the vendor name and address.

c) In the Vendor section, at top right, scroll to the vendor, click the ▼ select Create Invoice. The window fills with the vendor name and address.

We will use method c) for this transaction.

2 ➤		In the Vendors section, move to **Thomson Toy Makers**, click the ▼ select **Create Invoice**. The window fills with the vendor name and address, Tax code and Account number.
3 ➤	**Transaction**	⌨Tab to accept Invoice.
4 ➤	**Paid by**	Note that the choices are similar to the Receivables Journal. Accept **Pay Later**, ⌨Tab.
5 ➤	**Purchased From**	⌨Tab to accept **Thompson Toy Makers**, ⌨Tab.
6 ➤	**Order/ Quote No.**	⌨Tab ⌨Tab (a previous purchase order was not issued).
7 ➤	**Invoice**	Type **996**, the invoice number, ⌨Tab ⌨Tab.
8 ➤	**Date**	⌨Tab ⌨Tab to accept Apr 06, 2016 (the date of the purchase).
9 ➤	**Quantity**	Type **10**, ⌨Tab.
	Order	Not used if PO not issued.
	Back Order	Not used if PO not issued.
10 ➤	**Unit**	Type **each**, ⌨Tab.
11 ➤	**Description**	Type **Trucks large**, ⌨Tab.
12 ➤	**Price**	Type **30.00**, ⌨Tab.

When Tyson's Toys buys goods, the GST the business pays is recorded separately from the GST collected on Sales. Other companies may put the GST collected and GST paid in the same account.

At the end of a period (e.g., month, quarter) the business subtracts the GST PAID ON PURCHASES from the GST COLLECTED FROM SALES. (Calculation of GST amount shown in Exercise 3B-30.) If the GST collected (e.g., $800.00) is more than the GST paid (e.g., $300.00) the difference ($500.00) is sent to the government (shown in Exercise 3B-31 for remittance entry preparation and posting). If the GST collected (such as $700.00) is less than the GST paid (e.g., $900.00) the difference ($200.00) is requested from the government.

GST PAID ON PURCHASES is a Contra Liability account on the Balance Sheet, and has a debit balance.

13 ➤ Tax [Tab] to accept G.

14 ➤ GST The GST amount. We have purchased $300.00 of toy trucks to resell to customers, 5% GST on the $300.00 is calculated.

[Tab] to accept 15.00. (See side note box.)

PST The PST field should be blank because this purchase is PST-exempt.

15 ➤ Amount [Tab] to accept 300.00. The 300.00 is the calculated amount of Quantity multiplied by Price.

16 ➤ Acct [Tab] to accept the default account 5040 Purchases.

17 ➤ Terms Verify that the terms 2%/10, net 30 days are recorded correctly. Correct the terms if the record is incorrect.

18 ➤ Click **Report**, **Display Purchases Journal Entry**. The display window should appear as follows:

Purchases Journal Entry Apr 06, 2016 (J1)

Account Number	Account Description	Debits	Credits
2560	GST Paid On Purchases	15.00	-
5040	Purchases	300.00	-
2200	Accounts Payable	-	315.00
Additional Date:	Additional Field:		
		315.00	315.00

Notice the automatic credit to Accounts Payable. Check to ensure that the details on your screen are the same.

19 ➤ Exit from the Journal Entry window. Changes can be made to the invoice, if required, by clicking on the field to be changed, and entering the revised details. Make sure you display the entry again, after changes, to ensure that it is correct.

(See side note box below.)

20 ➤ Post when correct and **Exit** to the Home window.

To View a Vendor Account

To correct or cancel a recorded purchase quote, purchase order or posted purchase invoice, refer to Chapter 13. A procedure similar to Exercises 2A-18 and/or 3A-6 could also be followed.

Sometimes you may need to view a vendor account; e.g., you want to take advantage of a discount so you need to check the date of the invoice, or you want to know how much you owe a particular vendor. At any time, you can display or print the details in a vendor account.

As in the RECEIVABLES module, you can display a **Vendor Aged** report.

Exercise 3A-10 – To Display a Vendor Account

To display the Vendor Report for Thompson Toy Makers you have two choices:

a) If the Vendor Aged is listed in the *Recently Viewed Reports* area, click on it. This will display all vendors.

b) If the Vendor Aged is not listed in the *Recently Viewed Reports* area, use step 1 to display only Thompson Toy Makers.

1 ➤ Click **Report Centre**, from the Payables tab select, **Vendor Aged Detail**, click **Modify this report**, click on **Thompson Toy Makers** (it remains blue). The date should be Apr 06, 2016, click **OK**. The report could be displayed with Include Terms.

Notice that all invoices are in the Current (0 to 30 days) column.

2 ➤ **Exit** from the display window and return to the Home window.

Purchase of Services/Goods Not for Resale

Inevitably you need to purchase goods not for resale, such as shipping supplies. Although these items may be related to your sales, the items themselves are not for resale. Therefore, they should be recorded differently.

Other examples of items not for resale are office supplies, printed cheques for paying bills, customer bags, utilities (Electricity, Water), etc.

Journalizing Purchases with PST and GST

When a firm purchases goods or services that will be used by the business and not sold to customers, the PST, that is part of the invoice price, becomes part of the cost of the goods or services. The cost of the PST paid on these goods is not recoverable from the provincial government; e.g., supplies used in the office and store, telephone, electricity, etc.

GST is calculated on the invoice amount before PST. Remember, GST paid on purchases is recoverable from the federal government. For example:

Value of supplies purchased	300.00
PST not recoverable	24.00
True cost of supplies	**324.00**
GST to be recovered	15.00
Invoice amount paid for supplies	339.00

Simply allows you to record the cost price, PST and GST to match the information from the purchase invoice, and the software does the rest.

Exercise 3A-11 – Recording Purchase of Goods Not for Resale

Apr 06, 2016   Mr. Tyson ordered and received 1 box of 1,000 cheques, form style, number #10188 from NAS Business Forms. The special printing of cheques, on invoice #4556 dated today, is in the amount of $300.00, plus GST $15.00 and PST $24.00. Terms are 2/10, net 30. A purchase order number was not issued for this purchase. *Note*: Charge 1330 Prepaid Office Supplies because the cheques have not been used. The cost will be charged to an expense (adjustment) as they get used.

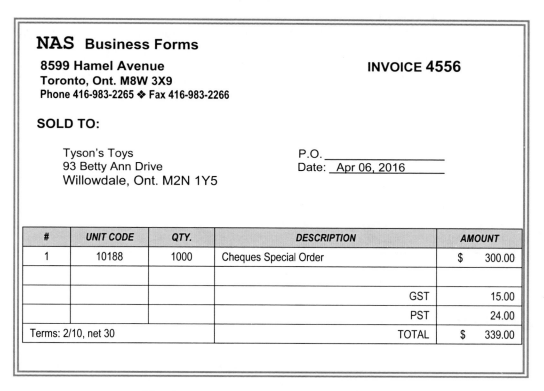

Fig. 3A-12: Purchase with PST and GST.

1 ➤ **Record** the entry as shown in Fig. 3A-13.

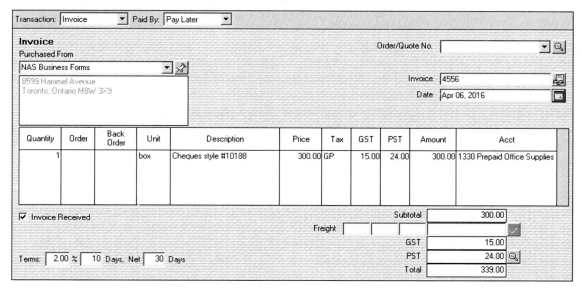

Fig. 3A-13: Purchases Journal window.

2 ➤ View the Purchases Journal Entry. Simply calculates the cost of the cheques correctly. PST is not recoverable; therefore, Simply added the PST value of $24.00 to the cost of the cheques ($300.00 + 24.00). The total cost of the goods before GST is $324.00.

If you make an error in a recorded purchase quote or order, or in a posted invoice, you can use the icon to adjust (Exercise 3A-6) or cancel the quote, order or invoice. You can also Reverse the entry. Refer to Exercise 2A-18 which would be similar, but use the appropriate Purchases Quotes, Orders or Invoices Journal instead. See also Chapter 13 to make corrections.

Purchases Journal Entry Apr 06, 2016 (J2)			
Account Number	Account Description	Debits	Credits
1330	Prepaid Office Supplies etc.	324.00	-
2560	GST Paid On Purchases	15.00	-
2200	Accounts Payable	-	339.00
Additional Date:	Additional Field:		
		339.00	339.00

3 ➤ When your entry is complete, **Post** the transaction and return to the Home window. (See side note box.)

Purchase of Services

Non-merchandise transactions such as rent, utility (electricity or water) expenses, accountant's fees, drawings, GST payments, etc., should be entered in the Purchases Journal, if it will be paid later just as any other purchase, or in the Payments Journal, if it is paid when you get the bill/invoice. A vendor subledger should be created for each non-merchandise supplier.

Exercise 3A-12 – Recording Purchase of Services – Cheque Issued

This exercise illustrates the steps to record a cheque issued for a service.

1 ➤ Advance the Session date to **Apr 07, 2016**.

Apr 07, 2016	**Mr. Tyson called you on his cell phone. He will pick up a cheque payable to Willowdale Mall Ltd. for $2,000.00 plus 5% GST cheque for the monthly mall rent at 93 Betty Ann Drive.**

The term Pay Expenses, is not exactly correct. You use this choice to pay expenses that are being paid without being recorded as a payable (rent cheques, office supplies that are purchased and not being used during this accounting period, Owner's Drawings, which is not a business expense and/or other miscellaneous expenses that are being paid by cheque).

2 ➤ From the Home window at the **Payments** icon, click the ▼ arrow and there are 6 choices.

Pay Purchase Invoices ➤ Pays Invoices previously posted

Pay Credit Card Bills ➤ Pays Credit Card bills previously posted

Pay Expenses ➤ Pays other bills not previously posted

Pay Remittances ➤ Pays Government amounts previously posted – GST (see Exercise 3B-31) and Income Tax, CPP, EI (see Chapter 7).

Find Payment ➤ Find payments previously posted.

Adjust Payment ➤ Adjust a payment previously posted. (See Exercise 3A-15.)

3 ➤ Select **Pay Expenses**. (See info note box.)

4 ➤ The choice at top left is Make Other Payment. Click the ▼ to see the choices available. Select **Make Other Payment**. [Tab].

5 ➤ **By**   Click the ⏷ to see the choices available. Select **Cheque**, ⎡Tab⎤.

6 ➤ **From**   If the company used more than 1 bank account you would click the ⏷ arrow and select a bank account. Tyson's Toys uses only 1 bank account. ⎡Tab⎤.

7 ➤ **To the Order of**   Select **Willowdale Mall Ltd.** ⎡Tab⎤.

Cheque No.   The next cheque number is 2511. Cheque #2511 was set up as part of the company defaults. You will learn how to do this in Chapter 4.

8 ➤ **Date**   Click this field. You could select a different date. ⎡Tab⎤ ⎡Tab⎤ to accept the date (see side box) and move to Acct. The Payments Journal window shows the cheque date as Apr 07, 2016, but the printed cheque will display the date as follows: 0 7 0 4 2 0 1 6 based on the CPA cheque guidelines. D D M M Y Y Y Y (See side note box.)

Note: Effective Jan 1, 2007, the Canadian Payments Association (CPA) has issued guidelines for cheque dates. Simply Accounting has adopted the same DDMMYYYY standard that Canadian cheque printers have adopted.

9 ➤ **Acct**   ⎡Tab⎤ to accept this field because this is the default expense account. If you need to change this column, you would double-click on **5310** and change it to the appropriate account number. DO NOT CHANGE.

10 ➤ **Description**   Type **Mall rent for April** ⎡Tab⎤.

11 ➤ **Amount**   Type **2000.00**. ⎡Tab⎤.

12 ➤ **Tax**   ⎡Tab⎤ to accept code G.

13 ➤ **GST**   ⎡Tab⎤ to accept GST calculated amount.

PST   This column is skipped because there is no PST on rent.

14 ➤ **Invoice Ref**   Type **Lease 04-2016** ⎡Tab⎤. This field will contain appropriate invoice numbers, memo codes, or other descriptive notations that help describe why the payment is being made. This information will display in the Vendor Aged Report. You cannot use the same Invoice Reference twice; therefore, **04-2016** would indicate the month and year of the lease payment.

15 ➤ **Comment**   Type **Mall rent for Apr at 93 Betty Ann Drive**. This field can be used to record an additional comment on the cheque at the bottom of the detail section. See the Make Other Payment window next. See next information note (under cheque) re printed journal.

Make Other Payment ▼	By Cheque ▼	From 1010 Bank Account ▼		Order cheques

Tyson'sToys-A, Student's Name   Cheque No.: 2511

Pay   Two Thousand One Hundred --00/100

To the Order of   Willowdale Mall Ltd. ▼   Date   Amount

1012 Finch Avenue West   Apr 07, 2016 $2,100.00
Willowdale, ON M2R 3K9

Acct	Description	Amount	Tax	GST	PST
5310 Rent Expense	Mall rent for April	2,000.00	G	100.00	

Subtotal	2,000.00
Tax	100.00
Total	2,100.00

Invoice/Ref. Lease 04-2016

Comment   Mall rent for Apr at 93 Betty Ann Drive   🔨 Post

In the printed Journal, the comment field will display to the right of the vendor name; e.g., 2511, Willowdale Mall Ltd.: Mall rent for Apr at 93 Betty Ann Drive .

16 ➤   Display the **Payments Journal Entry**. The window should appear as follows:

Payments Journal Entry Apr 07, 2016 (J3)

Account Number	Account Description	Debits	Credits
2560	GST Paid On Purchases	100.00	-
5310	Rent Expense	2,000.00	-
1010	Bank Account	-	2,100.00
Additional Date:	Additional Field:		
		2,100.00	2,100.00

Notice that Simply has automatically credited the BANK account.

17 ➤   **Exit** the display and **Post** when correct.

18 ➤   **Exit** to the Home window.

Exercise 3A-13 – Recording Purchase of Services – Pay Later

This exercise illustrates the steps necessary to record an invoice to be paid later. To record this transaction, the procedure is similar to Exercise 3A-9, but we will use the Purchase Invoices icon. (See side note box.)

> **Apr 07, 2016** The March telephone bill was received today. The bill, with no invoice number but dated Mar 31, was from Metro Phone Company. This bill was not accrued in the month of March. The amounts of the bill were: Phone service rental and long distance charges $352.00, PST $28.16 and GST $17.60. Phone bill is due for payment on Apr 24, 2016. Total amount owing $397.76.

A bill with amounts this large should be accrued as an adjustment at the end of each month. You have advised the accountant and they will begin recording monthly accruals starting at the end of this month. (Adjustments like this will be discussed in Chapter 9.)

1 ➤ From the Home window click the **Purchase Invoices** icon.

Use an appropriate code for other bills or memos that do not have an invoice number (e.g., for electricity bill use **Hydro0410**, for water bill use **Water0410**, etc.).

2 ➤ **Purchased From** Click the ▼ arrow and select **Metro Phone Co.,** Tab .

3 ➤ **Invoice** Type **PHMar31,** Tab Tab . This coding indicates that the invoice is from the phone company (PH), and that the date the information was sent by the phone company was March 31. (See side note box.)

Date: If you use a Mar 31, 2016 date and try to post the entry, you will get the following message:

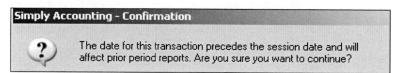

This means that the entry will go back to March 2016 data and change the account postings. The reports dated Mar 31, 2016 have already been printed and sent to the various managers and owners, and would now be incorrect. It is better to date this type of entry as being received on Apr 01, 2016.

The advanced date (Apr 1) would not have a significant effect on the financial results of April, the current month, yet it shows as a more recent report than the incorrect one (Mar 31).

This approach is reasonable as long as the amount is not significant. A significant transaction amount (large dollar value) would have to be recorded in March; otherwise, the reports may be misleading. Some companies may want to backdate this type of entry. If so, revised reports would be required for all managers and necessary staff. Be sure to provide an explanation to the managers and staff why the previous report was revised.

4 ➤ **Date** Select **Apr 01, 2016,** Tab to move to Quantity.

5 ➤ **Quantity** Type **1,** Tab Tab to Description.

6 ➤ **Description** Type **Phone bill to Mar 31,** Tab .

7 ➤ **Price** Type **352.00,** the invoice amount before taxes, Tab .

If the amounts for PST and/or GST are different from the amounts calculated by Simply, change the amounts in Steps 9 and 10 that require changing.

8 ➤ **Tax** Tab to accept GP code (GST and PST).

9 ➤ **GST** Tab to accept 17.60. (See side note box.)

10 ➤ **PST** Tab to accept 28.16. (See side note box.)

11 ➤ **Amount** Tab to accept 352.00.

12 ➤ Acct

The default account **5450 Telephone Expense** is displayed.

If you need to select a different account number press ⌈Enter⌉ or double-click. Remember, Simply will debit the account chosen, ⌈Tab⌉. The cursor moves to the next line of the purchase invoice. No more entries are required.

The total at the bottom should equal the total phone billing of **$397.76**.

13 ➤ Terms

Leave % blank, leave **Days** blank, type **23** in **Net _Days** box (payment due by Apr 24).

The Purchase Invoice window should appear as follows:

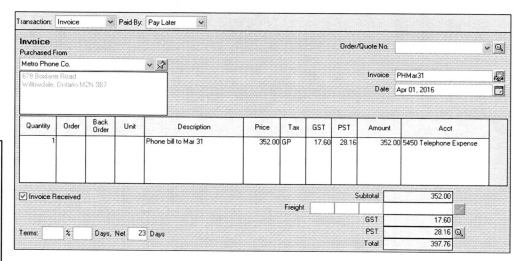

This transaction has been posted to Apr 2016. This does not follow the Matching Principle. However, if a March date is used, all of the reports for March will be changed. In cases like this, most companies would prefer to date this transaction as Apr 1, 2016 so that reports for Mar 2016 are not changed.

Monthly accruals should be recorded by the accountant.

14 ➤ Display the Purchases Journal Entry as follows:

Purchases Journal Entry Apr 01, 2016 (J4)

Account Number	Account Description	Debits	Credits
2560	GST Paid On Purchases	17.60	-
5450	Telephone Expense	380.16	-
2200	Accounts Payable	-	397.76
Additional Date:	Additional Field:		
		397.76	397.76

Simply has automatically credited Accounts Payable. Check the accuracy of the details.

15 ➤ Exit the Journal window, **Post** when correct and **Exit** from the Purchases Journal window. (See side note box at step 14.)

Recording Arrival of Goods Ordered on a Purchase Order

When goods on a purchase order arrive, an invoice usually accompanies them. This is now a purchase transaction; therefore, it should be recorded (and posted).

Exercise 3A-14 – Recording a Purchase Invoice from a PO

Apr 07, 2016 The items ordered from Markham Toy Manufacturing on purchase order #82 arrived today in good condition with Invoice #1693 dated Apr 06, 2016. Record the transaction with a purchase date of Apr 06, 2016 because the 2% discount period starts on the 6th. Mr. Tyson was aware the trucks would arrive late.

Enter the appropriate information into the fields as required.

1 ➤ From the Home window click the **Purchase Invoices** icon.

2 ➤ **Order/Quote No.** Click 🔍 **Look up an Order/Quote.** Select **82,** [Tab].

The screen should flicker and the information from the Purchase Order is displayed in the window.

3 ➤ **Invoice**   Type **1693,** [Tab] [Tab].

4 ➤ **Date**   Type or select **Apr 06, 2016,** [Tab].

5 ➤ **Quantity**   Type **40,** [Tab] or use the 🗹. The Backorder column is now blank because it shows the correct amount of items that have not been shipped as Nil. The complete order has been received.

The Purchases Journal window should appear as follows:

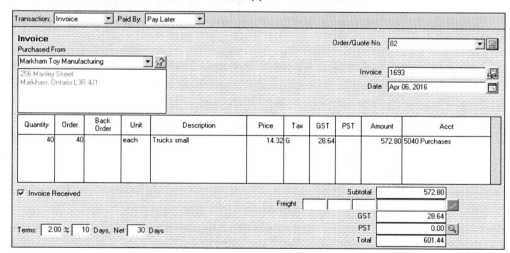

6 ➤ **View** the Purchases Journal entry. The display window should appear as follows:

Purchases Journal Entry Apr 06, 2016 (J5)

Account Number	Account Description	Debits	Credits
2560	GST Paid On Purchases	28.64	-
5040	Purchases	572.80	-
2200	Accounts Payable	-	601.44
Additional Date:	Additional Field:		
		601.44	601.44

7 ➤ **Exit** from the Journal entry window and **Post** when correct.

A message box appears.

> **Simply Accounting - Information**
>
> ⚠️ The purchase order has been filled and removed from the system.

8 ➤ Click **OK**. Click **OK** again, to accept the confirmation window. The window flickers and returns to a blank Purchases Journal.

9 ➤ **Exit** to the Home window.

Back up your data and update your logbook (located at the back of this textbook) now. **Remember, if it is important, back it up**.

Adjusting a cheque

There may be situations where a cheque was printed with the wrong amount, or to the wrong vendor. This exercise will show you how to adjust the Payment to the correct amounts. You could have cancelled the cheque (using the Reverse Cheque icon) and then issued a new cheque. In this exercise we will adjust the cheque and change the cheque number. You cannot reprint a cheque using the same cheque number.

Exercise 3A-15 – Adjusting a Posted Cheque

This exercise illustrates the steps to adjust a cheque.

> Apr 07, 2016   **Mr. Tyson arrived, and realized that he did not tell you the rent increased to $2,100.00 plus 5% GST as of April 1. Cancel cheque #2511 and issue a corrected cheque #2512 payable to Willowdale Mall Ltd. for the monthly mall rent at 93 Betty Ann Drive.**

1 ➤ From the Home window click the ▼ at the **Payments** icon.

2 ➤ Select **Adjust Payment**, and the Search window opens. Click **OK**.

3 ➤ Select **cheque 2511**, and a payment window with this header appears.

> **Payments Journal - Adjusting Other Payment 2511**

4 ➤ **Cheque No.**   Change the cheque number to **2512** (the next cheque) `Tab`.

If there was an error in the vendor name, you could click the ▼ arrow and select the correct vendor.

5 ➤ **Amount**   Type **2100.00**, `Tab`.

    GST   The amount changes to 105.00 (2,100.00 x 5%).

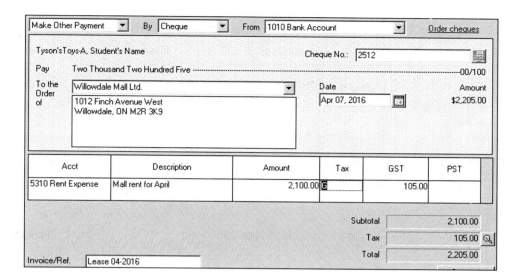

6 ➤ **View** the Payments Journal entry. The display window should appear as follows:

Account Number	Account Description	Debits	Credits
Payments Journal Entry Apr 07, 2016 (J7)			
2560	GST Paid On Purchases	105.00	-
5310	Rent Expense	2,100.00	-
1010	Bank Account	-	2,205.00
Additional Date:	Additional Field:		
		2,205.00	2,205.00

7 ➤ **Exit** from the Journal entry window and **Post** when correct.

8 ➤ **Exit** to the Home window.

9 ➤ Click **Report Centre**, **Banking**, **Cheque Log**, **Modify this report**, The Start Date should be **March 31** and a Finish Date of **April 7**, click **OK**.

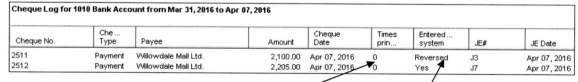

Cheque No.	Che... Type	Payee	Amount	Cheque Date	Times prin...	Entered... system	JE#	JE Date
2511	Payment	Willowdale Mall Ltd.	2,100.00	Apr 07, 2016	0	Reversed	J3	Apr 07, 2016
2512	Payment	Willowdale Mall Ltd.	2,205.00	Apr 07, 2016	0	Yes	J7	Apr 07, 2016

Cheque Log for 1010 Bank Account from Mar 31, 2016 to Apr 07, 2016

Notice that each cheque is shown as not being printed.

Good Audit Trail information, cheque 2511 is shown as Reversed, for the managers, accountants and owners.

10 ➤ **Exit** to the Home window.

Journalizing Purchase Returns

There are times when you may return merchandise for the same reasons that your customers would return goods you have shipped (they were damaged, defective, or not as ordered). This type of transaction should be recorded in the Purchase Returns account. You may send a return invoice (DEBIT MEMO) to the vendor along with the returned goods because you are **debiting** your ACCOUNTS PAYABLE account. The vendor would then credit the ACCOUNTS RECEIVABLE account in their books that corresponds to your company. They may send you a credit invoice (CREDIT MEMO) to verify the transaction.

Study this summary:

Transactions	Recorded in YOUR books	Transactions	Recorded in THEIR books
	They are a VENDOR to you		**You are a CUSTOMER to them**
Purchases from your vendor	Dr Purchases Cr Accounts Payable	Sale to you	Dr Accounts Receivable Cr Sales
Purchase Returns to your vendor (Receive their Credit Note)	Dr Accounts Payable Cr Purchase Returns/Allow	Sales Return from you (Issue Credit Note to the customer)	Dr Sales Returns/Allow Cr Accounts Receivable
	They are a CUSTOMER to you		**You are a VENDOR to them**
Sale to your customer	Dr Accounts Receivable CR Sales	Purchase from you	Dr Purchases CR Accounts Payable
Sales Returns from your customer (Issue a Credit Note to the customer)	Dr Sales Returns/Allow Cr Accounts Receivable	Purchase Return from you (Receive your Credit Note)	Dr Accounts Payable Cr Purchase Returns/Allow

---

Exercise 3A-16 – Recording Purchase Returns

> **Apr 07, 2016**   Returned 13 Trucks small, received this morning from Markham Toy Manufacturing due to paint peeling from the driver's side of truck. The cost of each returned item is $14.32, plus GST from invoice #1693. Markham Toy Manufacturing faxed us their credit memo #CM265 today in the amount of $-195.47.

Record the entry as follows:

1 ➤   From the Home window, click the **Purchase Invoices** icon.

2 ➤ **Purchased From**   Select **Markham Toy Manufacturing** vendors, `Tab`.

3 ➤ **Invoice**   Many firms would enter the old invoice number 1693 with an Rt code; i.e., **1693Rt**. Some firms, in addition, may also enter the credit memo number. Type **1693Rt CM265**. This coding method shows both the original invoice and the credit note. `Tab` `Tab` to Date.

4 ➤ **Date**   **Apr 07, 2016** is the date goods are returned. `Tab` `Tab` to Quantity.

5 ➤ **Quantity**   Type **-13** (minus), `Tab`. The minus sign represents the return of the trucks.

6 ➤ Unit   Type **each**, [Tab].

7 ➤ Description   Type **Trucks small - returned paint peeling**, [Tab].

8 ➤ Price   Type **14.32**, [Tab].

9 ➤ Tax   [Tab] to accept G.

10 ➤ GST   [Tab] to accept -9.31. The GST PAID ON PURCHASES account will be credited (reduced).

PST   Blank as the trucks were purchased PST- Exempt.

11 ➤ Amount   [Tab] to accept -186.16 (negative).

12 ➤ Account   You cannot use account 5040 because we are **returning** goods, not buying. Mr. Tyson wants to keep track of the goods returned in a separate account.

> A credit memo received is entered as a **negative** purchase invoice which reduces NET PURCHASES in the Income Statement.

Select **5050 Purchase Returns**, [Tab]. This account will be credited because of the minus amount. The cursor moves to the next line of the purchase invoice. No more entries are required. (See side note box.)

13 ➤ Terms   Change to **2%, 9 days, net 29 days** to match the original terms on invoice #1693. *Note:* Some firms would not change terms.

The lower portion of the window should appear similar to the following:

Quantity	Order	Back Order	Unit	Description	Price	Tax	GST	PST	Amount	Acct
-13			each	Trucks small - returned paint peeling	14.32	G	-9.31		-186.16	5050 Purchase Returns

☑ Invoice Received

		Subtotal	-186.16
Freight			
		GST	-9.31
Terms: 2.00 % 9 Days, Net 29 Days		PST	0.00
		Total	-195.47

14 ➤ Display the Purchases Journal Entry as follows:

> Entering a *negative* amount in the **Quantity** column results in a **debit** to **Accounts Payable**, and **credits** to **GST Paid on Purchases** and **Purchase Returns**.

Purchases Journal Entry Apr 07, 2016 (J8)

Account Number	Account Description	Debits	Credits
2200	Accounts Payable	195.47	-
2560	GST Paid On Purchases	-	9.31
5050	Purchase Returns	-	186.16
Additional Date:	Additional Field:		
		195.47	195.47

(See side note box.)

15 ➤ Post when correct. **Exit** from the Purchases Journal window and return to the Home window.

 Backup

Save your work on a regular basis and update your logbook.

To Review the Vendor Record

To view the return memo (negative purchase invoice) just recorded and posted, display the Vendor Aged detail as follows:

1 ➤ In the Vendors area, click ▼ at **Markham Toy Manufacturing, Display Vendor Aged Detail Report**, click **Modify, Report Options, Include Terms** and **OK** to display the detail for Markham Toy Manufacturing.

Notice that the return memo is displayed in the "Current" column because of the date used to enter the transaction.

Vendor Aged Detail As at Apr 07, 2016					
Source	Date	Transaction Type	Total	Current	31 to 60
Markham Toy Manufacturing					
1622	Mar 22, 2016	Invoice	1,073.10	1,073.10	-
1638	Mar 30, 2016	Invoice	1,047.90	1,047.90	-
1693	Apr 06, 2016	Invoice	601.44	601.44	-
1693Rt CM265	Apr 07, 2016	Invoice	-195.47	-195.47	-
Total outstanding:			2,526.97	2,526.97	-
Total unpaid invoices:			2,526.97	2,526.97	-
Total prepayments/prepaid order:			-	-	-
Total outstanding:			2,526.97	2,526.97	-

2 ➤ **Exit** from the display window.

Viewing/Printing Special Reports

Exercise 3A-17 – To View/Print a Pending Purchase Orders Report
---

Outstanding Purchase Orders

This report displays the outstanding Purchase Orders and the dates the goods are expected to be shipped. It is good to print this report periodically to ensure that no purchase orders are missed. The information in this report is also used for budgeting, particularly forecasting future receipts to ensure that cash is available for payment of bills.

1 ➤ To display this report, click **Report Centre, Payables, Pending Purchase Orders Detail by Vendor, Modify this report**, change the date to: **Apr 15, 2016** (just over 1 week in the future), **OK**. The Pending PO (A-Your Name Toys Parts) is displayed and includes a description of the items being purchased and Backordered quantity 100.00 (100 wheels have been ordered). Note that this report is different than the Summary report in Exercise 3A-7.

2 ➤ **Exit** from the Pending Purchase Orders window and return to Home window.

Another Transaction

1 ➤ **Record** and **Post** the following transaction: Return to the Home window.

> **Apr 07, 2016** Per special arrangements, Mr. Tyson sent back 30 trailer cars at $10.00 each plus GST, to Lanting Speciality Toys, that were originally purchased on invoice #6198 dated Feb 22, 2010. Total return including GST is -315.00 (negative). There are no terms on this return.

The Payments Journal

Payments to vendors for invoices that were previously recorded are entered in the **Payments** Journal. The Payments Journal is also used to record payments for prepayments and cash purchases where invoices are paid at time of purchase (invoices that have not been previously recorded and require a cheque). For cash purchases, you would record the invoice and the cheque at the same time.

Journalizing a Vendor Payment

When entering a vendor payment, Simply will automatically record a debit to ACCOUNTS PAYABLE and a credit to CASH IN BANK for the amount of the payment.

Simply can print cheques with an advice; however, Simply prints only the details of the cheque and advice. The cheques have to be formatted and printed with the bank codes according to bank specifications, ideally on preprinted cheques.

You can also select an option to display a reminder window to print cheques before posting. This has not been done for Tyson's Toys but will be covered in Chapter 4.

Exercise 3A-18 – Recording a Vendor Payment

---

1 ➤ Click the **Payments** icon from the Home window to open the Payments Journal.

The top menu options are the same as the Purchases Journal except for:

Payment   This drop-down menu shows the following options that are active and not grayed out:

- Enter Prepayments
- Include Fully Paid Invoices/Prepayments
- Adjust Payment
- Look Up Payment (previously posted invoices)
- Enter additional information
- Post

Toolbar Icons

The new icon in the Payments Journal is:

 Enter vendor prepayments   Allows you to record payments in advance of receiving goods and or services. Used without a purchase order. (See Exercise 3B-28.)

 The **Include Fully paid invoices prepayment** icon means that any invoice recorded as a Purchase Invoice (not paid using the Pay Expense selection) that was previously fully paid and not cleared (from the data file) will be displayed in the **Original Amt.** column. This feature allows a review of the invoice and payment activity for this vendor. (If you check the box while entering payments, the journal will be reset and amounts will have to be re-entered.)

Process the following transaction:

Apr 07, 2016 Mr. Tyson made arrangements to pay Lanting Speciality Toys for Invoice #6198 and the return of goods from that invoice. Cheque #2513 issued (see below).

As the information in Fig. 3A-14 indicates, cheque 2513 is paying only Invoice #6198 less the #6198 return. Invoice #6211 is not being paid at this time.

Enter the payment as follows:

2 ➤ To the Order of   Select **Lanting Speciality Toys**. Notice the program shows all unpaid invoices for this vendor (supplier). `Tab` .

Cheque No.   2513, is the next available cheque number for Tyson's Toys. If the cheque number is different, you would type the correct number.

3 ➤ Date   Click the date field. `Tab` `Tab` to accept Apr 07, 2016.

4 ➤ Due Date   The cursor is on Mar 23, 2016 for invoice 6198. `Tab` .

The Due Date column, displays the net 30 days due date, not the discount period date.

Invoice #	Invoice Date	Discount Date*	30 Days Due Date*
6198	Feb 22, 2016	Mar 03, 2016	Mar 23, 2016
6211	Feb 25, 2016	Mar 06, 2016	Mar 26, 2016
6198Rt	Apr 07, 2016	- none- **	Mar 23, 2016***

* February 2016 is a leap year.

**The 6198Rt (return) does not have a discount date, as the discount period for the original purchase has passed.

***Simply 2008 does not display the Due Date for negative invoices (returns and Allowances), therefore, the Mar 23, 2016 date is not shown.

Discount Available   The cursor does not stop in this field, as it is an information column that shows if a discount is available (this invoice is more than 10 days from the purchase date and, therefore, over the discount period).

5 ➤ Discount Taken   As discussed above, there is no discount on this invoice, `Tab` to leave blank.

6 ➤ Payment Amount   The amount **982.80**, which is the amount of invoice 6198, appears in this field and is highlighted. `Tab` to accept 982.80.

If the Disc. Available column has a **-6.00** discount showing, it was because you forgot to remove the terms from the return you recorded in the previous entry. Press ⏐ *Delete* ⏐ to remove the -6.00.

7 ➤ Discount Taken　　The cursor drops to the next invoice and the Discount Taken column. The current payment is for invoice 6198 and the return 6198Rt associated with the same invoice. Use the down arrow key ↓ to move to the **Discount Taken** field on the line for **6198Rt**. [Tab]. (See side note box.)

If you pressed [Tab] by mistake before moving down, and 3,162.60 appears in the Payment Amount column, press the ⏐ *Delete* ⏐ key to remove 3,162.60 from the column.

8 ➤ Payment Amount　　The amount of **-315.00** is highlighted, [Tab]. The total of the cheque to be issued is $667.80 If other invoices were listed and required payment, you would use the ↑ or ↓ key to move to the invoices that were being paid, and repeat the above procedure.

9 ➤ Comment　　This field (maximum 39 characters) could be used to record an additional comment which will appear at the bottom of the detail section on the cheque. (See Fig. 3A-14.)

Type **Payment as discussed with Mr. Lanting**, [Tab].

The lower portion window should display as follows:

The Due Date field does not display the date of the debit note (return or allowance). See Chapter 2, Exercise 2B-24, step 6.

Due Date	Invoice or Prepayment	Original Amount	Amount Owing	Discount Available	Discount Taken	Payment Amount
Mar 23, 2016	6198	982.80	982.80	0.00		982.80
Mar 26, 2016	6211	3,162.60	3,162.60	0.00		
	6198Rt	-315.00	-315.00	0.00		-315.00

Total　667.80

Comment　Payment as discussed with Mr. Lanting　　　　　🖊 Post

Fig. 3A-14 Lower portion of Payments Journal.

10 ➤　Display the Payments Journal Entry.

Payments Journal Entry Apr 07, 2016 (J10)

Account Number	Account Description	Debits	Credits
2200	Accounts Payable	667.80	-
1010	Bank Account	-	667.80
Additional Date:	Additional Field:		
		667.80	667.80

Notice that Simply has automatically debited Accounts Payable and credited the Bank Account.

11 ➤　**Exit** from the display window.

Do NOT print a cheque at this time. Pre-printed cheques can be printed on 8½ x 11 paper with one or two advice stubs. If the cheque has two stubs, one advice stub may be sent to the vendor and the second advice stub would be attached to the invoice with other documentation required to approve the payment. If only one advice stub is used, it will be sent to the vendor with the cheque.

12 ➤ **Post** when correct.

> Advisor: There are older outstanding invoices for this vendor. Are you sure you want to process this transaction?

The message box informs you that there are older invoices that should have been paid first. Mr. and Mrs. Tyson have made arrangements to pay invoice #6211 by Apr 16. In a business setting, the clerk would advise a supervisor that an older invoice has not been paid, and the supervisor would take appropriate action.

> To correct or cancel a vendor payment refer to Chapter 2, Exercise 2A-17, To Correct a Receipt Error, which would be similar, or see Chapter 13, for the PAYABLES correction.

13 ➤ We want to pay this invoice less the return; therefore, click **Yes**.

14 ➤ **Exit** to the Home window. (See side note box.)

To Review the Vendor Record

15 ➤ Display the **Vendor Aged Detail** report, without terms, for Lanting Speciality Toys.

Vendor Aged Detail As at Apr 07, 2016

Source	Date	Transaction Type	Total	Current	31 to 60	61 to 90
Lanting Speciality Toys						
6198	Feb 22, 2016	Invoice	982.80	-	982.80	-
2513	Apr 07, 2016	Payment	-982.80	-	-982.80	-
6211	Feb 25, 2016	Invoice	3,162.60	-	3,162.60	-
6198Rt	Apr 07, 2016	Invoice	-315.00	-315.00	-	-
2513	Apr 07, 2016	Payment	315.00	315.00	-	-
Total outstanding:			3,162.60	-	3,162.60	-

16 ➤ **Exit** from the display window to the Home page.

17 ➤ Advance the Session date to **Apr 15, 2016**.

Payment with Merchandise Discount

Many firms take a cash discount on the price of the goods before PST and GST are added. Most firms will not allow a discount on the PST and GST. You would set a default for the Simply program to specify how to calculate discounts (to include or not include PST and GST). Tyson's Toys has set Simply to allow cash discounts before taxes. You saw this step when you set up a new vendor in Exercise 3A-8.

Exercise 3A-19 – Recording a Payment with Merchandise Discount

> **Apr 15, 2016**   **Issued cheque #2514 to Thompson Toy Makers for $2,550.75 in payment of Invoice #886 and #996. Tyson's Toys took a cash discount on Invoice #996. Mr. Tyson wants the cheque to arrive before the end of the discount period.**

Tyson's Toys calculates the cash discount on the $300.00 merchandise purchased on invoice #996, before taxes; therefore, the discount available on this invoice is $6.00 which is 2% of $300.00.

1 ➤ Click the **Payments** icon from the Home window to display the Payments Journal.

2 ➤ To the Order of   Select **Thompson Toy Makers,** [Tab] .

Cheque No.   **2514** (the next cheque number).

Date   **Apr 15, 2016**.

The lower portion of the journal is displayed in Fig. 3A-15 and the Discount Available column shows 6.00.

Due Date	Invoice or Prepayment	Original Amount	Amount Owing	Discount Available	Discount Taken	Payment Amount
Apr 14, 2016	886	2,241.75	2,241.75	0.00		
May 06, 2016	996	315.00	315.00	6.00		

Fig. 3A-15: Payments Journal window showing discount.

3 ➤ Date   Change the date to **Apr 16, 2016**. The discount remains at 6.00.

4 ➤   Change the date to **Apr 17, 2016**. The Discount Available field now shows 0.00. (See side note box.)

> If you advance the date more than 10 days from the date of the invoice, the automatic discount calculation will report zero discount available.

5 ➤   Change the date back to **Apr 15, 2016,** [Tab] . The Discount Available field now shows 6.00.

6 ➤ Due Date   The cursor should be at Apr 14, 2016 in this field, [Tab] .

7 ➤ Discount Taken   There is no discount because it is more than 10 days from the invoice date for invoice #886. [Tab] .

8 ➤ Payment Amount   [Tab] to accept 2,241.75.

The cursor should be in the **Disc. Taken** field.

9 ➤   Double-click **6.00** in the **Disc. Available** field. The screen drills down to the original invoice. You can see the original purchase amount of $300.00 and can verify the discount of 2%. Simply does the calculation automatically.

10 ➤   **Exit** from the Purchases Journal - Invoice Lookup window, [Tab] .

11 ➤ Discount Taken [Tab] to accept 6.00.

12 ➤ Payment Amt. [Tab] to accept $309.00.

The amount of the cheque should be $2,550.75. The lower portion of the Payments Journal window should resemble Fig 3A-16:

Due Date	Invoice or Prepayment	Original Amount	Amount Owing	Discount Available	Discount Taken	Payment Amount
Apr 14, 2016	886	2,241.75	2,241.75	0.00		2,241.75
May 06, 2016	996	315.00	315.00	6.00	6.00	309.00
					Total	2,550.75

Fig. 3A-16: Payments Journal window.

13 ➤ Click **Report**, click **Display Payments Journal Entry**. The display window should appear as follows:

Account Number	Account Description	Debits	Credits
2200	Accounts Payable	2,556.75	-
1010	Bank Account	-	2,550.75
5080	Purchase Discounts	-	6.00
Additional Date:	Additional Field:		
		2,556.75	2,556.75

Payments Journal Entry Apr 15, 2016 (J11)

Notice the Debit to Accounts Payable and the Credit to Purchase Discounts.

14 ➤ **Exit** from the display window. If the cheque were printed on pre-printed forms, with Easy-Align, it would resemble Fig. 3A-17. You do NOT need to print the cheque.

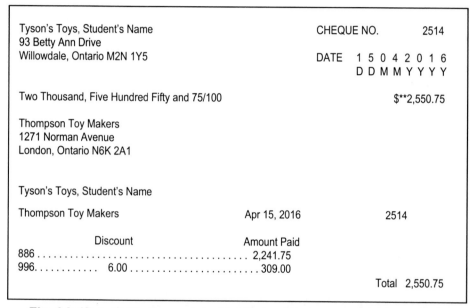

Tyson's Toys, Student's Name
93 Betty Ann Drive
Willowdale, Ontario M2N 1Y5

CHEQUE NO.   2514

DATE   1 5 0 4 2 0 1 6
       D D M M Y Y Y Y

Two Thousand, Five Hundred Fifty and 75/100 $**2,550.75

Thompson Toy Makers
1271 Norman Avenue
London, Ontario N6K 2A1

Tyson's Toys, Student's Name

Thompson Toy Makers   Apr 15, 2016   2514

          Discount   Amount Paid
886 . . . . 2,241.75
996 . . . . 6.00 . . . . 309.00

                                        Total 2,550.75

Fig. 3A-17: Information printed on Easy-Align pre-printed cheque form (note Discount).

15 ➤ **Post** when correct, and **Exit** the Payments Journal.

16 ➤ Display the **Vendors Aged Detail** Report (no terms) for this vendor at Apr 15, 2016.

The report should look like the following (note the Discount):

Vendor Aged Detail As at Apr 15, 2016

Source	Date	Transaction Type	Total	Current	31 to 60	61 to 90
Thompson Toy Makers						
886	Mar 15, 2016	Invoice	2,241.75	-	2,241.75	-
2514	Apr 15, 2016	Payment	-2,241.75	-	-2,241.75	-
996	Apr 06, 2016	Invoice	315.00	315.00	-	-
2514	Apr 15, 2016	Discount	-6.00	-6.00	-	-
2514	Apr 15, 2016	Payment	-309.00	-309.00	-	-
Total outstanding:			-	-	-	-

To display details of a recorded invoice, you could double-click on any item on the invoice **996** line. The invoice that created the $ values is displayed with a **PAID** image. This will assist you in not paying an invoice twice. To see the cheque that paid the invoice, you would double-click on the Payment line. The Cheque Lookup window will appear.

17 ➤ **Exit** from the Vendor Aged Detail display window.

Printing Reports when needed

It is normal to print some of the following reports during the month and file them for your audit trail:

- The Journal Entries - All of the transactions entered to date.
- The Vendor Aged Detail report, as at an appropriate date Apr 15, 2016.
- The Purchases Journal for the current period Apr 1 to Apr 15.
- The Payments Journal for the current period Apr 1 to Apr 15.
- The Cheque Log for the current period Apr 1 to Apr 15.

Exercise 3A-20 – Printing Period-End Reports

Make sure the printer is ready. You should be at the Tyson's Toys Home window to start this exercise.

1 ➤ **Print the All Journal Entries** report - as shown in previous chapters.

2 ➤ **Print the Vendor Aged Detail** at Apr 15, 2016. To ensure that everything is correct, you should compare the Balance Sheet Accounts Payable amount with the total of the Vendor Aged Detail report. They should be the same!

3 ➤ If required by your instructor, at Apr 15, refer to Exercise 3B-36 to View and/or Print the Purchases Journal, Payments Journal and/or Cheque Log.

Summary, Part A

Here is a summary of tasks and transactions in Chapter 3A:

Transaction	Journal	Remarks
Purchase Quote	Purchase Quotes	Enter amounts as positive including GST and PST where applicable. Does not update the General Ledger. Can be changed to a Purchase Order.
Purchase Order	Purchase Orders	Similar to Purchase Quote. Enter amounts as positive. A purchase order can be entered without a purchase quote being recorded. Does not update the General Ledger.
Purchase	Purchase Invoices	A purchase can be entered by changing a Purchase Order to an invoice, or can be recorded without recording a purchase order. Enter amounts as positive. GST and/or PST amounts are entered in appropriate fields. Updates the General Ledger.
Purchase Return	Purchase Invoices	Enter amount as a minus amount. GST is recorded as a negative amount. Updates the General Ledger.
Payment to Recorded invoice	Payments	Select the invoice(s) to be paid. Updates the General Ledger.
Payment with Discount	Payments	Applies a payment against the original invoice and the calculated discount.
New Vendor (Supplier)	Vendors Ledger	At the Taxes tab, change the Tax Exempt status for GST and PST where necessary and select the appropriate tax code. Select an appropriate default expense account.

Before Moving On..., Part A

Read the following questions and make sure you know the answers to them; otherwise, read the corresponding part in the chapter before moving on:

1. Name the types of transactions that are recorded in the PAYABLES module.

2. Describe the procedure for approving vendor invoices from the time they are received until they are paid. What is the significance of this procedure?

3. What types of entries are **not** recorded in the PAYABLES module? (ignore Sales entries)

4. When journalizing non-merchandise purchases with PST and GST, how is **PST** recorded?

5. Give the journal entry for a merchandise purchase return of $300.00 plus GST of $15.00.

6. Describe briefly the steps in recording an invoice payment in full, net of a cash discount. [Assume that a) merchandise for resale was purchased, and b) discounts are calculated on pre-tax amounts.]

7. What happens when you post journal transactions in the PAYABLES module?

8. When journalizing non-merchandise purchases with PST and GST, on what amount is **GST** based?

Refer to the second last page of Chapter 3B for the complete list of Accounting and Simply Accounting Terminology for the PAYABLES module.

Relevant Appendices, Part A

The following appendices are available on the Student Data CD.

Appendix 2009 CD-V   **Mini-Guide***

Appendix 2009 CD-Q   **Names Fields**

*******Refer to Mini-guide at the end of Chapter 3B for transactions.***

Note: After finishing Chapter 3A and Chapter 8, you can complete selected transactions from Chapter 3A, using the Perpetual INVENTORY module. See Challenge Exercise 08 C8-5 Toys-PI.

Challenge Exercise 03 C3A-1, Wheelchairs

PAYABLES and COMPANY Modules

Wheelchairs is a business that sells various kinds of wheelchairs to wholesale and retail customers.

Note: The business is open 7 days a week. GST is 5%, and PST is exempt for purchases of merchandise. PST is 8% for non-merchandise goods.

1 ➤ Refer to Exercise 1-1 to unzip the **03 C3A-1 Wheelchairs.exe** file.

2 ➤ Open the **C3A-1 Wheelchairs** file, and enter the following Accounts Payable transactions.

Mar 1   Issued Purchase order #81 to Your Name Chairs (Your name must appear) for 8 new model #CP-3 wheelchairs at $1,500 each, plus GST. Ship date is Mar 4. Other information: 156 Octavia Street, Belleville, Ontario, K8P 1H3, phone and fax numbers may be left blank. Terms are 2% 10 days, net 30 days, calculate discounts before tax.

Mar 1   Issued $2,250.00 plus GST cheque to Gordon Mall Management for lease rent for March.

Mar 4   Received 7 wheelchairs from Your Name Chairs from PO#81. Invoice #4568 received. The other chair is backordered and should be delivered by Mar 25th.

Mar 5   Returned 1 wheelchair from PO#81, as there is a crack in the metal frame. Credit note CN-56 received by fax.

Mar 6   Purchased and received from The Paper Place, 2 boxes of invoices with a new logo, that will be used during the year. Invoice #2256 received for $300 plus GST and PST, Terms 2/10, net 30.

Mar 7   We discovered that ¼ of the invoices (value $75.00) received on invoice #2256 were printed without logos. The Paper Place manager agreed to an allowance (2256Al) of $75.00 plus GST and PST which can be used to reduce the cost of the current order.

Mar 13   Received Belleville Hydro bill #1565-3 for $112.00 plus GST and PST. Service bill dated Mar 12, and payment date is Mar 27.

Mar 14   Issued next cheque to Your Name Chairs for amount owing, less the return.

Mar 17   Purchased from Avery Parts, 3 boxes of various repair parts for wheelchairs at $100.00 per box. Invoice #8897 in the amount of $300.00 plus GST. Terms 2/10, net 30.

Mar 20   Received a bank debit memo, dated today, regarding the loan payment of $400.00, which includes $67.00 of interest.

3 ➤ When you have recorded the above entries, **print** the following:
   a.   Vendor Aged Detail Report as at Mar 20
   b.   Journal Entries All, for Mar 1 to 20
   c.   Journal Entries-General, for Mar 1 to 20
   d.   Purchase Journal for Mar 1 to 20
   e.   Income Statement for Jan 1 to Mar 20
   f.   Pending Purchase Order report with an as at date of Mar 20

Challenge Exercise 03 C3A-2, Radios

PAYABLES and COMPANY Modules

Radios is a business that sells various kinds of radios to wholesale and retail customers.

Note: The business is open 7 days a week. GST is 5%, and PST is exempt for purchases of merchandise. PST is 8% for non-merchandise goods.

1 ➤ Refer to Exercise 1-1 to unzip the **03 C3A-2 Radios.exe** file.

2 ➤ Open the **03 C3A-2 Radios** file, and enter the following Accounts Payable transactions.

Aug 1   Issued $2,000 plus GST cheque to Royal Mall Management for lease rent for August.

Aug 1   Purchased from Town Printing Co, 4,000 advertising flyers at $.35 (35 cents each) plus GST and PST on invoice #9974 Terms 2/10, net 30. The flyers are being distributed today to homes and businesses in the local area.

Aug 4   Received 20 radios model #26583 from Radio Manufacturing Ltd., at $40.00 each plus GST on Invoice #2583 with terms 2/10, net 30.

Aug 4   Ordered on Purchase Order #135, 15 boom box radios at $83.00 plus GST, from new vendor Your Name Radio Wholesale. Your name must appear. Ship date is Aug 06. Other information: 688 Coleman Street, Belleville, Ontario, K8P 7P3, phone and fax numbers may be left blank. Terms are 2% 10 days, net 30 days, calculate discounts before tax.

Aug 6   Complete order received from Your Name Radio Wholesale on invoice #3865 dated today.

Aug 7   Returned 1 boom box from the Your Name Radio Wholesale order of Aug 6, as one of the speakers is broken. Credit note CN-86 received.

Aug 14   Issued next cheque to Radio Manufacturing Ltd. for invoice #2583.

Aug 15   Purchased from Oksana Radio Sales 2 specialty wide band radios at $150.00 each plus GST on invoice #3489. Terms 2/10, net 30.

Aug 15   Issued next cheque to Your Name Radio Wholesale for amount owing, less the return.

Aug 20   Issued next cheque to Gananoque Telephone for telephone service $160.00 and yellow pages advertising $40.00, plus GST and PST. Service bill dated August 19.

Aug 20   The owner does not want the cheque mailed to Gananoque Telephone as there is an error in the advertising amount. Reverse the cheque. We have requested a revised invoice.

   3 ➤ When you have recorded the above entries, **print** the following:
      a.   Vendor Aged Detail Report as at Aug 20
      b.   Journal Entries All, for Aug 1 to 20, **with Corrections**
      c.   Purchases Journal for Aug 1 to 20
      d.   Income Statement for Jan 1 to Aug 20

Chapter 3B

PAYABLES Module—Part B

Tyson's Toys

Learning Objectives

After completing Chapter 3B you will be able to:

- ☐ Continue to record purchase orders, invoices and returns.
- ☐ Continue to add new vendors and make changes to existing vendors.
- ☐ Record payments to vendors in full or partial payment of invoices with or without cash discounts.
- ☐ Record payments to other suppliers (one-time vendor, owner for drawings, etc.).
- ☐ Record tax payments for GST and PST to the appropriate government authority.
- ☐ Record prepayments to vendors.
- ☐ Display and print various payable reports (vendor balances outstanding, etc.) and journals.

This chapter is a continuation of Chapter 3A. You should download the 03 3B Toys-B data file for use with this chapter.

The contents of this chapter are as follows:

Opening the PAYABLES Module, Part B

In this chapter (3B), you will access the PAYABLES module of Tyson's Toys and enter transactions related to purchases, payments to vendors, one time payments and other payable transactions starting from April 16.

The 03 3B Toys-B.exe file contains the ending balances of the General Ledger accounts and Vendor files from Chapter 3A of this text (see Trial Balance on following page). These balances will be the starting point of the B file and journal entries will start at J1.

Slideshow 3B – PAYABLES Part B to prepare for more transaction processing in the PAYABLES module. Pay particular attention to the Accounting principles related to the various tasks.

Starting Simply for Payables

Exercise 3B-21 – To Open the 03 3B Toys-B data file

Review Exercise 1-2 if you need help to open a data file.

1 ➤ Refer to Exercise 1-1 to unzip the **03 3B Toys-B.exe** file. (See side note box.)

2 ➤ Start **Simply Accounting**.

3 ➤ At the Select Company window, click **Select an existing company** button and **OK**.

4 ➤ At the **Simply Accounting - Open Company** window, in the **Look in** box, locate your student location drive, and the Toys folder 🗀 03 3B Toys-B.

5 ➤ Double-click the 🗀 03 3B Toys-B folder and the 📠 Toys-B.SAI file will appear in the box below. (The image at the left of Toys may be different depending on the configuration of your computer and the SAI.)

6 ➤ Click the 📠 Toys-B.SAI icon. The **File name** box will change to Toys-B.SAI

7 ➤ Click **Open** to open the Toys-B.SAI file.

8 ➤ **Date**   Accept **Apr 15, 2016**.

9 ➤ Display the Trial Balance.

The following is the Tyson's Toys Trial Balance at the end of Chapter 3A.

Study Tyson's Trial Balance.

Tyson's Toys-B, Student's Name
Trial Balance As At Apr 15, 2016

		Debits	Credits
1010	Bank Account	6,001.45	-
1020	Bank Account US funds	580.60	-
1200	Accounts Receivable	12,899.00	-
1310	Toys and parts Inventory	6,907.29	
1330	Prepaid Office Supplies, etc.	949.00	-
1340	Prepaid Insurance	0.00	-
1510	Store Equipment	25,138.45	-
1515	Accum. Amort. Store Equipment	-	12,136.00
1520	Office Furniture/Equipment	2,812.60	-
1525	Accum. Amort. Office/Furniture/Equi	-	1,605.00
2200	Accounts Payable	-	7,842.27
2210	Visa Credit Card Payable	-	0.00
2550	GST Charged On Sales	-	1,738.25
2560	GST Paid On Purchases	807.07	-
2580	PST Payable	-	65.08
2610	Bank Loan Payable	-	14,310.86
3100	Capital Jerry Tyson	-	11,924.65
3120	Drawings Jerry Tyson	3,500.00	-
3200	Capital Helen Tyson	-	11,924.65
3210	Drawings Helen Tyson	3,500.00	
4100	Sales	-	34,126.00
4150	Sales - Discount	212.30	-
4200	Sales - Returns & Allowances	604.00	-
5010	Beginning Inventory	5,421.49	-
5040	Purchases	19,281.60	-
5050	Purchases Returns	-	786.16
5080	Purchase Discounts	-	295.80
5090	Ending Inventory	-	6,907.29
5310	Rent Expense	8,100.00	-
5340	Advertising Expense	516.00	-
5345	Bank Loan Interest	301.00	-
5350	Bank Charges	135.00	-
5355	Credit Card Charges	0.00	-
5360	Insurance Expense	303.00	-
5370	Auto Lease Expense	1,200.00	-
5440	Office/Store Supplies Expense	750.00	-
5450	Telephone Expense	1,292.16	-
5460	Utility Expense	1,250.00	-
5470	Bad Debts Expense	0.00	-
5480	Delivery Expense	1,200.00	-
		103,662.01	103,662.01

Fig. 3B-18: Trial Balance, Tyson's Toys-B.

Cash Flow Projection Report

The Cash Flow Projection report shows how the bank account is expected to change by anticipated payments to outstanding vendor accounts, and expected customer payments (receipts) to be received within the number of days specified, as well as, Recurring entries and Other payments that will affect the bank balance. (See Bank Account projection in step 1 and side note box beside step 1.)

Exercise 3B-22 – To View/Print a Cash Flow Report

> **Apr 15, 2016 Mr. Tyson is concerned about the amount of money he will have in the bank and the amount he owes his suppliers. He has asked you to print a Cash Flow report.**

The Cash Flow **Summary** report shows a summary of amounts that will affect the bank account balance. This chapter shows only Accounts Payable transactions and does not show any receipts from Accounts Receivable.

1 ➤ To display the Cash Flow report, click **Report Centre, Financials, Cash Flow Projection Summary, Display**. This report does not indicate when the account will be in a negative position.

1010 Bank Account. Cash flow projection from Apr 15, 2016 to May 15, 2016	
Description	Balance
Balance as of Apr 15, 2016	6,001.45
Total receipts	0.00
Total payments	-7,822.53
Total recurring general journal transactions	-884.20
Total recurring other payment transactions	0.00
Ending balance	-2,705.28
Net change in cash balance:	-8,706.74
Lowest balance in the account:	-2,705.29
Highest balance in the account:	6,001.45

An overdraft occurs when you have issued cheques for more money than you have in your bank account.

2 ➤ Click **Modify, Report Options**, select **Detail**, **1010 Bank Account** is selected, click **OK**. The report shows the balance per day (Total for the day) and that the bank account will go into a negative position, overdraft, on Apr 21 if current ACCOUNTS PAYABLE vendors are paid on time. Mr. and Mrs. Tyson are drafting a payment plan with the bank and all vendors. (See side note box.)

3 ➤ **Print** the Report.

4 ➤ **Exit** from the Cash Flow Projection window, return to the Home window.

Credit Card Purchase

Similar to credit card sales in the RECEIVABLES module, credit card purchases are considered cash purchases.

In Chapter 2, the credit card company charges the vendor (Mrs. Santos) a fee for each transaction for allowing a customer to use a credit card. In the case of the customer who uses a credit card to pay for a purchase, the customer does not pay a fee for every transaction. The credit card company usually collects an annual fee from the credit card holder. Study how the credit card purchase transaction is recorded in the next exercise.

Exercise 3B-23 – Recording a Credit Card Purchase

> **Apr 15, 2016**   **Mrs. Tyson purchased a second new briefcase (wide) for $135.00, plus 5% GST and 8% PST, for a total price of $152.55 from Santos Luggage. She is going to Vancouver for a toy conference and her old briefcase does not look good and needs some repairs. Mrs. Tyson used her business credit card to pay for the purchase. Received invoice 2401.**

Follow these steps to record the transaction:

1 ➤   From the Home window, click the **Purchase Invoices** icon.

Transaction   DO NOT CHANGE.

2 ➤ Paid by   Select **Visa Credit**, [Tab].

3 ➤ Purchased From   Type **Santos Luggage** [Tab], then **Continue**, then [Tab] [Tab].
The Tysons do not plan to buy other goods from Santos.

4 ➤   Type **635 Semple Avenue** [Tab], **Toronto, ON** [Tab], **M9L 1V5**. [Tab].

5 ➤ Invoice   For a credit card transaction, some vendors will issue a regular invoice and other vendors will issue a cash register receipt. Type **2401**, because Santos Luggage issued invoice 2401, [Tab] [Tab].

6 ➤ Date   [Tab] to accept **Apr 15, 2016**, [Tab] to Quantity.

7 ➤ Quantity   Type **1**, [Tab].

8 ➤ Unit   Type **each**, [Tab].

9 ➤ Description   Type **Briefcase wide**, [Tab].

10 ➤ Price   Type **135.00**, [Tab].

11 ➤ Tax   Select **GP**, [Tab]. (This is a retail purchase.)

12 ➤ GST   [Tab] to accept 6.75.

13 ➤ PST   [Tab] to accept 10.80.

14 ➤ Amount   [Tab] to accept 135.00.

15 ➤ Acct   Select **5440 Office/Store Supplies Expense**. (See side note box.)

Some firms may have specific expense accounts to charge this type of item. This item would not be charged to an asset account due to the low dollar value (the amount is not material). Your teacher will explain in more detail.

The lower portion of the window appears as follows:

Quantity	Order	Back Order	Unit	Description	Price	Tax	GST	PST	Amount	Acct
1			each	Briefcase wide	135.00	GP	6.75	10.80	135.00	5440 Office/Store Supplies Exp

The following is shown at the bottom of the Invoice window:

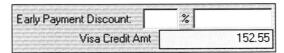

There is no Early Payment Discount on this purchase. The early payment discount referred to here is for a regular customer who has 2/10 terms, who pays when the purchase is made. The discount does not apply to a Visa purchase.

16 ➤ **Display** the entry as follows.

Purchases Journal Entry Apr 15, 2016 (J1)

Account Number	Account Description	Debits	Credits
2560	GST Paid On Purchases	6.75	-
5440	Office/Store Supplies Expense	145.80	-
2210	Visa Credit Card Payable	-	152.55
Additional Date:	Additional Field:		
		152.55	152.55

> Because you selected **Visa Credit** in the **Paid By** field, Simply automatically entered a credit to 2210 VISA CREDIT CARD PAYABLE, instead of a credit to ACCOUNTS PAYABLE.

(See side note box.)

17 ➤ **Post** when correct, and **Exit** to the Home window.

Payment with Non-Merchandise Discount

At this point, it is important to differentiate between **Purchase Discount** and **Cash Discount**.

A **Purchase Discount** account is used **ONLY** to show **reductions** (for paying within the discount period) to the cost of merchandise to be resold. When you are able to take a cash discount on goods or services that are **not for resale** (non-merchandise items, e.g., office supplies) and, therefore, not charged to the PURCHASES account, you should not record the discount to the Purchase Discount account.

Simply will allow an automatic discount entry to only 1 account. The Purchase Discount account has been set up as the default discount account.

Before you can record a payment with a discount on goods that are not for resale, (e.g., Office Supplies, Advertising Expense, etc.), you need to record a negative invoice. This invoice is charged to the same account, e.g., office supplies, which is a reduction to the original account where the cost was charged.

There are two steps to record a payment that involves a non-merchandise discount:

1. Record a negative purchase invoice for the discount. There are two ways to calculate the discount:

    i)   You can use the lookup feature to view the details of the original invoice, and manually calculate the discount.

    ii) You can use the Payment cheque icon to view the items that are owing for each vendor, and let Simply calculate the discount for you. ***Do not post the transaction. This method is used to calculate the discount only.***

2. Record the payment including the discount using method part (i) above.

Exercise 3B-24 – Recording a Payment with Non-Merchandise Discount

> **Apr 15, 2016**   **Paid $333.00 with your cheque #2515 to NAS Business Forms in payment of their invoice 4556 taking a cash discount because you are paying within the credit terms. The amount of the discount is $6.00 (2% of the $300.00 printing costs).**

The discount of $6.00 is a reduction of the cost of the printed cheques and is not charged to the Purchase Discounts account.

Note that this purchase of non-merchandise items was originally entered, in Chapter 3A Exercise 3A-11 Journal entry 2, as shown:

Purchases Journal Entry Apr 06, 2016 (J2)

Account Number	Account Description	Debits	Credits
1330	Prepaid Office Supplies etc.	324.00	-
2560	GST Paid On Purchases	15.00	-
2200	Accounts Payable	-	339.00
Additional Date:	Additional Field:		
		339.00	339.00

To record the payment with a cash discount:

Step One: Record the Discount

1 ➤   Click **Purchases Invoices** icon.

2 ➤ Paid by   Select **Pay Later** to match original invoice.

3 ➤ Purchased From   Select **NAS Business Forms**, `Tab`.

4 ➤ Invoice   Type **4556Di,** `Tab` `Tab`. (See side note box.)

5 ➤ Date   `Tab` to accept **Apr 15, 2016**, `Tab` to Quantity.

6 ➤ Quantity   Type **1**, `Tab` `Tab` to Description.

7 ➤ Description   Type **Discount on invoice 4556**, `Tab`.

8 ➤ Price   Type **-6.00**(negative amount to reduce the cost of supplies), `Tab`.

9 ➤ Tax   **Delete** the default GP tax code, as there are no taxes on a discount. `Tab` `Tab` to Acct.

10 ➤ Acct.   The default account 1330 Prepaid Office Supplies, etc., appears in this field. The cheques were originally charged (posted) to this account; therefore, `Tab` to accept. This will reduce the cost of the supplies.

11 ➤ Terms   Remove **2% 10 Days, Net 30 Days**. There are no terms when claiming a discount, `Tab`.

Di is added to the end of the invoice number to distinguish the discount as relating to a cash discount for non-merchandise items, and not a purchase discount for goods purchased for resale.

Your Purchases Journal display should be as follows:

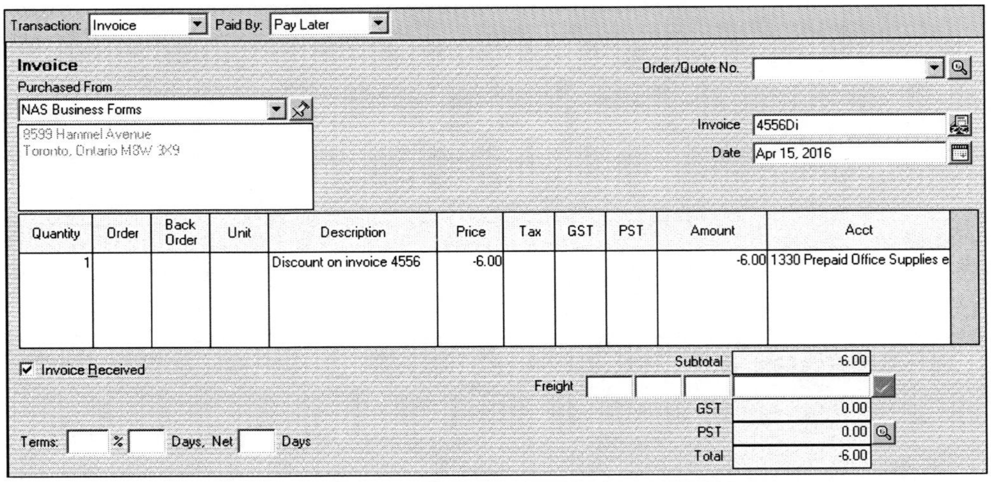

Fig. 3B-19: Purchases Journal showing discount.

12 ➤ **Display** the Journal entry, it should appear as follows:

Purchases Journal Entry Apr 15, 2016 (J2)

Account Number	Account Description	Debits	Credits
2200	Accounts Payable	6.00	-
1330	Prepaid Office Supplies etc.	-	6.00
Additional Date:	Additional Field:		
		6.00	6.00

Notice the **credit** to PREPAID OFFICE SUPPLIES, etc., and the **debit** to ACCOUNTS PAYABLE.

13 ➤ **Exit** from the Journal Entry window.

14 ➤ **Post** when correct, and **Exit** to the Home window.

Step Two: *Journalize the Payment*

15 ➤ Click the **Payments** icon.

16 ➤ **Pay to the order of**   Select **NAS Business Forms,** [Tab].

Cheque No.   2515 is the next cheque number.

Date   Apr 15, 2016 is the correct date.

17 ➤ **Due Date**   **Click** May 06, 2016. We want to pay invoice 4556 and 4556Di; therefore, press [Tab].

18 ➤ **Discount Taken**   Automatic calculation shows 6.00. Accepting the discount amount in this column means you want the discount to be charged to the Purchase Discount account. We have recorded a 6.00 non-merchandise discount on the next line. Press the *Delete* key to remove the 6.00, [Tab].

19 ➤ **Payment Amount**   [Tab] to accept $339.00, the amount of the original invoice.

20 ➤ **Discount Taken**   The cursor moves to the Discount Taken field for invoice 4556 [Tab].

21 ➤ **Payment Amount**   [Tab] to accept -6.00. This will charge the discount on non-merchandise to the account specified in step 10. The cheque amount total at the bottom is the correct amount (333.00) for this payment

The lower portion of the Payments Journal should resemble Fig. 3B-20.

Due Date	Invoice or Prepayment	Original Amount	Amount Owing	Discount Available	Discount Taken	Payment Amount
May 06, 2016	4556	339.00	339.00	6.00		339.00
	4556Di	-6.00	-6.00	0.00		-6.00
					Total	333.00

Fig. 3B-20: Payment with Prepaid Office Supplies discount.

22 ➤ **Display** the Journal entry, it should appear as follows.

The discount on this payment was charged to PREPAID OFFICE SUPPLIES in step 9.

Payments Journal Entry Apr 15, 2016 (J3)

Account Number	Account Description	Debits	Credits
2200	Accounts Payable	333.00	-
1010	Bank Account	-	333.00
Additional Date:	Additional Field:		
		333.00	333.00

23 ➤ **Exit** from the Payments Journal Entry window.

24 ➤ **Post** when correct and **Exit** to the Home window.

25 ➤ **Display** the Vendor Aged Detail report for NAS Business Forms at Apr 16, 2016 and it should appear as follows. Do *not* click Include Terms. The report should appear similar to Fig. 3B-21.

Vendor Aged Detail As at Apr 15, 2016

Source	Date	Transaction Type	Total	Current	31 to 60
NAS Business Forms					
4556	Apr 06, 2016	Invoice	339.00	339.00	-
2515	Apr 15, 2016	Payment	-339.00	-339.00	-
4556Di	Apr 15, 2016	Invoice	-6.00	-6.00	-
2515	Apr 15, 2016	Payment	6.00	6.00	-
Total outstanding:			-	-	-

Fig. 3B-21: Vendor Aged Detail.

26 ➤ **Exit** from the Vendor Aged Detail window.

27 ➤ Advance the date to **Apr 16, 2016**.

More Transactions

If you make an error in a cheque amount and realize it after you have posted the payment, refer to Exercise 2A-17 or Chapter 13. A cheque reversal in PAYABLES is similar to a reversal in RECEIVABLES.

1 ➤ **Record** and **Post** the following transactions: (See side note box.)

Apr 16, 2016	Received invoice #646 dated today, in the amount of **$357.68 for 15 Cars medium at $22.71 each plus GST, from Thompson Toy Makers. A PO was not issued. Terms 2/10, net 30.**

Apr 16, 2016	**The complete Purchase Order #83 of truck wheels from A-Your Name Toy Parts arrived in good condition with invoice # 65839 for $103.95 dated today.**

2 ➤ Advance the date to **Apr 18, 2016**.

Apr 18, 2016	**Cheque issued to pay Lanting Speciality Toys $3,162.60 on invoice #6211**.

Apr 18, 2016	**After receiving numerous telephone calls from Jason's Transport Service, Mr. Tyson paid their invoice #6691 with the next cheque.**

Apr 18, 2016	**Cheque issued to pay City Office Supplies for invoice #1235 in full**.

Purchase and Payment to a One-time Vendor

Similar to the RECEIVABLES options, Simply allows you to enter a purchase and payment to a vendor with whom you may not deal again (One-time vendor). For example, you may hire a company to deliver advertising flyers, or you may purchase curtains for the office from a store, etc.

You can enter this type of purchase/payment by either using the:

1. **Paid by Cheque** option in the **Purchase Invoices** Journal, or
2. **Make Other Payment** option in the **Payments** Journal.
3. Click the ▼ in **Payments**, select **Pay Expenses,** the Make Other Payment option is shown.

The Payments Journal option 2 will be used in this exercise.

Simply will record the transaction to the appropriate General Ledger account, but this type of entry will not be displayed in the Vendor Aged Detail report because no vendor was set up. The journal entry may be viewed in the Payments Journal or the Journal Entries-All report.

Exercise 3B-25 – Recording a Purchase from a One-time Vendor

1 ➤ Advance date to **Apr 19, 2016**.

> **Apr 19, 2016** Issued cheque to Alan Cohen & Associates, 2340 Eglinton Avenue East, Toronto ON M6E 2L6 for work done on setting up our website. The invoice #589 dated today, was for $412.00 plus GST $20.60 and PST $32.96 for a total invoice of $465.56. Mr. Tyson is not sure if he will deal with this firm again.

2 ➤ Click the **Payments** icon.

3 ➤ At `Pay Purchase Invoices ▼`, select **Make Other Payment**, `Tab`.

4 ➤ **Cheque**   Select **Cheque,** `Tab` `Tab`.

5 ➤ **To the**   Type **Alan Cohen & Associates,** `Tab`, click **Continue,**
        Order of   then `Tab`.

6 ➤ In the box, type the address as indicated above. This information would appear on the cheque if it were printed. Also, the payee name is recorded in the Payments Journal for audit trail purposes. `Tab`.

     Cheque No.   The next cheque is 2519.

     Date   Apr 19, 2016.

7 ➤ **Acct**   Select **5340 Advertising Expense**.

8 ➤ **Description**   Type **Setup Website,** `Tab`.

9 ➤ **Amount**   Type **412.00,** `Tab`.

10 ➤ **Tax**   Type **GP,** `Tab`.

11 ➤ **GST**   `Tab` to accept $20.60.

12 ➤ **PST**   `Tab` to accept $32.96.

13 ➤ **Invoice/Ref.**   Type **589,** `Tab`.

14 ➤ **Comment**   Type: **Alan Cohen & Associates created our website,** `Tab`.
                             (See side note box.)

15 ➤ The Payments Journal window should resemble the following:

> The **Comment** field replaces the **Vendor name** in the Journal entry display and printout. If you use the comment field, always use the vendor name as part of the comment.

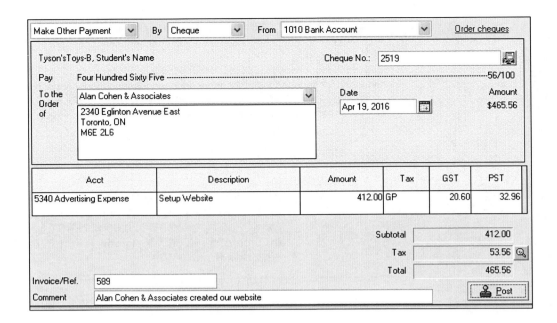

16 ➤ **View** the Payments Journal Entry. The display window should appear as follows:

Payments Journal Entry Apr 19, 2016 (J9)

Account Number	Account Description	Debits	Credits
2560	GST Paid On Purchases	20.60	-
5340	Advertising Expense	444.96	-
1010	Bank Account	-	465.56
Additional Date:	Additional Field:		
		465.56	465.56

To correct or cancel a vendor **Make Other Payment**, see Chapter 13.

17 ➤ **Exit** the Payments Journal Entry window.

18 ➤ **Post** after verifying accuracy, and **Exit** the Payments Journal.

Journalizing Bank Reconciliation Items

Bank charges and various items recorded on the bank statement (e.g., any special charges, etc.) but not recorded in the company accounting records would need to be entered in your Simply files. This type of entry would be entered in the General Ledger and would not affect the Vendors Ledger because it does not concern any vendor and a cheque is not issued.

Exercise 3B-26 – Recording Bank Reconciliation Entries

Study the next memo:

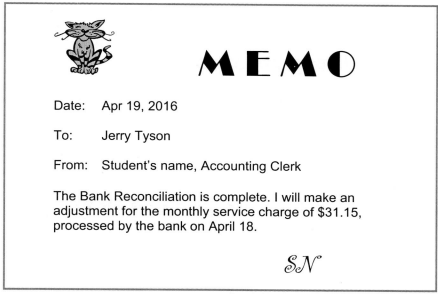

Fig. 3B-22: Memo about unrecorded item.

Entering Service Charges

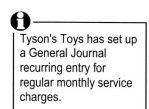

Tyson's Toys has set up a General Journal recurring entry for regular monthly service charges.

1 ➤ Click on the **COMPANY** module, click the **General Journal** icon. (See side note box.)

2 ➤ Click the **Recall Recurring Transaction** icon and the Recall Recurring Transaction window will appear as follows:

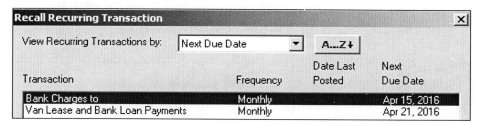

3 ➤ Select **Bank Charges to**, and the General Journal window will fill in with the recurring information.

Change the fields to resemble the following window. (See side note box.)

The entry date (Apr 18) is the date the bank took the bank charges from your account.

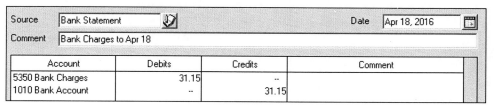

4 ➤ **Post** after verifying accuracy. A Confirmation box will appear.

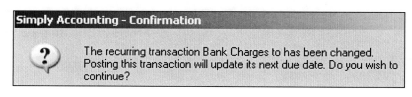

5 ➤ Click **Yes**. Click the **Recall Recurring Transaction** icon 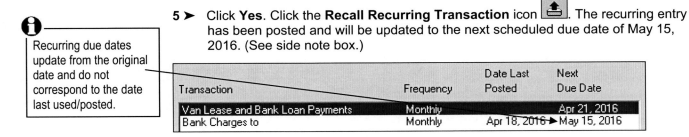. The recurring entry has been posted and will be updated to the next scheduled due date of May 15, 2016. (See side note box.)

> ⓘ Recurring due dates update from the original date and do not correspond to the date last used/posted.

Transaction	Frequency	Date Last Posted	Next Due Date
Van Lease and Bank Loan Payments	Monthly		Apr 21, 2016
Bank Charges to	Monthly	Apr 18, 2016 ➤	May 15, 2016

6 ➤ Click **Cancel** and **Exit** to the Home window.

Journalizing Partner's/Proprietor's Drawings

Although proprietorship withdrawals are not considered a normal vendor transaction, it is entered in **the PAYABLES module because this module is used to keep track of all payments made by the business.** Sole proprietorships or partnerships use an account called DRAWINGS or WITHDRAWALS when an owner withdraws money for personal use.

Jerry and Helen Tyson will be withdrawing money on a regular basis; therefore, vendor accounts should be set up. At any time Jerry or Helen can check their vendor account to see what amounts they have withdrawn during the year.

Exercise 3B-27 – Recording Owner's Drawings

1 ➤ Advance the Session date to **Apr 20, 2016**.

Study the following memo:

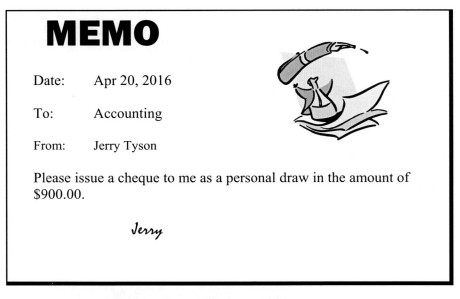

MEMO

Date: Apr 20, 2016

To: Accounting

From: Jerry Tyson

Please issue a cheque to me as a personal draw in the amount of $900.00.

Jerry

Fig. 3B-23: Memo requesting personal draw.

Apr 20, 2016   Issued next cheque to the owner, Jerry Tyson, for $900.00 as a drawing.

To Record the Withdrawal

Other payments that would use the **Make Other Payment** option are: Rent, GST payments to Receiver General, Insurance, purchases paid by cash, cheque and credit card.

2 ➤ From the Home window, click on **PAYABLES** module, click the **Payments** icon to display the Payments Journal. (See side note box.)

3 ➤ At | Pay Purchase Invoices ▼ |, select **Make Other Payment**, | Tab |.

4 ➤ **To the Order of**   Type **Jerry Tyson**, | Tab |.

5 ➤ Select **Full Add**. The **Address** tab (Home address), is **556 Betty Ann Drive, Willowdale, Ontario, M2N 1Y7**. Click **Options** tab, **Expense Account**, select **3120 Drawing**, click **Taxes** tab, change **Tax Exempt** to **Yes** for both **GST** and **PST**, select **-No tax** (there are no taxes on owner's withdrawals).

Click | Save and Close | when complete and you are returned to the Payments Journal, | Tab |.

Date   Apr 20, 2016.

6 ➤ **Description**   Type **Draw Apr 20, 2016**, | Tab |.

7 ➤ **Amount**   Type **900.00**, | Tab |.

Tax   Leave blank; there is no tax when an owner withdraws money from the business.

8 ➤ **Invoice/Ref**   Jerry or Helen would normally give you a memo to request a cheque indicating the reason for issuing the cheque. This is important for the audit trail. They will be giving you a number of memos during the year, and you will need to identify which memo was your authority to issue for each cheque. Type **Memo Apr 20** or Draw # 1, April (draw Apr, 1st draw of month), | Tab |.

Leave the **Comment** field blank for this and the other cheques that follow.

The Payments Journal should look like Fig. 3B-24.

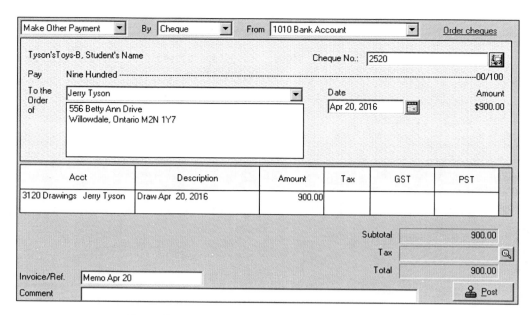

Fig. 3B-24: Jerry Tyson's Draw entry window.

9 ➤ Display the journal entry and it should appear as follows:

Payments Journal Entry Apr 20, 2016 (J11)

Account Number	Account Description	Debits	Credits
3120	Drawings Jerry Tyson	900.00	-
1010	Bank Account	-	900.00
Additional Date:	Additional Field:		
		900.00	900.00

10 ➤ **Exit** from the Payments Journal Entry window.

11 ➤ **Post** when correct.

A warning message box appears.

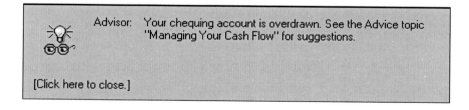

12 ➤ Mr. & Mrs. Tyson have previously made arrangements to issue cheques when they do not have enough money in their bank account. (This can be called a line of credit or overdraft protection.) You will see this message window when you post cheques later in this chapter. Accept the message by **clicking inside the box** to continue.

13 ➤ **Exit** from the Payments Journal.

This entry could be displayed in the **Vendor Aged Detail**. You do not need to view the Aged report at this time.

Recording a Purchase Order with a Prepayment to a Vendor

It is common business practice to give a prepayment to a vendor against future invoices to show the commitment to purchase items (special orders) or use their services.

In the Simply PAYABLES module, this type of transaction is called a **Prepayment**. In RECEIVABLES it is called a **Deposit**.

> Although we will use the Purchase Order paid by Cheque option, the cheque will not be issued in Simply. A manual cheque will need to be issued.

Exercise 3B-28 – Recording a Purchase Order and Prepayment Cheque

Apr 20, 2016	**A local service club has ordered 16 Orderly Vanline trucks. The trucks need to be received on Apr 29, 2016, as 10 of the trucks will be used as prizes in a children's contest, sponsored by the service club. Issue a Purchase Order (#84) to Thompson Toy Makers for these trucks at $25.66 each plus GST, Total $431.09. Terms 2/10, Net 30. Thompson requires a $200.00 prepayment, as this is a special order of trucks.**

To issue the Purchase Order and a prepayment cheque to Thompson:

1 ➤ Click the **Purchase Orders** icon from the home window.

      Transaction   **Purchase Order, do NOT change.**

2 ➤ **Paid by**   Select **Cheque,** a new field displays under Ship Date

        Prepay Ref. No. | 2521 | 2521 is the next cheque # or reference # for the prepayment.

3 ➤ **Purchased From**   **Select Thompson Toy Makers.**

4 ➤ **Ship date**   Select **Apr 28, 2016.**

5 ➤ **Order**   Type **16,** `Tab` `Tab` .

6 ➤ **Unit**   Type **each,** `Tab` .

7 ➤ **Description**   Type **Orderly Vanline Trucks,** `Tab` .

8 ➤ **Price**   Type **25.66,** `Tab` .

9 ➤ **Tax**   `Tab` to accept **G.**

10 ➤ Prepayment Paid | | Type **200.00,** `Tab` .

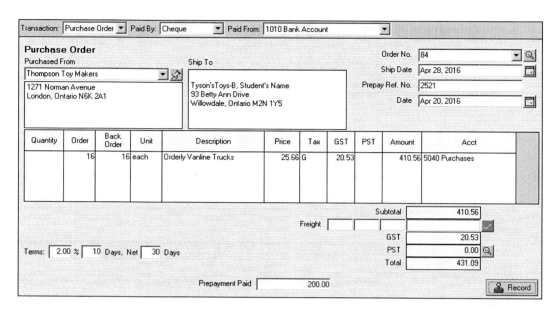

11 ➤ The Purchases Journal–Purchase Order Entry should appear as follows:

Purchases Journal Entry Apr 20, 2016 (J12)

Account Number	Account Description	Debits	Credits
2200	Accounts Payable	200.00	-
1010	Bank Account	-	200.00
Additional Date:	Additional Field:		
		200.00	200.00

12 ➤ **Exit** the Purchases Journal–Purchase Order Entry window.

13 ➤ **Record** when correct and **Exit** to the Home window.

14 ➤ Display the Vendor Aged Detail Report for **Thompson Toy Manufacturers** at Apr 20. The lower portion is shown next. The Prepayment (Prepaid order) is identified separately.

2521	Apr 20, 2016	Prepaid Order	-200.00	-200.00
Total unpaid invoices:			357.68	357.68
Total prepayments/prepaid order:			-200.00	-200.00
Total outstanding:			157.68	157.68

15 ➤ Advance the Session date to **Apr 21, 2016**.

Recording Lease Payments

Because Tyson's Toys pays the lease of their van on a monthly basis, they have set up a recurring transaction entry for this transaction.

Exercise 3B-29 – Recording a Lease Payment

Apr 21, 2016	**Received Bank Debit memo dated Apr 21, 2016 in the amount of $820.00 for the van lease payment ($400.00 plus $20.00 GST) and $400.00 payment on the bank loan ($304.59 to reduce the loan and $95.41 interest).**

You will use the **Recall Recurring Transaction** option, which has been set up for this transaction earlier.

1 ➤ Click on the **COMPANY** module. Click on the **General Journal** icon.

2 ➤ Click the **Recall recurring transaction** icon and the Recall Recurring Transaction window will appear as follows:

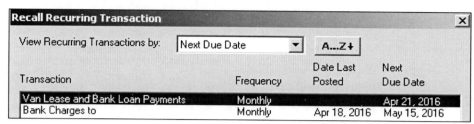

3 ➤ Select **Van Lease** and **Bank Loan Payments**, and the General Journal window is filled in.

4 ➤ Make necessary changes as shown in Fig. 3B-25.

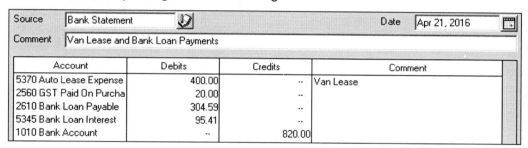

Fig. 3B-25: Van Lease and Bank Loan Payment entry.

5 ➤ In order to update the GST taxes properly, for the GST report when using the General Journal, click the Sales Taxes button.

6 ➤ **Enter** the information as shown next. This will update the GST report, which can be seen in the Appendix CD-D, *Printing a Tax (GST) Report* on the Student Data CD.

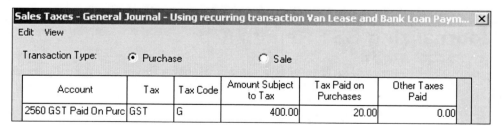

7 ➤ Click **OK**. You will notice a blue ✔ in the ✔ Sales Taxes button. This means that the Sales Taxes will be updated for the GST report.

8 ➤ **Post** when correct, click **Yes** to update the recurring entry.

9 ➤ **Exit** the General Journal to the Home page.

More Transactions

1 ➤ Advance the date to **Apr 29, 2016**.

2 ➤ **Record** and **Post** the three transactions below.

Apr 26, 2016 **Paid $101.97 to A-Your Name Toy Parts for invoice 65839**.

Apr 27, 2016 **Received 3 boxes of various coloured paper at $56.00 each, plus taxes and 3 binders ½ inch at $4.00 each plus taxes, from City Office Supplies. Invoice #2640 dated Apr 27, 2016 with terms of 2/10 n30. Total invoice $203.40.**

Apr 28, 2016 **Received 14 of the trucks ordered on PO #84, from Thompson Toy Makers. The other 2 trucks will be delivered on May 4, 2016. Invoice #1007 dated Apr 27, 2016 was received. Total invoice $377.20. You will need to change Paid by from Cheque to Pay later. See caution and information boxes.**

Simply remembers the last setting you used for the **Paid By** field.
You may have to click the **Paid By** ▼ and change it to **Pay Later**.

Prepay. Applied:	200.00	Total	377.20
		Amount Owing	177.20

Notice that the Prepayment made on Apr 21, has been applied to the invoice total of 377.20, which leaves an amount owing of 177.20.

Journalizing GST Remittance

The federal government (Canada Revenue Agency) requires that **GST CHARGED ON SALES** be paid to the government (**Receiver General**) on a regular basis.

Companies are allowed to subtract from the payment any **GST PAID ON PURCHASES** (this includes all goods and services). This is why many companies keep track of GST Paid on Purchases separately from GST Charged on Sales Invoices.

The balance of the GST PAID ON PURCHASES account is a **debit** (meaning **receivable**) and GST CHARGED ON SALES is a **credit** (meaning **payable**). However, both accounts are located in the Liabilities section of the Balance Sheet.

In a job situation, the task of reconciling GST PAID ON PURCHASES and GST CHARGED ON SALES and journalizing GST remittance may be part of your routine responsibilities. You may or may not receive a memo from your supervisor when it is time to do it. It depends on the procedure that has been set up at your company.

Exercise 3B-30 – Calculating the GST Remittance

Study the following memo:

MEMO

Date: Apr 29, 2016
To: Accounting Clerk
From: Helen Tyson

Please pay the Receiver General the net March 31 GST balance.

Helen

Fig. 3B-26: GST Remittance memo.

Apr 29, 2016	**Paid the Receiver General the net GST payable outstanding at the end of March 2016.**

First, you must find out the General Ledger account balances for GST CHARGED ON SALES and GST PAID ON PURCHASES at the end of March. In a normal business environment you would display the Balance Sheet or the Trial Balance at the end of March.

Chapter 3 was split into parts A and B. Because part B starts at Apr 15, 2016 you cannot display a Mar 31, 2016 Balance Sheet in Part B. In Exercise 3A-3 you were asked to print a Balance Sheet at Mar 31 and retain it for use in this Exercise. If you cannot locate the Mar 31, 2016 Balance Sheet, refer to the Mar 31, 2016 Trial Balance in Fig 3A-1 for the GST amounts.

In a business environment, you could also print a GST report as shown in Appendix CD-D, *Printing a Tax (GST) Report* on the Student Data CD. The Tyson's Toys 3A data file was started at Mar 31; therefore, there are no transactions recorded for March. There will be a message that there is no data to report.

Calculating GST Remittance

1 ➤ Refer to the Balance Sheet printed in Exercise 3A-3.

2 ➤ Circle the amounts for **GST CHARGED ON SALES** and **GST PAID ON PURCHASES**. The net GST amount owing should be $1,088.11.

GST Charged on Sales	1,738.25
GST Paid on Purchases	-650.14
Net GST amount owing	**1,088.11**

OR:

Refer to the Trial Balance (Fig. 3A-1) at the end of Mar 31, 2016, and write on a piece of paper the balances for GST CHARGED ON SALES and GST PAID ON PURCHASES, and calculate the difference. It should amount to **$1,088.11**.

There may be situations when the GST paid on purchases/services is higher than the GST collected on sales.

GST on Sales	$630.00
GST on Purchases/Services	$650.14
GST overpaid (refund requested)	$ 20.14

In this situation, the business would submit the GST return and claim a refund.

In a business environment you could also print the Balance Sheet or Trial Balance noted above as proof of the amounts used. Print the Income Statement for the dates specified on the GST Tax Form. The Sales and Purchase information will be used to fill in the tax form. This would be attached to the documentation for the cheque request and would be part of the audit trail information.

The Receiver General has been set up as a vendor for regular GST payments. Using a vendor will retain information in the PAYABLES module about payments made. This record can be used by Revenue Canada auditors to verify that a payment has been made.

Exercise 3B-31 – Recording the GST Remittance

To record the amount payable to the Receiver General, you would use the same procedure as in the payment to Mr. Tyson in Exercise 3B-27.

1 ➤ Click the **Payments** icon.

2 ➤ Select **Make Other Payment**, [Tab].

By Cheque	DO NOT CHANGE.
From 1010 Bank Account	DO NOT CHANGE.

3 ➤ To the Order of   Select **Receiver General** and [Tab].

4 ➤ Acct   The default account **2550 GST Charged on Sales** appears. GST Charged on Sales is a 2 series Liability account number. The program treats all 2 series numbers as **Liability** accounts, which have normal **credit** balances. We need to **debit** the GST CHARGED ON SALES account and transfer the amount to the ACCOUNTS PAYABLE account. [Tab].

5 ➤ Description   Type **Payment for Mar GST on Sales**, [Tab].

6 ➤ Amount   Type **1738.25**, [Tab]. (A positive number will debit the account used.)

7 ➤ **Tax**   `Tab` not used when paying the Receiver General.

8 ➤ **Acct**   Select **2560 GST Paid on Purchases**.

9 ➤ **Description**   Type **Payment for Mar GST on Purchases**, `Tab`.

10 ➤ **Amount**   Type negative **-650.14** (a negative amount will credit the account used), `Tab`.

11 ➤ **Invoice/Ref**   We need to create a visual record of what is taking place. Some companies would use codes similar to: GST@Mar 31 (Net GST at the end of March), Mar GST (March GST being paid) or GST1QTR (GST 1st Quarter of year).

Type **Mar GST**, `Tab`. The window should resemble Fig. 3B-27:

Acct	Description	Amount	Tax	GST	PST
2550 GST Charged on Sales	Payment for Mar GST on Sales	1,738.25			
2560 GST Paid On Purchases	Payment for Mar GST on Purchases	-650.14			

Subtotal	1,088.11
Tax	
Total	1,088.11

Invoice/Ref.   Mar GST

Comment

     🖊 Post

Fig. 3B-27: GST Payment window.

12 ➤ **Display** the Journal Entry and the window should appear as follows:

Payments Journal Entry Apr 29, 2016 (J17)

Account Number	Account Description	Debits	Credits
2550	GST Charged on Sales	1,738.25	-
1010	Bank Account	-	1,088.11
2560	GST Paid On Purchases	-	650.14
Additional Date:	Additional Field:		
		1,738.25	1,738.25

13 ➤ **Exit** from the Payments Journal Entry window. You could store this transaction as a recurring entry for future periods.

14 ➤ **Post** when correct and **Exit** from the Payments Journal.

Viewing the Vendor Aged Report

1 ➤ The above entry can be displayed using the Vendor Aged Detail report. Your screen display for the Receiver General, should be similar to:

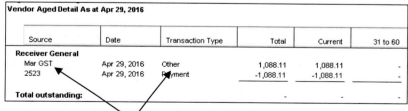

Vendor Aged Detail As at Apr 29, 2016

Source	Date	Transaction Type	Total	Current	31 to 60
Receiver General					
Mar GST	Apr 29, 2016	Other	1,088.11	1,088.11	-
2523	Apr 29, 2016	Payment	-1,088.11	-1,088.11	-
Total outstanding:			-	-	-

Notice the Source **Mar GST** information.

Also notice **Other** in the Transaction Type column. Future payments should have similar good audit trail information.

2 ➤ **Exit** the Vendor Aged Detail report.

Journalizing an Invoice without GST

Current Federal GST legislation exempts insurance from GST; therefore, at present there is no GST on insurance. However, this legislation may change, so watch for GST changes in the future.

Insurance is normally paid in advance, and the cost is charged to PREPAID EXPENSES and then charged to INSURANCE EXPENSE every accounting period over the life of the insurance policy.

Exercise 3B-32 – Recording an Invoice without GST

Study this transaction and the invoice below:

Apr 29, 2016	**Received the following invoice #4799 from Meadows Insurance Brokers Inc. GST is not applicable on insurance invoices.**

Meadows Insurance Brokers Inc.
197 Larange Avenue, Suite 125
Toronto, Ontario M8Z 4R9
Phone/Fax (416) 233-5886

INVOICE
4799

SOLD TO:
Tyson's Toys
93 Betty Ann Drive
Willowdale, Ont M2N 1Y5

Date:___Apr 28, 2016_

COVERAGE	
Renewal Policy #3224321	
To insure building at 93 Betty Ann Drive, Willowdale, Ontario	
Coverage for the period Apr 01, 2016 through Mar 31, 2017	$1,200.00

	GST	N/A
	PST	96.00
Terms: upon receipt	TOTAL	$1,296.00

Fig. 3B-28: Insurance Invoice.

Because the company will be buying additional insurance during the year, you will set up **Meadows Insurance Brokers Inc.** as a vendor, using the Full Add option.

The invoice will be allocated to prepaid expense based on the following:

- (Remember, PST is part of the cost to the company.)

- $1,296.00 divided by 12 months equals $108.00 per month.

- April expense (#5360 Insurance Expense) account will be $108.00, and as the remaining $1,188 prepaid amount expires (gets used), it will be charged to INSURANCE EXPENSE.

You could set up a recurring adjusting General Journal entry for the insurance expense portion for future use.

To Record Payment for Insurance

1 ➤   Click the **Payments** icon.

2 ➤   Select **Make Other Payment**.

3 ➤   **To the**   Type **Meadows Insurance Brokers Inc.**, `Tab`.
          Order of

4 ➤   Click `Full Add`. Use Invoice information to complete the data fields.

5 ➤   Click the **Options** tab. Expense Account field, select **1340 Prepaid Insurance**.

6 ➤   Click the **Taxes** tab. **Tax Exempt** field for GST, click in the column to change to **Yes**.

7 ➤   **Tax code**. Select **P** (GST Exempt, PST at 8%). Click `Save and Close` when complete. `Tab`.

          Cheque No.   2524, the next cheque number.

          Date   Apr 29, 2016, the date the cheque is being issued.

          Acct   Account 1340 Prepaid Insurance is shown since you created this in step 5.

8 ➤   **Description**   Type **Insurance - Building Prepaid**, `Tab`.

9 ➤   **Amount**   Type **1,100.00**, `Tab`.

10 ➤ **Tax**   `Tab` to accept P.

11 ➤ **PST**   `Tab` to accept 88.00. (See side note box.)

12 ➤ **Acct**   Select **5360 Insurance Expense**.

13 ➤ **Description**   Type **Insurance - Building Expense**, `Tab`.

14 ➤ **Amount**   Type **100.00**, `Tab`.

15 ➤ **Tax**   `Tab` to accept P.

16 ➤ **PST**   `Tab` to accept 8.00.

17 ➤ **Invoice/Ref**   Type **4799**, `Tab`.

The lower portion of the Payments window should appear as follows:

> The $1,188 charged to **Prepaid Expenses** is for the 11 months from May 1, 2016 to Mar 31, 2017. As the insurance expires in future months, this amount will be reduced and allocated to **Insurance Expense**.

Acct	Description	Amount	Tax	GST	PST
1340 Prepaid Insurance	Insurance - Building Prepaid	1,100.00	P		88.00
5360 Insurance Expense	Insurance - Building Expense	100.00	P		8.00

	Subtotal	1,200.00
	Tax	96.00
	Total	1,296.00

Invoice/Ref.   4799

Comment

Post

18 ➤ Display the Payments Journal Entry. It should look like the following:

Payments Journal Entry Apr 29, 2016 (J18)

Account Number	Account Description	Debits	Credits
1340	Prepaid Insurance	1,188.00	-
5360	Insurance Expense	108.00	-
1010	Bank Account	-	1,296.00
Additional Date:	Additional Field:		
		1,296.00	1,296.00

19 ➤ **Exit** from the Payments Journal Entry window.

20 ➤ **Post** after verifying accuracy, and **Exit** to the Home window.

More Transactions

Record and **Post** the following transactions:

RST refers to **Retail Sales Tax**, the official name is **PST** (Provincial Sales Tax). Click the **Options** tab, for **Expense Account:** select **2580 PST Payable. Click** the **Taxes** tab, make both **Taxes Exempt** and choose tax code **No tax.** Follow similar procedure used to pay the Receiver General as in Exercise 3B-30 and 3B-31.

Apr 29, 2016	**Pay the Ministry of Finance, RST Taxation Data Centre, PO Box 620, Oshawa, Ontario, L1H 8E9, the $65.08 PST Payable amount from March 31.** In the Vendor ledger you will need to use the **Street 1**: field to record the RST Taxation Data Centre information.

Apr 29, 2016	**Returned 3 binders ½ inch at $4.00 each plus taxes, to City Office Supplies. Original Invoice #2640. Binders too small.**

Apr 29, 2016	**Purchased various parts, odd size wheels, doors, etc., which will be sold as parts (record as 1 lot of various parts) from A-Your Name Toy Parts. PO was not issued. Received their invoice #9765 dated today, for $169.21 (including $8.06 for GST), terms net 30 for this invoice.**

1 ➤ Advance the date to **Apr 30, 2016**.

Apr 30, 2016	**Paterson's Wood Working, 698 Beech Avenue, Suite 6, Toronto, Ontario, M4E 9A3, delivered and installed 2 new Store Equipment (display) cabinets. They were ordered by Mrs. Tyson to display new and current toys. A PO was not issued. The cabinets cost $900.00 each, plus GST and PST. Received $2,034.00 invoice #2696 dated today, with terms net 10 days.**

Printing Reports

An Income Statement shows the current financial position re SALES, COST OF GOODS SOLD and EXPENSES. This chapter deals with PURCHASES; therefore, there will be no change to the Revenue (Sales) section of the Income Statement. (See side note box.)

Exercise 3B-33 – Printing Reports

---

1 ➤ Print the following and compare them to the same report you printed at the beginning of this chapter, Mar 31, 2016, at Exercise 3A-3.

a. Income Statement for period **Jan 01, 2016** to **Apr 30, 2016**.

b. Balance Sheet at **Apr 30, 2016**.

2 ➤ Print a Trial Balance. Click **Reports, Financials, Trial Balance**, Date: **Apr 30, 2016**. Click **OK**, then **Print** Report.

You should notice that in both Income Statements, ENDING INVENTORY accounts (#5090) have the same negative -$6,907.29. You should also notice that both Balance Sheets have a Current Asset TOYS AND PARTS INVENTORY account (#1310) in a value of $6,907.29.

In business, it is extremely unlikely that inventory values would not change from one month to the next, especially with sales and purchases being made during the month. The ending inventory value $6,907.29 needs to be updated to reflect the actual cost value of goods on hand.

Adjusting Ending Inventory – Periodic Method in Simply

There are three inventory values (one on the Balance Sheet and two on the Income Statement) needed to complete financial statements. They include:

Balance Sheet:

- Asset Inventory on the Balance Sheet (what is "owned" on that date).

Income Statement:

Cost of Goods Sold (COGS) Calculation.

- COGS Beginning Inventory
- COGS Ending Inventory

How inventory accounting is recorded will depend on:

1. Which system is used (perpetual or periodic), and
2. If the company uses manual bookkeeping or computerized bookkeeping (e.g., Simply Accounting).

Review the comparison between Periodic Inventory System and Perpetual Inventory System. Remember that in this chapter we are using a **Periodic** inventory system in a **computerized** bookkeeping environment.

Periodic Inventory System

For companies that are still using manual bookkeeping, there are no inventory entries until closing entries at fiscal year-end. Interim financial statements are prepared with inventory information supplied by management, but inventory amounts are not recorded in the accounting records.

For companies that use computerized bookkeeping (e.g., Simply Accounting), inventory values must be recorded in the Simply system for all reports. This means inventory entries (to adjust inventory values) are required every time financial statements are produced.

Review the following comparison between **manual** and **computerized** environments assuming a company uses the calendar year as its fiscal year.

Manual Bookkeeping

For the entire fiscal year, the value for inventory in the G/L INVENTORY (Asset) account as of January 1 will not change. For financial statement reporting throughout the year, it is reported as the value of **COGS Beginning Inventory** on the **Income Statement**.

In order to properly reflect the amount of inventory still "owned" versus "sold" each month, a physical count is conducted at month-end and reported:

1. On the **Balance Sheet** as the **asset** INVENTORY value to accurately report what is "owned", and
2. On the **Income Statement** as the **COGS Ending Inventory** value. The ending inventory as part of the COGS calculation (which includes the COGS **Beginning Inventory** value and **Net Purchases**), will ensure accurate reporting of what has been "sold" to date.

There are NO entries made in the company files for either of 1 or 2 above.

After the physical inventory count at fiscal year-end has been approved and reported, the asset INVENTORY value in the General Ledger will be updated to the new count and closing entries are posted. As in the year just finished, this value will be in the General Ledger INVENTORY Asset account for the entire next fiscal year.

During the **next** fiscal year, it will be "used" for Income Statement reporting as the "COGS Beginning Inventory."

Computerized Bookkeeping

In contrast, computers cannot "borrow" information from G/L accounts to complete the financial statements. The information must be recorded in the system. Therefore, we need to use three inventory accounts to parallel the one account we use in manual systems. These accounts are:

Financial Statement	Type of Account	Account Name
Balance Sheet	Asset	Inventory
Income Statement	COGS	Beginning Inventory (See side box.)
Income Statement	COGS	Ending Inventory

> **BEGINNING INVENTORY** is also referred to as **OPENING INVENTORY**.

The **INVENTORY** value as of January 1 is reported in the **COGS Beginning Inventory** account. This balance does NOT CHANGE during the year.

The asset **INVENTORY** value and the **COGS Ending Inventory** value are the actual physical count, usually on a monthly basis. At the end of each month, you update these two accounts by removing last month's values and replacing them with the current month's values. This will be shown to you in Exercise 3B-34. Again, this is done to ensure accurate reporting of what is "owned" on the Balance Sheet and what has been "sold" on the Income Statement.

Perpetual Inventory System

See the 'Comparison of Periodic and Perpetual Inventory Methods' chart at the beginning of Chapter 8, for a visual display of entries required in both the Perpetual and Periodic inventory methods. You will also be able to record the transactions in 3A using the 08 C8-5 Toys-PI data file using the Perpetual Inventory method (after you have completed Chapter 8).

In Chapter 8, you will have a chance to work with the **perpetual** inventory system. In contrast to a **periodic** inventory system, a perpetual inventory system's features include:

1. Updating Asset INVENTORY and COGS balances as inventory is bought and sold.
2. Using inventory adjustment entry to update the accounts to match the actual inventory on hand; e.g., adjust inventory value based on the physical count and/or record decrease due to lost/damaged items, etc.

As you have seen, when you record purchase of goods for resale (or purchase of goods to make goods for resale), the INVENTORY accounts, as mentioned above, do not change. They are adjusted only at period-end or when you want to produce accurate financial statements.

Study this information:

The **Mar 31, 2016** and **Apr 30, 2016 inventory balances** are as follows:

Section	Name of Account	Debit	Credit
ASSET	1310 Toys and parts Inventory	$6,907.29	
COGS*	5010 Beginning Inventory	$5,421.49	
COGS*	5090 Ending Inventory		$6,907.29

*Cost of Goods Sold

Just as inventory values are adjusted and closed in a manual accounting system, inventory amounts need to be adjusted in Simply. Management decides the time period for the financial statements, (e.g., monthly, quarterly, etc.), and by an actual count or estimate, a reasonable dollar value ENDING INVENTORY must be determined.

You are provided with the new INVENTORY value by the following memo:

MEMO

Date: Apr 30, 2016

To: Accounting Clerk

From: Jerry Tyson

Would you please print a year-to-date Income Statement for me.

The ending inventory on Apr 30, 2016 rounded to nearest dollar is $8,297.00 based on an inventory count taken.

Jerry

Fig. 3B-29: ENDING INVENTORY memo.

There are two methods to adjust the inventory:

Method 1 requires two steps. 1 Remove the previous inventory $6,907.29 2 Set up the new inventory value $8,297.00	**This method is recommended by the authors**. You can see the old value removed and the new value entered.
Method 2 requires only one step: Adjust the inventory for the $1,389.71 difference between the two inventory amounts.	This method can cause problems because you may deduct from the inventory when you should have added to inventory, or vice versa.

Method 1 will be explained in this chapter. Method 2 will be explained in Chapter 9.

Exercise 3B-34 – Adjusting Inventory

To Remove Previous INVENTORY Value

To remove the old ENDING INVENTORY, the General Journal is used, because the entry does not affect Receivables or Payables.

1 ➤ Click the **COMPANY** module, and click the **General** icon.

2 ➤ Source   Type **Memo Apr-JT** (Memo Apr- Jerry Tyson), `Tab` to Comment.

3 ➤ Comment   Type **Remove March ending inventory**, `Tab`.

4 ➤ Account   Select **5090** (Ending Inventory in Cost of Goods Sold), `Tab`.

5 ➤ Debit   Type **6,907.29**. `Tab` `Tab` to accept 6,907.29 and bypass the **Comment** column field.

The 5 series accounts normally have a **debit** balance, but closing inventory (a contra account) has a **credit** balance. It reduces the cost of goods available for sale to what was actually sold. We need to debit #5090 to reduce the account. Enter as a Debit (positive) amount.

6 ➤ Account   Select **1310** Toys and parts Inventory (Asset), `Tab`.

7 ➤ Credits   The cursor is in the **Credits** column to balance the entry.

`Tab` to accept 6,907.29 and bypass the **Comment** column. The 1 series accounts normally have a **debit** balance. We need to credit the account to reduce the ASSET account amount to nil.

8 ➤ **Display** the General Journal Entry. The screen should resemble the following:

General Journal Entry Apr 30, 2016 (J23)

Account Number	Account Description	Debits	Credits
5090	Ending Inventory	6,907.29	-
1310	Toys and parts Inventory	-	6,907.29
Additional Date:	Additional Field:		
		6,907.29	6,907.29

9 ➤ **Exit** the General Journal entry and **Post** when correct.

This inventory entry and the next, which happen monthly, are excellent examples of entries that could be set up as recurring entries.

This procedure has reduced both accounts to nil. You need to record the new inventory value of $8,297.00 (estimated) by reversing the above procedure.

To Enter the New Inventory Value

10 ➤ Source   Type **Memo Apr-JT** (Memo Apr- Jerry Tyson), `Tab`.

11 ➤ Comment   Type **Set up April ending inventory**, `Tab`.

12 ➤ Account   Select **1310** (Toys and parts Inventory) (Asset), `Tab`.

13 ➤ Debit   You need to set up as an asset the amount of inventory that is on hand. Type **8297.00**, `Tab` `Tab` to accept 8,297.00 and bypass the **Comment** column field.

14 ➤ Account   Type **5090** (Ending Inventory) (Cost Of Goods Sold), `Tab`.

15 ➤ Credits The cursor is in the **Credits** column. [Tab] [Tab] to accept. The 5 series accounts normally have a **debit** balance, but ENDING INVENTORY needs a **credit** balance. It reduces the cost of goods available for sale to what was actually sold.

16 ➤ Display the General Journal entry:

General Journal Entry Apr 30, 2016 (J24)			
Account Number	Account Description	Debits	Credits
1310	Toys and parts Inventory	8,297.00	-
5090	Ending Inventory	-	8,297.00
Additional Date:	Additional Field:		
		8,297.00	8,297.00

17 ➤ Exit the General Journal entry and **Post** when correct.

18 ➤ Exit to the Home window.

Apr 30, 2016 trial balance would contain the following values:

Section	Name of account	Debit	Credit
ASSET	1310 Toys and parts Inventory	$ 8,297.00	
COGS*	5010 Beginning Inventory	$ 5,421.49	
COGS*	5090 Ending Inventory		$ 8,297.00

*Cost of Goods Sold
Notice that account #5010 Beginning Inventory (Jan 1, 2016) did NOT change.

To see the effect each of the above transactions had on each of the INVENTORY accounts, drill down to each of the accounts. You will see that each account shows the opening balance; the first adjustment reduces the account to nil, and the second adjustment updates the account with the new balance.

Study this next example:

General Ledger Report Apr 15, 2016 to Apr 30, 2016 Sorted by: Transaction Number							
Date	Comment	Source #	JE#	Debits	Credits		Balance
1310 Toys and parts Inventory							6,907.29 Dr
Apr 30, 2016	Remove March ending inventory	Memo Apr-JT	J23	-	6,907.29		- Dr
Apr 30, 2016	Setup April ending inventory	Memo Apr-JT	J24	8,297.00	-		8,297.00 Dr
				8,297.00	6,907.29		

Exercise 3B-35 – Printing Statements

1 ➤ Print an **Income Statement** with starting date of **Jan 01, 2016** and finish date **Apr 30, 2016**. The statement should now show the new ending inventory. Exit to the Home page.

When you start a new fiscal year the inventory entries are slightly different. See Chapters 9 and 10 for discussion on this topic.

Mr. Tyson wants to see the Income Statement activity from Apr 16 as well as the year-to-date activity.

The Comparative Income Statement

To print a Comparative Income Statement follow these steps:

1 ➤ Click **Report Centre**, **Financials**, click the **+** at **Income Statement**, select **Comparative 2 Period**, click **Modify this report**. A new Options window appears.

2 ➤ To see what changes occurred in the period Apr 16 to April 30, as well as the year-to-date information, change the **First Period Start** date to **Apr 16, 2016**, Tab, change the Report On item as shown, then click **OK**.

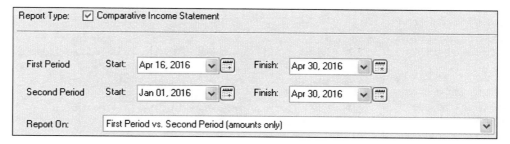

The Comparative Income Statement is displayed. The first column of amounts is the activity that occurred from the entries you recorded from April 16 to the 30th. The other column is the year-to-date values in the accounts.

3 ➤ **Exit** to the Home window.

The BEGINNING INVENTORY account value in the first group of columns is 0.00. This is because there was no change in the account for the period requested, namely April 16 to the 30th. Beginning Inventory will not change throughout the fiscal year.

The ENDING INVENTORY account value in the first group of columns is -1,389.71. This is because there was a credit increase from 6,907.29 to 8,297.00 to this account for the period requested, namely April 16 to the 30th.

Other Period-End/Month-End Reports

At the end of the month it is normal to print the following additional reports for the month and file them for your audit trail:

- The All Journal Entries for the transactions entered in the month.
- The Balance Sheet as at Apr 30, 2016.
- The General Ledger for Apr.
- The Vendor Aged Detail report, as at Apr 30, 2016.
- The Purchases Journal for the month of Apr - includes cash purchases.
- The Payments Journal for the month of Apr.
- The Cheque Log for the month of Apr.

Exercise 3B-36 – Printing Period-End Reports

Make sure the printer is ready. You should be at the Tyson's Toys Home window to start this exercise.

1 ➤ **Print the All Journal Entries** as shown in previous chapters.

2 ➤ **Print the General Ledger for Apr 16-30** as shown in previous chapters.

3 ➤ **Print the Vendor Aged Detail** at **Apr 30, 2016.** To ensure that everything is correct, you should compare the Balance Sheet Accounts Payable amount with the total of the Vendor Aged Detail report. They should be the same!

To View and Print the Purchases Journal

When you see the magnifying glass with the + sign in any of the reports, it means you can drill down (if you click the Journal entry number) to see the original invoice that made the entry.

If you drill down from the account number or name, you will see the ledger account and all entries that make up the account. Try drilling down for one or two entries.

To print the **Purchases Journal** for Apr 2016:

1 ➤ Click **Report Centre, Payables, Purchases Journal Entries, Modify this report**.

    By Date   DO NOT CHANGE.

2 ➤ **Start**   Select **Apr 15, 2016,** ⌨Tab .

3 ➤ **Finish**   ⌨Tab to accept Apr 30, 2016.

4 ➤ Click **Corrections** or **Additional Information** if required. Click **OK** to display the Purchases Journal.

5 ➤ **Print** the report.

6 ➤ **Exit** from the display window. (See side note box.)

To View and Print the Payments Journal

To print the **Payments Journal** for Apr 2016:

1 ➤ Click **Report Centre, Payables, Payments Journal Entries, Modify this report.**

    By Date   DO NOT CHANGE.

2 ➤ **Start**   Select **Apr 15, 2016,** ⌨Tab .

3 ➤ **Finish**   ⌨Tab to accept Apr 30, 2016.

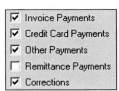

Click the boxes shown, even though you have not made a credit card payment or corrections. The Remittance Payments option will be discussed in Chapter 7 (Payroll).

4 ➤ Click **OK** to display the Payments Journal.

5 ➤ **Print** the report.

6 ➤ **Exit** from the display window.

To View and Print a Cheque Log

1 ➤ Click **Report Centre, Banking, Cheque Log, Modify this report**, select the options as shown next:

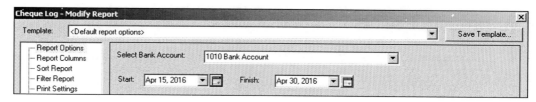

2 ➤ Click **OK** and the cheque log will display.

3 ➤ You may **Print** this report, and return to the Home window.

Cheque Log for 1010 Bank Account from Apr 15, 2016 to Apr 30, 2016

Cheque No.	Che... Type	Payee	Amount	Cheque Date	Times prin...	Entered... system	JE#	JE Date
2515	Payment	NAS Business Forms	333.00	Apr 15, 2016	0	Yes	J3	Apr 15, 2016
2516	Payment	Lanting Speciality Toys	3,162.60	Apr 18, 2016	0	Yes	J6	Apr 18, 2016
2517	Payment	Jason's Transport Service	1,260.00	Apr 18, 2016	0	Yes	J7	Apr 18, 2016
2518	Payment	City Office Supplies	155.94	Apr 18, 2016	0	Yes	J8	Apr 18, 2016
2519	Payment	Alan Cohen & Associates	465.56	Apr 19, 2016	0	Yes	J9	Apr 19, 2016
2520	Payment	Jerry Tyson	900.00	Apr 20, 2016	0	Yes	J11	Apr 20, 2016
2522	Payment	A-Your Name Toy Parts	101.97	Apr 26, 2016	0	Yes	J14	Apr 26, 2016
2523	Payment	Receiver General	1,088.11	Apr 29, 2016	0	Yes	J17	Apr 29, 2016
2524	Payment	Meadows Insurance Broker...	1,296.00	Apr 29, 2016	0	Yes	J18	Apr 29, 2016
2525	Payment	Ministry of Finance	65.08	Apr 29, 2016	0	Yes	J19	Apr 29, 2016

The cheque log (from Part 3A) is shown below:

Cheque Log for 1010 Bank Account from Mar 31, 2016 to Apr 15, 2016

Cheque No.	Che... Type	Payee	Amount	Cheque Date	Times prin...	Entered... system	JE#	JE Date
2511	Payment	Willowdale Mall Ltd.	2,100.00	Apr 07, 2016	0	Reversed	J3	Apr 07, 2016
2512	Payment	Willowdale Mall Ltd.	2,205.00	Apr 07, 2016	1	Yes	J7	Apr 07, 2016
2513	Payment	Lanting Speciality Toys	667.80	Apr 07, 2016	0	Yes	J10	Apr 07, 2016
2514	Payment	Thompson Toy Makers	2,550.75	Apr 15, 2016	0	Yes	J11	Apr 15, 2016

This report displays the cheque numbers, amounts and dates the entries were recorded. As noted early in the chapter, you would not print cheques in order to conserve paper, unless your instructor requires you to do so.

In the 3A report above, cheque 2511 was recorded and reversed. Cheque 2512 was printed. In a job situation, the **Times prin** (Times Printed**)** column would indicate a **1** (for cheques printed) and perhaps **2** if there was a printer jam and the cheque had to be reprinted. The report would ensure that management knew the number of times cheques were printed in order to prevent fraud (the same cheque printed more than once). The manager would want to see all damaged cheques and make sure that they were voided and unusable.

4 ➤ Compare your printed reports to the reports for Tyson's Toys in the data files from your instructor.

To View Graphs

You may find information on using the graph feature (pie and bar charts) for PAYABLES comparisons in Appendix CD-K on the Student Data CD.

Summary, Part B

Here is a summary of tasks and transactions in Chapter 3, Part B.

Transaction	Journal/Ledger	Remarks
Prepayment	Purchase Orders	Record a Vendor prepayment with a Purchase Order.
New Vendor (Supplier)	Vendors Ledger	At the Taxes tab, change the Tax Exempt status for GST and PST where necessary and select the appropriate tax code. Select an appropriate default expense account.
Drawings	Payments	Create owner's Vendor record. Use Make other Payment option to record a memo and a cheque together.
GST Remittance	Payments	Create Receiver General as a Vendor. Use Make other Payment option to record a memo and a cheque together. Determine balance of GST Charged On Sales and GST Paid on Purchase accounts to be paid. Enter a negative amount to GST paid on Purchases account.
Inventory Adjustment	General	Remove and set up inventory values as required.

Review **Slideshows 3A** and **3B** now. They will help you better understand the next chapter on **Setting Up a Company**.

Before Moving On..., Part B

Read the following questions and make sure you know the answers to them; otherwise, read the corresponding part in the chapter before moving on.

1. When journalizing non-merchandise purchases with PST and GST, how is **PST** recorded?

2. Give the journal entry for a purchase return of $300.00 plus GST of $15.00:

    a) for merchandise for resale.

    b) for merchandise not for resale, plus $24.00 PST (non-purchase items - office supplies).

3. Describe briefly the steps in recording a payment of an invoice when taking a cash discount, using as the base the cost before taxes:

   a) for merchandise for resale.

   b) for merchandise not for resale (Office Supplies).

4. Give the journal entry for a prepayment of $100.00 to a vendor.   How is it entered in Simply?

5. Describe briefly how the GST remittance is calculated.

6. What happens when you post journal transactions in the PAYABLES module?

7. When journalizing non-merchandise purchases with PST and GST, on what amount is **GST** based?

8. The month-end inventory adjustment consists of two entries. What is the Journal entry for the reversal of the old inventory?

9. What would a manager look for when reviewing the cheque log?

10. What is the difference in the periodic inventory method of accounting between the Simply process and the manual books process? Which method requires more inventory accounts?

Relevant Appendices, Part B

The following appendices are available on the Student Data CD.

Appendix 2009 CD-D   **Printing a Tax (GST) Report**

Appendix 2009 CD-K   **Graphs Feature**

Challenge Exercise 03 C3B-1, Network

(PAYABLES and GENERAL Ledger)

1 ➤ Refer to Exercise 1-1 to unzip the **03 C3B-1 Network.exe** file.

2 ➤ Open the **03 C3B-1 Network** file and enter **PAYABLES transactions for Mar** for a company that sells various computer parts. Apply GST of 5% and PST of 8%, when needed. Network Company does *not* print cheques.

The business is open every day. You worked on March 5, 12, 19, 26, and March 31.

3 ➤ Record and **Post** the following transactions:

Mar 2   Ordered on PO# 651, 28 Ethernet cable-ready network cards for $75.00 each, plus GST, from PC Cards Company. Shipping date to be Mar 12. Terms 2/10, net 30 days. PO total $2,205.00.

Mar 3   A $300.00 cheque is issued to Umax Cables as a prepayment for a special order of 80 RJ45 cables at $21.50 each, plus GST. Total cost $1,720.00, plus GST. Issue next PO. These cables are required by Mar 28. Terms are 2/10, net 30.

Mar 9   Purchased from new vendor, Your Last Name (surname) Supplies, various store supplies for $145.00, plus GST and PST. Goods arrived and were placed in the storage cabinet. Invoice #8261, terms 2/10, net 30, calculate discounts before tax. The default Expense Account field in the Vendor Setup, Options tab window, can be an Asset or other account type. Select an appropriate account for this field.

Mar 10   Next cheque issued to J.D. Long for 2 Network Hubs at $81.00 each, plus GST, invoice #10005 received.

Mar 12   Received 28 Ethernet cable-ready network cards from PC Cards Company ordered on PO# 651. Invoice #6638 was received totaling $2,205.00. Terms 2/10, net 30 days.

Mar 15   Issued cheque to the Receiver General for the GST owing at the end of February. Note that the Trial Balance GST amounts at February month-end are correct.

Mar 16   Returned 1 Ethernet cable-ready network card to PC Cards Company because it is damaged. Our technician could not get it to work. PC Cards accepted the return with a credit note 6638RT.

Mar 19   Issued cheque to Your Last Name (surname) Supplies, for invoice #8261.

Mar 22   Issued cheque to PC Cards Company as payment in full for invoice #6638, after return.

Mar 28   80 RJ45 cables arrived with invoice #8964 from Umax Cables Company (P.O. #652). Each cable cost $21.50, plus GST. Terms on the order are 2%10, net 30.

Mar 30   Bank statement as of March 29 arrived with debit note that the bank charge for the period ending March 29 is $19.35. No GST or PST.

Mar 31   The manager advised you that the ending inventory value was $84,286.00. Adjust the inventory to allow you to prepare accurate financial statements.

4 ➤ When you have recorded the above entries, **print** the following:

  a) Vendor Aged Detail report as at Mar 31.
  b) All Journal Entries for the monthly activity with ✓ Show Corrections
  c) Journal Entries-General for the monthly activity with ✓ Show Corrections
  d) Purchases Journal for Mar.
  e) Payments Journal for Mar.
  f)   Income Statement for the year to date.
  g) Cheque log for the month.

Challenge Exercise 03 C3B-2, China

(GENERAL, PAYABLES and RECEIVABLES)

1 ➤   Refer to Exercise 1-1 to unzip the **03 C3B-2 China.exe** file.

This exercise is a review of the 3 modules (GENERAL, PAYABLES and RECEIVABLES).

2 ➤   Open the the **03 C3B-2 China** file.

The China Company sells various kinds and sizes of china for everyday use and for special occasions. 5% GST and 8% PST are applied for retail sales. Terms for non-retail sale customers are 2/10, net 30. Vendor invoices normally have terms of 2/10, net 30, except where additional information is given.

All sales invoices and cheques are issued in numerical order. China Company does not print invoices or cheques. The company does not use the **Shipped** field in Purchase Invoices. Cash discounts when appropriate are calculated on the cost price before GST and PST. You normally work on March 5, 12, 19, 26 and March 31. You advance the session date when you open the data file.

3 ➤   **Record** and **Post** the following transactions:

Ignore phone and fax numbers for new customers and vendors.

Mar 1	Issued Purchase order #106 to BNS Printing Ltd. for new invoices with a revised logo. Delivery date is Mar 5. Cost of the new invoices will be $100.00, plus GST and PST, with terms 2/10, net 30.
Mar 1	Advertisement in today's issue of Yourtown Newspaper, a new vendor, 5569 Ace Avenue, Yourtown, Ontario L5N 1X6, contact Eugene Korobok. Invoice #1099 received for $200.00, plus PST and GST. Terms Net 15 days. Use an appropriate account for the default Expense field.
Mar 2	Purchased 30 dinner plates at $25.00 each, plus GST, from Specialty Manufacturer. All plates were received in good condition. Invoice #361 dated today with terms of 2/10, net 30.
Mar 3	Sold on invoice #5270, one specialty item, a British luncheon service set, to a new customer, **Your Actual Name**, 85 Lake Avenue, Rockton, Ontario L6N1B9. The service set selling price is $1,000.00, plus GST and PST. **Your Actual Name** will pay the net amount in 15 days. Credit limit $2,000.00.
Mar 5	The new invoices from BNS Printing ordered on PO#106 are received in good condition with invoice #875 dated today.
Mar 5	We returned 4 plates from the Mar 2 order from Specialty Manufacturer Ltd., because the pattern is not centered properly. Original cost of the plates was $25.00 each, plus GST.
Mar 6	Sold 1 dozen soup bowls at $15.00 per bowl, plus GST, to Plates and More. Normal terms.
Mar 6	Issued cheque to pay Receiver General the GST owing at the end of February.
Mar 7	Plates and More returned 5 of the soup bowls because they arrived damaged. We have called the shipping company to determine what happened. Plates and More purchased replacement bowls from another store and have requested a reduction to their account. We accepted the returned bowls by issuing a credit note with the original Invoice number as a reference.

Mar 8   Issued an $800.00 cheque to Mary Opal, owner, based on a memo received. The money is for personal expenses.

Mar 12   Issued cheque to Specialty Manufacturer Ltd. to pay only for dinner plates purchased, after returns, on invoice #361.

Mar 15   Issued cheque to pay BNS Printing Ltd. for invoice #875.

Mar 16   Received $108.15 cheque #789 from Plates and More re: invoice #5271.

Mar 16   Issued cheque to Yourtown Newspaper for outstanding invoice #1099.

Mar 19   Received cheque #788 from Your Actual Name for invoice #5270.

Mar 19   The bank manager called and requires an Income Statement as of business today. The manager advised you by memo to adjust the ending inventory as counted by staff to $12,380.00.

4 ➤ **Print** the following reports:

   a)   Year-to-date Income statement.
   b)   Journal Entries - All for the transactions above.
   c)   Journal Entries General, Mar 1 – Mar 19.
   d)   Accounts Receivable - Aged Detail for all customers.
   e)   Accounts Payable - Aged Detail for all vendors.
   f)   Cash Flow Projection (detail) for the next 30 days.

Challenge Exercise 03 C3B-3, Dance Studio

(GENERAL, PAYABLES and RECEIVABLES)

1 ➤   Refer to Exercise 1-1 to unzip the **03 C3B-3 Dance.exe** file.

2 ➤   Open the **03 C3B-3 Dance** file and enter transactions for Mar.

The Dance Studio instructs students in various types of dance classes (Tap, Scottish, Irish, Ballet, etc.). Dance lessons are PST-Exempt.

Terms for customers are net 5 days with a few customers being given 2/10, net 30. Vendor invoices normally have terms of 2/10, net 30, except where additional information is given. Discounts for paying vendor invoices early are charged to Cleaning and Repairs Expense. All sales invoices and cheques are issued in numerical order. Dance Studio Company does not print invoices or cheques. Ignore Shipped by field. GST is 5% and PST is 8%.

You work on a weekly basis, Mar 5, 12, 19, 26 and Mar 31, therefore, advance the date as needed. Ignore phone and fax numbers for new customers and vendors.

3 ➤   Enter the following transactions:

Mar 1   Purchased 10 boxes of special wax (Cleaning & Repairs Expense) at $32.00 each, plus GST and PST for the new dance practice studio floor from new vendor Speciality Services (any address information). These will be used in the next two weeks. Invoice #748 received with terms 2/10, net 15 days, calculate discounts before tax.

Mar 2   Issued cheque #897 to pay for invoice #1962 owing to Quinton Cleaning Services.

Mar 5   Sold on invoice #426, dance lessons for the week $40.00 plus GST, to **Your Actual Name**. You paid with a Universal credit card.

Mar 5   Returned 1 box of the special wax to Speciality Services, as the wax was too oily. Credit note #748RT received.

Mar 8   The owner, Rajwinder Opuku, issued a memo requesting an $800.00 cheque to cover personal expenses. Cheque #898 is issued.

Mar 14   Purchased 1 box of sales invoices from NAJ Printing Ltd. Invoice #875, $100.00, plus GST and PST. Terms, net 20 days.

Mar 15   Paid Speciality Services with cheque #899, for invoice #748 after taking off the return.

Mar 19   Sold on invoice #427 dance lessons, for the week $40.00, plus GST to **Your Actual Name**. You paid with your cheque #158.

Mar 26   The bank advised by $428.00 debit memo dated today that the bank interest on the loan was $28.00 and the loan payment was $400.00.

Mar 29   Sold on invoice #428 dance lessons for the week $55.00, plus GST, to Ying Zhu. Ying paid cash for the invoice.

Mar 30   Received invoice #456 in the amount of $80.00, plus GST and PST, for cleaning of classroom from Quinton Cleaning Services. Terms 2/10, net 20.

Mar 30   Received $175.00 plus PST (GST-Exempt) insurance bill #A4589 from Metro Insurance (any address information) for the month of March. Bill to be paid in 5 days.

4 ➤   Advance the date to **Mar 31** and **print** the following:

    a)   Income Statement for Jan 1 to Mar 31.
    b)   Journal Entries-All, for Mar 1 to Mar 31.
    c)   Journal Entries-General, for Mar 1 to Mar 31.
    d)   Accounts Receivable - Aged Detail for all customers, for Mar 1 to Mar 31.
    e)   Accounts Payable - Aged Detail for all vendors, for Mar 1 to Mar 31.

Challenge Exercise 03 C3B-4, Chairs

This exercise is a review of 3 modules – COMPANY, PAYABLES & RECEIVABLES

1 ➤ Refer to Exercise 1-1 to unzip the Chairs exe file that is appropriate for your province or territory. The exe file is located on the Student CD under: **Chapter Data files\Chairs-Provincial Data Files.**

Chairs-Alberta.exe   Chairs-Nova Scotia.exe
Chairs-British Columbia.exe   Chairs-Ontario.exe
Chairs-Manitoba.exe   Chairs-Prince Edward Island.exe
Chairs-New Brunswick.exe   Chairs-Quebec.exe
Chairs-Newfoundland.exe   Chairs-Saskatchewan.exe
Chairs-North West Territories.exe   Chairs-Yukon.exe

2 ➤ Open the appropriate **Chairs** file.

3 ➤ Locate the **Chairs document** folder on the Student Data CD.

4 ➤ **Print** the appropriate **Chairs Adobe PDF file** for your province or territory, with information about the company and a list of the transactions.

If you do not have Adobe Reader on your computer, check the **Open me FIRST** Microsoft Word document (under the Appendices folder on your Student Data CD) for instructions on how to download Adobe Acrobat Reader.

Each data file has the GST, PST or HST rates appropriate for that province or territory.

A list of GST and PST rates are shown below and can also be found in Chapter 15, *Taxes.*

The GST rate of 5% is used in this text and reflected in the solutions. This rate, however, may have changed since the publication date. When on the job be sure to use the appropriate GST and PST rates.

5 ➤ **Record** the transactions listed in the PDF document.

6 ➤ **Print** the reports required in step 4 of the PDF document.

GST, PST and HST rates by Province & Territory (at May 31, 2009)	GST	PST	HST	Total
Prince Edward Island	5.0	10.0	-	15.0
New Brunswick	-	-	13.0	13.0
Newfoundland & Labrador	-	-	13.0	13.0
Nova Scotia	-	-	13.0	13.0
Ontario	5.0	8.0	-	13.0
Quebec	5.0	7.5	-	12.5
British Columbia	5.0	7.0	-	12.0
Manitoba	5.0	7.0	-	12.0
Saskatchewan	5.0	5.0	-	10.0
Alberta	5.0	-	-	5.0
North West Territories	5.0	-	-	5.0
Yukon	5.0	-	-	5.0

Accounting and Simply Accounting Terminology

Approval Stamp: A stamp on the back of the vendor invoice on which an authorized person in the purchasing department indicates the G/L account number(s) to which the invoice must be charged. It is approved usually by showing the person's name or initials, and dated.

Clear: To remove (delete) paid vendor invoices from the data records.

Credit Memo: A memorandum sent by a vendor to the purchaser to indicate that the purchaser's account has been **reduced**, usually because of a return of the purchased goods. It is a **credit** memo because the vendor is crediting **their** customer's ACCOUNTS RECEIVABLE account; therefore, the purchaser would **debit** ACCOUNTS PAYABLE in their books.

Deposit: *See Prepayment.*

Expense: Purchase of goods not for resale or services used in running a business.

GST: **G**oods and **S**ervices **T**ax. In the PAYABLES module, GST paid to vendors is posted to the account GST PAID ON PURCHASES. It is based on 5% of the invoice amount (excluding PST).

GST Remittance: GST paid on purchases is deducted from GST collected from sales. If GST collected from sales is larger, the difference must be paid (remitted) to the government. If the reverse is true, a GST refund will be requested. The GST remittance may be made monthly, quarterly, or annually depending on volume of business.

Manual Cheque: A cheque written by hand and not printed by Simply. A numbering system different from computer-generated cheques may be used for manual cheques.

Matching Principle: This accounting principle requires that if revenues earned in an accounting period are recorded, then expenses incurred to earn those revenues must also be recorded in that period.

Prepayment: An advance payment made to a vendor against a future invoice to show a commitment to purchase. In the RECEIVABLES module Simply refers to advance payments from a customer as a **deposit**.

PST: **P**rovincial **S**ales **T**ax. Many firms are exempt from paying PST if the goods are purchased for resale. If the goods are not for resale, then PST is added to the purchase invoice amount (the original price), and is considered a normal business expense. For example, supplies $100 plus $8 PST and $5 GST. The business expense is $108.00.

Purchase: Includes transactions involving purchase of merchandise for resale, or the purchase of goods used to produce goods for resale.

Purchase Order (PO): A business form issued by a company, usually the Purchasing Department, to place an order for goods or services with a vendor or supplier. A purchase order, usually abbreviated PO, is a formal request for goods or services to be shipped at a specified date, price and quantity.

Purchase Quote: A business form issued by the vendor (supplier) to advise the customer that it can and will supply the products and/or services listed at the prices quoted by the date specified.

Purchase Returns: A company may return goods purchased for a number of reasons; damaged goods, wrong items, late shipment, or over shipment. Purchase returns reduce PURCHASES and are recorded as a negative purchase invoice. This account refers only to goods purchased for resale. Returned items that are not for resale are recorded as a reduction to the original account charged when purchased. (e.g., Office Supplies).

Purge: To delete (remove) from the disk file.

Supplier: See Vendor.

Vendor: A business from which another firm buys goods or services. May also be called Supplier.

Vendor Aged Report: A report of all amounts owing to each vendor in the VENDORS subledger aged according to specified aging period; e.g., **Current, 30 days overdue, 60 days overdue,** etc. The report may be listed in **Summary** (total owed to each vendor) or **Detail** (individual outstanding invoices per vendor not paid in full).

Mini-Guide for Chapter 3

Mini-guide for transactions in Simply Accounting 2009***
Not all types of transactions listed here.

***Study Suggestion – Add additional transactions from your chapters.

Purchase Events	Entry	Module	Journal	Comments	You fill in the Text Ref
You ask vendor for price quote	No entry	PAYABLE	Purchases, Orders & Quotes	No Purchase, you are asking for prices	
You confirm quote & place order for later delivery	No entry	PAYABLE	Purchases, Orders & Quotes	No Purchase, price confirmed for future delivery	
Purchase of merchandise	Purchases	PAYABLE	Purchases, Orders & Quotes	may be preceded by purchase quote	
	GST on Purchases			may be preceded by purchase order	
	Accounts Payable			may be a purchase without prior quote or order	
Purchase Rtn of Merchandise	Accounts Payable	PAYABLE	Purchases, Orders & Quotes	Add "Rt" to invoice number	
	Purchase Rtns & Allowances			If credit memo listed, then add "CMxxx"	
	GST on Purchases				
Payment (no discount)	Accounts Payable	PAYABLE	Payment	-can be partial or full payment	
	Cash			-can be after a return	
Payment, with discount	Accounts Payable	PAYABLE	Payment	-full payment	
	Purchase Discount			-can be after a return	
	Cash				

Chapter 4

Setting Up a New Company

Sarah's Kitchen Stores

Learning Objectives

After completing this chapter you will be able to:

☐ Set up a company from scratch.
☐ Add account names with specific account types for displaying reports.
☐ Modify and delete accounts as required.
☐ Set up links from modules to the General Ledger.
☐ Record opening balances for General Ledger accounts.
☐ Set up Tax Classes, Codes and Rates.
☐ Set up Receivable and Payable accounts and balances.
☐ Turn the modules to Ready mode.
☐ Display and Print reports.

In this chapter you will create (SET UP) a company's data file from scratch. You will convert a manual set of accounting records to a computerized accounting system.

If you are setting up a recent new company or one that has been in business for some time, refer to Appendix CD-H, *New Business Guide* for a Checklist of forms or registration items the company should be aware of.

Before you can use Simply Accounting software to process company transactions, you need to create the data file, enter defaults and various settings, add accounts, customers, vendors and balances and set the module to READY. It is important to prepare the system carefully, to avoid problems when you start processing transactions.

This chapter explains the typical procedure in setting up a company in Simply. Since every company is different, some of these requirements may vary. To help you learn the setup procedures, we will guide you in setting up the COMPANY, PAYABLES and RECEIVABLES modules for **Sarah's Kitchen Stores**, a business that buys and sells kitchen cabinets and accessories.

The contents of this chapter are as follows:

Run **Slideshow 4 – Setting Up a New Company**. You will get a good idea of what is involved in setting up a new company from scratch and how to link the various modules.

Step 1: Creating Company Files

Creating Simply Files

A company data file must be created in Simply for Sarah's Kitchen Stores that is the same as the existing company's manual system. This is known as the **CONVERSION** process. Simply provides a selection of sample companies, with General Ledger Chart of Accounts already set up (called templates). One of these company templates may be copied to a new Simply company folder to save the time required to enter the G/L accounts.

Normally, these sample companies are located in a folder called **SAMDATA**. You would select a company that has a chart of accounts most similar to that of your own company. A template chart of accounts for the Retail Company contains 167 accounts.

Using the template, you would have to delete accounts you do not need, such as 1920 Goodwill, 1930 Incorporation Costs and others. You would then modify account names to match your own Chart of Accounts, such as 1060 Chequing Bank Account to 1060 Nova Scotia Bank Account and others. You would add accounts that are not on the list, such as 5010 Beginning Inventory, and 5340 Ending Inventory and others.

The text will show you how to set up a company from scratch. This structure will start with one account 3600 Current Earnings, which will allow for the transfer of the Net Income or Loss from the Income Statement to the Balance Sheet Equity section.

To start a company from a template is covered in Appendix CD-AA, *Setting Up a New Company File using a Template*.

As you are going through this chapter, remember to save at regular intervals.

Account Number Structure

It is important that you understand how the Simply account numbering structure works to make sure that the program processes transactions properly.

Simply uses an Account Number Range shown next to identify the type of account and how to process each accordingly.

Study the next example regarding the position of account numbering in Simply:

Account Type	Account # Range	Normal Balance		Amount Entered
Assets	1000 – 1999	Debit		positive
Liabilities	2000 – 2999		Credit	positive
Equity	3000 – 3999		Credit	positive
Revenue	4000 – 4999		Credit	positive
Expense *	5000 – 5999	Debit		positive

* Includes **Cost of Goods Sold** and **Expenses**.

Simply will allow account numbers up to 8 digits. This text uses 4 digits in account numbers, therefore, you cannot use an account number outside of this structure, i.e., a number lower than 1000 or higher than 5999.

Account Types

If you use a template to create your company file, print the chart of accounts before you make changes to the structure.

View the structure of the Current Assets section shown below. The complete financial statements with account codes (HASGT) are shown in Fig. 4-37b. The displayed or printed Chart of Accounts shows only the account code.

Look carefully at the type of account and where it is located in the statement structure; i.e., column 1, the first dollar value on the left (coded as **A** 'Subgroup **A**ccount' [values that accumulate]), or column 2, the second dollar value column which is on the right (coded as **S** '**S**ubgroup Total,' **G** '**G**roup Account' or **T** '**G**roup **T**otal').

Acct #	Description	Type	Code	Column 1 Amount	Column 2 Amount
1000	Current Assets	Group Heading	H		
1005	Petty Cash	Subgroup Account	A	100.00	
1010	Bank Account Chequing	Subgroup Account	A	17,106.00	
1011	Bank Account Credit Card	Subgroup Account	A	0.00	
1080	**Cash Total (subtotal)**	**Subgroup Total**	**S**		17,206.00
1200	Accounts Receivable	Subgroup Account	A	12,173.90	
1210	Allowance for Bad Debts	Subgroup Account	A	-550.00	
1219	**Net Accounts Receivable**	**Subgroup Total**	**S**		11,623.90
1240	Store/Office Supplies/Prepaid	Group Account	G		400.00
1260	Inventory of Goods	Group Account	G		102,500.00
1299	**Total Current Assets**	**Group Total**	**T**		131,729.90

It is very important that you understand the use of the Simply type of accounts:

Group **H**eadings   Group Headings start each section. They provide descriptions of section account types, are **not postable** and have no balances.

Acct #	Description	Type	Code	Amount	Amount
1000	Current Assets	Group Heading	H		

Other Examples:

     1400   Capital Assets
     2000   Current Liabilities
     2300   Long Term Liabilities

Subgroup **A**ccount	**Postable** accounts. Subgroup **A**ccounts are used when you need to add accounts together to get a subtotal. **A** accounts can have opening balances and are updated whenever debits and credits from journal entries are posted to them.

They are not in Debit or Credit columns. They are printed in the left column of the appropriate group on the financial statement.

Subgroup Total (Accumulates **A** accounts)	Subgroup Total accounts are used when you want to subtotal **A** accounts. **S** type of accounts are **not** **postable** and create a subtotal of **A** accounts above the **S**. **S** accounts are printed in the right column of the appropriate group on the financial statement. This makes your financial statement easier to understand.

Study the example below regarding the position of the **A**, **S** accounts.

Example:

Acct #	Description	Type	Code	Amount	Amount
1005	Petty Cash	Subgroup Account	A	100.00	
1010	Bank Account Chequing	Subgroup Account	A	17,106.00	
1011	Bank Account Credit Card	Subgroup Account	A	0.00	
1080	**Cash Total (subtotal)**	**Subgroup Total**	**S**		17,206.00

The **A** type of accounts **are postable** and their balances are printed in the left column of the appropriate group on the financial statement. **A** type of accounts require an **S** type of account to subtotal the amounts.

The **S** account **1080 Total Cash**, is the subtotal of the **A** type of accounts (#'s 1005, 1010 and 1011) and it is printed in the right column of the appropriate group on the financial statement.

Another example:

Acct #	Description	Type	Code	Amount	Amount
1200	Accounts Receivable	Subgroup Account	A	12,173.90	
1210	Allowance for Bad Debts	Subgroup Account	A	-550.00	
1219	**Net Accounts Receivable**	**Subgroup Total**	**S**		11,623.90

Group Account	**Postable** accounts. **Group** accounts are used when there are no **A** accounts to be subtotaled. These accounts are in the right column and can have an opening balance and are updated with debits and credits from journal entries posted to them.

Study the example below regarding the position of the **G** accounts.

Acct #	Description	Type	Code	Amount	Amount
1240	Store/Office Supplies/Prepaid	Group Account	G		400.00
1260	Inventory of Goods	Group Account	G		102,500.00

Notice that the amounts for the **G** accounts 1240 and 1260 are placed at the right column, whereas amounts for the **A** accounts were placed in the left column.

Group Total   Used to end each section. They are **not postable**, and will
                         subtotal all the **G** and **S** accounts in the section above it.
                         They are descriptions only of the section above.

Acct #	Description	Type	Code	Amount	Amount
1299	Total Current Assets	Group Total	T		131,729.90

Other examples of **T**otals are:

    1499   Net Capital Assets
    2299   Total Current Liabilities
    2399   Total Long Term Liabilities

Important things to remember:

1) Each section must begin with an **H** (Heading) and end with a **T** (Total account). You
    cannot have 2 Hs or 2 Ts together.

2) **A** (Subgroup accounts) and **G** (Group accounts) are the only postable account types.

3) **A** (Subgroup accounts) must be followed by an **S** (Subgroup Total) account. **Always**.

4) The Group Total **T** account adds all **G** (Group accounts) and **S** (Subgroup Total
    accounts) between the **H** (Heading; e.g., 1000 Current Assets) and the **T** (Total
    account; e.g., 1299 Total Current Assets).

Current Earnings X   **Not Postable**. The **X** account is like the manual accounting
                         INCOME SUMMARY account. It is used only to move
                         dollar values from the Income Statement to the Balance Sheet.

                         Simply assigns the number 3600 **Current Earnings** to the **X**
                         account. **This cannot be changed**. It automatically adds the
                         Net Revenue Earned and subtracts the **Cost of Goods Sold**
                         and **Expenses**. The difference, the **Net Profit or Loss**, is
                         carried forward to the Balance Sheet in the Equity Section.

Setting Up a New Company File from Scratch

You will now set up the company file for Sarah's Kitchen Stores using the Scratch
method.

Exercise 4-1 – Setting Up a New Company File from Scratch

This exercise will demonstrate the creation of a new company data file from scratch.
If you want to use a template, refer to Appendix CD-AA, *Setting Up a New Company
File using a Template,* in case you need to use one in the future.

1 ➤ Start **Simply Accounting** the normal way.

Simply Accounting Premium

Welcome to Simply Accounting. What do you wish to do?

- ⦿ Open the sample company to help you learn Simply Accounting.
- ○ Create a new company.
- ○ Restore from backup.
- ○ Select an existing company.
- ○ Open the last company you worked on:

Fig. 4-1: What do you wish to do window.

You may not see ○ Open the last company you worked on: at the bottom.

2 ➤ Click the **Create a new company** button, then **OK**.

Fig. 4-2a: New Company Setup Wizard using School Edition.

This window informs you that the wizard will help in setting up the new company, and that changes may be made to any options chosen. If you click the Help button, you will see a checklist of steps to complete when setting up a new company using the scratch method.

If you are using the **Student** version that came with the text, you will see Fig. 4-2b. As noted in Appendix A, Installation Instructions, the links shown (Customer Support and Accounting expert) are not available for Students. The links require an upgrade to the retail version.

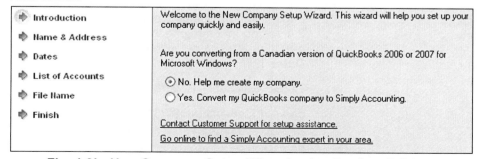

Fig. 4-2b: New Company Setup Wizard using Student Edition.

3 ➤ Click **Next >**.

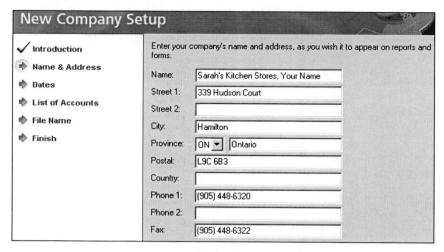

Fig. 4-3: Company Name and information.

4 ➤ **Type the information** from Fig. 4-3 into the fields in your window. Remember to type your actual name, in place of Your Name, to identify your printouts. When complete click **Next >**.

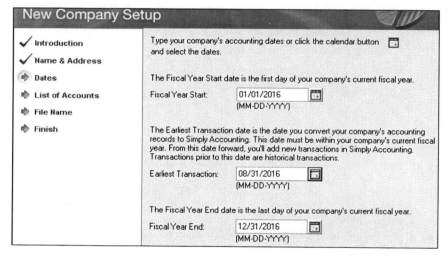

Fig. 4-4: Dates window. (See side note box.)

If your computer has been set up to display dates as DD/MM/YYYY, then the dates would appear as follows:
Start   01/01/2016
Earliest   31/08/2016
Year End 31/12/2016

5 ➤ Sarah's Kitchen Stores, a single-owner business, has a calendar fiscal year ending Dec 31 of each year. Enter the dates shown in Fig. 4-4. You will see the setting for changing the dates display to show the month name in Exercise 4-3, step 25. The default setting for dates when starting a company is **Short Dates** (01/01/2016).

Fiscal Year Start	**01/01/2016**	(Jan 1, **Start date** of the fiscal year.)
Earliest Transaction	**08/31/2016**	(Aug 31, this is the last date the accounting records were completed manually, or were completed on another computer system, or the day the records were converted to Simply. This may also be called a **conversion date**. The records are being created in Simply as of this date.)
Fiscal Year End	**12/31/2016**	(Dec 31, **End date** of the fiscal year.)

6 ➤ When complete click **Next >**.

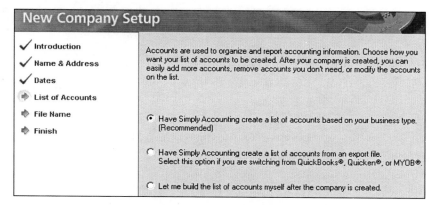

Fig. 4-5: Setup Method.

> ⊙ Have Simply Accounting create a list of accounts based on your business type.
> (Recommended)

With this option, Simply will create a company with approximately 167 General Ledger accounts that would be used by similar businesses. Using a template may save time in setting up a company; however, if you have a small company, using a template may take more time because you have to modify, delete and/or add new accounts and change the default settings using **Setup, Simply Settings, Settings** window. Refer to Appendix CD-AA, *Setting Up a New Company File Using a Template*.

> ○ Have Simply Accounting create a list of accounts from an export file.
> Select this option if you are switching from QuickBooks®, Quicken®, or MYOB®.

Using this option, Simply will create a list of General Ledger accounts *from a Quickbooks®, Quicken®, MYOB® export file* ® (other accounting software programs). This means that Simply will convert the data from the export file to a Simply data file structure.

> ⊙ Let me build the list of accounts myself after the company is created.

Using this method, Simply will create a company with only 1 General Ledger account (i.e., **3600 Current Earnings)** in the chart of accounts. You would create (add) accounts into each section as needed. In the authors' view, this is the best way for students to create a company as you will build each section containing the H A S G T accounts.

This is the method you will be using in this chapter.

7 ➤ Click method **c) Let me build the list of accounts myself after the company is created,** then **Next >**.

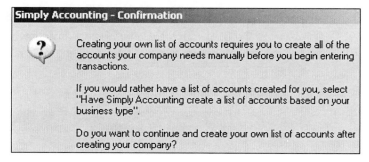

Fig. 4-6: Warning Message.

8 ➤   This window informs you that you have chosen to create your own list of
accounts method. Click **Yes**.

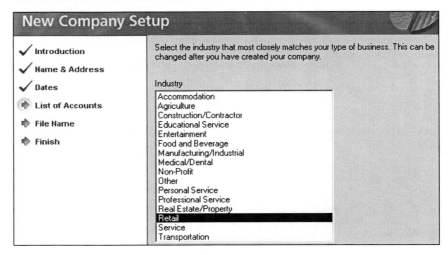

Fig. 4-7: Type of Business window (Choose a Template).

This window lists a number of different types of businesses.

9 ➤   Select the **Retail Industry** (type of business). Click **Next >**.

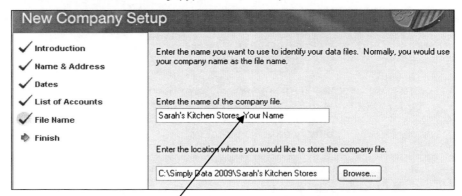

Fig. 4-8: Enter the name of company file window.

10 ➤   **Type the information** from Fig. 4-8 into the fields in your window (see
caution box).

Remove your name here. Do NOT type your name here as part of the company file
name. If you type your name here, it will become part of the company data file name;
e.g.,

Sarah's Kitchen Stores Oliver Megan.SAI

Change the **C:** to your drive letter. Delete any other information that may remain in
the boxes. Maximum 52 characters including spaces.

11 ➤   When Fig. 4-8 is complete, click **Next >**.

12 ➤ Simply informs you that the folder and file do not exist in the location you have specified. Verify the location and when correct, click **Yes** and Simply will create the folder and file. (See side note box.)

C:\Simply Data 2009\ **Sarah's Kitchen Stores** means that Simply will create on the **C:** drive, inside the Simply Data 2009 folder, a folder named **Sarah's Kitchen Stores.SAJ**, and will create the **Sarah's Kitchen Stores.SAI** file in the Kitchen folder.

.SAI may also be lower case, as in **.sai.**

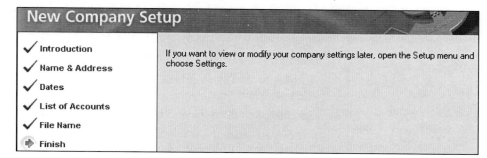

13 ➤ The above display informs you that in order to view or modify settings after continuing, you need to change settings. Click **Finish** to have Simply set up the files for the company.

After you click Finish, a message box will appear to advise you, ***Creating new database***, similar to the following.

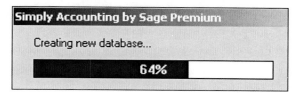

The creating database procedure can take up to *3 minutes or more*, depending on the type of computer system you are using – it might look as if the computer has stalled at the 10% or other point. Closing the Simply program or shutting the computer off can cause a major problem to the data file and you will have to redo the setup procedure again. Moreover, it is possible that the file cannot be deleted from your storage space. **Wait until the system has set up the data file before proceeding.**

When Simply has created the data files, the program will display the next window.

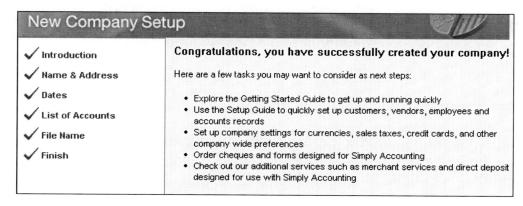

Fig. 4-9: Successfully created the company data file.

This window lists some of the tasks that may be needed to finish setting up the company data file.

   a.   Explore the Getting Started Guide to view tutorials that are available.

   b.   Modify the company settings to those needed by the company (Exercise 4-2a, 4-2b, 4-3 and 4-4).

   c.   Use the Setup Guide to add and link General Ledger accounts with open balances (Exercise 4-5 to 4-10 inclusive).

   d.   Add list of vendors and record unpaid invoices (Exercise 4-12). Note the text adds vendors first.

   e.   Add list of customers and record unpaid invoices (Exercise 4-13).

   f.   If required, add inventory items and services, with quantities. Sarah's Kitchen Stores does not require the INVENTORY module at this time.

   g.   Get customized cheques, quotes, orders and invoices from a printer.

14 ➤   Click **Close**, then **OK**, then **Close** the Getting Started window.

> The menu bar may be on two lines. You can resize the window by placing your mouse over the right edge of the outside border of the Simply window; when it changes to ↔, drag the edge to the right to widen the window so the menu bar can be on one line.

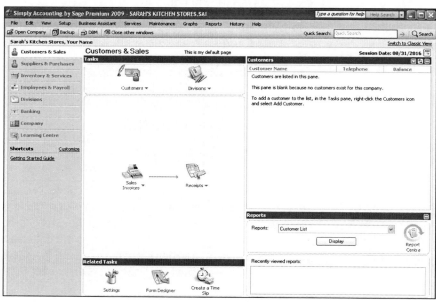

Fig. 4-10: Sarah's Kitchen Stores Home window (see side note box).

> Note that Purchases and Sales do not indicate Orders & Quotes. You will make these selections in Exercise 4-3, step 10.

The Customers & Sales window does not display Sales Quotes or Sales Orders.

The Suppliers & Purchases window does not display Purchase Quotes or Purchase Orders. (See side note box.)

The following modules display the History symbol, (quill pen): CUSTOMERS & SALES, SUPPLIERS & PURCHASES, INVENTORY & SERVICES, EMPLOYEES & PAYROLL, AND COMPANY.

15 ➤   You can view the Chart of Accounts created for a scratch company, using two methods:

   a) Click the **Report Centre**, **Accounts**, **Chart of Accounts**, click **Display**.

   b) Click the **COMPANY** module, click the **Chart of Accounts** icon.

   Use method a) to view the **Chart of Accounts**.

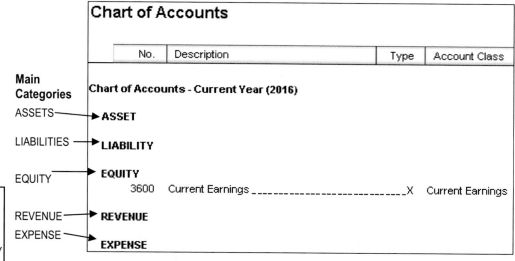

Fig. 4-11: Chart of Accounts from scratch.

The Chart of Accounts structure is created with the five main financial statement categories and the X account **3600 Current Earnings**. You will be adding accounts to this structure to create Sarah's Kitchen Stores Chart of Accounts before linking accounts. Remember, if you use the template, you would have to remove (delete) the accounts you don't need, change (modify) the names of accounts to those that your firm would use, and add other accounts that are not listed. If you decide to use a template, you should print the default Chart of Accounts to determine which accounts to keep, delete, modify or add. (See side note box.)

Congratulations! You have successfully set up the scratch company files in your data location!

At the end of this chapter, after setting up the company, you will be shown how to turn the COMPANY, PAYABLES, and RECEIVABLES modules to READY.

You will also set up the linked accounts to the General Ledger that will be used by the PAYABLES and RECEIVABLES modules. This will be explained in Exercise 4-9.

16 ➤ Click **X** and **Close** to return to the Home window.

> If you had used the template option (see Appendix CD-AA, *Creating a New Company using a Template)* Simply would have created a set of standard default General Ledger accounts (167 or more) for the company and created the linked accounts.

Step 2: Setting User Preferences Defaults

A **default** is a pre-selected option that is automatically set until you choose a different option. Each of the next windows will allow you to either accept the defaults or select new options to set as defaults for various windows and reports.

Exercise 4-2a – To Set User Preferences–View Defaults

We are going to hide the modules that we will not use in this chapter. The procedure can be reversed later to reveal the modules as you need them.

1 ➤ To hide modules, click **Setup**, **User Preferences**.

2 ➤ In the left pane click on the **View** item.

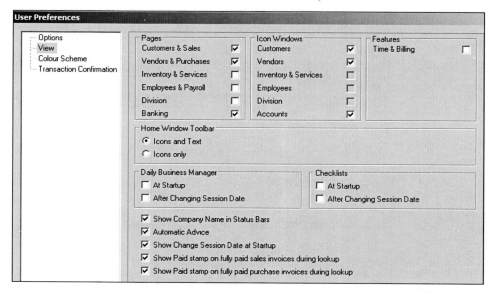

Fig 4-12 User Preferences View window (after changes).

Window (Fig. 4-12) will allow you to choose the modules you plan to use for your company. Unclick a Pages item (e.g., Division ✓ and the corresponding Icon Windows ✓ is unchecked as well.

Customers & Sales	Allows you to keep track of your Accounts Receivable.
Vendors & Purchases	Allows you to keep track of your Accounts Payable.
Inventory & Services	Allows you to maintain individual records using the perpetual inventory method. (Shown in Chapter 8.)
Employees & Payroll	Allows you to record employee paycheques with payroll deductions and prepare government reports (T-4s). (Shown in Chapter 7.)
Division	This option allows you to maintain records of cost centres (projects, jobs, departments, etc.) for sale of goods and/or sale of services you provide to others. (Shown in Chapter 11.)
Banking	Allows you to Receive Payments (Receipts from Chapter 2), make Deposits, Pay various bills (Payments Chapter 3), Transfer funds between Company bank accounts and Reconcile accounts (Chapter 12).
Time and Billing	Used with Customers & Sales, Employees & Payroll. Allows you to maintain time for employees and using the information to bill the customer. Shown in Appendix CD-AD, *Time & Billing Module.*
3 ➤ Pages	Remove the ✓ at **Inventory & Services, Employees & Payroll** and **Division**. This will hide the modules in the Home window.
4 ➤ Features	Remove the ✓ at **Time & Billing**.

Home Window Toolbar

Leave the selection as ⟨ ⊙ Icons and Text ⟩. If you select icons only the home window icons will display without wording.

Daily Business Manager

The default setting is to display the Daily Business Manager ✓ **After Changing the Session Date**.

5 ➤ Click ✓ **After Changing the Session Date** to NOT display the Daily Business Manager. The ✓ has been removed.

> ┌─ Daily Business Manager ──────────────────┐
> │ ☐ At Startup   │
> │ ☐ After Changing Session Date   │
> └───┘

Checklists

You can find information on Checklists in Appendix CD-I, *Checklists for Task Completion* on the Student Data CD.

The default setting is to display the **Checklists After Changing the Session Date**.

6 ➤ To change the Checklists to not display, click on ✓ **After Changing Session Date**. The ✓ has been removed.

> ┌─ Checklists ──────────────────────────────┐
> │ ☐ At Startup   │
> │ ☐ After Changing Session Date   │
> └───┘

Checklists will not display unless you repeat the procedure.

Lower section

> ☑ Show Company Name in Status Bars
> ☑ Automatic Advice
> ☑ Show Change Session Date at Startup
> ☑ Show Paid stamp on fully paid sales invoices during lookup
> ☑ Show Paid stamp on fully paid purchase invoices during lookup

 Do NOT change. The default is to have the company name displayed at the bottom of each journal.

☑ Automatic Advice Do NOT change. This will provide advice on the Help menu if requested.

7 ➤ ☑ Show Change Session Date at Startup Click this field. This will provide the change session date window when you open a company data file.

☑ Show Paid stamp on fully paid sales invoices during lookup
☑ Show Paid stamp on fully paid purchase invoices during lookup Do NOT change. This will display the Paid stamp on fully paid invoices during lookup.

Colour scheme

Many businesses use different background colours for quotes, orders and invoices. It is easier to see and know that you are in the correct window by the colour of the window.

8 ➤ In the left pane, click on the **Colour scheme** item. You will see the current colours used in journal windows. Simply allows the user to change the background colour of the Journals.

The network system at your school may not allow you to change the background colour settings. You can change the colour background (appearance) of any window (from the default) by clicking the ▼ to see the various choices available from the list. Many of the default windows already have different colour backgrounds. There is no exercise for changing the settings. (See side note box.)

Transaction Confirmation

9 ➤ In the left pane, click on the **Transaction Confirmation**.

Do NOT change. This choice will provide a window advising you the entry was posted or recorded. You may uncheck this box if you do not want the advice window.

Exercise 4-2b – To Set User Preferences–Options Defaults

---

1 ➤ In the left pane, click **Options** to move to the Options window.

Changing Preferences Settings

Use the following procedure to customize the options for your data file. If a row or rows of information is not discussed, leave the default unchanged.

Terminology

Fig. 4-13: Terminology window.

2 ➤ Click **Use Accounting Terms** button. This will allow you to display familiar accounting terms.

Microsoft Excel Language

Microsoft® Excel Language
⊙ English   ○ French   ○ Spanish

Do NOT change from English.

Print Button

The Print Button in the Invoice Window Always Prints
⊙ An Invoice   ○ A Packing Slip   ○ An Invoice and a Packing Slip

3 ➤ Leave the choice as **An Invoice**. Printing of Packing slips will be shown in Appendix CD-W, *Printing Packing Slips*.

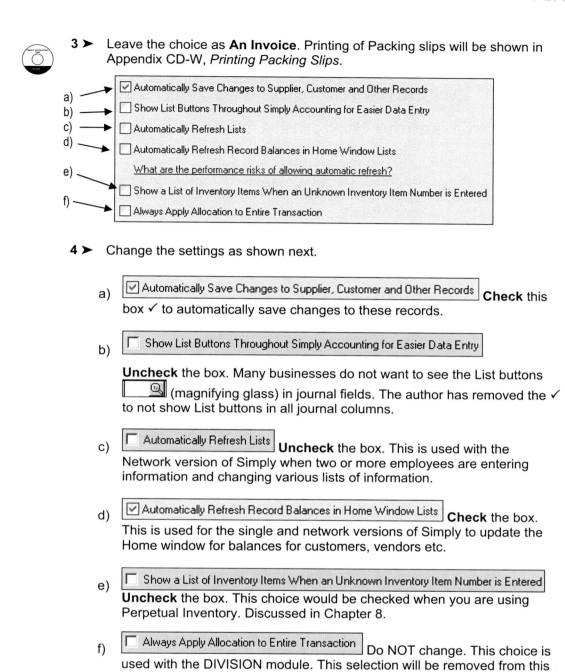

a)
b)
c)
d)
e)
f)

☑ Automatically Save Changes to Supplier, Customer and Other Records

☐ Show List Buttons Throughout Simply Accounting for Easier Data Entry

☐ Automatically Refresh Lists

☐ Automatically Refresh Record Balances in Home Window Lists

    What are the performance risks of allowing automatic refresh?

☐ Show a List of Inventory Items When an Unknown Inventory Item Number is Entered

☐ Always Apply Allocation to Entire Transaction

4 ➤ Change the settings as shown next.

a) ☑ Automatically Save Changes to Supplier, Customer and Other Records **Check** this box ✓ to automatically save changes to these records.

b) ☐ Show List Buttons Throughout Simply Accounting for Easier Data Entry

Uncheck the box. Many businesses do not want to see the List buttons 🔍 (magnifying glass) in journal fields. The author has removed the ✓ to not show List buttons in all journal columns.

c) ☐ Automatically Refresh Lists **Uncheck** the box. This is used with the Network version of Simply when two or more employees are entering information and changing various lists of information.

d) ☑ Automatically Refresh Record Balances in Home Window Lists **Check** the box. This is used for the single and network versions of Simply to update the Home window for balances for customers, vendors etc.

e) ☐ Show a List of Inventory Items When an Unknown Inventory Item Number is Entered **Uncheck** the box. This choice would be checked when you are using Perpetual Inventory. Discussed in Chapter 8.

f) ☐ Always Apply Allocation to Entire Transaction Do NOT change. This choice is used with the DIVISION module. This selection will be removed from this window when you click OK in step 5.

5 ➤ Click **OK** to return to the Home window.

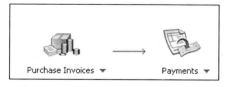

Purchase Invoices ▼ ⟶ Payments ▼

Fig. 4-14: Sarah's Kitchen Stores Payable display before Update Exercise 4-3.

The program, based on your choices earlier, has amended the scratch company data file and displays the RECEIVABLES, PAYABLES, BANKING and COMPANY modules, and the LEARNING CENTRE Module.

Since you did not use a template, you will need to add accounts and link appropriate accounts for the COMPANY, PAYABLES, and RECEIVABLES modules.
This window does not display the EMPLOYEES, INVENTORY, DIVISION or TIME and BILLING modules, because you removed the ✓ in Exercise 4-2a, step 3.
See View item information Fig. 4-12, User Preferences View window.

Step 3: Changing System Defaults

In this section, you will be confirming and/or changing some of the system settings defaults. If you need to change any settings in the future (e.g., comments to appear on sales quotes, orders or invoices), this section is where you would come to make the change.

In this section, you will be looking at new settings that were not shown before in Exercise 4-1 and/or 4-2.

Exercise 4-3 – Changing System Defaults

---

1 ➤   **Related Tasks**   From the Home window, area, click on **Settings**.

Information

2 ➤   In the left pane, click the ⊞ at Company. Click on **Information**.

3 ➤   **Business No.**   Type **R4675 2567**. `Tab`. Some companies have one registration number for both GST and Employee payroll. This number is issued by Canada Revenue Agency (CRA) [formerly called Canada Customs and Revenue Agency (CCRA)] and needs to be printed on Sales invoices and T4 slips.

Industry Type

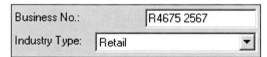

Fig. 4-15: Business Number window.

4 ➤   Click the ▾ to view the choices available. *Note*: These are the same choices available in Fig. 4-7. Select **Other**.

System

5 ➤   In the left pane, click on **System**. You will see the following confirmation.

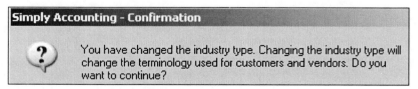

6 ➤   Click **No** to return to the Retail setting. You do not want to change the Industry type settings. In the left pane, click on **System**.

```
┌─ Cash-Basis Accounting ──────────────────────────────────────────────┐
│                                                                        │
│   ☐ Use Cash-Basis Accounting        Cash Accounting Date: [        🗓]│
│                                                                        │
│                                                                        │
│                                                                        │
│   ☑ Use Cheque No. as the source code for cash purchases and sales     │
│   ☐ Do not allow transactions dated before:  [              🗓]        │
│   ☐ Allow transactions in the future (beyond the session date)         │
│        ☐ Warn if transactions are  [        ] days in the future       │
│   ☐ Warn if accounts are not balanced when entering a new month        │
└────────────────────────────────────────────────────────────────────────┘
```

Fig. 4-16: Settings window – System.

Cash-Basis Accounting Recognizes revenue when cash is received, and recognizes expenses when cash is paid. The cash basis of accounting is used by farmers and fishermen and is *Not* covered in this text.

Sarah's Kitchen Stores uses **Accrual Based** accounting. Do NOT click the box.

☑ Use Cheque No. as the source code for cash purchases and fees DO NOT CHANGE this field. It should be ✓. When using the Reconciliation and Deposits journal, it is useful to know the cheque number for a cash purchase or sale. Checking this option results in Simply using the cheque number as the source code rather than the invoice number.

☐ Do not allow transactions dated before: DO NOT CHECK THIS BOX. This feature will allow you to post transactions in previous months (e.g., May, July, or previous years). If you check this box ✓, the date field and box will be available to change. Sarah's Kitchen Stores does not plan on using this feature.

7 ➤ ☐ Allow transactions in the future (beyond the session date) Remove the ✓ from this box. This feature would allow you to record transactions in the future (e.g., post-dated cheques). At this time Sarah's Kitchen Stores does not want to allow future postings. Information on *Post-Dated Cheques* can be found in Appendix CD-M on the Student Data CD.

☐ Warn if accounts are not balanced when entering a new month DO NOT CHANGE. This feature will allow the user to buy and install the software and immediately start to record transactions before putting in the previous month's General Ledger balances and CUSTOMERS and PAYABLES invoice details called **History**. If you record transactions in a new month, a warning message will appear to advise you that the subledger(s) do not balance with the General Ledger. Do not change the settings.

Backup

8 ➤   In the left pane, click on **Backup**.

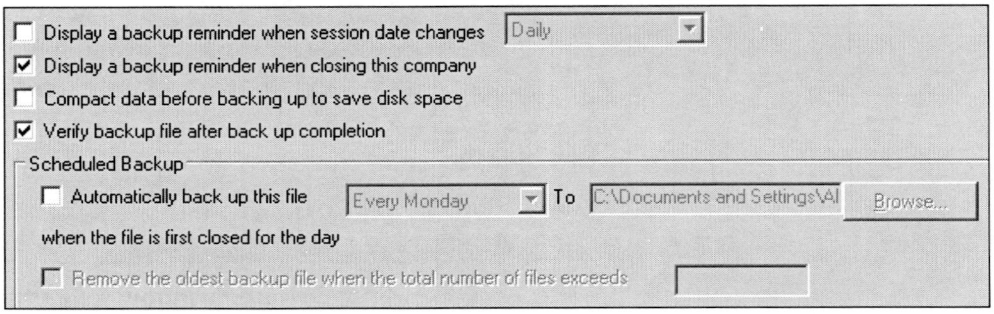

Fig. 4-17: Backup window.

This feature assumes you are backing up as shown in Exercise 1-23.

9 ➤   Change the settings as shown in Fig. 4-17.

If you are using a different backup procedure (e.g., creating backups outside of Simply), then these settings would not be required.

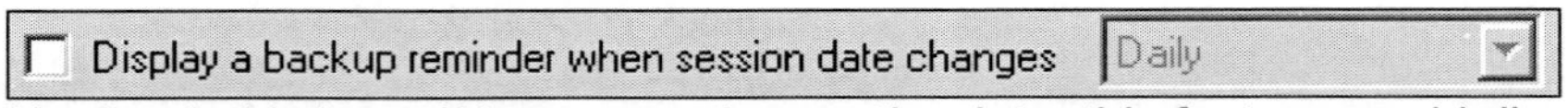

Uncheck this item. When you advance the date, this feature would display a backup reminder window.

In a business setting, this item could be used, but in a classroom environment it is not required.

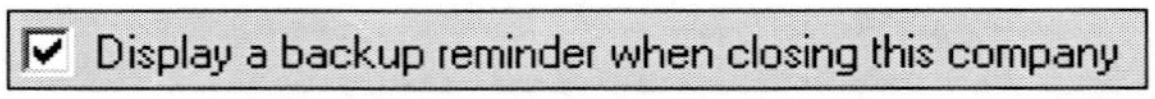

DO NOT CHANGE. When closing the company (exiting), you will be reminded to back up before exiting. Discuss a backup procedure with your instructor.

The authors recommend that daily backups be completed, and a copy of the data on USB storage device, CD or other media be taken off-site to ensure safety of the material. There are many cases where a business has suffered losses due to fire, etc., and has recovered because the accounting records were backed up and stored away from the business location. See Exercise 1-23.

DO NOT CHANGE. In a classroom environment there is no need to Compact Data when exiting. In a business environment when the file contains hundreds of entries, there would be a need to compact the data file.

DO NOT CHANGE. When using any backup procedure, it is recommended that you maintain a setting to verify the backup data.

Uncheck this item. In a classroom environment, there is no need to schedule backups. In a business environment, it is recommended that you schedule backups daily.

Features

10 ➤   In the left pane, click on **Features**.

Sarah has decided that she will not use Purchase Quotes for vendors/Suppliers. She will use only Purchase Orders to confirm orders placed with vendors. She will use customer Quotes and Orders and will not use Packing Slips.

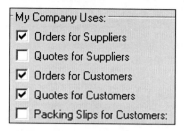

Fig. 4-18: Orders, Quotes and Packing Slips.

11 ➤ Change the selections as shown in Fig. 4-18.

Language

DO NOT CHANGE. Sarah's Kitchen Stores does not have any customers using French.

Credit Cards, Sales Taxes

The following items in the left pane will be left for a later exercise as they need account number information to proceed. **Sales Taxes** (Exercise 4-11) **Credit Cards** (Exercise 4-14).

Currency

12 ➤ In the left hand pane, click on **Currency**.

You will notice that the Home Currency is Canadian Dollars. You will also notice that the window has a column for Foreign Currency, but you cannot enter information unless you click the `☐ Allow Transactions in a Foreign Currency`

Click the **Allow Transactions in a Foreign Currency** box, a ✓ appears and the `Enter your home currency` changes to `Enter your home currency and the account used to track exchange differences`. The `Track Exchange and Rounding Differences in:` field is not grayed out.

13 ➤ Double-click on the **Foreign Currency** column, to see a list of foreign currencies available in Simply. You could select a foreign currency or click cancel.

14 ➤ Click **Cancel** in the Select Foreign Currency list window. Sarah's Kitchen Stores does not plan to sell to the U.S. or any other country at the current time. See Chapter 14 for information on Multi-Currency.

15 ➤ Click the box again to remove the ✓ in `☐ Allow Transactions in a Foreign Currency`.

Forms

16 ➤ In the left pane, click on **Forms.**

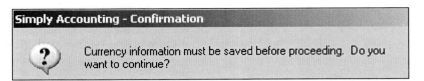

Simply needs to save currency information, even though you changed the setting to the original default setting.

17 ➤   Click **Yes**.

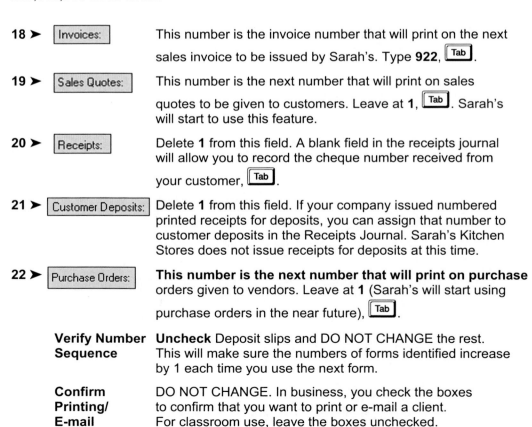

	Next Form Number	Verify Number Sequence	Confirm Printing/E-mail	Print Company Address on	Print in Batches	Check for Duplicates
Invoices:	922	☑	☐	☑	☐	☑
Sales Quotes:	1	☑	☐	☑	☐	--
Sales Order Confirmations:	--	--	☐	☑	☐	--
Receipts:		☐	☐	☑	☐	☐
Statements:	--	--	--	☑	--	--
Customer Deposits:		☐	--	--	--	--
Purchase Orders:	1	☑	☐	☑	☐	--
Cheques:	--	☑	☐	☑	☐	--
Deposit Slips:		☐	☐	--	--	--

Fig. 4-19: Settings – Forms tab (see side note box).

> There is no box for Cheque Number. The next cheque number will be entered when you set up bank accounts (see Exercise 4-8, step 6).

The number entered in these fields is the next number that will print on the appropriate form. Simply has the capability to print any number from 1 to 200,000,000 on all forms.

18 ➤ | Invoices: | This number is the invoice number that will print on the next sales invoice to be issued by Sarah's. Type **922**, [Tab].

19 ➤ | Sales Quotes: | This number is the next number that will print on sales quotes to be given to customers. Leave at **1**, [Tab]. Sarah's will start to use this feature.

20 ➤ | Receipts: | Delete **1** from this field. A blank field in the receipts journal will allow you to record the cheque number received from your customer, [Tab].

21 ➤ | Customer Deposits: | Delete **1** from this field. If your company issued numbered printed receipts for deposits, you can assign that number to customer deposits in the Receipts Journal. Sarah's Kitchen Stores does not issue receipts for deposits at this time.

22 ➤ | Purchase Orders: | **This number is the next number that will print on purchase** orders given to vendors. Leave at **1** (Sarah's will start using purchase orders in the near future), [Tab].

Verify Number Sequence   **Uncheck** Deposit slips and DO NOT CHANGE the rest. This will make sure the numbers of forms identified increase by 1 each time you use the next form.

Confirm Printing/ E-mail   DO NOT CHANGE. In business, you check the boxes to confirm that you want to print or e-mail a client. For classroom use, leave the boxes unchecked.

Print Company Address on	DO NOT CHANGE. When this option is ✓, the company name and address (as set up in the Company Information window) will print on forms. Note: This field, is ✓ for classroom/lab use to identify students' work. In a business setting the name and address would be on the pre-printed document.
Print in Batches	DO NOT CHANGE. You can enter many invoices during a day and then print them at one time. For classroom use, leave the boxes unchecked so you can print individual forms, as required. You will find information in Appendix CD-F, *Printing in Batches* on the Student Data CD.

If you click on the bottom computer link, "Order cheques and forms" you would be taken to a Simply Accounting Business Services window with more information about buying customized forms.

23 ➤ Check for Duplicates   Click the **Invoice** box ✓. This will verify that duplicate numbers are not used on invoices.

(See side note box.)

E-mail

24 ➤ Click the **E-mail** item.

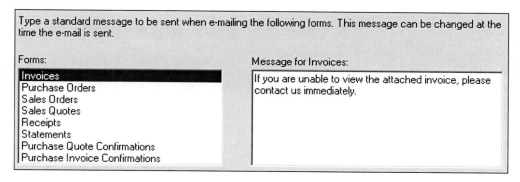

Fig. 4-20: Settings – E-mail.

DO NOT CHANGE. This text does not have an exercise to send or receive e-mail, Sarah's Kitchen Stores will not be e-mailing documents to customers or vendors. Click each of the forms and notice the wording in the message box. This wording can be changed when the form is being e-mailed.

DO NOT CHANGE. You can send e-mail documents to your customers and vendors in either of the two formats shown. This text does not have an exercise to send the different forms.

Dates

25 ➤ Click the **Date Format** item.

Select the choices as shown. The dates will display and print in words (e.g., Aug) instead of 08.

Shippers

26 ➤ Click the **Shippers** item.

Sarah's Kitchen Stores is not going to record Shipper information at this time. You can return here at a later date and add information as required.

Logo

27 ➤ Click the **Logo** item.

Sarah's Kitchen Stores is not going to use a logo on forms. There is no exercise to use this feature.

Names

28 ➤ Click the **Names** item.

DO NOT CHANGE. Refer to Appendix CD-Q, *Names Fields*.

General Accounts

29 ➤ Click the **+** at General (Accounts), the list is expanded.

Budget

30 ➤ Click the **Budget** item.

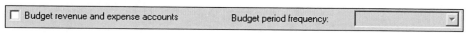

Budget revenue and expense accounts	You would record budgeted amounts for reporting and control purposes. You can select the frequency of the budget period from a drop-down list. If this option is checked, each Revenue and Expense account can be modified to include budgeted amounts by budget period. (See side note box.)

You can find information on using the *Budget Feature* in Appendix CD-E on the Student Data CD.

The Income Statement can then be displayed with a comparison of actual to budget for the period.

At this time, Sarah's Kitchen Stores is not planning to set up a budget. DO NOT CHANGE. **Leave** the box **unchecked**. This default can be changed at a later date, if desired.

Numbering

31 ➤ Click **Numbering**. DO NOT CHANGE.

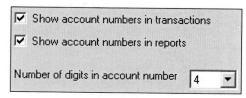

Fig. 4-21: Numbering.

Show account numbers in reports	DO NOT CHANGE. If you select this selection, account numbers (e.g., 5330 for Telephone Expense) will not appear in the General Ledger printouts.
32 ➤ Number of digits in account number	Click the ▼. You can extend the account number up to 8 digits. **Change** to 8 digits. **Change** back to 4 digits. This text will use only 4 digits in all account numbers DO NOT CHANGE.

Departments

33 ➤   Click **Departments**.

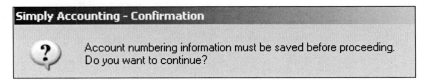

34 ➤   This confirmation is aware that you clicked the [▼], and assumes that you changed a setting. Click **Yes** to continue.

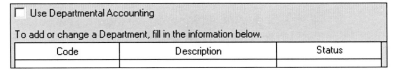

Fig. 4-22: Departmental Accounting.

35 ➤   Click **Use Departmental Accounting**, the following warning appears.

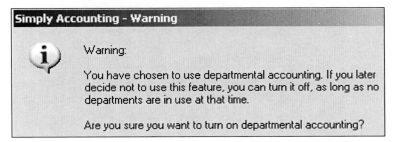

36 ➤   Select **Cancel**. Sarah's Kitchen Stores has decided not to use Departmental Accounting at this time.

Names

37 ➤   Click the **Names** item, and the following warning message appears.

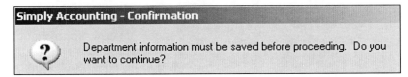

This message appears because you changed a setting in Departments and changed it back to the default. Click **Yes** to continue without creating Departments. Simply does not realize there is no change.

   A list of 5 Field Names appears. DO NOT CHANGE. See Appendix CD-Q, *Names Fields* on the Student Data CD for a discussion on this topic.

Linked Accounts

38 ➤   Click the **Linked Accounts** item.

You will return here after entering the General Ledger accounts.

Payables

39 ➤   In the left pane, click on + at **Payables**, the list is expanded.

Address

40 ➤ Click the **Address** item.

```
┌─────────────────────────────────────────────────┐
│ Enter default address information for new suppliers. │
│                                                   │
│  City:      │Hamilton                        │   │
│                                                   │
│  Province:  │Ontario                         │   │
│  Country:   │                                │   │
└─────────────────────────────────────────────────┘
```

41 ➤ Change the information as shown. This default information will appear when you add new suppliers (vendors).

Options

42 ➤ Click the **Options** item.

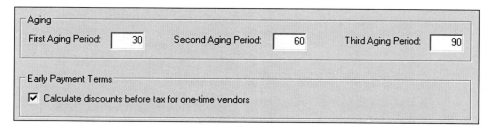

Fig. 4-23: Settings – Payables Options.

Aging	DO NOT CHANGE. Aging is a process of sorting Accounts Payable transactions in the Vendor Aged reports using predefined categories; e.g., 30, 60, or 90 days based on the current session date. Aging enables you to easily see which invoices are due within the time periods.
	Some companies use 10, 30, and/or 60 days as the aging periods. If you wish to change the aging period, you would click on the appropriate box, and type in the new setting. The second number must be larger than the first, and the third larger than the second.
43 ➤ Early Payment Terms	Click the **Calculate discounts before tax for one-time Vendors** field. A ✓ appears. This will allow cash discounts for early payments to be taken from One-time Vendors (when appropriate) on the value of goods purchased before GST and PST were added to the invoice value.

Duty

44 ➤ Click **Duty**.

```
┌─────────────────────────────────────────────────┐
│  ☐ Track duty on imported items                  │
│                                                   │
│  Import Duty Account: │                      │▼│ │
└─────────────────────────────────────────────────┘
```

DO NOT CHANGE. Sarah's Kitchen Stores does not plan on importing merchandise at this time.

Names

> Ignore Additional Information Titles at this time. See Appendix CD-Q, *Names Fields* on the Student Data CD for a discussion on this topic.

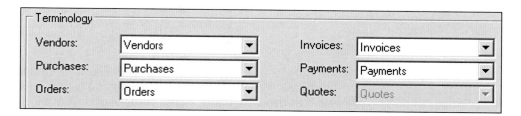

45 ➤ Click **Names**. Click each of the ▼ to see the various choices. Change the settings as shown.

Linked Accounts

You will return here after entering the General Ledger accounts.

Receivables

46 ➤ You may need to scroll down in the left hand pane to see Receivables. Click the **+** at **Receivables**. The list is expanded.

Address

47 ➤ Click the **Address** item.

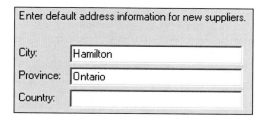

48 ➤ Change the information as shown. This default information will appear when you add new customers.

Options

49 ➤ Click the **Options** item.

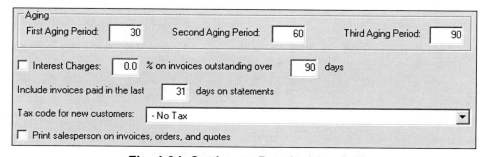

Fig. 4-24: Settings – Receivables Options.

Aging	DO NOT CHANGE (see Payables Aging).
Interest Charges	DO NOT CHANGE. Interest on overdue invoices can be calculated by checking this box. If desired, you may enter an interest rate and the number of days the invoice is overdue before interest applies. The interest charges will appear on the customer statement. When this is used, Simply shows only the amount on the statement. It does not automatically post it as an interest charge to the account. Leave the default blank.
Include invoices paid in the last 31 days on statements	DO NOT CHANGE. You can print details of paid invoices with receipts on customer statements for the selected number of days with this option. If you have cleared paid invoices from the system, no paid invoices will be printed.
Tax code for new customers	You are unable to change this field as you have not set up individual tax codes. You will set up Sales Tax codes in Exercise 4-11.

☐ Print salesperson on invoices, orders, and quotes Refer to Appendix CD-AC, *Adding a Salesperson's Name to an Invoice* on the Student Data CD.

Discount

50 ➤ Click on **Discount**.

> ┌─ Early Payment Terms ──────────────────────────────────────┐
> │ [2.00] % discount if paid within [10] days. Net amount due within [30] days. │
> │ ☑ Calculate early payment discounts before tax │
> │   │
> │ ☑ Calculate line item discounts on invoices, orders and quotes │
> └──┘

51 ➤ Early Payment Terms	Add the following in each box: **2**%, **10** days, net **30** days. This will allow these terms to be applied to all future invoices. However, the default can be changed in individual invoices, if desired.
52 ➤ Calculate early payment discounts before tax	Click **this field**. A ✓ appears. This will allow cash discounts for early payment to be taken on the value of goods purchased before GST and PST are added to the invoice value.
53 ➤ Calculate line item discounts on invoices, orders & quotes	This field should have a ✓. If there is no ✓, click this field. A ✓ appears. This will allow a Disct (Discount) % to appear in Sales Invoices. See Fig. 2A-5 in Chapter 2.

Comments

54 ➤ Click the **Comments** item.

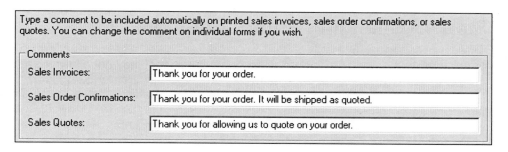

Fig. 4-25: Settings – Comment tab.

55 ➤ **Type** the comments as shown in Fig. 4-25. They will appear on the appropriate form when recording quotes, orders and invoices.

Names

56 ➤ Click the **Names** item. DO NOT CHANGE. Click each of the ▼ to see the various choices.

Ignore Additional Information Titles at this time. See Appendix CD-Q, *Names Fields* on the Student Data CD for a discussion on this topic.

Linked Accounts

You will return here after entering the General Ledger accounts.

57 ➤ Click **OK** to accept the setting changes and return to the revised Home window, shown next.

Study the Home window in Fig. 4-26. Modules CUSTOMERS & SALES, and VENDORS & PURCHASES are changed to RECEIVABLES and PAYABLES. The following modules are hidden: INVENTORY & SERVICES, EMPLOYEES & PAYROLL and DIVISIONS. The middle Tasks diagram displays the Sales Quotes icon.

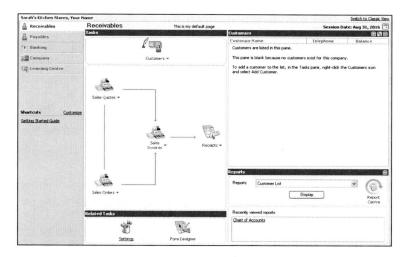

Fig. 4-26: Revised Kitchen Home window after changes.

58 ➤ Click the PAYABLES module. Notice the icon **Purchase Quotes** is not displayed as a result of the setting made in step 11, Fig. 4-18 to not use Quotes.

Step 4: Changing Printer Settings

The Network system at your school may not allow you to change the printer settings. Check with your teacher. If you click Printer Settings by mistake, the Simply program may exit and you may have to restart the Setup procedure again.

If you are NOT able to change the Printer Settings, go to Step 5: Conversion Process with Accounts.

Exercise 4-4 – Changing Printer Settings

Report & Form Options

1 ➤ If you are able to change printer settings, on the menu bar, click **Setup**, **Reports & Forms**. The Report & Form Options window is displayed.

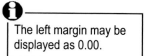

The left margin may be displayed as 0.00.

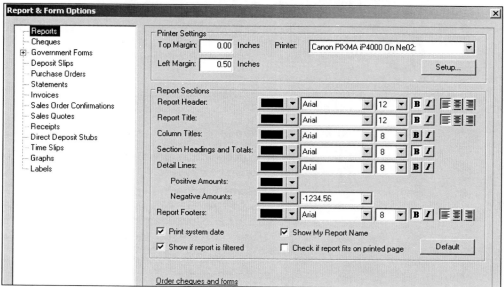

Fig. 4-27: Printer Settings window before changes. (See side note box.)

Reports

The left pane lists the various reports and forms that are available to change. The right pane lists the various selections that can be changed within the various reports and forms.

Printer Settings

This section allows you to select Top and Left Margin settings and a printer.

Left Margin   The left margin should be **0.50** (reports will indent one-half inch from the left edge of the paper).

2 ➤ **Printer**   Click on the ▼ arrow to view the printers available. In most cases do not change the default printer. If a different printer is to be used, your instructor will advise you. On some networks the printer font and size may not be changed. DO NOT CHANGE the default.

Reports Sections

> You are not able to change printer settings for cheques as bank accounts have not been set up at this time. Refer to Exercise 4-8.

This section allows you to customize the colour of various headings and titles, change the font and font size, and see the various printer settings available for each report identified. Sarah's Kitchen Stores prints with default settings, except those noted below. Sarah may change settings in the future. Cheques and invoices are not printed.

If you are able to, you will change settings for Reports and Purchase Orders. If not, it would still be worthwhile going through the steps below (without setting the defaults) in order to see the available options in each step. (See side note box.)

3 ➤ **Report Headers** — **Colour** . Click on the ▾ arrow. You will see a Colour chart window. Click **Cancel** to leave the settings.

Change *only* the Report Header and Report Title font and size in steps 4 and 5. Do not change other items.

4 ➤ **Arial** — Click on the ▾ arrow beside Arial to display the fonts that are available for the printer selected. Choose **Arial**.

5 ➤ **12** — Click on the ▾ arrow beside 12 to see the various font sizes available. You must select a size that will print the reports clearly on the paper for your printer. This may require some test prints. Choose size **10**.

6 ➤ Repeat steps 4 and 5 for Report Title.

Settings for Bold and Italics

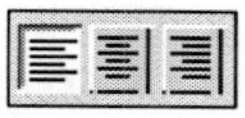
Settings for left, centre and right justified.

Print system Date — DO NOT CHANGE. The current date (the computer system date) will appear at the bottom of each printed report, e.g., Printed On: Aug 31, 2010.

This will enable you to know the date the report was printed.

Show if report is filtered — DO NOT CHANGE. If reports are filtered, a note, "This report has been filtered" will appear at the bottom-right corner of each printout.

Show My Report Name — DO NOT CHANGE. The template report name can be saved (e.g., Mrs. Kafa report) in the My Reports section of Simply. When selecting a report from **Report Centre, My Reports**, you can select the appropriately named report. When you display the report, you will see the report name in the title section of the report as follows.

Balance Sheet As at Aug 31, 2010 - Mrs. Kafa report

7 ➤ **Check if report fits on printed page** — If this choice is not ✓**,** click on this choice. When printing, a message box will inform you if the printout will print over the right margin.

Purchase Orders

8 ➤ In the left pane click the **Purchase Orders** item.

9 ➤ In the right pane the selection should be ◉ Pre-printed. If not, click on Pre-printed.

10 ➤ **Form Type** — Click ▾ and you will see 2 choices.

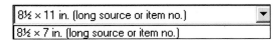

Selection **8½ x 11 in**. (**long source or item no**.) will allow more space to record information in invoice no. and other boxes. The report will print on a regular size paper. If you are using the Student version, select **8½ x 11 in**. (long source or item no.)

Selection **8½ x 7 in**. (**long source or item no**.) will allow more space to record information in invoice no. and other boxes, but will print on a smaller size page.

☐ Warn when there are less than	0	forms remaining. There are	0	forms on hand.

This option would be ✓ if Simply was checking on the remaining blank forms available. There is no exercise for this feature.

In the E-mail Form section at the bottom, you will see the Form box grayed out. This is where the e-mail Purchase Order form is located on the hard drive.

11 ➤ Click **OK** to return to the Home window.

Step 5: Conversion Process with Accounts

The next step is to enter accounting data such as accounts and account balances from the manual records of the company. This is required not only for Sarah's Kitchen Stores, but also for any company converting to Simply.

Conversion, in this chapter, means changing from one accounting system to another. There are two types of conversion:

1.   Changing from a manual system to a computerized system.
2.   Changing from one computerized system to another computerized system.

When a company buys the Simply software program it has two choices:

a)   After setting up the Chart of Accounts, the company can record transactions immediately without entering previous history balances in the General Ledger, and Customer and/or Vendor subledgers. They would add previous history during the next month(s), but before a year-end.

b)   The company can set up the Chart of Accounts, then record their previous history balances at a specific time, normally from the end of a month. This is done when all accounting records from the original accounting system have been updated, and the Trial Balance and financial statements have been prepared.

Regardless of the method the company chooses, the new computerized Chart of Accounts should accurately reflect the company's Chart of Accounts. Then the Trial Balance amounts, and customers' and vendors' balances are entered in the computer records.

It is possible to have more than one conversion date. A company may decide to use a computerized GENERAL LEDGER on one date; e.g., January 1, and could start to use the computerized RECEIVABLE subledger on another date, e.g., March 1. In either case, the accounts and balances for the manual system and computer system must be the same on the dates when information is converted.

At this time, both the manual and computer records should agree. This specific time is called the **Conversion Date**. Simply refers to it as the **Earliest Transaction Date**. When all information and dollar values have been entered in Simply and they agree with the old records, you will change the system from a HISTORY mode to a READY mode. After this date, the company would stop using the manual records and start to enter transactions using the computer system. (See side note box.)

Sarah's Kitchen Stores has decided to use method **b)** described previously and take the time to set up the complete company records, COMPANY, ACCOUNTS PAYABLE and ACCOUNTS RECEIVABLE modules before recording new transactions.

The Chart of Accounts

Part of the conversion process is to ensure that the General Ledger accounts are the same for the manual system and the computerized system. The G/L accounts for Sarah's Kitchen Stores need to be set up.

Using the COMPANY module of Simply you can add, change or delete the G/L accounts. Before making any changes, it is important to understand how Simply sets up the chart of accounts.

The following is a summary of the information provided at the beginning of the chapter: Step 1 Account Number Structure.

Account Numbering System in Simply

The account numbering system for this company and all companies in this text starts with 1000 and ends with 5999. Each section of a classified statement must always:

- start with an **H** account (Group Heading), and
- end with a **T** (Group Total) account.

Postable accounts that require a subtotal are shown in the first dollar value column on the left as an **A** (subgroup Account).

The account that adds the **A** type of accounts is the **Subgroup Total** account and is shown in the second dollar column.

Postable accounts that do not require a subtotal are shown in the second dollar value column on the right as a **G** (group account).

Leave spaces between account numbers for adding accounts in the future without having to make new account groups to accommodate the new accounts. For example, if you start **Cash In Bank** at 1050, and the next account Is Accounts Receivables, assign Accounts Receivable number 1060 so that if you need to insert other bank accounts in the future, you can assign them numbers close to the first bank account.

You will now start setting up Sarah's Kitchen Stores, Chart of Accounts. You will be starting with the scratch Chart of Accounts, which Simply sets up when you select the option to start the Chart of Accounts from scratch (shown next). You will add accounts under each account category. Refer to Fig. 4-33 (Chart of Accounts) to see the accounts and structure that you will be setting up.

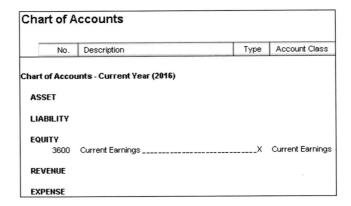

Exercise 4-5 – Setting Up (Adding) the Chart of Accounts

To Add an Account

For illustrative purposes, you will add 3 accounts:

> **1000 Current Assets**
> **1005 Petty Cash**
> **1010 Bank Account Chequing**

There are 3 ways to enter new accounts:

A. From the Home window, click on the **COMPANY** module, click the ▾ at Chart of Accounts to view the 4 choices. The blue quill pen icon (History) means this module is still in History mode. Select Add Account or click on the Chart of Accounts icon to display Fig. 4-28a.

B. From the Home window, click the Chart of Accounts icon to open the Accounts window, click the Create 🔳 icon. The General Ledger window (Fig. 4-28a) will be displayed. This method will be shown for information purposes for Ex 4-5.

C. Click **Setup**, **Setup Guide**, click on **Accounts** to open new window, Fig 4-28b.

   1 ➤ You will use method **B** to display the General Ledger window, as you will be using the Accounts window in step 18.

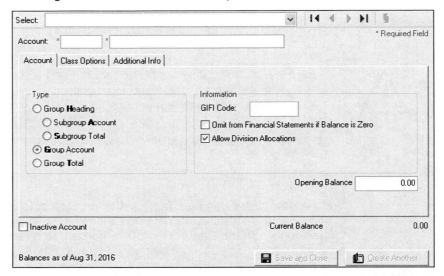

Fig. 4-28a: New Account window. *Note the red * referencing Required Field.*

2 ➤ Account

Notice that there are 3 tabs. Type **1000** a number within the Asset section. Notice that three new tabs appear: [Reconciliation & Deposits], [Related Historical Accounts] and [Notes]. The [Reconciliation & Deposits] tab is covered in Chapter 12.

The [Related Historical Accounts] tab information is created by Simply when you move into a new fiscal year. The information for this tab is only available when you have recorded transactions in Premium in a previous fiscal year.

[Notes].A feature to add Notes to display and print on Financial Statements. See Appendix CD-U *Add Notes/Footer to Statements* for more information.

[Tab] to move to the next field which is the Account Name field. Type **Current Assets**, [Tab].

3 ➤ Type

Click [○ Group Heading]. Current Assets is the heading (H) for the Current Assets section on the Balance Sheet.

You will see that some of the options (under GIFI Code) are now hidden. They will be seen and explained in step 13.

Information

GIFI Code:

DO NOT CHANGE. This field is used for electronic filing of Corporate Tax Returns.

4 ➤ Click on [Class Options] tabs.

> There are no Class Options for accounts which are used as a Group Heading, Subgroup Total, or Group Total.

5 ➤ Click on the [Additional Info] tab. You can add up to 5 additional lines of description about this account (e.g., the manager or assistant manager responsible for the account). See Appendix CD-Q *Names Fields* for information about these fields.

6 ➤ Click on the [Reconciliation & Deposits] tab.

> Account Reconciliation cannot be performed on Group Heading, Subgroup Total, Group Total, and most linked accounts.

The Options are available only for **postable** type accounts (**A** and **G**).

7 ➤ Click on the [Related Historical Accounts] tab.

> There are no Related Historical Accounts for accounts which are used as a Group Heading, Subgroup Total, or Group Total.

8 ➤ Click on the [Notes] tab. As mentioned in step 2, you can add notes to display and print on Financial statements.

9 ➤ Click once again on [Account] tab. Click **Save and Close**, **X** to return to the Home window.

10 ➤ From the menu bar, click **Setup, Setup Guide, Accounts** to display the Accounts window (Fig 4-28b).

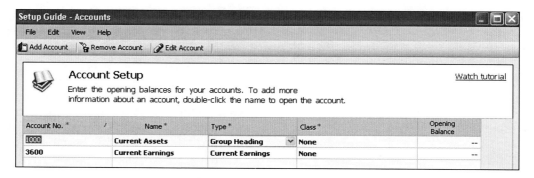

Fig. 4-28b: New Account Setup window. *Note the red * Required Fields.*

Account 1000 is there from the previous steps.

11 ➤ Account   Below account 3600 Type **1005**, [Tab].

12 ➤ Name   Type **Petty Cash**, [Tab].

13 ➤ Type   Click the [▼]. Select **Subgroup Account** because this account will require a subtotal. [Tab].

Remember: If you use a **Subgroup Account (A)**, then you must also use a **Subgroup Total (S)** after the last A in a group.

14 ➤ Class   Click the [▼]. A list of account classes displays. They can be used for sorting and filtering reports in later versions of the Simply program. Enter the classes as indicated. (See side note box.)

Not all classes are discussed below. (See side note box.)

Asset:	All Items owned by a company.
Cash:	Amount of cash on hand.
Bank:	A bank account (chequing or savings).
Credit Card Receivable:	Amount owed by credit card company to you for sales made to customers.
Accounts Receivable:	Amount that is owed to you for goods and services sold on credit.
Other Receivable:	Amount that is owed to you that is not a normal sale of goods and services (e.g., sale of old office equipment).
Inventory:	Goods on hand for sale to customers.
Current Asset:	Assets that will be replaced/or used up within a year (e.g., Prepaid Items, Investments, etc.).
Capital Asset:	An asset that will be used for a long period of time (e.g., Building, Computer Equipment, etc.).
Other Asset:	An asset that does not fit into any of the other categories.

15 ➤ Sarah has decided to keep a minimum number of classes of accounts as shown with the names of the accounts (see Fig. 4-33). Simply requires certain types with specific accounts such as the Accounts Receivable ledger account to be an Accounts Receivable Option type. Select **Cash**. [Tab].

Opening Balance   DO NOT CHANGE. Sarah's Kitchen Stores has decided to add all the accounts and the account structure (**H A S G T**)

The author has used a minimum number of account class options in the setup of accounts to allow you to understand the basic setup of the account classes without spending too much time on it.

Account classes can be changed at a later time if the business needs to break down the accounts into specific groupings.

ℹ️

You may also add each
account's balance as you
create the account.
Accounts and Class
Options are entered in
this exercise, and
Account Balances will be
entered in Exercise 4-10.
When you become more
comfortable with account
types and contra
balances, you may try to
add the account
balances as you create
the accounts.

before adding the account balances in Exercise 4-10. See side box.

16 ➤   Name *   Double-click on **Petty Cash** to display the General Ledger window.

Information Section

GIFI Code	DO NOT CHANGE.
Omit from Financial Statements if Balance is Zero	DO NOT CHANGE. If you click this box and the account has a zero balance, it will not show when viewing or printing the financial statements. Sarah's Kitchen Stores has decided to show all accounts when viewing or printing statements.
Allow Division Allocation	DO NOT CHANGE. Sarah's Kitchen Stores will not use the DIVISION module. The DIVISION OR PROJECT module will be discussed in Chapter 11. Leave blank.

Class Options Tab

17 ➤   Next Deposit No. [   ] Sarah will not keep track of receipts by deposit numbers. Remove **1**, [Tab].

To see information about the different types of classes, you would click on the **Help** menu, **Contents**, **Search**, and in the top field, type **classes**. You will see a list of categories below classes. Click on any one that you would like information about. **Exit** the Help window. Click Save and Close.

18 ➤   Create account **1010 Bank Account Chequing**, with **Subgroup Account** type and with a **Class Option of Bank**. Double-click on **Name**, and click the **Class Options** tab.

19 ➤   Institution: Click on ▼ and you will see a list of banks that allow electronic transfer of funds using Simply. Select **Other**.

DO NOT CHANGE the Branch, Transit Number, and Account Number fields.

20 ➤   Next Deposit No. [   ] Sarah will not keep track of receipts by deposit numbers. Remove **1**, [Tab].

Fig. 4-29: Bank Class Options window.

If you choose the Account Class Option: Cash, you will be able to link the Principal Bank Account in Exercise 4-9 (Figures 4-35 and 4-36), but you will not be able to record the Next Cheque No. as shown in Exercise 4-8, step 6.

When you attempt to record a Payments Journal entry, you will see the following warning message.

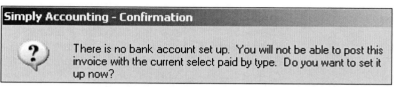

Fig. 4-30: Bank Confirmation window.

If you choose an Account Class Option other than Cash or Bank (e.g., Asset, Current Asset), the Principal Bank Account in Exercise 4-9 (Figures 4-35 and 4-36) will not display the Bank account for linking.

21 ➤   Click **Save and Close** to add the account.

22 ➤   After reviewing the possible warning messages below, turn to the next page to create the remaining accounts from the lists (2 pages).

Note: If you attempt to add an account number that has already been set up, you may see the following error message. If you see this message, click OK to continue.

You should see a message similar to the following:

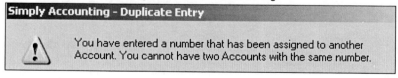

Click **OK**. Remember that the account number has already been entered/created.

Note: Simply may not allow you to enter more accounts after entering the first screen or later. If this happens, click Close. You will see an error message about accounts are not in logical order or the accounts are not balanced. Click Yes, Continue or click Save my Opening Balances as entered. You are returned to the Setup Guide. Click Accounts and continue entering accounts.

Some users prefer **HEADING** and **TOTAL** names in all capital letters, while others capitalize only the first letter (**Heading** and **Total**). Sarah's Kitchen Stores uses the latter format.

When you create account 1080 Cash Total, select type Subgroup Total account **S**.

To **delete** an account set up in error, see Exercise **4-6**. To **modify** an account, see Exercise **4-7**.

Acct #	Account Name	Type of Account	Code	Class
1011	Bank Account Credit Card Receivable	Subgroup Account	A	Credit Card Receivables (no other changes)
1080	Cash Total	Subgroup Total	S*	(See side note box.)
1200	Accounts Receivable	Subgroup Account	A	Accounts Receivable
1210	Allowance for Bad Debts	Subgroup Account	A	Allowance for Bad Debts
1219	Net Accounts Receivable	Subgroup Total	S	
1240	Store/Office Supplies/Prepaid	Group Account	G	Current Asset
1260	Inventory of Goods	Group Account	G	Inventory
1299	Total Current Assets	Group Total	T	
1400	Capital Assets	Group Heading	H	
1410	Display Equipment	Subgroup Account	A	Capital Asset
1415	Accumulated Amortization Display Eq	Subgroup Account	A	Accum. Amort. & Depreciation
1419	Display Equipment: Net Value	Subgroup Total	S	
1420	Office Furniture/Equipment	Subgroup Account	A	Capital Asset
1425	Accumulated Amort. Office Fur/Eq	Subgroup Account	A	Accum. Amort. & Depreciation
1429	Office Furniture/Equipment: Net Value	Subgroup Total	S	
1499	Net Capital Assets	Group Total	T	

The **Liabilities** section heading is automatically put in by the program. Create the Liability accounts as shown next:

2000	Current Liabilities	Group Heading	H	
2010	Accounts Payable	Group Account	G	Accounts Payable
2030	Visa Credit Card Payable	Subgroup Account	A	Credit Card Payable*

> * DO NOT CHANGE other fields in the Class Options tab for this account.

2210	GST Charged on Sales	Subgroup Account	A	Sales Tax Payable
2220	GST Paid on Purchases	Subgroup Account	A	Sales Tax Payable
2230	Net GST Owing/Receivable	Subgroup Total	S	
2240	PST Payable (Prov Sales Tax)	Group Account	G	Sales Tax Payable
2299	Total Current Liabilities	Group Total	T	
2300	Long Term Liabilities	Group Heading	H	
2310	Bank Loan Payable	Group Account	G	Long Term Debt
2399	Total Long Term Liabilities	Group Total	T	

The **Equity** section heading is automatically put in by the program. Create the Equity accounts as shown next:

3000	Owner's Equity	Group Heading	H	
3020	Capital Beginning Sarah Kafa	Subgroup Account	A	Retained Earnings
3030	Capital Additional Investments	Subgroup Account	A	Equity
3040	Drawings Sarah Kafa	Subgroup Account	A	Equity
3050	Net Capital before Current Earnings	Subgroup Total	S	
3699	Total Owner's Equity	Group Total	T	

Notice that the full details of the Statement of Owner's Equity have been built into the equity section of the Balance Sheet (including the Current Earnings account #3600).

The **Revenue** section heading is automatically put in by the program. Create the Revenue accounts below:

4000	Sales Revenue	Group Heading	H	
4010	Sales Kitchen Cabinets	Subgroup Account	A	Revenue
4020	Sales Kitchen Sinks	Subgroup Account	A	Revenue
4030	Sales Kitchen Accessories	Subgroup Account	A	Revenue
4099	Sales Total	Subgroup Total	S	Revenue
4210	Sales Returns	Subgroup Account	A	Revenue
4220	Sales Discounts	Subgroup Account	A	Revenue
4229	Sales Deductions Total	Subgroup Total	S	Revenue
4399	Sales Net	Group Total	T	

The **Expense** section heading is put in by the program. Create the Cost of Goods Sold and Expense accounts next.

5000	Cost of Goods Sold	Group Heading	H	
5020	CGS Beginning Inventory	Subgroup Account	A	Cost of Goods Sold
5030	Purchases	Subgroup Account	A	Cost of Goods Sold
5040	Purchase Returns	Subgroup Account	A	Cost of Goods Sold
5050	Purchase Discounts	Subgroup Account	S	Cost of Goods Sold
5060	Goods Available for Sale	Subgroup Total	S	
5090	CGS Ending Inventory	Group Account	G	Cost of Goods Sold
5099	Total Cost of Goods Sold	Group Total	T	

5300	Store Expenses	Group Heading	H	
5310	Rent Expense	Group Account	G	Expense
5320	Store Salaries Expense	Group Account	G	Expense
5330	Telephone Expense	Group Account	G	Expense
5340	Advertising Expense	Group Account	G	Expense
5350	Amortization Expense-All	Group Account	G	Expense
5360	Delivery Cost to Customers	Group Account	G	Expense
5370	Bad Debts Expense	Group Account	G	Expense
5380	Utilities (Hydro/Water) Expense	Group Account	G	Expense
5399	Total Store Expenses	Group Total	T	
5500	Other Expenses	Group Heading	H	
5510	Bank Charges Expense	Group Account	G	Expense
5520	Credit Card Charges	Group Account	G	Expense
5530	Bank Interest on Loan	Group Account	G	Expense
5599	Total Other Expenses	Group Total	T	

You will not be able to view the Income Statement or Balance Sheet until all sections are set up.

If you place an account in a wrong section, refer to Appendix CD-X *Removing an Account from a Wrong Section* on the Student Data CD to correct the account.

You should be aware that there are many different ways to number and structure accounts. Some companies would subtotal accounts 5510 and 5520 to show bank costs before Interest on loans. (See side note box.)

23 ➤ When you have entered all the accounts click on the **Validate** button. If everything is okay, you will see Fig. 4-31. If your accounts are not in logical order, Exercise 4-6 will provide some insight as to what needs to be done to resolve these issues.

To Delete an Account

To delete an account, complete the following steps:

Exercise 4-6 – Deleting an Account

This exercise is used to show you the steps involved in removing an account.

1 ➤ Click on account **5530 Bank Interest on Loan**, to highlight the account in blue.

2 ➤ Click 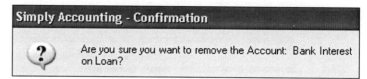 icon, and the following message box will request confirmation that you want to remove the account.

Simply Accounting - Confirmation

> Are you sure you want to remove the Account: Bank Interest on Loan?

3 ➤ Click **No**. If you wanted to remove the account, you would click **Yes** and the account would be removed.

Review and Check Account Coding Changes Made

There are three ways to verify that the account structure you added is correct.

a) Use the Validate button.

b) Display an Income Statement or Balance Sheet to indicate the structure is correct.

c) From the Home page, click on the Chart of Accounts icon, and click the 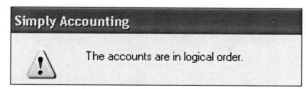 validity of accounts icon.

4 ➤ Click the **Validate** button. If there are no errors you will see the message box Fig. 4-31.

Simply Accounting

> The accounts are in logical order.

Fig. 4-31: Accounts in order.

5 ➤ Click **OK**.

6 ➤ **Display** an Income Statement or Balance Sheet. If there are any errors in your account coding (accounts not in logical order) the message box Fig. 4-32 will advise you where the account coding error has occurred. If there are a number of coding errors, you may see a similar message box a number of times.

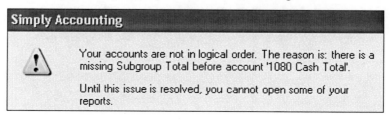

Simply Accounting

> Your accounts are not in logical order. The reason is: there is a missing Subgroup Total before account '1080 Cash Total'.
>
> Until this issue is resolved, you cannot open some of your reports.

Fig. 4-32: Example of an Account Coding Error window.

It may be helpful to display or print the Chart of Accounts and check your structure near the account number given. You would then change the account coded in error and try again.

You may need to do this a number of times due to an incorrect **H A S G T** structure.

    7 ➤ You may need to repeat steps 4, 5 and 6 until such time as your **H A S G T** account structure is validated as "logical."

To Modify an Account

Sarah has decided that she wants to change the name of account 3600 Current Earnings, using a different way from the Setup guide.

Exercise 4-7 – To Modify an Account

---

    1 ➤ From the Account Setup window, locate and double-click the **3600 Current Earnings** Account No. or Name column.

        The General Ledger window similar to Fig. 4-28a will appear.

    2 ➤ **Account**   Change the name to: **Net Income from Income Statement,** `Tab`.

As explained earlier, this account will transfer the balance of the Net Income from the Income Statement to the Owner's Equity section of the Balance Sheet.

The Account with no Type coding cannot be changed. If you clicked the Class Options tab, you will see the grayed out Account Class as Current Earnings. (See side note box.)

Other types of accounts could be changed; however, the Current Earning **X** account cannot be changed.

    3 ➤ **GIFI Code**   Remove **3620**. A single-owner non-incorporated business does not use GIFI codes.

    4 ➤ Click the ▶ or ◀ to save the changes. On the last account to be modified use the **Save and Close** button.

All the accounts have been added. Refer to Fig. 4-33.

    5 ➤ **Exit** to the Home window.

Sarah's Kitchen Stores - Student Name
Chart of Accounts

ASSETS

1000 Current Assets..H
   1005   Petty Cash ....A Cash
   1010   Bank Account Chequing ....A Bank
   1011   Bank Account Credit Card Receivable ....A Credit Card Receivable
   1080   Cash Total...S
   1200   Accounts Receivable.................................A Accounts Receivable
   1210   Allowance for Bad Debts ....A Allowance for Bad Debts
   1219   Net Accounts Receivable...........................S
   1240   Store/Office Supplies/Prepaid ....G Current Asset
   1260   Inventory of Goods ....G Inventory
1299 Total Current Assets..T

1400 Capital Assets..H
   1410   Display Equipment....................................A Capital Asset
   1415   Accumulated Amortization Display Eq........A Accum. Amort & Depre
   1419   Display Equipment: Net Value....................S
   1420   Office Furniture/Equipment........................A Capital Asset
   1425   Accumulated Amort. Office Fur/Eq ....A Accum. Amort & Depre
   1429   Office Furniture/Equipment Net Val...........S
1499 Net Capital Assets...T

LIABILITIES

2000 Current Liabilities...H
   2010   Accounts Payable.....................................G Accounts Payable
   2030   Visa Credit Card Payable ....G Credit Card Payable
   2210   GST Charged on Sales...............................A Sales Tax Payable
   2220   GST Paid on Purchases ....A Sales Tax Payable
   2230   Net GST Owing/Receivable........................S
   2240   PST Payable (Prov Sales Tax)............... G Sales Tax Payable
2299 Total Current Liabilities ....T

2300 Long Term Liabilities ....H
   2310   Bank Loan Payable....................................G Long Term Debt
2399 Total Long Term Liabilities ....T

EQUITY

3000 Owner's Equity ....H
   3020   Capital Beginning Sarah Kafa ....A Retained Earnings
   3030   Capital Additional Investments...................A Equity
   3040   Drawings Sarah Kafa.................................A Equity
   3050   Net Capital before Current Earnings ....S
   3600   Net Income from Income Statement...........X Current Earnings
3699 Total Owner's Equity ....T

REVENUE

4000 Sales Revenue ....H
   4010   Sales Kitchen Cabinets ....A Revenue
   4020   Sales Kitchen Sinks..................................A Revenue
   4030   Sales Kitchen Accessories.........................A Revenue
   4099   Sales Total...S
   4210   Sales Returns...A Revenue
   4220   Sales Discounts..A Revenue
   4229   Sales Deductions Total ....S
4399 Sales Net...T

EXPENSE

5000 Cost of Goods Sold ....H
   5020   CGS Beginning Inventory...........................A Cost of Goods Sold
   5030   Purchases..A Cost of Goods Sold
   5040   Purchase Returns.....................................A Cost of Goods Sold
   5050   Purchase Discounts ....A Cost of Goods Sold
   5060   Goods Available for Sale............................S
   5090   CGS Ending Inventory...............................G Cost of Goods Sold
5099 Total Cost of Goods Sold ....T

5300 Store Expenses..H
   5310   Rent Expense...G Expense
   5320   Store Salaries Expense..............................G Expense
   5330   Telephone Expense ....G Expense
   5340   Advertising Expense..................................G Expense
   5350   Amortization Expense - All ....G Expense
   5360   Delivery Costs to Customers......................G Expense
   5370   Bad Debts Expense...................................G Expense
   5380   Utilities (Hydro/Water) Expense ....G Expense
5399 Total Store Expenses ....T

5500 Other Expenses ....H
   5510   Bank Charges Expense..............................G Expense
   5520   Credit Card Charges ....G Expense
   5530   Bank Interest on Loan ....G Expense
5599 Total Other Expenses.......................................T

H =	Group Heading
A =	Subgroup Account
S =	Subgroup Total
G =	Group Account
T =	Group Total

Fig. 4-33: Sarah's Kitchen Stores Chart of Accounts before linking accounts.

Exercise 4-8 – Change Next Cheque Number & Settings

You were not able to change the Payment Cheque Information in Exercise 4-3, because the bank accounts were not set up at that time. The bank accounts are now set up and you can update the next cheque number.

1 ➤ Click **Setup, Reports & Forms,** in the left pane click **Cheques**, in the right pane click 1010 Bank Account Chequing. The window contains the default settings for Payment Cheque, Payroll Cheque and Cheque Settings.

Payment Cheque Setting

2 ➤   In the right pane ensure the selection is  .

3 ➤   At Form Type select the following to conform to the Canadian Payments Association guidelines for cheques. Information on the guidelines can be seen at Exercise 3A-12, step 8.

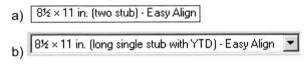

Payroll Cheque Setting

4 ➤   In the right pane ensure the selection is Pre-printed .

5 ➤   At Form Type there are two Easy-Align form types available to conform to the Canadian Payments Association guidelines for cheques.

a)   8½ × 11 in. (two stub) - Easy Align

b)   8½ × 11 in. (long single stub with YTD) - Easy Align

Select **b**, with 1 stub.

Cheque Setting

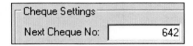

6 ➤   Type **642** for the next cheque number.

7 ➤   Click **OK** to return to the Home window.

   8 ➤   *This is a good time to do a **backup**.* Your structure is correct. Use a folder name for your backup similar to **Sarah's Kitchen Stores_with_accts**.

The next step is to link the accounts before entering the $ values to the accounts from the Trial Balance.

Step 6: Linking Modules/Accounts

The Simply program allows you to copy information (Debits and Credits) from the RECEIVABLES and/or the PAYABLES modules to the General Ledger. This process called **Linking** permits the modules to talk to each other to ensure information is up-to-date across the modules.

Remember that earlier in the RECEIVABLES and PAYABLES modules you entered only one side of an entry; e.g., when you entered a SALES amount for a sales transaction on credit, Simply automatically debited ACCOUNTS RECEIVABLE and credited GST ON SALES. This is because these accounts have been linked from the RECEIVABLES module (see linked windows in this exercise). The person setting up the linked accounts determines which account data needs to be copied to General Ledger linked accounts.

One thing to remember: you can change the account structure and links **before** setting the module to **Ready**.

If you have to change the account structure and the links after setting the module to READY, you need to be very careful as you adjust the links. If you had posted transactions to a Sales Discount account and then had to change the account number, you will also need to change the links.

You can change the links between General Ledger accounts at any time.

 When a General Ledger account is linked, it is impossible to delete the account without deactivating the link of the accounts. A General Ledger account cannot be deleted if it contains posted transactions.

If you had used a template to create a company, Simply would have created a set of linked accounts for you.

When using a template, there are two ways to set up or change the links:

1. Remove the links before changing the accounts.
2. Change the accounts while using the default links.

The author believes it is easier to use method 1. Remove the links, then change the default chart of accounts to the company's needs. Then you would return and link the appropriate accounts.

Changes or deletions to the linked accounts are made by using the **Setup** options from the menu bar. A link to a General Ledger account can be removed (deactivated) or changed. A deactivated linked account cannot be deleted if the Ledger account contains posted transactions.

You now need to set up your own linked accounts because you have not used a template. This will allow you to better understand the process of linking accounts.

Linking the Modules

The next step in the setup process is to make the modules "talk" to each other. Before transactions can be entered in the appropriate subledger modules, links to General Ledger accounts must be specified. This procedure is also called **Integration**.

Exercise 4-9 – Linking the Modules

COMPANY Module Links

1 ➤ From the Home window Related Tasks area, click **Settings**, click on **General (Accounts)**, in the right pane select **Linked Accounts**, and a window similar to the following is displayed.

When you start a new fiscal year, the balances from your income and expense accounts are moved to the Retained Earnings account.

Retained Earnings: 3020 Capital Beginning Sarah Kafa ▼

Current Earnings: 3600 Net Income from Income Statement

☐ Record opening balances in my Retained Earnings account

Fig. 4-34: COMPANY Linked Accounts window.

2 ➤ Retained Earnings:

In a single-owner business, the proper account name is Capital (account 3020). Simply will not allow you to change the program heading **Retained Earnings**. Account 3020 accumulates the profits of the firm from prior years. It is automatically updated by the program when a new accounting year is started.

When you start a new fiscal year, the program closes the prior year's accounting records and transfers the balance in the Net Income from the Income Statement or Current Earnings (account 3600) to the identified Retained Earnings account.

Select **3020 Capital Beginning Sarah Kafa,** Tab .

You cannot change the program heading **Retained Earnings**.

Do not click Record opening balances in my Retained Earnings account, as it will update the account automatically. You want to record your own balance.

Current Earnings:

The program transfers the year-to-date Net Income or Loss from the Income Statement, and adds the value to the Equity section of the Balance Sheet.

3 ➤ When your window resembles Fig. 4-34, move to the PAYABLES module as shown next.

PAYABLES Module Links

1 ➤ In the left pane click **Payables,** in the right pane select **Linked Accounts,** to display the Payables Linked Accounts window.

Fig. 4-35: Payables Linked Accounts window.

2 ➤ Select the accounts shown above.

Principal Bank Account

1010 Bank Account Chequing. This will allow the program to credit the bank account in the General Ledger when you record a cheque being issued in the PAYABLES module.

Accounts Payable	**2010 Accounts Payable**. This will allow the program to credit ACCOUNTS PAYABLE in the General Ledger when you purchase goods or services on credit. It will also debit ACCOUNTS PAYABLE when you return goods and issue cheques.
Freight Expense	Leave this field blank. This account is used for freight costs that cannot be included in purchases. Sarah's Kitchen Stores does not use this account.
Purchase Discount	**5050 Purchase Discounts**. This is the account Simply will credit when a purchase discount is taken on a purchase merchandise for resale invoice.
Prepayments and Prepaid Orders	**2010 Accounts Payable**. This is the account Simply will debit when a prepayment is made on a purchase order.

3 ➤ In the left pane, click **Receivables**. In the right pane select **Linked Accounts**, to display the Receivables Linked Accounts window.

RECEIVABLES Module Links

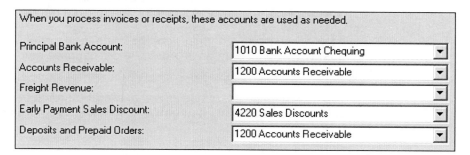

Fig. 4-36: RECEIVABLES Linked Accounts window.

4 ➤ Select the accounts shown above.

Principal Bank Account	**1010 Bank Account Chequing**. Receipts from customers entered in the Receipts journal will be debited to this account in the General Ledger.
Accounts Receivable	**1200 Accounts Receivable**. This account will be automatically debited and credited when entering sales transactions for customers.
Freight Revenue	Leave this field blank. This account is used for **freight** revenue that is not part of sales. Sarah's Kitchen Stores does not use this account.
Sales Discount	**4220 Sales Discount,** for paying early (within discount terms), is taken off a sales invoice.
Deposits and Prepaid Orders	**1200 Accounts Receivable**. This account will be automatically credited when a deposit is received on a Sales Order.

5 ➤ Click **OK** and you are returned to the Home window.

Step 7: Entering Opening G/L Account Balances (History)

Important: Back up your data before proceeding.

You have now set up the chart of accounts, but the ledger accounts do not have the current manual record dollar balances. We need to enter the August 31, 2016 Trial Balance so that the starting point in the computerized system is the ending point of the manual records.

As you have learned before, Simply structures G/L accounts into five categories (or groups):

1. Assets
2. Liabilities
3. Equity
4. Revenue
5. Expense

Simply also breaks up the previous categories into subgroups (class options) as seen in Exercise 4-5, step 14. How does Simply know whether an amount entered is a debit or a credit? The answer is based on the **normal balance** of the account.

If the account has a normal **debit balance** (e.g., asset – OFFICE SUPPLIES), then a **positive** amount entered is a **debit** and a negative amount, for a contra account, is entered for a **credit**.

Similarly, if the account has a normal **credit balance** (e.g., SALES) then a **positive** value entered is a **credit** and a **negative** amount, for a contra account, is entered for a **debit**.

VERY IMPORTANT:

To enter a **contra balance** (a decrease) to an Asset, Liability, Equity or Revenue account (normal debit balance) you must enter the amounts with a **negative**. For example, DRAWINGS is an Equity section contra account. **Equity** normally has a credit balance. When you enter the Drawings amount with a **negative** sign it will cause Simply to **debit** it.

To enter a **Sales Return** or a **Purchase Return**, you would enter the amount with a **negative** sign. As SALES RETURNS is a contra (decrease) balance to SALES (with a normal credit balance), entering a negative amount will cause Simply to **debit** it. On the other hand, PURCHASE RETURNS is a contra (decrease) balance to PURCHASES (with a normal debit balance), so entering a negative amount will cause Simply to **credit** it.

Here are the rules for entering debits or credits to accounts:

#	Category/ Group	Normal Balance	Normal Balance to be entered	Contra Balance to be entered
1	Asset	Debit	Positive	Negative (Credit)
2	Liability	Credit	Positive	Negative (Debit)
3	Equity	Credit	Positive	Negative (Debit)
4	Revenue	Credit	Positive	Negative (Debit)
5	Cost of Goods and/or Expenses	Debit	Positive	Negative (Credit)

Sarah's Kitchen Stores – Your Name
Trial Balance As At Aug 31, 2016

		Debits	Credits
1005	Petty Cash	100.00	-
1010	Bank Account Chequing	17,106.00	-
1011	Bank Account Credit Card Receivable	0.00	-
1200	Accounts Receivable	11,946.50	-
1210	Allowance for Bad Debts	-	550.00
1240	Store/Office Supplies/Prepaid	400.00	-
1260	Inventory of Goods	102,500.00	-
1410	Display Equipment	30,700.00	-
1415	Accumulated Amortization Display Eq	-	11,000.00
1420	Office Furniture/Equipment	8,125.00	-
1425	Accumulated Amort. Office Fur/Eq	-	3,450.00
2010	Accounts Payable	-	11,297.45
2030	Visa Credit Card Payable	-	0.00
2210	GST Charged on Sales	-	3,517.50
2220	GST Paid on Purchases/Services	1,410.00	-
2240	PST Payable (Prov Sales Tax)	-	4,020.00
2310	Bank Loan Payable	-	51,256.00
3020	Capital Beginning Sarah Kafa	-	79,411.55
3030	Capital Additional Investments	-	0.00
3040	Drawings Sarah Kafa	16,900.00	-
4010	Sales Kitchen Cabinets	-	338,165.00
4020	Sales Kitchen Sinks	-	22,560.00
4030	Sales Kitchen Accessories	-	53,289.00
4210	Sales Returns	6,200.00	-
4220	Sales Discounts	5,731.00	-
5020	CGS Beginning Inventory	91,500.00	-
5030	Purchases	308,986.00	-
5040	Purchase Returns	-	12,600.00
5050	Purchase Discounts	-	7,212.00
5090	CGS Ending Inventory	-	102,500.00
5310	Rent Expense	16,800.00	-
5320	Store Salaries Expense	46,980.00	-
5330	Telephone Expense	3,216.00	-
5340	Advertising Expense	7,468.00	-
5350	Amortization Expense-All	0.00	-
5360	Delivery Cost to Customers	9,645.00	-
5370	Bad Debts Expense	0.00	-
5380	Utilities (Hydro/Water) Expense	1,796.00	-
5510	Bank Charges Expense	743.00	-
5520	Credit Card Charges	9,842.00	-
5530	Bank Interest on Loan	2,734.00	-
		700,828.50	700,828.50

Fig. 4-37a: Sarah's Kitchen Stores Trial Balance.

Note: This information will be recorded in Exercise 4-10.

Sarah's Kitchen Stores, Student's Name
BALANCE SHEET As at Aug 31, 2016

ASSETS		Column 1 Subgroup	Column 2 Group Subtotal Total
Current Assets	H		
Petty Cash	A	100.00	
Bank Account Chequing	A	17,106.00	
Bank Account Credit Card Receivable	A	0.00	
Cash Total	S		17,206.00
Accounts Receivable	A	11,946.50	
Allowance for Bad Debts	A	-550.00	
Net Accounts Receivable	S		11,396.50
Store/Office Supplies/Prepaid	G		400.00
Inventory of Goods	G		102,500.00
Total Current Assets	T		131,502.50
Capital Assets	H		
Display Equipment	A	30,700.00	
Accumulated Amortization Display..	A	-11,000.00	
Display Equipment: Net Value	S		19,700.00
Office Furniture/Equipment	A	8,125.00	
Accumulated Amortization – Office F..	A	-3,450.00	
Office Furniture/Equipment: Net Val	S		4,675.00
Net Capital Assets	T		24,375.00
TOTAL ASSETS			155,877.50
LIABILITIES			
Current Liabilities	H		
Accounts Payable	G		11,297.45
Visa Credit Card Payable	G		0.00
GST Charged on Sales	A	3,517.50	
GST Paid on Purchases/Services	A	-1,410.00	
Net GST Owing/Receivable	S		2,107.50
PST Payable (Prov Sales Tax)	G		4,020.00
Total Current Liabilities	T		17,424.95
Long Term Liabilities	H		
Bank Loan Payable	G		51,256.00
Total Long Term Liabilities	T		51,256.00
TOTAL LIABILITIES			68,680.95
EQUITY			
Owner's Equity	H		
Capital Beginning Sarah Kafa	A	79,411.55	
Capital Additional Investments	A		0.00
Drawings Sarah Kafa	A	-16,900.00	
Net Capital before Current Earning	S		62,511.55
Net Income from Income Statement	X		24,685.00
Total Owner's Equity	T		87,196.55
TOTAL EQUITY			87,196.55
LIABILITIES AND EQUITY			155,877.50

Sarah's Kitchen Stores, Student's Name
INCOME STATEMENT Jan 01, 2016 to Aug 31, 2016

REVENUE		Column 1 Subgroup	Column 2 Group Subtotal Total
Sales Revenue	H		
Sales Kitchen Cabinets	A	338,165.00	
Sales Kitchen Sinks	A	22,560.00	
Sales Kitchen Accessories	A	53,289.00	
Sales Total	S		414,014.00
Sales Returns	A	-6,200.00	
Sales Discounts	A	-5,731.00	
Sales Deductions Total	S		-11,931.00
Sales Net	T		402,083.00
TOTAL REVENUE			402,083.00
EXPENSE			
Cost of Goods Sold	H		
CGS Beginning Inventory	A	91,500.00	
Purchases	A	308,986.00	
Purchase Returns	A	-12,600.00	
Purchase Discounts	A	-7,212.00	
Goods Available for Sale	S		380,674.00
CGS Ending Inventory	G		-102,500.00
Total Cost of Goods Sold	T		278,174.00
Store Expenses	H		
Rent Expense	G		16,800.00
Store Salaries Expense	G		46,980.00
Telephone Expense	G		3,216.00
Advertising Expense	G		7,468.00
Amortization Expense-All	G		0.00
Delivery Cost to Customers	G		9,645.00
Bad Debts Expense	G		0.00
Utilities (Hydro/Water) Expense	G		1,796.00
Total Store Expenses	T		85,905.00
Other Expenses	H		
Bank Charges Expense	G		743.00
Credit Card Charges	G		9,842.00
Bank Interest on Loan	G		2,734.00
Total Other Expenses	T		13,319.00
TOTAL EXPENSE			377,398.00
NET INCOME			24,685.00

Fig. 4-37b: Balance Sheet and Income Statement after changes (with codes).

Account names with boxes around them, ASSETS   TOTAL REVENUE   and others, are automatically put in by the computer program. You cannot delete or change them.

Note: This information will be recorded in Exercise 4-10.

Exercise 4-10 – Entering Opening G/L Balances (History)

One **VERY IMPORTANT thing to remember:** You may change the balances you have entered for G/L accounts up until you set the modules to **Ready** (ready to record transactions). Once the modules are **Ready**, balances can be changed only by making journal entries. Setting modules to **Ready** is covered in Exercise 4-15.

1 ➤ From the menu bar, click **Setup, Setup Guide, Accounts**.

Group Heading (H) type of accounts, (a non-postable account), do not have amounts associated with it.

Subgroup Accounts (S) and **Group Accounts (G)** accounts have amounts posted to them.

Subgroup Total (S) and **Group Totals (T)** and the **Current Earnings (X)** account balances are non-postable accounts, but have amounts that are calculated by Simply based on the balances you enter for the corresponding postable accounts.

2 ➤ Click on the **Opening Balance** field for **1005 Petty Cash** (from Fig. 4-37a).

3 ➤ Opening Balance Type **100** ⌨`Tab`. Simply puts in .00 to input 100.00.

If you make a mistake in entering the dollar amount or you forgot to press the negative (minus) key for an opposite balance, you can return to the field and correct the amount. The new amounts will replace the incorrect values you entered before.

4 ➤ Move down the **Opening Balance column**, where the 0.00 fields are, and **continue entering balances** from the Trial Balance (Fig. 4-37a), subject to the Contra Account Balance notes in the next section. If the account does *not* have a 0.00 displayed, it is a non-postable account like an H (Group Heading), S (Subgroup Total), or T (Group Total).

5 ➤ See steps 6 and 7 for entering a contra account balance.

Contra Account Balance

As you have learned earlier, **Contra** means **opposite**. For example, a **contra asset account** (e.g., ACCUMULATED AMORTIZATION of an asset account such as a truck or computers) is placed in the Asset section, but since it **decreases** the value of the asset, it is entered with a **negative** sign, causing Simply to **credit** this account, instead of the normal debit entry for Assets.

Other examples of Contra accounts are:

Section	*Contra Account Name*
Asset	Allowance for Bad Debts
	Accumulated Amortization Display Eq
	Accumulated Amortization Office Fur/Eq
Liability	GST Paid on Purchases
Equity	Owner's Withdrawals (**Drawings** in a sole proprietorship)
	Dividends Declared (used in a corporation)
Revenue	Sales Returns & Allowances
	Sales Discounts

Cost of Goods Sold	Purchase Returns & Allowances
	Purchase Discounts
	Ending Inventory

6 ➤ Click on the **0.00** field, for the **Allowance for Bad Debts** account.

7 ➤ Opening   Type **-550 (negative)**, Tab . The -550.00 shows up in
Balance   the Accounts window in the Debit column with a negative
        -550.00. If you display a Trial Balance, you will see the
        amount in the Credit column.

        Continue entering the **other accounts**.

Only **postable** accounts [Subgroup (**A**) and Group (**G**)] have balances.

Subgroup totals and Group Totals are calculated automatically. The **X** account balance is calculated automatically based on the total of revenues less expenses (net income).

If you do not enter all the account balances during one session and you need to quit, or if you have an error in the amounts you entered, you will receive a message window similar to the following:

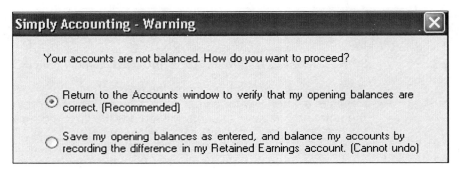

8 ➤ Select the first choice and check the amounts entered. *Note*: Verify that you have recorded the Contra accounts with negative amounts. If the amounts appear correct, see step 9.

9 ➤ Select the 2nd choice: Save my opening balances as entered.

This window will allocate the amount difference to the 3020 Capital Beginning Sarah Kafa (Retained Earning account). The 'Cannot undo' means that you can't undo the balance at this time. You can amend amounts that are in error.

10 ➤ Print a Trial Balance and check the amounts agree with the amounts in Fig 4-37a.

11 ➤ Return to the Setup Guide and correct the Opening Balance amounts.

You can take your time to locate the error(s). When the account with the error is found (e.g., Sales discount entered as a positive amount and should have been a negative amount), return to the Setup Guide and update the accounts that have the errors.

12 ➤ When all corrected account balances have been entered, Click Close and you are returned to the Setup Guide window, without the error message from step 7. **Exit** to the Home window.

Displaying the Trial Balance

13 ➤ Display the **Trial Balance**. Check that the amounts agree with the Trial Balance in Fig. 4-37a and correct if necessary.

14 ➤ It would be a good idea to print the Trial Balance, Income Statement and Balance Sheet. Compare them to Fig. 4-37a and Fig. 4-37b. This would be done in an office setting to prove that the starting computer General Ledger accounts agree with the manual General Ledger.

15 ➤ Back up your data before moving on. Identify the backup with a name similar to Sarah's Kitchen Stores_B4_Ready. You are returned to the Home window when the backup is complete. Make a note in your logbook similar to **Starting balances, not ready**. If you make a major mistake and want to start back at this point, it will be easy with a backup data file.

Step 8: Setting Up Tax Classes, Codes, Rates & Customization

In this section, you will enter the appropriate taxes (GST and PST) with their corresponding linked accounts. You will also set up abbreviated tax codes for each tax class.

Exercise 4-11 – *Setting Up Tax Classes, Codes, Rates & Customization*

Taxes

1 ➤ Click **Setup, Settings,** in the left pane click ⊞ at **Company**, click ⊞ at **Sales Taxes**, click **Taxes** and enter the information shown in the Fig. 4-38.

To add a tax, enter the tax name on a new line in the Tax column.

Tax	Tax ID Included on Forms	Exempt from this tax?	Is this Tax taxable?	Acct. to track tax paid on purchases	Acct. to track tax charged on sales	Report on taxes
GST	R4675 2567	No	No	2220 GST Paid on Purchase	2210 GST Charged on Sale:	Yes
PST		No	No		2240 PST Payable (Prov Sa	No

Fig. 4-38: Sales Tax Information window.

Tax	**GST** and **PST**.
Tax ID Included on Forms	**R4675 2567** (the Business registration number), .
Exempt from this tax?	**No**. The business must **collect** GST on Sales and **pay** GST on Purchases/Services.
Is this Tax taxable?	**No**. In the province of Ontario, you do not pay PST on GST.
Acct. to track tax paid on purchases	Double-click in the field and scroll down and select **2220 GST Paid on Purchases/Services.**
Acct. to track tax charged on sales	Double-click in the field and scroll down and select **2210 GST Charged on Sales**.
Report on taxes	Press the **spacebar**, or click on the field to change it to **Yes** for GST. (See side note box.)
	Complete the requirements for PST as per Fig. 4-38 noting there is no recoverability of PST taxes paid.

Tax Codes

2 ➤ In the left pane, click on **Tax Codes** and enter the information shown.

To add a tax code, enter in a code and description.

To see tax code details, double-click on a tax code or description.

Code	Description	Use In
	No Tax	All journals
G	GST added at 5% and PST Exempt	All journals
GP	GST added at 5% and PST at 8%	All journals
P	GST Exempt, and PST at 8%	All journals

Code   An abbreviation for the tax code.

Description   A description of the tax being collected.

Use In   Select All Journals.

3 ➤ Code   Double-click the **GP** field and the Tax Code Details window appears. **Type** the information as shown. The tax code GP is shown first, as it contains both GST and PST codes with relevant information.

When entering the tax rate (e.g., **5.0**, the **.0** does not show). If the rate does not have a decimal point, the .0 does not display even if you type it in.

The **Is Refundable** column (for GST) is set to **Yes** because the GST **collected** is deducted from the GST **paid** and the difference can be recovered (receive a refund) from the federal government.

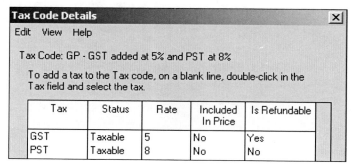

(See side note box.)

Tax Code Details

Edit   View   Help

Tax Code: GP - GST added at 5% and PST at 8%

To add a tax to the Tax code, on a blank line, double-click in the Tax field and select the tax.

Tax	Status	Rate	Included In Price	Is Refundable
GST	Taxable	5	No	Yes
PST	Taxable	8	No	No

4 ➤ Click **OK** to accept the information, codes and rates.

5 ➤ Repeat **steps 3** and **4** to enter the information for the G and P codes as follows:

- Code **G** Set up GST the same as shown in step 3, but the PST Status is **Exempt**.

Tax	Status	Rate	Included In Price	Is Refundable
GST	Taxable	5	No	Yes
PST	Exempt			

The **Is Refundable** column (for PST) is set to **No** as it is not refundable from the provincial government.

- Code **P** Set up PST the same as shown in step 3, but the GST Status is **Exempt**.

Tax	Status	Rate	Included In Price	Is Refundable
GST	Exempt			
PST	Taxable	8	No	No

6 ➤ Click **OK** and return to the Home window.

Changing Settings for Item Number and Allocations

The Journal columns are not set the way we are used to. We are going to change some of the column fields.

1 ➤ Click the **RECEIVABLES** module, click on the **Sales invoices** icon. The Journal columns do not resemble what you have used in previous chapters.

2 ➤ With a Transaction **Invoice** and Style **Standard**, click on the Customize **Journal** icon, in the left pane click **Columns** and change the items as shown next.

Sales Invoices

3 ➤ In the right pane, click on **Item Number** (the ☐ Account is grayed out), and **Allocations**, to insert a ✓ to NOT display both items.

Sales Orders

4 ➤ In the left pane, click **+** at **Sales Orders** and **Columns**. **Repeat step 3** to NOT display Item Number and Allocations.

Sales Quotes

5 ➤ In the left pane, click **+** at **Sales Quotes** and **Columns**. **Repeat step 3** to NOT display Item Number and Allocations.

Purchase Invoices

6 ➤ In the left pane near the top, click **+** at **Purchase Invoice** and **Columns**. **Repeat step 3** to NOT display Item Number and Allocations.

Purchase Orders

7 ➤ Click on the **Purchase Orders** and **Columns**. **Repeat step 3** to NOT display Item Number and Allocations.

Make Other Payment

8 ➤ Click on the **Make Other Payment** and **Columns**. **Repeat step 3** to NOT display Allocations.

9 ➤ Click **OK**. You do not need to change the other settings. The Invoice window columns will now resemble the ones you used previously. Note, you may have to repeat Exercise 2A-3 to Customize columns to widths that you want.

10 ➤ **Return** to the Home window.

Step 9a: Setting Up Subledgers–Vendors

Another part of the conversion process is to enter **vendors** and **vendor history** into the Vendors subledgers. The subledgers in Simply have the same purpose as those in a manual accounting system.

Detailed vendor balances in the Vendors subledger are compared in total to the balance of the ACCOUNTS PAYABLE account in the G/L.

Before setting up Vendors & Customers it is strongly recommended that you review Appendix CD-Y, *To Cancel a History Invoice*, as this is a common mistake in Setting up invoices.

The following are the vendor details for Sarah's Kitchen Stores at Aug 31, 2016.

Exercise 4-12 – Setting Up Vendor Subledgers

Entering the Vendor Accounts

Create an account for each vendor as follows:

1 ➤   From the Home window, click **Setup, Setup Guide, Vendors**. You are in the Vendor Setup window

2 ➤   Create the first vendor, with the following information.

Vendor	Office Stationery Plus
Contact	Owen Cliff
Telephone	905-675-6628
Street 1	987 Emerson Street
City	Hamilton
Province	Ontario
Postal Code	L8S 4W3

3 ➤   Before entering Balance Owing amounts, you will enter other Vendor information. Double-click the Vendor, **Office Stationery Plus**. This is using the same procedure as discussed in Chapter 3 – Exercise 3A-8 after step 16 information section, Creating a New Vendor Account.

4 ➤   Click the **Options** tab. Enter the information shown next.

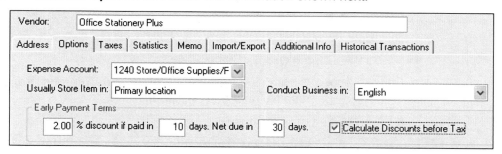

5 ➤   Click the **Taxes** tab. GST and PST Exempt NO. Select Tax code **GP**.

6 ➤   Click the **Historical Transactions** tab.

7 ➤   Click the **Invoices** button. The Historical Invoices window is displayed.

Historical Invoices	
Vendor:	Office Stationery Plus
Invoice No.:	5628
Date:	Aug 25, 2016
Terms:	2.00 % 10 Days, Net 30 Days
Pre-tax Amount:	278.27
Tax:	36.18
Invoice Total:	314.45

Fig. 4-39: Historical Invoices window.

8 ➤ Type the information from Fig. 4-39 into the fields in your window.

Pre-tax Amount	This field and the Tax field will not display if the vendor does not have Calculate Discounts before Tax field ✓. (See Exercise 4-12, step 4.) Only an amount field will display.

> Amount: [   ]

If there is no discount available, the program does not need a breakdown in the amount.

Tax	You would type the amount of the tax, GST or GST and PST where applicable. Note: the cost of the office goods purchased was 278.27. The 36.18 tax cost is PST and GST.

9 ➤ When your window resembles Fig. 4-39, click the **Record** button.

There are no other invoices to be entered for Office Stationery Plus.

10 ➤ Close Click on the **Close** button when finished.

At the bottom of the window the vendor | Balance Owing   314.45 | now shows 314.45 for Office Stationery Plus. (See side note box.)

> *To cancel or correct a historical invoice, refer to Appendix **CD-Y** on the Student Data CD.*

11 ➤ Click **X** to Exit.

12 ➤ Enter the other vendors information and outstanding balances (referred to as **History**).

Vendor	Custom Cabinets Ltd.	Kitchen Gadgets Inc.	Your Name Landlord
Contact	Toby Aharonhi	Sarah Ditlove	Carol Smith
Telephone	905-819-4751	905-623-3926	905-569-2863
Street 1	3890 Barton Street	200 Lakeshore Blvd	16 Main Street West
City	Hamilton	Hamilton	Hamilton
Province	Ontario	Ontario	Ontario
Postal Code	L8E 8Q2	L2X 4C3	L8S 4J1
Expense	5030	5030	5310
Terms	See Fig 4-41	See Fig 4-41	Net 3 days
Discounts	✓	✓	No
GST	Exempt No	Exempt No	Exempt No
PST	Exempt Yes	Exempt Yes	Exempt Yes
Tax code	G	G	G

Fig. 4-40: Vendor Names and Addresses.

Accounts Payable Outstanding Balances - August 31, 2010

Vendor	Inv. #	Date	Terms	Pre-Tax Amount	Tax Amount	Invoice Total
Custom Cabinets Ltd.	3620	Aug 16, 2016	2/10, net 30	7,810.00	390.50	8,200.50 (GST only)
Kitchen Gadgets Inc.	600	Aug 20, 2016	2/10, net 30	2,650.00	132.50	2,782.50 (GST only)
**Office Stationery Plus	5628	Aug 25, 2016	2/10, net 30	278.27	36.18*	314.45 (GST & PST)

* 36.18 includes GST and PST	---------------
** "New wording" entered in Exercise 4-12	$ 11,297.45

Fig. 4-41: Vendor Names and History.

History for vendors can be entered in detail by entering individual invoices and payments, or entered as one balance carried forward. The detail method provides an accurate aging of the payable balance.

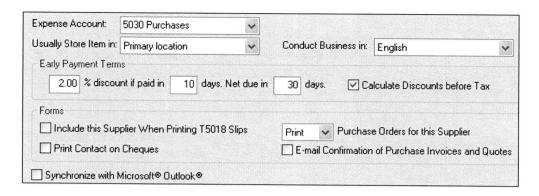

 Remember to record the terms and ✓ the Calculate Discounts before Tax box for vendors that allow discounts to be taken on the purchase price of the goods before PST and GST.

 When you add the invoice details for an invoice that has no discount for paying early, the Pre-tax Amount box does not show. Record the full amount of the invoice owing.

 Do NOT change any information for other fields. You may find information on what goes in the **Additional Info** tab in the Appendix CD-Q, *Names Fields* on the Student Data CD.

13 ➤ When all vendors have been entered, you should see the following at the bottom. The amounts agree.

Accounts Payable Balance: $11,297.45   equals ⓘ Total Balance Owing: $11,297.45

14 ➤ Close the Setup Guide and return to the Home window.

 Depending on the configuration of your computer, the Home window Vendors Opening Balance amounts may not be updated. You will have to exit Simply and reopen the data base to update the amounts.

15 ➤ It would be a good idea to print the Vendor Aged Detail report and compare vendor totals. Using the Report Centre, display the **Vendor Aged Detail, Modify this report,** all vendors should be **selected**, click **Include Terms, OK** to display the aged vendor balances. ($11,297.45 to G/L ACCOUNTS PAYABLE account 2010. The amounts must be the same (**$11,297.45**). This is done to prove that the starting PAYABLES module agrees with the COMPANY module (General Ledger).

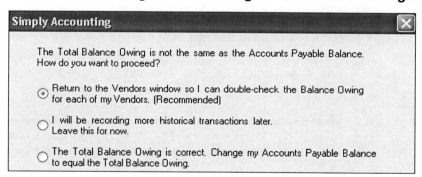

Vendor Aged Detail As at Aug 31, 2016

Source	Date	Terms	Transaction Type	Total	Current
Custom Cabinets Ltd.					
3620	Aug 16, 2016	2%/10, Net 30	Invoice	8,200.50	8,200.50
Total outstanding:				8,200.50	8,200.50
Kitchen Gadgets Inc.					
600	Aug 20, 2016	2%/10, Net 30	Invoice	2,782.50	2,782.50
Total outstanding:				2,782.50	2,782.50
Office Stationery Plus					
5628	Aug 25, 2016	2%/10, Net 30	Invoice	314.45	314.45
Total outstanding:				314.45	314.45
Total unpaid invoices:				11,297.45	11,297.45
Total prepayments/prepaid order:				-	-
Total outstanding:				11,297.45	11,297.45

Fig. 4-42: Vendor Aged Detail Aug 31, 2016.

16 ➤ Exit the Vendor Aged Detail window.

17 ➤ Exit the Report Centre window.

The history for the PAYABLES module is now complete.

18 ➤ Back up (save) your work before proceeding.

When the Vendors Ledger Does Not Agree with General Ledger

Simply Accounting

The Total Balance Owing is not the same as the Accounts Payable Balance. How do you want to proceed?

○ Return to the Vendors window so I can double-check the Balance Owing for each of my Vendors. (Recommended)

○ I will be recording more historical transactions later. Leave this for now.

○ The Total Balance Owing is correct. Change my Accounts Payable Balance to equal the Total Balance Owing.

What would you do if the Vendor Aged Detail total does not agree with the General Ledger ACCOUNTS PAYABLE account 2010? Simply will not allow you to change from History to **Ready**. You would then take steps to find the error(s). Errors could be caused by:

a) one or more missing vendor information records.

b) one or more incorrect outstanding balances in the payable detail.

c) an error in the manual General Ledger (posting error).

Most companies would like to get the Simply system working as soon as possible. In the event that an error occurred, the business may enter an **UNKNOWN VENDOR** account for the difference between the Vendor Aged Detail total and the ACCOUNTS PAYABLE account.

If you see the above window, select the 2nd choice. **I will be recording more historical transactions later**. This will allow you to print the Aged Detail report and compare it to the manual records. You would then return to the Vendors area and add the missing amount(s) or correct an amount. See Student Data CD **CD-Y**, *To Cancel a History Invoice*.

Difference	General Ledger Balance	Accounts Payable Detail	Difference To GL	Difference	Unknown Vendor Adjustment required
Short	$11,297.45	$11,087.45	$-210.00	Short	Positive Invoice
Over	$11,297.45	$11,612.45	$ 315.00	Over	Negative Invoice

The UNKNOWN VENDOR would be entered with an invoice number as:

a) **Unknown**, or
b) ? ? ? or
c) 9999999 or something similar to indicate an unknown invoice number.

You can get the Simply program working with the subledgers balanced; meanwhile, you will have time to find and correct the error. The error may be found when a vendor called for payment, a missing vendor card was located, a posting error was corrected, etc.

Step 9b: Setting Up Subledgers–Customers

Follow the same procedure that you used in Exercise 4-12 to create the Customer Ledger and enter Customer balances to add the dollar value to each customer history.

Exercise 4-13 – Setting Up Customer Subledgers

Entering Customers

1 ➤ From the Home window, click **Setup, Setup Guide, Customers.** You are in the Customer Setup window.

2 ➤ Create the following customers, with the following information.

Customer	Chaiken's Home Depot	Lee's Department Store
Contact	Marion Chaiken	Michael Lee
Telephone	519-745-1481	613-748-6358
Street 1	268 Grandview Street	2075 Heron Road
City	Kitchener	Ottawa
Province	Ontario	Ontario
Postal Code	N2B 2B9	K1N 2A4

3 ➤ Before entering Balance Owing amounts, you will enter other custom information. Double-click **Chaiken's Home Depot**. This is using the same procedure as discussed in Chapter 3 – Exercise 3A-8 after step 16 information section, Creating a New Vendor Account.

Options tab		
Revenue Account	4010	4010
Terms	2/10, net 30	2/10, net 30
Taxes tab		
PST	Tax Exempt, Yes	Tax Exempt, Yes
PST Tax ID	Ex5-8956	Ex4-1283
Tax code	G	G
Statistics tab		
Credit Limit	15,000.00	15,000.00

Customer	Inv. #	Date	Terms	Pre-tax Amount	Tax Amount	Invoice Total
Chaiken's Home Depot	598	Aug 23, 2016	2/10, n30	4,760.00	238.00	4,998.00 (GST)
Lee's Department Store	613	Aug 28, 2016	2/10, n30	6,510.00	325.50	6,835.50 (GST)

						$11,833.50

Fig. 4-43: Customer Outstanding Invoices.

Entering Customer Balances (History)

1 ➤ Click the **Historical Transactions** tab.

2 ➤ Click the **Invoices** button. The Historical Invoices window is displayed. Enter the invoice information in Fig. 4-43 for each customer. When complete, click **Record** and **Close** for each customer.

3 ➤ When you have entered both customers' historical transactions, **exit** the RECEIVABLES Ledger.

At the bottom of the Customer Setup window you will see:

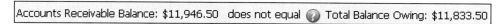

Accounts Receivable Balance: $11,946.50   does not equal ⓘ Total Balance Owing: $11,833.50

You will notice that the total of the Customer Aged Detail report (Total Balance Owing) is $11,833.50 and **does not balance with** the $11,946.50 balance of the G/L ACCOUNTS RECEIVABLE Balance account 1200.

4 ➤ Click **Close** to exit to the Home window.

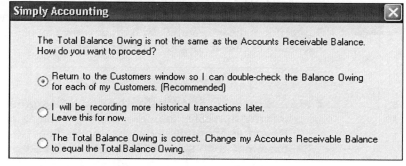

5 ➤ Click the 2nd choice as you will return to record another customer, and exit to the Home window.

6 ➤ From the top menu, click **Reports, Receivables, Customer Aged, Detail,** Both customers should be selected, **Include Terms, OK** to display the aged customer balances.

Customer Aged Detail As at Aug 31, 2016					
Source	Date	Terms	Transaction Type	Total	Current
Chaiken's Home Depot					
598	Aug 23, 2016	2%/10, Net 30	Invoice	4,998.00	4,998.00
Total outstanding:				4,998.00	4,998.00
Lee's Department Store					
613	Aug 28, 2016	2%/10, Net 30	Invoice	6,835.50	6,835.50
Total outstanding:				6,835.50	6,835.50
Total unpaid invoices:				11,833.50	11,833.50
Total deposits/prepaid order:				-	-
Total outstanding:				11,833.50	11,833.50

Fig. 4-44: Customer Aged Detail – not balanced.

Difference	General Ledger Balance	Accounts Receivable	Difference Detail	Difference To GL	Unknown Customer Adjustment required
Short	$11,946.50	$$11,833.50	$-113.00	Short	Positive Invoice

As discussed in the vendor section, you may create an UNKNOWN CUSTOMER account to record the missing balance. This will allow the module to be turned to Ready and will give you time to locate the missing invoice.

A search of invoices issued has located all invoices except 615. Invoices 613, 614 and 616 were issued on Aug. 28, 2016; therefore, invoice 615 would have been issued on the same day. The Sales Journal on Aug. 28, 2016 has an entry for $100.00, plus 5% GST and 8% PST, for Kitchen Accessories for a total invoice of $113.00. However, the customer's name was not recorded, and the staff cannot remember to whom the sale was made.

The above invoice (615) was recorded correctly in the General Ledger.

You will enter the sales invoice information you have and try to locate the missing invoice.

You may not be able to locate information about the missing invoice(s) before turning the module to **Ready**. A suggested solution is to add an **Unknown Customer**, similar to step 8, with an unknown invoice number or other code as discussed in step 9, for the missing amount.

7 ➤ Add a customer ledger for **Unknown Customer,** with **no address information**, Ship to Address is the **same as mailing address**, leave **Revenue Account** field blank as you do not know what Revenue account this customer normally uses. Terms **2/10, net 30** given to all customers. Click the **Taxes** tab, GST **No**, PST **No**, Tax Code **GP**. Click the **Statistic** tab, Credit Limit **$113.00**.

8 ➤ Add historical invoice number **#615** with the following: Date **August 28, 2016**, Pre-tax Amount **$100.00**, Tax **13.00**, Invoice total **113.00**. If the invoice number is not known, use a code similar to **Unknown, ? ? ?,** or **999999,** etc., as discussed in Exercise 4-12 after step 18.

9 ➤ After entering the Unknown Customer, **exit** the Receivable Ledger. At the bottom of the Customer Setup window you will see:

Accounts Receivable Balance: $11,946.50   equals ⓘ   Total Balance Owing: $11,946.50

The sub-ledger now agrees to the General ledger balance. Click **Close** and **Exit** to the Home window.

10 ➤ Display the **Customer Aged Detail** report as shown:

Customer Aged Detail As at Aug 31, 2016

Source	Date	Terms	Transaction Type	Total	Current
Chaiken's Home Depot					
598	Aug 23, 2016	2%/10, Net 30	Invoice	4,998.00	4,998.00
Total outstanding:				4,998.00	4,998.00
Lee's Department Store					
613	Aug 28, 2016	2%/10, Net 30	Invoice	6,835.50	6,835.50
Total outstanding:				6,835.50	6,835.50
Unknown Customer					
615	Aug 28, 2016	2%/10, Net 30	Invoice	113.00	113.00
Total outstanding:				113.00	113.00
Total unpaid invoices:				11,946.50	11,946.50
Total deposits/prepaid order:				-	-
Total outstanding:				11,946.50	11,946.50

Fig. 4-45: Customer Aged Detail – after correction.

Compare the Customer Aged Detail $11,946.50 to the General Ledger again to prove that the starting CUSTOMERS module agrees with the General Ledger.

11 ➤ **Exit** to the Home window.

The history for the CUSTOMERS module is now complete.

Step 10: To Add Credit Card Information

To process credit card transactions, you must set up the information for the specific credit card company that your firm accepts.

Exercise 4-14 – To Add Credit Card Information

The following procedure is used to add credit card information:

1 ➤ At the bottom, Related Tasks, click **Settings,** click ➕ at **Company,** click **Credit Cards.**

Credit Cards Used

2 ➤   In the right pane, click **Used**. The blank Settings window for **Credit Cards Used** appears.

Enter the credit cards you use to make purchases.
Under Payable Acct, enter the account that tracks the amount you owe the credit card company.
Under Expense Acct, enter the account you want to charge any fees, such as interest charges and annual fees, against.

Credit Card Name	Payable Acct	Expense Acct
Visa	2030 Visa Credit Card Payable	5520 Credit Card Charges

Fig. 4-46: Credit Cards used window.

Sarah's Kitchen Stores uses a business credit card from the Visa Credit Card Company for their purchases.

3 ➤   Type the information as shown in Fig. 4-46.

Credit Card Name   **Visa**. Sarah will use this card to make purchases for the business. She may apply for other business credit cards later.

Payable Acct   **2030 Visa Credit Card Payable** is the account where the amounts owing to the credit card company will be charged.

Expense Acct   **5520 Credit Card Charges** is the account where the amounts that the credit card company charges the business for annual fees, etc., will be recorded. This is the same account to which the discount fee on customer credit card sales is charged. Sarah's Kitchen Stores has decided to use one account for all credit card fees and charges.

Credit Cards Accepted

4 ➤   In the left pane, click the **Credit Cards Accepted** item.

Enter the credit cards you accept from customers.
Under Discount Fee, enter the % fee the credit card company charges on transactions.
Under Expense Acct, enter the account you want to charge the discount fee against.
Under Asset Acct, enter the account that tracks the amount the credit card company owes you.

Credit Card Name	Discount Fee %	Expense Acct	Asset Acct
Visa	3.50	5520 Credit Card Charge	1011 Bank Account Cre

Fig. 4-47: Credit cards accepted window.

5 ➤   Type the information as shown in Fig. 4-47.

Credit Card Name   **Visa** (maximum 13-characters). Sarah has decided to accept only the Visa Credit Card for use by her customers. Other credit cards may be added later.

Discount Fee %   When you entered the Visa name above, a 0.00 appeared in this column. The rate would be the discount fee the credit card company charges the business for using the credit card. The Visa credit company charges a fee of **3.5%** on the sales value including taxes. (e.g., Sale 100.00, plus $5.00 GST and $8.00 PST = $113.00.) The discount fee would be $3.96 (3.5% of $113.00).

Expense Acct	**5520 Credit Card Charges** is the account where the discount fee will be charged as an expense.
Asset Acct	**1011 Bank Account Credit Card Receivable** is the asset account where the receivable (cash) amount from the credit card company will be charged.

6 ➤ Click **OK** to Exit.

VERY IMPORTANT: Back up your data before proceeding.

Step 11: Setting Modules to Ready

The final step in the setup process is to set the modules to **Ready** (change from History). The journals can be used for transaction entries from September 1, 2016 onwards. The modules that are being used for Sarah's Kitchen Stores are COMPANY, PAYABLES and RECEIVABLES.

Here's a last-minute checklist:

1. All sections in the Chart of Accounts must begin with an **H** and end with a **T**.

2. All **A** type accounts must be followed by an **S**.

3. All Accounts must be in logical order.

4. All Linked accounts needed should have been set up. You may change or modify the linked accounts at any time in the future, as the need arises.

5. Before the system can be made **Ready**, all subledger module balances must agree with the associated Linked account balances in the General Ledger. They now agree.

6. It is best to print a Trial Balance, Income Statement, Balance Sheet, Schedules of Accounts Payable and Accounts Receivable, and verify that the balances agree.

Mistakes made in entering History **cannot** be changed once the module is set to **Ready**.

Back up your data and use the backup to correct History errors. Once the errors are corrected, another backup must be made before setting to Ready.

Remember, **BACK UP** before proceeding. Make *TWO* backup copies of your data. *THIS IS VERY IMPORTANT.* In Chapter 5, Sarah's Kitchen Stores is used to enter transactions. An extra backup, *before setting the modules to Ready*, could be vital. It should be kept in case you have to start Chapter 4 again, or fix errors when entering transactions.

If the above conditions are met, you can turn the modules to **Ready**.

Setting the System to READY

The following procedure will turn the COMPANY, RECEIVABLES and PAYABLES modules to **Ready**, and the quill pens (History icons), will disappear from the window.

Exercise 4-15 – To Set the System to READY

---

1 ➤ On the menu bar, click on **History**, and then **Finish Entering History**.

If the PAYABLES or RECEIVABLES do not balance with the General Ledger, you will receive an error message similar to the following:

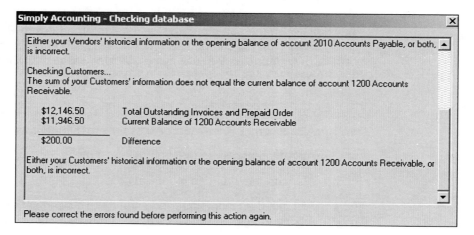

The Simply database verifies that all modules displayed are error-free. If errors exist, the program identifies the area where the error occurred (see above).

You will need to go back to the module that is not balanced and correct the error.

If you have not set up the Chart of Accounts in a logical order, an error message similar to the following is displayed, preventing you from changing to Ready and continuing. The error must be fixed before you can turn the Modules to Ready.

> Checking Accounts...
> Your accounts are not in logical order. The reason is: there is a missing Subgroup Account before account '2240 PST Payable (Prov Sales Tax)'. Until this issue is resolved, you cannot open some of your reports.

When the subledger balances agree with the G/L, you will see the following window and warning message to back up your data files:

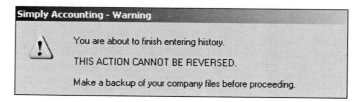

2 ➤ Click **Proceed**.

The screen will flicker and the quill pens will disappear. The RECEIVABLES, PAYABLES, BANKING and COMPANY modules, with all historical data, are now in READY mode and are **Ready** to use.

CONGRATULATIONS! The Journals in RECEIVABLES (Sales Quotes, Sales Orders, Sales Invoices and Receipts), PAYABLES (Purchase Orders, Purchase Invoices, and Payments), COMPANY (Chart of Accounts and General Journal) and BANKING (Reconcile Accounts) are ready to use. If you wish to use other modules, the setup and conversion process must be performed for the module before making the module **Ready**. The setup for other modules is covered in later chapters in this book.

3 ➤ Exit Simply.

Chapter 5 continues to use the Sarah's Kitchen Stores data file, and will provide a review of journalizing transactions in the COMPANY, PAYABLES and RECEIVABLES modules using simulated source documents.

Exercise 4-16 –Verify Information in SAI Data File

This procedure will allow you to verify/confirm the SAI data file information that you entered in the Sarah's Kitchen Stores data file, or can be used to verify other data files. This exercise does not take the place of an up-to-date log book.

1 ➤ Open Windows Explorer.

2 ➤ In the left pane, **locate** and **click** on the + beside the **C:\Simply Data 2009** folder.

3 ➤ In the left pane, click on the **Sarah's Kitchen Stores** folder containing the SAI file you want information about.

4 ➤ In the right pane, **click** on the ⬚ Sarah's Kitchen Stores.SAI file, then **right-click**.

5 ➤ Select **Properties**. The Sarah's Kitchen Stores.SAI properties window appears.

6 ➤ Click on the **Simply Accounting** tab. Information about the SAI file will display.

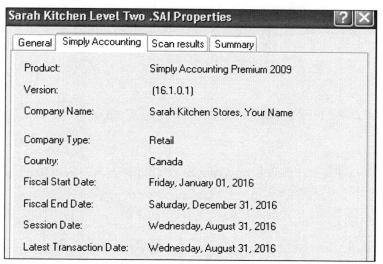

This window will confirm the information you entered in this file, or any other Simply SAI file. This exercise does not take the place of an up-to-date log book.

7 ➤ Exit the window.

In future exercises, refer to **Slideshow 4** when creating a new G/L account, setting up a new vendor or a new customer.

Before Moving On...

Read the following questions and make sure you know the answers to them; otherwise, read the corresponding part in the chapter before moving on.

1. Explain the differences between the following dates: **Fiscal Start**, **Fiscal End**, **Earliest Transaction**, **Session**, **Latest Transaction** and **Historical Transactions**.

2. Before assigning account numbers, why is it important to know what accounts go with each account group number; e.g., 1000, 2000, 3000, 4000 or 5000?

3. What is the difference between **postable** and **non-postable** accounts? How do you designate a postable account?

4. Assume that mistakes have been made in entering the history balances and the system has been changed to **Ready**. What are two ways to correct this problem?

5. What does setting a module to **Ready** mean?

6. What is a **Linked** account?

7. Briefly explain each category of the account types **H A S G T** and **X**.

8. What is the purpose of the **X** account in the chart of accounts?

9. Would you enter the history balance of GST Paid on Purchases account as a positive or a negative number? Explain why.

10. Briefly explain what is meant by **Class Options** in Accounts.

Challenge Exercise 04 C4-1, Balloons Store

Conversion to Simply Accounting (G/L, A/R & A/P)

1 ➤ Use the **Wizard** to create a new company from scratch.

The trial balance provided shows only postable accounts. It is expected that you will use the techniques shown in Sarah's Kitchen Stores (Chapter 4) to:

- a) Add Headings (**H**), Postable accounts (**A** and **G**) with Subtotal (**S**) accounts and Total (**T**) accounts. You should have a minimum of 3 **S**-type accounts.
- b) Use a **Difference at Startup** account.
- c) Create **Linked accounts** for the COMPANY, PAYABLES and RECEIVABLES modules.
- d) Select **Class Options** required.
- e) Add **Vendor** and **Customer** invoice information.

Balloons Store is assumed to be a sole proprietorship business. It sells various kinds of party balloons.

This review assignment does not use all accounts that may be used by a typical business – it uses only the RECEIVABLES (Customers), PAYABLES (Vendors), and COMPANY modules. Balloons Store does not use the budget feature, credit cards, or shippers. When all data has been entered, turn the related modules to **Ready**.

A) The business using a calendar fiscal year has the following important dates:
   Opened for business   **Sep 12, 1987**
   Year-end this year   **Dec 31, 2012**
   Year-end last year   **Dec 31, 2011**
   Manual books stopped   **Apr 30, 2012.** This will be the conversion date the manual accounting records will be transferred to Simply.

B) The business is: Balloons Store, Your Name, 936 Alfred St., Sarnia, Ontario N7V 3K7

> *Remember, your name must appear on all reports.*

C) Business number is Z345

D) Forms use the next number on:
   Invoices (342)
   Cheques (384)
   All other forms start at **1**, except for:
          Receipts (# blank)
          Customer Deposits (# blank)
          Direct Deposit Stubs (# blank)

E) Discounts are calculated **before tax** for both customer and vendor invoices, with Customer early payment terms **2/10 net 30**.

F) The computer financial statements should be set up with the following sections:
Current Assets	Owner's Equity
Capital Assets	Revenue
Current Liabilities	Cost of Goods Sold
Long Term Liabilities	Store Expenses

The **normal** account balances from the Apr 30, 2012, Balloons Store Trial Balance are listed below. Use appropriate **account classes** in setting up your accounts.

Account Names	Balance	Class	Other
Bank Account	$ 3,187	Bank	Cheque #384
Accounts Receivable	6,780	Accounts Receivable	
Supplies Store & Office	800		
Inventory	See below		
Store Furniture	34,400		
Accumulated Amortization	6,100		
Accounts Payable	9,030	Accounts Payable	
GST on Sales	1,600		
GST on Purchases	900		
PST Payable	863		
Bank Loan Payable	24,600	Long Term Debt	8 year loan
Capital, your actual name	27,192		
Capital, Additional Investments	0		
Drawings, your actual name	6,500		
Sales Revenue	186,000		
Sales Returns	3,046		
Sales Discounts	312		
Beginning Inventory	See below		
Purchases	148,000		
Purchase Returns	2,000		
Purchase Discounts	2,086		
Ending Inventory	See below		
Rent Expense	16,221		
Advertising Expense	1,325		
Amortization Expense	0		
Inventory at Beginning of fiscal year	was $38,000		
Inventory at April 30, 2012	is $61,360		

G) Tax Classes, Codes and Rates:

    GST rate is 5%, GST registration # R1234, and GST is refundable.
    PST rate is 8%, PST is not charged on GST.

    G   code is GST at 5% and PST Exempt.
    GP code is GST at 5% and PST at 8%.
    P   code is GST Exempt, PST at 8%.

H) Customize the Journals as shown in Exercise 4-11, Setting up Tax Classes, Codes, Rates & Customization.

I) Set up Customers and Vendors:

Accounts Receivable Customers	**Accounts Payable Vendors**
Belair Hospital (balloons for rooms & patients)	"Your Last Name Here" Balloon Supply
Contact: Jordan Royes	Contact: Kylie Lunn
85 Colborne Road	289 Talford Street
Sarnia, Ontario, N7V 5B3	Sarnia, Ontario, N7T 6L4
Phone: (519) 826-7520, Fax –None	Phone: (519) 726-7520, Fax –None
Terms: 2/10, net 30. Credit Limit $10,000.	Terms: 2/10, net 30.
Revenue Account: Sales Revenue	Invoice #349 April 24, 2012, $8,500
Price List: Regular	GST $425. Total invoice: $8,925.
Invoice #340 April 26, 2012 $6,000;	Expense Account: Purchases
GST $300; PST $480. Total invoice $6,780	Tax Code G
Tax Code GP	

J) Set the related modules, accounts, vendors and customers to **Ready** mode.

2 ➤ Print the following reports.

    As of Apr 30, 2012
      a) Income Statement Jan 1- Apr 30
      b) Balance Sheet
      c) Customer Aged Detail report
      d) Vendor Aged Detail report

3 ➤ **Record** and **post** the next two transactions.

May 1   Purchase return (from original invoice # 349) of 10 cases of Red 40th Birthday balloons at $10.00 each plus GST, to "Your Last Name Here" Balloon Supply.

May 1   Sold to retail customer, Mirella Nostopolis, 3 party packages of children's balloons at $15.00 per package plus GST and PST. Received her cheque #315 as payment in full.

4 ➤ **Print** the following reports.

    As of May 1, 2012

      a) Income Statement Jan 1- May 1
      b) Balance Sheet
      c) Customer Aged Detail report
      d) Vendor Aged Detail report
      e) All Journal Entries

Challenge Exercise 04 C4-2, Kojokaro

(Setup of a company file, using G/L, A/R & A/P)

1 ➤ Refer to Exercise 1-1, to unzip the **04 C4-2 Kojokaro.exe** file.

2 ➤ Open the **04 C4-2 Kojokaro** file with a date of Jan. 01.

This exercise is a review of the setup of a company file.

The account structure – Chart of Accounts, with many errors, was created by an employee of Kojokaro Sales Company. Account classes have not been shown in the information below. As a consultant hired to help with the setup of the company you will:

1 ➤ Identify the errors.

2 ➤ Add, Modify and Delete accounts necessary to fix the account structure.

3 ➤ Print the Balance Sheet.

4 ➤ Print the Income Statement.

5 ➤ Print the Chart of Accounts List.

Chart of Accounts

ASSETS

1000 Current Assets .... **H**	
1001 Cash in Bank............................A	
1030 Total Cash ....S	
1050 Accounts Receivable ....A	
1059 Accounts Receivable Net..........S	
1100 Store Supplies ....A	
1299 Total Current Liabilities ....S	
1400 Capital Assets .... **H**	
1410 Equipment ....A	

LIABILITIES

2000 Current Liabilities .... **H**	
2005 Accum Amortization/Deprec. .... G	
2100 Accounts Payable .... G	
2200 Drawings by Owner................... G	
2500 Long Term Liabilities............... **H**	
2530 Bank Loan -Mortgage .... G	

EQUITY

3010 Owner's Equity...........................A	
3020 Inventory ....A	
3030 Capital ....A	
3600 Current Earnings.......................X	

REVENUE

4010 Sales ....H	
4020 Sales -All....................................A	
4040 Sales Discounts ....A	
4050 Sales Returns ....G	
4100 GST on Sales ....G	

EXPENSE

5000 Cost of Goods Sold ....H	
5020 Purchases ....A	
5030 Purchase Discounts ....A	
5040 Purchase Returns....................A	
5050 GST on Purchases ....A	
5080 Ending Inventory......................A	
5090 Beginning Inventory.................A	
5099 Cost of Goods Sold.................G	
5200 PST Payable ....G	
5300 Rent Expense ....G	
5310 Amortization/Deprec Expense .G	
5325 Telephone Expense.................A	
5390 Other Expenses ....S	

Challenge Exercise 04 C4-3, Skates Stores

Conversion to Simply Accounting, using G/L, A/R & A/P

1 ➤ Use the **Wizard** to create a new company from scratch.

The trial balance provided shows only postable accounts in alphabetical order. It is expected that you will use the techniques shown in Sarah's Kitchen Stores (Chapter 4) to:

a) Add Headings (**H**), Postable accounts (**A** and **G**) with Subtotal (**S**) accounts and Total (**T**) accounts. You should have a minimum of 3 **S**-type of accounts.
b) Use a **Difference at Startup** account.
c) Create **Linked accounts** for the COMPANY, PAYABLES and RECEIVABLES modules.
d) Select **Class Options** required.
e) Add **Vendor** and **Customer** invoice information.

Skates Stores is assumed to be a sole proprietorship business. It sells figure skates and hockey skates.

This review assignment does not use all accounts that may be used by a business, and uses only the COMPANY, PAYABLES (Vendors) and RECEIVABLES (Customers) modules. Skates Stores does not use the budget feature, credit cards, or shippers. When all data has been entered, turn the related modules to **Ready**.

A) The business using a calendar fiscal year has the following important dates:
   Opened for business   **February 15, 1986**
   Year-end this year   **December 31, 2012**
   Year-end last year   **December 31, 2011**
   Manual books stopped   **May 31, 2012**. This will be the conversion date the manual accounting records will be transferred to Simply.

B) The business is: Skates Stores, Your Name, 514 Semple Avenue, Your Town, Ontario, L0N 1B0.

> **Remember, your name must appear on all reports.**

C) Business Registration # R1176.

D) Forms: use the next number on:
   Invoices (#983)
   Cheques (#468)
   All other forms start at **1**, except:
   Receipts (# blank)
   Customer Deposits (# blank).

E) Discounts are calculated **before tax** for both customer and vendor invoices, with Customer early payment terms **2/10 net 30**.

F) The computer financial statements should be set up with the following sections:

Current Assets	Owner's Equity
Capital Assets	Revenue
Current Liabilities	Cost of Goods Sold
Long Term Liabilities	Store Expenses

The <u>normal</u> account balances from the May 31, 2012, Skates Stores. Trial Balance in alphabetical order is next:

Account Name	Balance	Class	Other
Accounts Payable	$ 1,260.00	Accounts Payable	
Accounts Receivable	1,155.00	Accounts Receivable	
Accumulated Amortization	4,100.00		
Amortization Expense All	0.00		
Beginning Inventory Jan 1	3,900.00		
Capital – Additional Investments	0.00		
Capital –Your last name	9,240.00		
Cash in Bank	416.00	Bank	Cheque #468
Drawings –Your last name	1,000.00		
Ending Inventory	6,100.00		
GST on Sales	252.00		
GST Paid on Purchases	136.00		
Inventory	6,100.00		
Notes Payable (Long Term)	21,400.00		
PST on Sales	0.00		
Purchases	15,730.00		
Purchase Discounts	125.00		
Purchase Returns	345.00		
Rent Expense	3,200.00		
Sales Discounts	300.00		
Sales Returns	350.00		
Sales Revenue	14,165.00		
Store Equipment	23,700.00		
Store Supplies	200.00		
Telephone Expense	800.00		

G) Tax Classes, Codes and Rates:

GST rate is 5%, GST registration # R1234, and GST is refundable.

PST rate is 8%, PST is not charged on GST.

G   code is GST at 5% and PST Exempt.

GP   code is GST at 5% and PST at 8%.

P code is GST Exempt, PST at 8%.

H) Customize the Journals as shown in Exercise 4-11, Setting up Tax Classes, Codes, Rates & Customization.

l) Set up Customers and Vendors:

Accounts Receivable customers:
Elvis Skates Corp., Contact Elvis Schafer
2 Huron Street
Woodstock, Ontario, N4S 1A5
Phone 519-546-8588 - Fax: none
Terms 2/10, net 30
Invoice #980, date May 24, 2012
Invoice amount $1,155.00 (including $55.00 GST)
Revenue Account: Sales Revenue
Tax: PST Exempt
Tax ID: 3785-4
Tax: G
Credit Limit: $5,000.00

Accounts Payable vendors:
Skates Supply Ltd., Contact Greg Johnson
43 McKay Avenue
Windsor, Ontario, N9B 1A4
Phone: 519-675-8940
Terms 2% 10, net 30
Fax: 416-675-8930
Invoice # 6512, date May 10, 2012
Invoice amount $735.00 (including $35.00 GST)
Expense Account: Purchases
Tax: G

Manufacture Supply Inc., Contact Jessie Grant
645 Bancroft Drive
Sudbury, Ontario, P3B 8T4
Phone: 705-672-4860 - Fax: 705-672-4860
Terms 2% 10, net 30
Invoice # 1431, date May 28, 2012
Invoice amount $525.00 (including $25.00 GST)
Expense Account: Purchases
Tax: G

2 ➤ Turn the system to **Ready** and **Record** the inventory adjustment entry for May 31, 2012. Ending inventory at close of business is $3,000.00.

3 ➤ After the ending inventory has been recorded, **print** the following reports:
   a) Income Statement, year-to-date
   b) Balance Sheet
   c) Vendor Detail report
   d) Customer Detail report
   e) Journal Entries-General

Back up your file regularly.

Challenge Exercise 04 C4-4, R. Park Uniforms
(Conversion to Simply Accounting, using the G/L)

1 ➤ Refer to Exercise 1-1 to unzip the **04 C4-4 Uniforms.exe** file.

2 ➤ Open the Simply file **04 C4-4 Uniforms**. This file contains only the account 3600 Current Earnings account. See Fig. 4-11 as a reference.

Mr. Roland Park has asked for your assistance in setting up the General Ledger in Simply. The manual paper records were dropped on the floor and mixed up and are not in the proper order, but he knows that the Trial Balance which he cannot find now was balanced.

The bookkeeper had to leave this morning to attend to an important family matter in another province and will not be back for a week. The individual Accounts Receivable customer and Payable vendor pages are in her car. She will need your help with the PAYABLES and RECEIVABLES modules when she returns.

3 ➤ Set up the General Ledger accounts with balances using appropriate H A S G T account classes.

Other information:

The business opened	June 1, 2001
Year-end this year	December 31, 2018
Year-end last year	December 31, 2017
Manual books stopped	July 31, 2018

Business Name is R. Park Uniforms, any address (file created with Ontario)
Business number is R56-B37
GST rate is 5%, registration #R1234 and GST is refundable
PST rate is 8%, PST is not charged on GST
G   code is GST at 5% and PST Exempt
GP   code is GST at 5% and PST at 8%
P   code is GST Exempt and PST at 8%
Next Cheque # and all Forms start at 1
Discounts are all 2/10, net 30

R. Park Uniforms: List of accounts (not in order) at July 31, 2018

GST Charged on Sales	1,280
PST Payable	1,462
Bank	24,700
Inventory Asset	39,900
Beginning Inventory	16,500
GST Paid on Purchases/Services	712
Ending Inventory	39,900
Salaries Expense	78,600
Prepaid Insurance	750
Accounts Payable	7,350
Advertising Expense	9,000
Capital R. Park	11,000
Mortgage Payable (Due March 2020)	31,020
Rent Expense	19,500
Purchases	117,580
Sales/Revenue	226,960
Accounts Receivable	8,400
Drawings R. Park	0
Sales Discounts	5,000
Purchase Returns	1,670

4 ➤ Print the following:
    a) Trial Balance as at July 31
    b) Income Statement, year-to-date
    c) Balance Sheet as at July 31

Accounting and Simply Accounting Terminology

Account Class: An identification for specific groups of accounts. The class identifies each group's main purpose or function; Cash, Bank, Payable, Debt, Expenses, etc. (refer to Exercise 4-5, step 14 and Fig. 4-33). This is different from Account Types or Account Numbers.

Account Numbers: A range of numbers established by Simply for each particular type of account (Asset, Liability, Equity, Revenue and Expense). This system is used by Simply in determining the normal balance of each account, and where the account is located in the Balance Sheet or Income Statement.

Account Type: An identification code, or category, for each account; e.g., Asset, Liability, Equity, etc. Each code has a specific function and placement on financial statements.

Conversion: The change from one accounting system to another, usually from manual accounting to a computerized system, or from one computerized accounting software to another.

Conversion Date: See *Earliest Transaction Date*.

Default: A value or course of action that Simply has preset. A default could be a display format; e.g., mmddyy for date format, a number (6 lines for labels), a Yes/No state, etc. A default can be changed; then the new setting is referred to as the default.

Earliest Transaction Date: This is the date when the manual books are converted to the computer system, or converted from one computerized system to another; e.g., May 31 month-end conversion. This is the conversion date as defined by Simply Accounting.

Export: A feature that allows you to transfer reports produced in Simply into a format that can be used by other software programs; e.g., Lotus 1-2-3, Excel, SuperCalc, most word processing, etc.

Finish Date: The end of the fiscal year.

History: Account balances and other pertinent information in a module. Historical information needs to be entered before the module can be set to **Ready**.

Integration: See *Linking*.

Linking: A feature of Simply that allows you to enter a transaction in one module and automatically update other modules.

Ready: The last step in the conversion process is to set the module to **Ready** for recording transactions. Before setting up a module from History to Ready mode, the total of individual subledger balances must agree with the corresponding General Ledger control accounts.

Start Date: The beginning of the current calendar year, or fiscal year, or the date when the business started this year.

Template: A data file supplied with the software that contains a set of linked and non-linked General Ledger accounts with section and group headings. Each of the templates has accounts that are similar in nature to specific businesses.

Wizard: A smart step-by-step help feature that takes you through the necessary procedure in completing a process (e.g., setting up a new company).

Relevant Appendices

The following appendices are available on the Student Data CD.

Appendix 2009 CD-E	**Budgets — General Ledger**
Appendix 2009 CD-F	**Printing in Batches**
Appendix 2009 CD-H	**New Business Guide**
Appendix 2009 CD-I	**Checklists for Task Completion**
Appendix 2009 CD-M	**Post-Dated Cheques**
Appendix 2009 CD-Q	**Names Fields**
Appendix 2009 CD-U	**Add Notes/Footer to Statements**
Appendix 2009 CD-X	**Removing an Account from a Wrong Section**
Appendix 2009 CD-Y	**To Cancel a History Invoice**
Appendix 2009 CD-AA	**Setting Up a New Company File using a Template**
Appendix 2009 CD-AD	**Time and Billing Module**

Chapter 5

Review of COMPANY, PAYABLES and RECEIVABLES Modules

Sarah's Kitchen Stores

Learning Objectives
After completing this chapter you will be able to:

☐ Use the data file created in Chapter 4.
☐ Record transactions from source documents, in the COMPANY, ACCOUNTS RECEIVABLE and ACCOUNTS PAYABLE modules.
☐ Display and print various reports and journals.

This chapter contains transactions that will allow you to review the concepts and procedures you have learned so far. You will be presented with source documents, and will need to determine what type of transaction each of them represents, and which module to use to process them. After processing the transactions, you will be required to print financial statements and reports.

The setup of the COMPANY, PAYABLES and RECEIVABLES modules for Sarah's Kitchen Stores was covered in Chapter 4. The modules have been set to **Ready**; therefore, you can start entering transactions in the various modules at any time.

Sarah's Kitchen Stores Profile

Before starting work in this chapter, display the Sarah's Kitchen Stores Balance Sheet and Income Statement and be sure that they are the same as those shown in Fig. 4-37b in Chapter 4. If you have any differences, check with your instructor.

1 ➤ The following source document transactions should be recorded using appropriate modules with dates in September 2016. If you are not sure which module to use, look back to Chapters 1, 2A, 2B, 3A and 3B, or ask your instructor for assistance. Begin recording the transactions assuming you work only 1 day a week, starting on Friday, September 3, 2016. Advance your Session Date appropriately.

Note: **SD** refers to Source Document.

Some important points to note are as follows:

- Make sure that you enter appropriate descriptions, and invoice credit or debit note numbers with proper codes where required.

- You may have to create new vendors, customers and G/L accounts.

- There is no GST on discounts.

- Discount on Office Supplies should be charged to the Office Supplies account.

- Late payment amounts on Utilities should be charged to the Utilities account.

- Remember that the GST remittance is calculated from the difference between the GST CHARGED ON SALES account and the balance of GST PAID ON PURCHASES account in previous months.

2 ➤ When you have finished, print the following reports:

- Trial Balance as of	Sep 30
- Income Statement for	Sep 01 to 30
- Vendor Detail report as of	Sep 30
- Customer Detail report as of	Sep 30
- All Journal Entries	Sep 01 to 30
- General Ledger from	Sep 01 to 30
- Cash Projections as of	Sep 30

Compare your reports to those given in the Solutions Manual provided to your instructor. If you have any differences, try to find out which transaction(s) caused the difference. To correct any errors, you must enter adjusting (or correcting) entries. You cannot change the existing entries once they have been posted. Refer to Chapters 1, 2A, 2B, 3A and 3B, or 13 for correcting errors.

Transactions

Transactions are recorded using the original date of the document to ensure that our records match the records of our suppliers and customers for discount periods, etc. (e.g., a 2%/10, net 30 day purchase invoice dated September 23, received on September 24, and approved on September 25, would be recorded as a purchase using the September 23 date, as this is the date the discount starts.)

SD-1

Quote

Sarah's Kitchen Stores   339 Hudson Court, Hamilton ON L9C 6B3

To: Chaiken's Home Depot
268 Grandview Street
Kitchener ON N2B 2B9

Ship To:
(Same)

Quote NO.	DATE
1	Sep 01, 2016

Qty.	Order	Back Order	Description	Base Price	Disc. %	Price	Tax	Amount
	1		Set Kitchen Cabinets Model L45	$3,675.00		$3,675.00	G	3,675.00
	1		Sink Model D256	300.00		300.00	G	300.00
	1		Group Specialty Drawers & Knives	325.00		325.00	G	325.00

Subtotal	4,300.00
GST #R4675 2567 GST 5%	215.00
PST 8%	

TOTAL DUE
$4,515.00

Shipping Date: Sep 07, 2016
Terms: 2%/10, Net 30 days

SD-2

RECEIVED   Sep 02 2016

FOR DEPOSIT ONLY

Chaiken's Home Depot

268 Grandview Street
Kitchener, ON N2B 2B9

CHEQUE NO.   **791**

DATE   0 1 0 9 2 0 1 6
D D M M Y Y Y Y

PAY   Four Thousand Nine Hundred two and 80/100 $**4,902.80
To The
Order Of   Sarah's Kitchen Stores

Bank of Nova Scotia
936 Grandview Street
Kitchener, ON N2B 2D3

Chaiken's Home Depot
Marion Chaiken

⑈79⑈⑈ ⑈⑈028⑈⑈006⑈ 11⑈⑈9335⑈⑈2

DETACH BEFORE CASHING

Chaiken's Home Depot   CHEQUE NO.   **791**

Date	Description	Amount
Sep 01, 2016	#598	$ 4,902.80

SD-3

Sarah's
Kitchen Stores

339 Hudson Court, Hamilton ON L9C 6B3

CHEQUE NO.   **642**

DATE   0 1 0 9 2 0 1 6
D D M M Y Y Y Y

PAY   Two Thousand Two Hundred five and 00/100 $**2,205.00

To   Your Name Landlord
The   16 Main Street West
Order   Hamilton ON L8S 4K1

Toronto Dominion Bank   *Sarah's Kitchen Stores*
2 Palace Rd.
Hamilton, Ontario L3X 1T3   *S. Kafa*
                                           _____

⑆642⑈   ⑈2644⑉007⑈   192⑈991⑈2⑈

Please Detach Before Cashing

Sarah's Kitchen Stores   CHEQUE NO.   **642**
   Your Name Landlord   Sep. 01, 2016
                                             $2,205.00

Note: Rent $2,100, plus 5% GST payment for month based on lease.

SD-4

Order

Sarah's
Kitchen Stores   339 Hudson Court, Hamilton ON L9C 6B3

To: Chaiken's Home Depot   Ship To:
    268 Grandview Street   (Same)
    Kitchener ON N2B 2B9

Order NO.	DATE
1	Sep 02, 2016

Qty.	Order	Back Order	Description	Base Price	Disc. %	Price	Tax	Amount
	1		Set Kitchen Cabinets Model L45	$3,675.00		$3,675.00	G	3,675.00
	1		Sink Model D256	300.00		300.00	G	300.00
	1		Group Specialty Drawers & Knives	325.00		325.00	G	325.00

GST #R4675 2567

	Amount
Subtotal	4,300.00
GST 5%	215.00
PST 8%	

TOTAL DUE
$4,515.00

Shipping Date: Sep 07, 2016
Terms: 2%/10, Net 30 days

SD-5

Sarah's
Kitchen Stores
339 Hudson Court, Hamilton ON L9C 6B3

CHEQUE NO. **643**

DATE 0 2 0 9 2 0 1 6
D D M M Y Y Y Y

PAY   Three Hundred eight and 88/100 $**308.88

To   Office Stationery Plus
The   987 Emerson Street
Order   Hamilton ON L8S 4W3

Toronto Dominion Bank
2 Palace Rd.
Hamilton, Ontario L3X 1T3

Sarah's Kitchen Stores

S. Kafa

⑆643⑆ ⑈2614⑈007⑉ 192⑈991 2⑈

- -

Please Detach Before Cashing

Sarah's Kitchen Stores		**Discount**	**Cheque No.**	**643**
Office Stationery Plus	Inv. 5628	5.57		Sep. 02, 2016
				$308.88

SD-6

J̶ack D̶aly
614 Manley Street
Hamilton, ON L9K 3A5

CHEQUE NO.   **501**

DATE   0 6 0 9 2 0 1 6
D D M M Y Y Y Y

PAY One Hundred Eleven and 00/100 $**111.00

To The   Sarah's Kitchen Stores
Order   339 Hudson Court
Of   Hamilton, ON L9C 6B3

Central Bank
601 Main St.
Hamilton, ON L9Z 1M2

J. Daly

⑆0501⑆ ⑈11330501⑈ 91   890⑉

RECEIVED Sep 06, 2016   *FOR DEPOSIT ONLY*

Note: This is the cheque from the missing customer. Change the name and customer information to Mr. Daly and increase credit limit to $200.00.

SD-7

FOR DEPOSIT ONLY
RECEIVED   Sep. 07, 2016

LEE'S Department Stores   CHEQUE NO.   **4680**

2075 Heron Road
Ottawa, ON K1N 2A4

D A T E   0 6 0 9 2 0 1 6
               D D M M Y Y Y Y

To the
Order Of   Sarah's Kitchen Stores $**6,705.30

PAY   Six thousand seven hundred five ---30/100 DOLLARS

Bank of Montreal   LEE'S Department Stores
618 Main St.
Erinvale, ON N0Z 1Z0   *M. Lee*

⑆4680⑆   ⑆00031⑈012⑈   180232⑆5

DETACH BEFORE CASHING

Date	Description	Amount	Discount	CHEQUE NO. **4680**
Sep 06, 2016	Payment re: 613	$6,705.30	130.20	LEE'S Department Stores

---

SD-8

INVOICE

**Sarah's
Kitchen Stores**   339 Hudson Court, Hamilton ON L9C 6B3

To: Chaiken's Home Depot
     268 Grandview Street
     Kitchener ON N2B 2B9

Ship To:
   (Same)

Invoice NO.	DATE
922	Sep 07, 2016

Qty.	Order	Back Order	Description	Base Price	Disc. %	Price	Tax	Amount
1			Set Kitchen Cabinets Model L45	$3,675.00		$3,675.00	G	3,675.00
1			Sink Model D256	300.00		300.00	G	300.00
1			Group Specialty Drawers & Knives	325.00		325.00	G	325.00

                                Subtotal   4300.00

GST #R4675 2567   GST 5%   215.00
                                 PST 8%

Reference: Sales Order 1
Shipped: Sep 07, 2016
Terms: 2%/10, Net 30 days

TOTAL DUE
$4,515.00

Order

**Sarah's
Kitchen Stores**　　339 Hudson Court, Hamilton ON L9C 6B3

To: Connoisseur Gadgets Ltd.
896 Shaw Park Road
Belfountain ON L0N 1B3

Ship To:
Sarah's Kitchen Stores
339 Hudson Court
Hamilton ON L9C 6B3

Order NO.	DATE
1	Sep 07, 2016

Qty.	Order	Back Order	Description	Base Price	Disc. %	Price	Tax	Amount
	10		Specialty Knives	$36.75		$36.75	G	367.50
	8		Specialty Cutting Gadgets	9.95		9.95	G	79.60
	9		Food Processor Blades	12.00		12.00	G	108.00

	Amount
Subtotal	555.10
GST 5%	27.76
PST 8%	

Shipping Date: Sep 10, 2016
Terms:　2%/10, Net 30 days

TOTAL DUE
$582.86

- CREDIT MEMO -

**Sarah's
Kitchen Stores**　　　339 Hudson Court, Hamilton ON L9C 6B3

To: Chaiken's Home Depot
268 Grandview Street
Kitchener ON N2B 2B9

Ship To:
(Same)

Invoice NO.	DATE
922Rt	Sep 08, 2016

Qty.	Order	Back Order	Description	Base Price	Disc. %	Price	Tax	Amount
-1			Returned: Sink Model D256 Small crack in fittings	$300.00		$300.00	G	-300.00

GST #R4675 2567

	Amount
Subtotal	-300.00
GST 5%	-15.00
PST 8%	

Total Credit
$ -315.00

SD-11

Connoisseur Gadgets Ltd.
896 Shaw Park Road,
Belfountain ON L0N 1B3

GST# 118 112 113

Invoice # 15838

TO:
   Sarah's Kitchen Stores
   339 Hudson Court
   Hamilton ON L9C 6B3

DATE	CUSTOMER #	TERMS	P.O. #
Sep 08, 2016	4040	2/10 n30	1

QUANTITY	UNIT	BACKORDERED	DESCRIPTION	UNIT PRICE	TOTAL
10	sets		Specialty Knives	36.75	367.50
7	sets	1	Specialty Cutting Gadgets	9.95	69.65
8	sets	1	Food Processor Blades	12.00	96.00
				Subtotal	533.15
				GST	26.66
				PST	
				TOTAL	$ 559.81

SD-12

Sarah's Kitchen Stores
299 Hudson Court, Hamilton ON L9C 6B3

CHEQUE NO.   **644**

DATE   0 8 0 9 2 0 1 6
       D D M M Y Y Y Y

PAY   One Hundred Thirteen and 00/100 $**113.00

To
The   Auto-Rite Mechanics
Order   6589 Rexford Drive
         Hamilton ON L8W 7P3

Toronto Dominion Bank
2 Palace Rd.
Hamilton, Ontario L3X 1T3

Sarah's Kitchen Stores

S. Kafa

⑈644⑈ ⑈2644⑈007⑈ 192⑈991 2⑈

- -
Please Detach Before Cashing

Sarah's Kitchen Stores
   Auto-Rite Mechanics
   Re: Invoice 3396 ($100.00 +PST $8.00 +GST $5.00
       maintenance husband's personal car)

Cheque No.   **644**
Sep. 08, 2016
$113.00

SD-13

Connoisseur Gadgets Ltd.   ▸ **CREDIT MEMO** ◂

896 Shaw Park Road,
Belfountain, ON L0N 1B3

GST# 118 112 113

TO:
Sarah's Kitchen Stores
339 Hudson Court
Hamilton ON L9C 6B3

▸ **DEBIT MEMO** ◂

DATE	CUSTOMER #	TERMS	INVOICE #
Sept. 10, 2016	*4040*	*2/8, n 28*	*15838Rt*

QUANTITY	UNIT	BACKORDERED	DESCRIPTION	UNIT PRICE	TOTAL
-3	*sets*		*Returned Food Processor Blades*	*12.00*	*-36.00*
			- Original Invoice 15838		
				Subtotal	*-36.00*
				GST	*-1.80*
				PST	
				TOTAL	*$- 37.80*

SD-14

INVOICE

Sarah's Kitchen Stores   339 Hudson Court, Hamilton ON L9C 6B3

To: Kurpreet Gilbert
Visa Credit Card

Ship To:
Pickup

Invoice NO.	DATE
923	Sep 11, 2016

Qty.	Order	Back Order	Description	Base Price	Disc. %	Price	Tax	Amount
8			Kitchen Gadgets	$8.95		$8.95	GP	71.60

GST #R4675 2567

Subtotal	71.60
GST 5%	3.58
PST 8%	5.73
TOTAL DUE	
	$80.91

Shipped: Sep 11, 2016

SD-15

Metro Hydro

55223 Electric Drive, Hamilton ON L6Y 3B3

Sarah's Kitchen Stores	Phone (905) 448-6320
339 Hudson Court	Date: Sept 13, 2016
Hamilton ON L9C 6B3	

Service to Sept. 8	$212.39
G.S.T. R142887665	10.62
PST Tax *	16.99**
Current charges including tax.	**$240.00** DUE BY SEPT. 20
If paid after DUE DATE	**$250.00**

APPROVAL
Date <u>Sep 14, 2016</u>
Acct. <u># Utilities</u>
Approved *SW*

RECEIVED   Sep. 14, 2016

Note: PST may not be charged by your province on this type of service. This bill is shown to represent a bill where PST is charged. For this bill, record PST.

****Note:*** PST is part of the cost of electricity bill; refer to Chapter 3. Record $240.00 amount. It is anticipated that we can pay this invoice by the due date.

SD-16

Sarah's Kitchen Stores

339 Hudson Court, Hamilton ON L9C 6B3

CHEQUE NO.   **645**

DATE   1 5 0 9 2 0 1 6
          D D M M Y Y Y Y

PAY   Two Thousand One Hundred Seven and 50/100

$**2,107.50

To The Order   Receiver General
875 Heron Road
Ottawa ON K1A 1A3

Toronto Dominion Bank
2 Palace Rd.
Hamilton, Ontario L3X 1T3

Sarah's Kitchen Stores

S. Kafa

⑈645⑈ ⑈2614⑈007⑈ 192⑈991⑈2⑈

--- Please Detach Before Cashing ---

Sarah's Kitchen Stores
  Receiver General
  Re: GST at end of Aug 31, 2016

CHEQUE NO.   **645**
Sep 15, 2016
$2,107.50

SD-17

INVOICE

Sarah's Kitchen Stores
339 Hudson Court, Hamilton ON L9C 6B3

To: Mr. Lennie Bercovitch
Visa Credit Card

Ship To:
612 Harmony Avenue
Hamilton ON L8H 1P6

Invoice NO.	DATE
924	Sep 15, 2016

Qty.	Order	Back Order	Description	Base Price	Disc. %	Price	Tax	Amount
1			Set Kitchen cupboards (includes installation)	$5,300.00	10	$4,770.00	GP	4,770.00

Subtotal	4,770.00
GST #R4675 2567 GST 5%	238.50
PST 8%	381.60

TOTAL DUE

$5,390.10

Shipped: Sep 11, 2016
* 10% Senior Discount

SD-18

Sarah's Kitchen Stores
339 Hudson Court, Hamilton ON L9C 6B3

CHEQUE NO.   **646**

DATE   1 6 0 9 2 0 1 6
          D D M M Y Y Y Y

PAY   Five Hundred Twelve and 07/100 $**512.07

**To
The
Order**   Connoisseur Gadgets Ltd.
896 Shaw Park Road
Belfountain ON L0N 1B3

**Toronto Dominion Bank
2 Palace Rd.
Hamilton, Ontario L3X 1T3**

Sarah's Kitchen Stores

S. Kafa

⑇646⑇   ⑈2614⑈007⑈   192⑈991 2⑈

- -
Please Detach Before Cashing

Sarah's Kitchen Stores
Connoisseur Gadgets Ltd.
Re: Invoice 15838, 15838Rt

CHEQUE NO.   **646**
Sep. 16, 2016
$512.07

SD-19

Sarah's Kitchen Stores
339 Hudson Court, Hamilton ON L9C 6B3

CHEQUE NO. **647**

DATE 3 0 0 9 2 0 1 6
DD MM YYYY

PAY Two Hundred Fifty and 00/100 $**250.00

To   Metro Hydro
The   55223 Electric Dr.
Order   Hamilton ON L6Y 3B3

Toronto Dominion Bank   Sarah's Kitchen Stores
2 Palace Rd.
Hamilton, Ontario L3X 1T3   _S. Kafa_

⑈647⑈ ⑈26⑈⑈007⑈ ⑈192⑈991⑈2⑈
- -
Please Detach Before Cashing

Sarah's Kitchen Stores   CHEQUE NO.   **647**
  Metro Hydro   Sep. 30, 2016
  Re: Sep. 13 bill. Includes late payment $10 (Utility Expense) $250.00

SD-20

Smith & Sons Tool Company
SCO – 06-6168
159 Main Street, North York ON M6W 4X6

Date: Sep. 30, 2016	Inv. # 515807
Time: 11:10 am	By: Al
Type: Visa	

281-8275 Various tools $83.00 B

------------------------SUBTOTAL ---------------------- 83.00
GST: 5.00%   4.15
PST: 8.00%   6.64
----------------------------TOTAL ------------------------ 93.79

===========AMOUNT(S) TENDERED================

VISA   93.79

==================SOLD TO ===================
Sarah's Kitchen Stores
339 Hudson Court,
Hamilton ON L9C 6B3
VISA Account: Z320-011-007
Exp.Date: 02/20

S. Kafa
Customer's Signature

Note: Students should make a
new account:
#5390 Tools Expense
Type: G
Class Option: Expense

Chapter 6

CHALLENGE
COMPANY, RECEIVABLES, PAYABLES
Setup and Transactions

Shirts & Ties

Learning Objectives
After completing this chapter you will be able to

☐ Create a new data file using knowledge gained from Chapter 4.
☐ Record transactions from source documents, in the COMPANY, RECEIVABLES, and PAYABLES modules.
☐ Display and print various reports and journals.

This chapter provides a challenge for you to set up the COMPANY, RECEIVABLES and PAYABLES modules for a company, and process transactions using source documents in the appropriate modules.

Study the information for the company and set up the various modules. Use your last name followed by Shirts & Ties as the company name (e.g., Smith Shirts & Ties) with the following address: 8 Shirt Drive, Ottawa, ON K2Z 1Z1. Supply all other missing details.

Analyze and process the source documents that follow.

You can also complete this Challenge exercise using the Perpetual Inventory method, after you complete Chapter 8.

See Challenge Exercise 08 C8-6 Shirts & Ties–PI.

(Your Last Name) Shirts & Ties: Company Profile

(Your Last Name) Shirts & Ties (business number R133922445) sells special shirts and ties to other businesses. The company has recently experienced rapid growth both in sales dollars and in sales volume, forcing management to look into another more efficient accounting system. The company books, up to this point, had been kept manually by your friend, but the increased size of the company has forced the business to computerize the accounting records. You are to convert this manual system to Simply Accounting, and help your friend with the first month of computerized operation (August 2016).

The company follows a **calendar fiscal year** and would like to convert after business closed on July 31, 2016.

The July 31, 2016 Trial Balance and details of Accounts Receivable and Accounts Payable are shown on the next two pages.

Some points to remember:

- Suggested company data file name is Shirts.

- The Trial Balance provided shows only postable accounts. You will have to create headings, subtotals and total accounts so that the appropriate financial statements can be printed.

- The Discount Fee percentage for credit cards accepted is 3.5%.

- Remember to make a backup before setting the modules to Ready.

- Remember to enter appropriate invoice numbers, cheque numbers, descriptions, etc., for the transactions (audit trail).

- When you allocate account numbers for your system, always leave a gap of at least 5 to 10 numbers to allow for future accounts to be inserted. Here is an example of why this is so important:

  Assume your number sequencing is similar to:

  > 5110 Purchases
  > 5120 Purchase Returns
  > 5130 Ending Inventory

  You discover after turning the system to **Ready** mode that you missed adding the "Purchase Discounts" account into your chart of accounts.

  You will be able to easily insert Purchase Discounts as account number 5125 or any number between 5121 and 5129.

> If you had numbered the above three accounts as:
> > 5110 Purchases
> > 5111 Purchase Returns
> > 5112 Ending Inventory
>
> You would have a lot of work to do to fix all four of the accounts.

(Your Last Name) Shirts & Ties
Trial Balance Jul 31, 2016

	Debits	Credits
Bank Account Chequing	21,430.00	-
Accounts Receivable	15,350.32	-
Credit Card Receivables	0.00	-
Inventory	21,265.00	-
Prepaid Expenses	1,420.00	-
Warehouse Equipment	63,650.00	-
Accum Amortiz Warehouse Equip	-	21,300.00
Office Equipment	25,800.00	-
Accum Amortiz Office Equip	-	7,400.00
Accounts Payable	-	6,273.75
Universal Credit Card Payable	-	0.00
GST Charged on Sales	-	3,100.00
GST Paid On Purchases	950.00	-
PST Payable (Prov Sales Tax)	-	3,428.00
Bank Loan Payable (Long Term)	-	75,000.00
Capital Your Last Name	-	13,847.57
Drawings Your Last Name	7,000.00	-
Sales	-	269,385.00
Sales Returns	2,650.00	-
Sales Discounts	2,800.00	-
Beginning Inventory	38,200.00	-
Purchases	88,800.00	-
Purchase Returns	-	3,000.00
Purchase Discounts	-	1,628.00
Ending Inventory	-	21,265.00
Wages Expense	98,030.00	-
Warehouse/Office Supplies Expense	1,790.00	-
Other Office Expenses	1,850.00	-
Travel & Entertainment Expense	2,630.00	-
Utilities Expense	2,800.00	-
Telephone Expense	2,400.00	-
Legal Expenses	1,600.00	-
Amortization Expense-All	2,900.00	-
Rent Expense	14,000.00	-
Credit Card Charges	7,512.00	-
Insurance Expense	800.00	-
	----------------	----------------
	425,627.32	425,627.32
	==========	==========

Accounts Receivable Details   [Credit limit - all customers $15,000.00]
Jul 31, 2016

	Tax Code	Invoice Number	Invoice Date	Amount	Taxes	Inv. Amt	Terms
Flight Airways Inc. 2983 Somerset Street W Ottawa ON K2P 3W2 (613) 889-8855 Contact: John Stammers	GP	5686	Jul 30, 2016	4,184.35	543.97	$4,728.32	Net 30
McBurger Chain 903 Wheeler Street Ottawa ON K2J 5J3 (613) 554-2236 Contact: Jim Muir	GP	5681	Jul 26, 2016	2,400.00	312.00	$ 2,712.00	2/10, net 30
Radisser Hotels Inc. 3865 Pickford Drive Ottawa ON K2J 5Z6 (613) 554-8833 Contact: Sandra Wilson	GP	5683	Jul 30, 2016	7,000.00	910.00	$ 7,910.00	2/10, net 30
						$15,350.32	

Accounts Payable Details
Jul 31, 2016

	Tax Code	Invoice Number	Invoice Date	Amount	Taxes	Inv. Amt	Terms
Arrow Clothing Centre 2830 Appollo Way Ottawa ON K4A 6N8 (613) 938-4220 Contact: Legoria Simmons	G	2531	Jul 24, 2016	3,975.00	198.75	$ 4,173.75	2/10, net 30
Polo Accessories 36 Canter Blvd Ottawa ON K2G 4L7 (613) 338-4322 Contact: Kiran Kenth	G	6528	Jul 27, 2016	2,000.00	100.00	$ 2,100.00	2/10, net 30
						$ 6,273.75	

Transactions

Transactions are recorded using the original date of the document to ensure that our records match the records of our suppliers and customers for discount periods, etc. (e.g., a 2%/10, net 30 day purchase invoice dated August 23, received on August 24, and approved on August 25, would be recorded as a purchase using the August 23 date, as this is the date the discount starts.)

1 ➤ The following transactions took place in August 2016. Enter them in the appropriate journals.

SD-1

Shirts & Ties

8 Shirt Drive
Ottawa ON K2Z 1Z1

CHEQUE NO. **5001**

DATE 0 1 0 8 2 0 1 6
D D M M Y Y Y Y

PAY   One Thousand Seven Hundred Twenty two and 00/100 $**1,722.00

To The	McTavish Building Management
Order	80 Scott Street
Of	Ottawa ON K4Z 1K9

Shirts & Ties

Bank of Central Ontario
601 Duke St.
Ottawa, ON K0Z 1Z2

Per_____*YST*_____
Authorized Signature

⑆00500 1⑈ ⑈11330501⑉ 91⑈1055⑉

- -

Shirts & Ties Inc.   *Please Detach Before Cashing*   CHEQUE NO. **5001**

Aug 1, 2016   Re: Lease ($1,640.00 plus GST) $1,722.00

SD-2

Shirts & Ties

8 Shirt Drive
Ottawa ON K2Z 1Z1

CHEQUE NO. **5002**

DATE 0 2 0 8 2 0 1 6
D D M M Y Y Y Y

PAY Four Thousand Ninety Four and 25/100 $**4,094.25

To The	Arrow Clothing Centre
Order	2830 Appollo Way
Of	Ottawa ON K4A 6N8

Shirts & Ties

Bank of Central Ontario
601 Duke St.
Ottawa, ON K0Z 1Z2

Per_____*YST*_____
Authorized Signature

⑆00500 2⑈ ⑈11330501⑉ 91⑈1055⑉

- -

Shirts & Ties Inc.   *Please Detach Before Cashing*   CHEQUE NO. **5002**

Aug 2, 2016   Paid #2531   Discount $79.50 $4,094.25

SD-3

Shirts & Ties

8 Shirt Drive
Ottawa ON K2Z 1Z1
Phone: (613) 927-3838

INVOICE

Sold: To	Flight Airways Inc. 2983 Somerset St. West Ottawa ON K2P 3W2	Ship To: (Same)

Invoice NO.	DATE
5694	Aug 04, 2016

Qty.	Order	Back Order	Description	Base Price	Disc. %	Price	Tax	Amount
250			Shirts style FA-6	$21.00		$21.00	GP	$5,250.00

Subtotal	5,250.00
GST 5%	262.50
PST 8%	420.00

R133922445

TOTAL DUE
$5,932.50

Shipping Date: Aug 04, 2016
Terms: Net 30 days

SD-4

Ottawa Hydro Company

55223 Electric Drive, Ottawa ON K6Y 3I3

Shirts & Ties
8 Shirt Drive
Ottawa ON K2Z 1Z1

Phone: (613) 445-8875
Date: Aug 04, 2016

Service to July 29	$403.54
G.S.T. R142887665	20.18
PST Tax	32.28
Current charges including tax	**$456.00**
If paid after August 19 pay	**$466.00**

Note...
Record 456.00 amount owing. If payment is late, the additional cost is charged to Other Office Expenses.

APPROVAL
Date Aug 5, 2016
Acct. # Utilities
Approved GK

RECEIVED   Aug 05, 2016

SD-5

McBurger Chain
903 Wheeler Street
Ottawa ON K2J 5J3

CHEQUE NO.   **665**

DATE   0 5 0 8 2 0 1 6
D D M M Y Y Y Y

To the order of
Shirts & Ties
8 Shirt Drive
Ottawa ON K2Z 1Z1

Pay: Two Thousand Six Hundred Sixty Four and 00/100 $**2,664.00

Canadian City Bank
125 Mavis Dr., Ottawa ON K3Y 2M9   *JH Smith*

⑆665⑈   ⑆2500 250080⑈   ⑆89662⑈

McBurger Chain   **665**

DATE	INV.NO.	DISCOUNT	AMOUNT PAID
Aug. 05, 2016	#5681	48.00	$2,664.00

RECEIVED   Aug 06, 2016

For Deposit Only

SD-6

Springman & Associates

6990 Winston Churchill Road
Caledon ON L0P 1P6
519-927-8885
GST Number: R222444666
Anne Springman

PURCHASE ORDER
 # 2180

Date: Aug 9, 2016
Ship Date: Aug 11, 2016

To: Shirts & Ties
8 Shirt Drive
Ottawa ON K2Z 1Z1

Ship To:
(Same)

Ordered	Description	Unit Price	Unit	Tax	Total
38	Shirts Mod-36	$20.00	Each	GP	$ 760.00
38	Ties VA-Mac	$32.00	Each	GP	1,216.00
				Subtotal	$ 1,976.00
				GST	98.80
				PST	158.08
	Terms: 2/10, net 30			**TOTAL**	$ 2,232.88

SD-7

Radisser Hotels Inc.
3865 Pickford Drive
Ottawa ON K2J 5Z6

CHEQUE NO.   **93288**

DATE   0 9 0 8 2 0 1 6
       D D M M Y Y Y Y

PAY	Seven Thousand Seven Seventy and 00/100	$**7,770.00

To The
Order   Shirts & Ties
Of   8 Shirt Drive
        Ottawa ON. K2Z 1Z1

Canadiania Bank
19 Moore Avenue
Nepean ON K4C 2A1

B.J.Radisser

⑈93288⑈   ⑈0426⑈004⑈   112⑈181. 8⑈

DETACH BEFORE CASHING

Radisser Hotels Inc.   **93288**

DATE	DESCRIPTION	AMOUNT
Aug 09,2016	RE: Payment of Invoice #5683, less $140.00 discount	$ 7,770.00

RECEIVED   Aug 09, 2016
For Deposit Only

SD-8

Shirts & Ties

8 Shirt Drive
Ottawa ON K2Z 1Z1
Phone: (613) 927-3838

INVOICE

Sold: Springman & Associates   Ship To:
To   6990 Winston Churchill Road   (Same)
         Caledon ON L0P 1P6

Invoice NO.	DATE
5695	Aug 13, 2016

Qty.	Order	Back Order	Description	Base Price	Disc. %	Price	Tax	Amount
38			Shirts Mod-36	$20.00		$20.00	GP	$ 760.00
38			Ties, VA-Mac	32.00		32.00	GP	1,216.00
							Subtotal	1,976.00
			R133922445	GST 5%				98.80
				PST 8%				158.08

PO 2180 Attn: Ann Springman
Shipping Date: Aug 13, 2016
Terms: 2%10, Net 30 days

TOTAL DUE
$2,232.88

SD-9a

Arrow Clothing Centre

2830 Appollo Way
Ottawa ON K4A 6N8
GST# 53842

Aug 15, 2016

Invoice 2689

To: Shirts and Ties
      8 Shirt Drive
      Ottawa ON K2Z 1Z1

Terms: 2/10, net 30

30 Shirts Model 42	24.25 each	$ 727.50
	GST	36.38
	Total	$ 763.88

Received a $30.00 Canadian mail-in rebate form on this purchase. See SD-9b.

SD-9b

REBATE CHECKLIST	CUSTOMER $30 MAIL-IN REBATE

Purchase $200 or more to receive a $30.00 mail-in rebate.
 	
To qualify for this rebate, you must submit:
 	
❏ This completed rebate form.
 	
❏ Copy of the dated invoice, or transaction record for qualifying purchase.
	PLEASE PRINT CLEARLY IN CAPITAL LETTERS
	
	SHIRTS MODEL 42
	Product description
	
	SHIRTS AND TIES
	Name
	
	2830 APPOLLO WAY
	Street Address (required)
	
	OTTAWA ON K4A 6N8
	City **Province** **Postal Code**
	
	613-281-0967 (blank)
	Phone Number **E-mail address**
	
	Mail to: Rebate Centre
	              81 Booth Street
	              Ottawa ON K2R 5P2
	
	This offer expires: October 31, 2016

Assume that this form was completed and mailed today. Create a customer "Rebate Centre." Use invoice 5696 to record this receivable.

SD-10

Shirts & Ties

8 Shirt Drive
Ottawa ON K2Z 1Z1
Phone: (613) 927-3838

INVOICE
Credit Memo

Sold:	Springman & Associates	Ship To:
To	6990 Winston Churchill Road	(Same)
	Caledon ON L0P 1P6	

Invoice NO.	DATE
5695Rt	Aug 15 2016

Qty.	Order	Back Order	Description	Base Price	Disc. %	Price	Tax	Amount
-2			Shirts Mod-36	$20.00		$20.00	GP	$-40.00

	Subtotal	-40.00
R133922445 GST 5%		-2.00
PST 8%		-3.20
	TOTAL DUE	
		$-45.20

PO 2180 Attn: Ann Springman
Shipping Date: Aug 15, 2016
Terms: 2%8, Net 28 days

SD-11

Shirts & Ties

8 Shirt Drive
Ottawa ON K2Z 1Z1

CHEQUE NO.   **5003**

DATE   1 5 0 8 2 0 1 6
D D M M Y Y Y Y

PAY   Two Thousand One Hundred Fifty and 00/100 $**2,150.00

To The	Receiver General
Order	875 Heron Road
Of	Ottawa ON K1A 1A3

Shirts & Ties

Bank of Central Ontario
601 Duke St.
Ottawa, ON K0Z 1Z2

Per _____*YST*_____
Authorized Signature

⑈005003⑈   ⑈113050⑈ ⑈91⑈1055⑈

- -

Shirts & Ties Inc.   *Please Detach Before Cashing*   **CHEQUE NO.   5003**

Aug 15, 2016   Re: GST to July 31 $2,150.00

SD-12

Shirts & Ties

M E M O

August 19, 2016

To: Your Name

From: Robert Amber, Manager

Issue cheque today to pay the August 4, 2016 Ottawa Hydro (utilities) bill.
This must be paid today to save $10.00.

Robert

SD-13

Shirts & Ties

8 Shirt Drive
Ottawa ON K2Z 1Z1
Phone: (613) 927-3838

I N V O I C E

Sold:	Your Name	Ship To:
To	Staff – Credit Card Sale	(Same)

Invoice NO.	DATE
5697	Aug 19 2016

Qty.	Order	Back Order	Description	Base Price	Disc. %	Price	Tax	Amount
2			Shirts Mod-36	$20.00	30	$14.00	GP	$28.00

	Subtotal	28.00
R133922445	GST 5%	1.40
	PST 8%	2.24

Staff discount 30%
Shipping Date: Aug 19, 2016
Terms: Today

TOTAL DUE
$31.64

SD-14

Springman & Associates
6990 Winston Churchill Rd.
Caledon, ON L0P 1P6

CHEQUE NO.   556

DATE 2 3 0 8 2 0 1 6
        D D M M Y Y Y Y

To the order of

Shirts & Ties
8 Shirt Drive
Ottawa ON K2Z 1Z1

Pay: Two Thousand One Hundred Forty-eight and 96/100- - - - - - - - - - - - - $**2,148.96

Canadian City Bank
125 Mavis Dr., Ottawa, ON K3Y 2M9

S Springman

⑈00556⑈   ⑈2500 2080⑈ 8966 2⑈

Springman & Associates   CHEQUE NO. 556

DATE	INV.NO.		AMOUNT
Aug 23, 2016	#5695, 5695Rt	Paid order less return, discount	$2,148.96

RECEIVED   August 24, 2016
                              For Deposit Only

SD-15

Meadows Insurance Brokers Inc.   **INVOICE 5395**
197 Larange Avenue, Suite 125
Ottawa, ON K8Z 4R9
 Phone/Fax (613) 233-5886

SOLD TO:
    Shirts & Ties
    8 Shirt Drive   Date:___Aug 31, 2016___
    Ottawa ON K2Z 1Z1

COVERAGE		
Renewal Policy #365654325 Fire and Theft Insurance at 8 Shirt Drive, Ottawa, Ontario		
Coverage period Aug 1, 2016 through Jul 31, 2017		1,365.00
	GST	N/A
	PST	109.20
Terms: upon receipt	TOTAL	$1,474.20

Shirts & Ties

Aug 31, 2016

To: Your Name
From: Robert Amber, Manager

Please enter the following in the Simply system:

- Andrea Mosely, the new bank accounting clerk, completed the bank reconciliation to August 23 and advised that there are 2 items (Bank Charges $100.00 and Bank Interest Expense $500.00 on our loan) that have not been recorded. Please create 2 new accounts to record these 2 charges.

- The current ending inventory as counted by the stock department is $39,800.00. Record the proper inventory entries to adjust the new inventory value for the Asset Inventory account and the ending inventory in the Cost of Goods Sold section of the Income Statement.

2 ➤   At the end of the month, **print** the following:

- Income Statement   Jan 01 to Aug 31
- Balance Sheet at   Aug 31
- Vendor Aged Detail report at   Aug 31
- Customer Aged Detail report at Aug 31
- Journal Entries—All for   Aug 01 - Aug 31
- Journal Entries General   Aug 01 - Aug 31

Chapter 13

Correcting Transaction Errors After Posting

Learning Objectives

After completing this chapter, you will be able to:

☐ Reverse and adjust posted entries or other information (quotes or orders).

The contents are as follows:

No one is perfect, and we all make mistakes from time to time. This chapter will help you correct errors in invoices, quotes, orders and/or journal entries after you have posted your transactions.

You can avoid having to do these corrective steps if you view each entry before posting. See Exercise 1-7 if you wish to review the procedure.

Errors in wrong vendor, customer, employee, wrong number of items shipped, wrong description of item being sold, wrong general ledger account number, etc., may all be corrected. Remember, that it is **very** important to document any corrections you make. Write a memo explaining the original error, including the posting entry number (e.g., J125), how the entry was corrected, including the new posting entry number (e.g., J147). This memo notation is part of what is called an **Audit trail**. This trail is how someone else can trace or track what has happened in accounting records.

Always use codes to identify corrections made to entries. See Exercise 2A-14 for a sample listing of error codes. Companies may use many other codes to identify corrections. The secret of effective use of these codes is **consistency**.

There are three ways to correct entries:

a) You may use the 🖾 Lookup icon to locate the entry that needs correcting. The window changes and the header will be similar to: Sales Journal – Invoice.

   Lookup. You would then click on 🖾 Adjust icon and the header changes to: Sales Journal -Adjusting Invoice No. 2310. You make the necessary changes and post when correct.

   Using this method the original and reversing entries **Do NOT** show in the Customer or Vendor aged detail listings. Only the corrected invoice will show in the report.

   When you display journal entries (with corrections) that have been corrected and posted, you will see the reversing entry with a source field similar to: ADJ2310, Reversing J3, Correction is J5. The correcting entry will have a source field based on the changes that you have made.

b) If you want to see the original, reversal and correcting entries in the Customer or Vendor aged detail reports, you will need to record and post:

   i.   A reversing entry with a code similar to 2310Rv (2310 Reversed). In the reversing entry, accounts that were originally debited are credited, and accounts that were credited originally are now debited.

   ii. The correct entry, new invoice 2314 [assumed new invoice number], will display the way it should have been recorded.

   The Aged Detail report will show the original 2310, the 2310Rv and 2314.

c) If you want to reverse an entry (cancel) because the entry was in error and there is no correction (new entry not needed), you may use the 🖾 Reverse icon.

The Adjustment icon method (a) and Reverse an entry icon will be shown in this chapter. You will see:

   1. information about the original entry.
   2. a screen display of the original entry.
   3. a screen display of the original posted journal entry.
   4. correcting screen display.
   5. correcting screen display of the revised entry.

Remember to **view** the reversing entry before posting. This will allow you to verify that the reversing entry you are making is correct; otherwise, you will complicate the problem even further.

1 ➤ Refer to Exercise 1-1 to unzip the **13 Corrections.exe** file.

2 ➤ Open the **13 Corrections** file and accept the date of **Jan 02, 2014**.

The **Corrections Prizes Company** sells various games and prizes for home and office party loot bags.

The Corrections Prizes Company was opened on January 2, 2014. Unfortunately the bookkeeper was tired from partying on New Year's Day and made many mistakes. He was going to correct the errors, but was called out of town for a personal family situation. You were called in, for the afternoon, to print the entries that he made and correct them.

You will be shown how to correct each type of error using the Adjustment icon and/ or Reversing icon.

Exercise 13-1 – Print General Journal Entries

The first thing you need to do is to print the General Journal entries to identify the entries that need to be corrected.

1 ➤ **Print** Journal Entries - All for January 2, 2014.

Correcting General Journal Entries

Jan 02, 2014	**The bank faxed the debit memo for printing new cheques. Information on the fax was New cheques $43.00, PST $3.44, GST $2.15, total debit to the account $48.59.**

The General Journal entry recorded in error was:

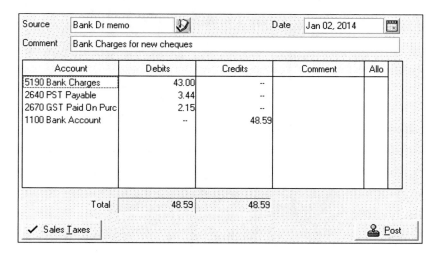

New cheques are normally charged to a Prepaid Office Supplies account and expensed as they are used. In this situation the cost of printing the cheques is not a large amount (immaterial amount) and is charged to Office Supplies Expense account. Cheques are normally not charged to Bank Charges. The PST should be part of the cost because it is not recoverable from the provincial government. (See Chapter 15, *Taxes*.)

In Chapter 1 (Photos Company), there were no taxes (GST or PST) recorded when using the General Journal. The following correction entry will show you how Sales taxes are recorded in the General Journal.

Exercise 13-2 – Correcting General Journal Entries

1 ➤ To correct this entry, click the **COMPANY** module, click the **General Journal** icon.

2 ➤ Click the 🔏 **Adjust a previously posted entry** icon.

3 ➤ At the Search window, do not change dates, click **OK**.

4 ➤ At the Select Entry to Adjust window, select **Journal # 1**, with a description of Bank charges for new cheques. Notice that only General Journal entries recorded show in this display.

5 ➤ Change the **accounts, amounts and comments** to reflect the journal shown next. **Do not change the date**. The bank withdrew the money on January 2.

6 ➤ To remove the previous 2640 PST Payable line, click on the line, then click **Edit**, **Remove Line**.

Source	Bank Dr memo		Date	Jan 02, 2014	
Comment	Bank Charges for new cheques				

Account	Debits	Credits	Comment	Allo
5220 Office Supplies	46.44	--	New cheques	
2670 GST Paid On Purc	2.15	--		
1100 Bank Account	--	48.59		

7 ➤ **View** the entry before posting.

General Journal Entry Jan 02, 2014 (J10)

Account Number	Account Description	Debits	Credits
5220	Office Supplies	46.44	-
	New cheques		
2670	GST Paid On Purchases	2.15	-
1100	Bank Account	-	48.59
Additional Date:	Additional Field:		
		48.59	48.59

As discussed in Exercise 1-12, all adjusting entry numbers will be increased due to the automatic reversing entry, therefore, after posting, J9 would be the reversing entry and J10 would be the correction.

Jan 02, 2014	J9	ADJBank Dr memo, Reversing J1. Correction is J10.

8 ➤ Click the **Sales Tax** button (with the blue✔). See the information field after step 9.

9 ➤ The Sales Taxes- General Journal – Adjusting Bank Dr Memo window displays.

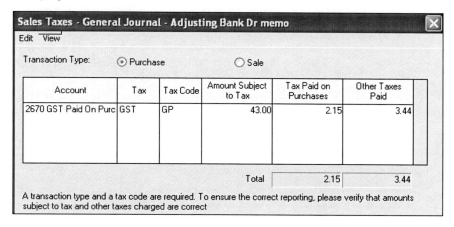

The window records amounts affecting linked tax accounts. In order for the GST Tax report to be correct, the cost of the cheques and taxes must be recorded properly.

 If the original entry did not use the sales taxes button and, therefore, the linked tax accounts did not get recorded properly, you would see the following window.

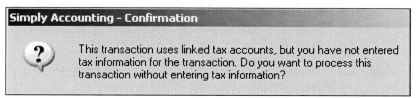

You should click No, to record taxes properly. The tax information window appears and should be filled in as noted in step 9.

GP Tax Code would be the appropriate code for this transaction.

The **Amount Subject to Tax** and **Other Taxes Paid** column amounts appear as shown.

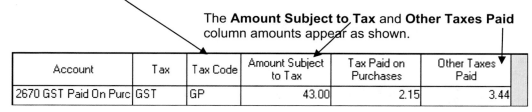

Simply divides the GST amount (Tax Paid on Purchases) $2.15 by .05 (the GST rate) to determine the amount subject to GST tax ($43.00).

10 ➤ Click **OK** to continue. The Sales Tax button has the blue ✔ to indicate that Sales Tax (purchase taxes) information will be updated for the report.

11 ➤ **Post** when correct.

12 ➤ Return to the Home window.

Correcting or Canceling Sales Orders or Quotes

Exercise 13-3 – Correcting a Sales Order or Quote

> The bookkeeper recorded a Sales Quote for 10 Prizes Adults-metal (P20). This should have been a quote for 15 prizes.

Sales Quote recorded in error

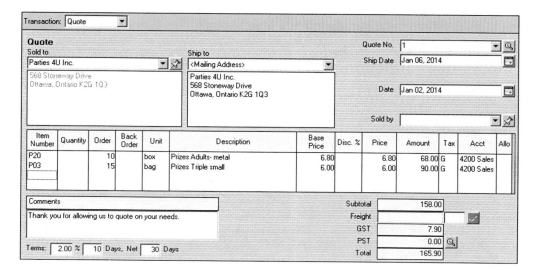

To Change a Sales Order or Quote

1 ➤ Click the **RECEIVABLES module,** click the **Sales Quotes** icon.

2 ➤ **Quote No.** Click the ▼, select **1** and Tab. The original Quote is displayed.

3 ➤ Click on 🔲 **Adjust quote** icon and change the order for P20 Prizes Adults-metal to **15** Tab.

4 ➤ The new total is $201.60. **Record** when correct, click **OK** to return to the Home window.

To Cancel (Remove) a Sales Order or Quote

1 ➤ Click the **Sales Quotes** icon.

2 ➤ **Quote No.** Click the ▼, select **1,** Tab. The revised quote is displayed.

3 ➤ Click on 🔲 **Remove quote** icon.

4 ➤ You will be asked: Are you sure you want to remove this Quote? Click **No** to leave the Sales Quote with 15 units of each item ordered, and Return to the Home window.

Correcting Sales Journal Entry for Merchandise

There are two scenarios shown below, illustrating different ways to adjust or reverse a Sales journal entry for goods for resale.

Scenario: Invoice with errors has **not** been sent to the customer.

Method one

To correct

Use the Simply **Adjust Invoice** feature that will allow you to change the item(s) that are in error, and post. This will reverse the original customer's invoice and prepare a correct invoice.

Method two

Use the **Reverse** icon feature to cancel the original entry if there are many errors. This will allow you to create a new invoice with the correct amounts.

As discussed earlier, methods one and two do not provide an audit trail for the customer, because the original and reversing entries will not show in the customer's ledger record. Only the new corrected invoice will appear in the Journals All report.

Method three

Scenario: Invoice with errors has **been** sent to the customer.

If the invoice has been sent to the customer, method one and two are not appropriate because the original and reversing entries will not show in the customer's ledger record. Only the new corrected invoice will appear. This discrepancy between your company records and those of the customer could present a problem later.

There are two ways to resolve the problem:

a) **Assuming there are a few items on the invoice.**

    (1)   Reverse the original invoice entry to cancel the original invoice (Method 2).

    (2)   Record a correct invoice with appropriate comments to reference the original invoice.

b) **Assuming there are many items on the invoice.**

Record an invoice reversing only the item with the error. This in effect is canceling the sale of those items with the error. On the next line, record the **correct** item with the correct information. This is similar to Exercise 8-19.

An example of b) is shown in Exercise 13-4.:

Exercise 13-4 – Correcting a Sales Invoice

The original sales entry (invoice #11504) was recorded to the Rideau Social Club. Their manager called stating that the price given by our manager for the Prizes Adults-metal should be $6.70. Your manager confirmed the price. You will create an invoice adjustment for the Prizes Adults-metal item.

Original Sales Journal

Item Number	Quantity	Order	Back Order	Unit	Description	Base Price	Disc. %	Price	Amount	Tax	Acct	Allo
P20	30			box	Prizes Adults- metal	6.80		6.80	204.00	GP	4200	
P04	20			bag	Prizes Double Bag	5.60		5.60	112.00	GP	4200	

Comments		
Thank you for your order.	Subtotal	316.00
	Freight	
	GST	15.80
	PST	25.28
Terms: 2.00 % 10 Days, Net 30 Days	Total	357.08

Original Sales Journal entry

Sales Journal Entry Jan 02, 2014 (J6)

Account Number	Account Description	Debits	Credits
1200	Accounts Receivable	357.08	-
5080	Cost Of Sales - Prizes	159.08	-
1280	Inventory -Prizes	-	159.08
2640	PST Payable	-	25.28
2650	GST Charged On Sales	-	15.80
4200	Sales - Prizes	-	316.00
Additional Date:	Additional Field:		
		516.16	516.16

1 ➤ Click the **Sales Invoices** icon.

2 ➤ Create a **Partial Revised** Sales invoice #11504 as shown next. Invoice number code **PtCo** refers to **Part correction**. Comments section can also contain relevant information.

Revised Sales Invoice

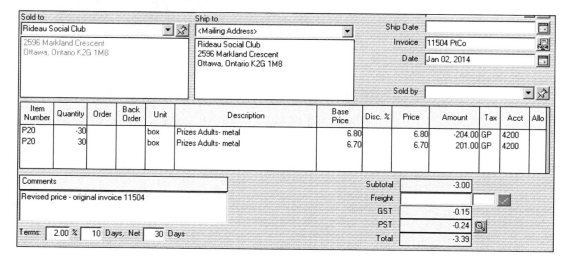

Sold to	Ship to	
Rideau Social Club	<Mailing Address>	Ship Date
2596 Markland Crescent Ottawa, Ontario K2G 1M8	Rideau Social Club 2596 Markland Crescent Ottawa, Ontario K2G 1M8	Invoice 11504 PtCo
		Date Jan 02, 2014
		Sold by

Item Number	Quantity	Order	Back Order	Unit	Description	Base Price	Disc. %	Price	Amount	Tax	Acct	Allo
P20	-30			box	Prizes Adults- metal	6.80		6.80	-204.00	GP	4200	
P20	30			box	Prizes Adults- metal	6.70		6.70	201.00	GP	4200	

Comments		
Revised price - original invoice 11504	Subtotal	-3.00
	Freight	
	GST	-0.15
	PST	-0.24
Terms: 2.00 % 10 Days, Net 30 Days	Total	-3.39

Revised Sales Invoice Journal entry

Sales Journal Entry Jan 02, 2014 (J11)

Account Number	Account Description	Debits	Credits
2640	PST Payable	0.24	-
2650	GST Charged On Sales	0.15	-
4200	Sales - Prizes	3.00	-
1200	Accounts Receivable	-	3.39
Additional Date:	Additional Field:		
		3.39	3.39

3 ➤ **Post** when correct. Return to the Home window.

Correcting Sales Receipt Entry

Exercise 13-5 – Correcting Sales Receipt Entry

The original receipt of **$370.80** was recorded as shown below.

The clerk forgot to record the **$7.20** discount.

Before correcting this Receipt, note that the Customers area displays an outstanding balance of **$7.20**. Simply has converted the **$7.20** Discount Available in the Original Receipt window (below), to an Outstanding Receivable balance of **$7.20**.

Original Receipt window

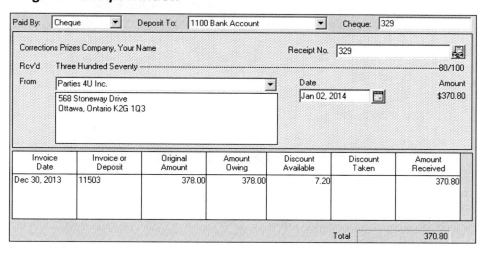

Original Receipt entry

Receipts Journal Entry Jan 02, 2014 (J8)

Account Number	Account Description	Debits	Credits
1100	Bank Account	370.80	-
1200	Accounts Receivable	-	370.80
Additional Date:	Additional Field:		
		370.80	370.80

To Reverse the original entry:

1 ➤ Click the **Receipts** icon.

2 ➤ Click the 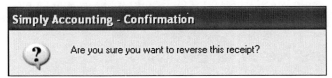 **Lookup** icon.

3 ➤ At the Search window, do not change dates, click **OK**.

4 ➤ At the Select a Receipt window, select **Journal #8**, with customer Parties 4U Inc.

5 ➤ Click on the **Reverse Receipt** icon. You will see the following window.

Simply Accounting - Confirmation

? Are you sure you want to reverse this receipt?

6 ➤ You want to reverse this receipt. Click **Yes.** You are returned to a blank Receipts Journal. The original receipt has been reversed as shown next.

Jan 02, 2014	J12	ADJ329, Parties 4U Inc.: Reversing J8. Correction is J12.		
		1200	Accounts Receivable	370.80	-
		1100	Bank Account	-	370.80

You will notice that the debit entry is to Accounts Receivable.

7 ➤ **Rec'd From**   Select **Parties 4U Inc.** in the Receipts window; you will now record the proper cheque amount with a cheque number of **329Co** as shown next.

Correct Receipts window

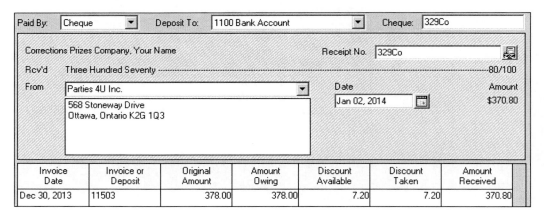

Correct Receipts entry

Receipts Journal Entry Jan 02, 2014 (J13)

Account Number	Account Description	Debits	Credits
1100	Bank Account	370.80	-
4290	Sales Discounts, all items	7.20	-
1200	Accounts Receivable	-	378.00
Additional Date:	Additional Field:		
		378.00	378.00

8 ➤ **Post** when correct. Return to the Home window.

Canceling or Correcting Purchase Orders or Quotes

Exercise 13-6 – Canceling or Correcting Purchase Orders or Quotes

> A Purchase order issued for 55 boxes of Games Wooden Medium size 1 was recorded as 50 boxes in error as shown next.
>
> You will be adjusting the quantity ordered in this exercise.

Original Purchase Order window

Transaction: Purchase Order ▼   Paid By: Pay Later ▼

Purchase Order

Purchased From   Order No. 1 ▼ 🔍
Games Manufacturing Inc. ▼ ✎   Ship Date Jan 10, 2014
899 Des Epinettes Avenue
Ottawa, Ontario K1C 0P7

Ship To
Corrections Prizes Company, Your Name
7905 Bank Street
Ottawa, Ontario K2P 2A9

Date Jan 02, 2014

Item Number	Quantity	Order	Back Order	Unit	Description	Price	Tax	GST	PST	Amount	Acct	Allo
G-W-1		50	50	box	Games Wooden Medium size 1	5.2813	G	13.20		264.07	1260 Inventc	

Subtotal 264.07
Freight
GST 13.20
Terms: 2.00 % 10 Days, Net 30 Days
PST 0.00 🔍
Total 277.27

To Change a Purchase Order or Quote

1 ➤ Click the **PAYABLES** module, click **Purchase Orders** icon.

2 ➤ Order No.   Click ▼, select 1 `Tab`. The original Purchase order is displayed.

3 ➤ Click on 🔲 **Adjust purchase order** icon and change the order quantity to **55**. `Tab`.

Item Number	Quantity	Order	Back Order	Unit	Description	Price	Tax	GST	PST	Amount	Acct	Allo
G-W-1		55	55	box	Games Wooden Medium size 1	5.2813	G	14.52		290.47	1260 Inventc	

4 ➤ The new total is $304.99. **Record** when correct.

5 ➤ Return to the Home window.

To Cancel (Remove) a Purchase Order or Quote

1 ➤ Click the **Purchase Orders** icon.

2 ➤ Order No.   Click ▼, select **1,** `Tab`. The original Purchase order is displayed.

3 ➤ Click on **Remove purchase order** icon.

4 ➤ You will be asked: Are you sure you want to remove this order? Click **No** to leave Purchase Order 1 with 55 items ordered.

5 ➤ Return to the Home window.

Correcting Purchase Journal Entries for Goods for Resale (Merchandise)

Exercise 13-7 – Correcting Purchase Journal Entries for Merchandise

If you wanted the vendor record to show the original incorrect entry, the reversal and the correction entry, you will need 2 entries to correct the original:

1. Record a negative invoice (negative quantity) to reverse the original invoice.
2. Record the correct entry.

This exercise, using the Adjusting icon method, will demonstrate how to adjust purchase invoices, assuming that the quantity amount should have been 35.

(See side note box.)

The Purchase Journal Invoice entry for merchandise for resale that was recorded in error is shown next.

Original Purchase Invoice entry

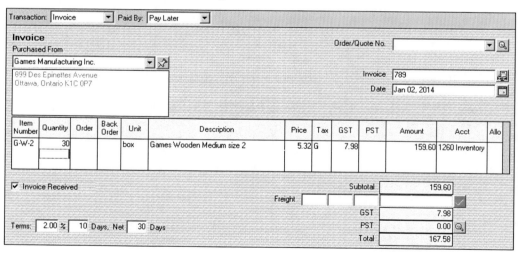

Purchase Journal entry

Account Number	Account Description	Debits	Credits
1260	Inventory -Games	159.60	-
2670	GST Paid On Purchases	7.98	-
2200	Accounts Payable	-	167.58
Additional Date:	Additional Field:		
		167.58	167.58

Purchases Journal Entry Jan 02, 2014 (J2)

1 ➤ Click on **Purchase Invoices** icon.

2 ➤ Click on 🖳 **Lookup an invoice** icon.

3 ➤ At the Search window, do not change dates, click **OK**. Outstanding invoices from the year 2013 and 2014 are listed. Select **Games Manufacturing Inc.** entry dated **Jan 02, 2014** (invoice **789**) in the amount of $167.58.

4 ➤ Click on the **Adjust invoice** icon and change the Quantity amount to **35**, ⌨ Tab . The invoice total changes to 195.51.

Purchase Journal Adjusted

Item Number	Quantity	Order	Back Order	Unit	Description	Price	Tax	GST	PST	Amount	Acct	Allo
G-W-2	35			box	Games Wooden Medium size 2	5.32	G	9.31		186.20	1260 Inventory	

☑ Invoice Received

Subtotal	186.20
Freight	
GST	9.31
PST	0.00
Total	195.51

Terms: 2.00 % 10 Days, Net 30 Days

Purchase Journal Adjusted entry

Purchases Journal Entry Jan 02, 2014 (J15)

Account Number	Account Description	Debits	Credits
1260	Inventory -Games	186.20	-
2670	GST Paid On Purchases	9.31	-
2200	Accounts Payable	-	195.51
Additional Date:	Additional Field:		
		195.51	195.51

5 ➤ **Post** when correct. Return to the Home window.

To cancel the Invoice (Information only)

To cancel the invoice completely, click on 🖳 Lookup icon, and select the invoice to be reversed.

Click on 🖳 Reverse icon.

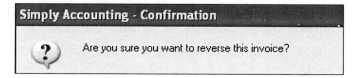

Click Yes, if this is the correct invoice to cancel.

The entry is reversed (Cancelled).

End of Information section.

Correcting Purchase Journal Entries for Non-Merchandise

Exercise 13-8 – Correcting Purchase Journal Entry for Non-Merchandise

> This exercise assumes the wrong price of 300.00 was recorded. The price should have been 200.00.

Purchase Journal (Non-merchandise) entry that was recorded in error.

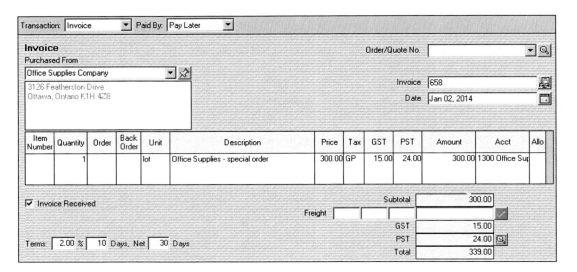

Account Number	Account Description	Debits	Credits
1300	Office Supplies On Hand	324.00	-
2670	GST Paid On Purchases	15.00	-
2200	Accounts Payable	-	339.00
Additional Date:	Additional Field:		
		339.00	339.00

Purchases Journal Entry Jan 02, 2014 (J3)

1 ➤ Click the **Purchase Invoices** icon.

2 ➤ Click the ⬚ **Lookup** icon.

3 ➤ At the Search window, do not change dates, click **OK**. Outstanding invoices from the year 2013 and 2014 are listed.

4 ➤ Select **Office Supplies Company** entry **#3,** dated **Jan 02, 2014** (invoice **658**) in the amount of $339.00. Note: There are 2 journal entries #3. One in 2013 and 1 in 2014.

5 ➤ Click on the **Adjust invoice** icon and change the Price amount to **200.00,** ⬚ Tab . The invoice total changes to 226.00.

Purchase Journal Adjusting Invoice

Item Number	Quantity	Order	Back Order	Unit	Description	Price	Tax	GST	PST	Amount	Acct	Allo
	1			lot	Office Supplies - special order	200.00	GP	10.00	16.00	200.00	1300 Office Sup	

☑ Invoice Received

Terms: 2.00 % 10 Days, Net 30 Days

Freight

Subtotal	200.00
GST	10.00
PST	16.00
Total	226.00

Purchase Journal entry

Purchases Journal Entry Jan 02, 2014 (J17)

Account Number	Account Description	Debits	Credits
1300	Office Supplies On Hand	216.00	-
2670	GST Paid On Purchases	10.00	-
2200	Accounts Payable	-	226.00
Additional Date:	Additional Field:		
		226.00	226.00

6 ➤ **Post** when correct. Return to the Home window.

Correcting Vendor Payments

Exercise 13-9 – Correcting Vendor Payments

The clerk issued a cheque to Games Manufacturing to pay invoice #731, but he entered $566.00 in the Payment field. He did not accept the $566.50 amount Simply was showing.

You will cancel (Reverse) the original payment (with the error) and record a correct payment.

When you look up the payment made, you will not be able to see 2 invoices that were not paid.

Original Payment

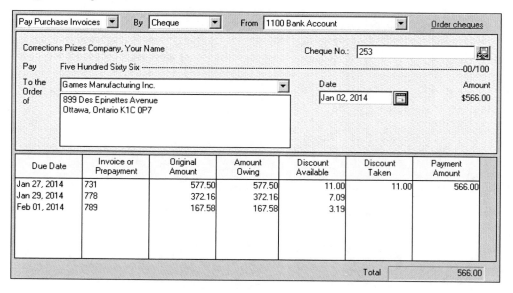

Original Payment entry

Account Number	Account Description	Debits	Credits
2200	Accounts Payable	577.00	-
1100	Bank Account	-	566.00
5090	Purchase Discounts	-	11.00
Additional Date:	Additional Field:		
		577.00	577.00

Payments Journal Entry Jan 02, 2014 (J5)

1 ➤ Click the **Payments** icon.

2 ➤ Click the [icon] **Lookup** icon.

3 ➤ At the Search window, do not change dates, click **OK**, journal entry payment #5 is listed.

4 ➤ Select **Games Manufacturing Inc.**, entry **#5,** dated **Jan 02, 2014** in the amount of $566.00.

5 ➤ Click on **Reverse payment** [icon] icon. You will see the following:

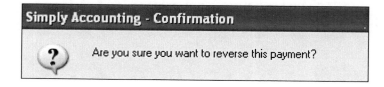

6 ➤ You want to reverse this payment. Click **Yes.** Return to a blank Payments journal window.

Record the Correct Payment

7 ➤ **Record** a correct payment to Games Manufacturing Inc. Issue replacement **cheque #254** as shown next.

Due Date	Invoice or Prepayment	Original Amount	Amount Owing	Discount Available	Discount Taken	Payment Amount
Jan 27, 2014	731	577.50	577.50	11.00	11.00	566.50
Jan 29, 2014	778	372.16	372.16	7.09		
Feb 01, 2014	789	195.51	195.51	3.72		
					Total	566.50

Correct Payment entry

Payments Journal Entry Jan 02, 2014 (J19)			
Account Number	Account Description	Debits	Credits
2200	Accounts Payable	577.50	-
1100	Bank Account	-	566.50
5090	Purchase Discounts	-	11.00
Additional Date:	Additional Field:		
		577.50	577.50

8 ➤ Post when correct. Return to the Home window.

Correcting Payments (Make Other Payment)

Exercise 13-10 – Correcting Payments (Make Other Payment)

In this exercise, the GST on Sales and GST on Purchases amounts on a payment entry were not recorded correctly. Fortunately, the cheque has not been mailed. Reverse original cheque 252, and issue a new cheque for the correct amounts.

Original Payment

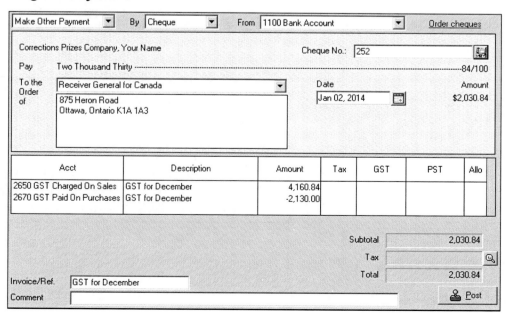

Payment Journal entry

Account Number	Account Description	Debits	Credits
	Payments Journal Entry Jan 02, 2014 (J4)		
2650	GST Charged On Sales	4,160.84	-
1100	Bank Account	-	2,030.84
2670	GST Paid On Purchases	-	2,130.00
Additional Date:	Additional Field:		
		4,160.84	4,160.84

1 ➤ Click the **Payments** icon.

2 ➤ **Pay Purchase Invoices**   Select **Make Other Payment**.

3 ➤ Click the ▣ **Lookup** icon.

4 ➤ At the Search window, do not change dates, click **OK**. Payments are listed.

5 ➤ Select **entry #4 dated Jan 02, 2014** (cheque 252) in the amount of $2,030.84.

6 ➤ Click on ▣ **Reverse payment** icon. You will see the Reverse confirmation window.

7 ➤ You want to reverse this payment. Click **Yes.** Return to a blank Payments journal window.

Record the Correct Payment

8 ➤ **Record** a correct Receiver General payment, cheque number **255,** as shown next.

Payment correction

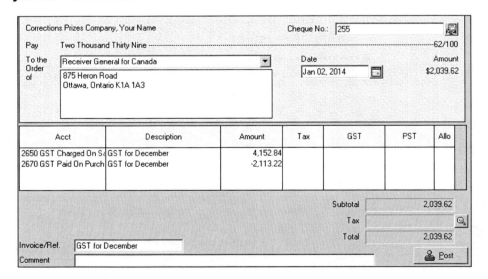

Payment correction entry

Payments Journal Entry Jan 02, 2014 (J21)			
Account Number	Account Description	Debits	Credits
2650	GST Charged On Sales	4,152.84	-
1100	Bank Account	-	2,039.62
2670	GST Paid On Purchases	-	2,113.22
Additional Date:	Additional Field:		
		4,152.84	4,152.84

9 ➤ Post when correct. Return to the Home window.

Correcting Payroll Cheque Items

You can **NOT** use the Payroll Cheque Run journal to correct payroll cheques. You must use the Paycheques journal to cancel (reverse) a cheque. See Exercise 7-16a and 16b.

Correcting Inventory Adjustments Journal Entries

There is no Adjust icon in the Inventory Adjustments Journal.

There are two ways to adjust INVENTORY adjustment errors:

1. Reverse the original entry, then record the correct entry.
2. Reverse and correct the entry in one step (shown below).

Exercise 13-11 – Correcting Inventory Adjustments

This adjustment assumes method 2 will be used to correct the error in one step.

The manager's memo stated that the Prizes Double bag should be reduced by 15 units. In error, the Prizes Single was reduced by 5 units.

Incorrect Inventory Adjustment

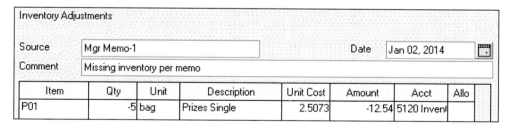

Incorrect Inventory Adjustment journal entry

Inventory Adjustments Journal Entry Jan 02, 2014 (J7)			
Account Number	Account Description	Debits	Credits
5120	Inventory Adjustments	12.54	-
1280	Inventory -Prizes	-	12.54
Additional Date:	Additional Field:		
		12.54	12.54

You need to record a correction entry as shown next:

1 ➤ Click the **INVENTORY & SERVICES** module, click the **Adjust Inventory** icon.

2 ➤ Enter the **correct** entry shown as follows:

Inventory Adjustments								
Source	Correct J7				Date	Jan 02, 2014		
Comment	Correction of missing inventory per memo							

Item	Qty	Unit	Description	Unit Cost	Amount	Acct	Allo	
P01	5	bag	Prizes Single	2.5073	12.54	5120 Invenl		
P04	-15	bag	Prizes Double Bag	2.8056	-42.08	5120 Invenl		

Correcting entry

Inventory Adjustments Journal Entry Jan 02, 2014 (J22)			
Account Number	Account Description	Debits	Credits
1280	Inventory -Prizes	-	29.54
5120	Inventory Adjustments	29.54	-
Additional Date:	Additional Field:		
		29.54	29.54

3 ➤ **Post** when correct. Return to the Home window.

Correcting Build from Inventory Assembly Journal Entries

Exercise 13-12 – Correcting Build from Inventory Assembly

The manager sent a memo to set up 10 Games Loot Bag #1 as a promotional sales item using the Bill of Materials Journal.

This adjustment assumes the bookkeeper used the Build from Item Assembly Journal. This procedure may also be used to set up or cancel inventory items that do not occur on a regular basis.

The clerk set up the loot bag in error as shown next. There is no Adjust icon, and you cannot display a posted Item Assembly Journal.

Original Item Assembly Journal

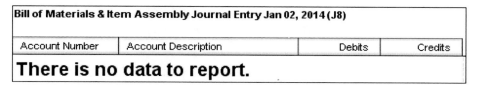

Build from Item Assembly	▼					
Source	Mgr Memo-2			Date	Jan 02, 2014	🗓
Comment	Set up Games Loot Bags					

Assembly Components

Item	Qty	Unit	Description	Unit Cost	Amount
G-W-1	10	box	Games Wooden Medium size 1	5.2813	52.81
G-P-1	10	box	Games-Plastic Medium size 1	5.50	55.00
G-M1	10	box	Games-Metal Spring	6.5205	65.21

	Additional Costs	
	Total	173.02

Assembled Items

Item	Qty	Unit	Description	Unit Cost	Amount
GLB-1	10	Each	Games Loot Bag 1	17.302	173.02

	Total	173.02

Original Item Assembly entry

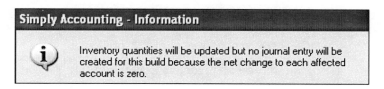

Bill of Materials & Item Assembly Journal Entry Jan 02, 2014 (J8)

Account Number	Account Description	Debits	Credits

There is no data to report.

It appears that journal entry #8 with no amounts is created when the original entry is posted, but entry #8 is not created.

> **Simply Accounting - Information**
>
> ⓘ Inventory quantities will be updated but no journal entry will be created for this build because the net change to each affected account is zero.

It is a transfer within the INVENTORY module. The Games Loot Bags use the same General Ledger linked accounts as the individual games items and there is no Journal entry created.

To Reverse an Item Assembly

1 ➤ Click the **Build from Item Assembly** icon. Leave the choice as **Build from Item Assembly**.

2 ➤ To **reverse** the setup of the Games Loot Bag, type the following information into the Item Assembly Journal as shown next.

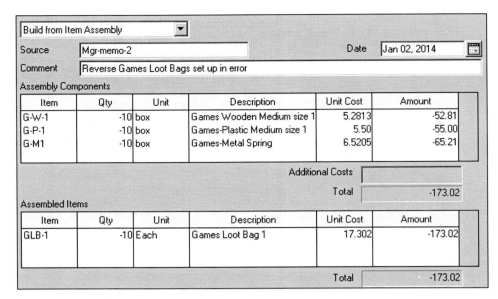

If you display the Journal, you will see:

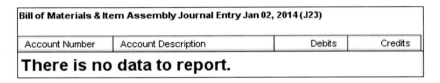

3 ➤ Post the entry when correct.

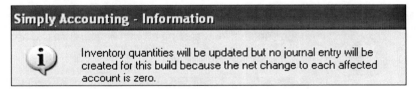

4 ➤ Click **OK** to continue. Click **OK** again.

You will see an Inventory Low report.

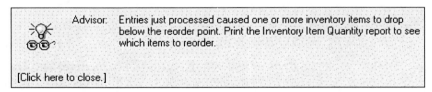

5 ➤ Ignore this report for this exercise. Click in the **box** to continue. **Return** to the Home window.

To set up the proper 10 Games Loot Bag #1 as a promotional sales item using the Bill of Materials Journal, complete the following steps. Refer to Exercise 8-21.

To set up the Build from Bill of Materials Loot Bag Build Information

1 ➤ Click the **Inventory & Services** icon (in Tasks area).

2 ➤ Locate and double-click **Games Loot Bag 1 GLB-1** icon.

3 ➤ Click on the **Build** tab.

4 ➤ Type the information as shown.

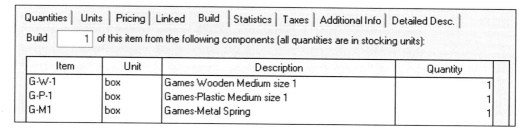

5 ➤ Click the Save and Close button. **Exit** to return to the Home window.

To Create the Loot Bag Using the Build from Bill of Materials Journal

1 ➤ Click the **Build from Bill of Materials** icon.

2 ➤ Type the information shown next.

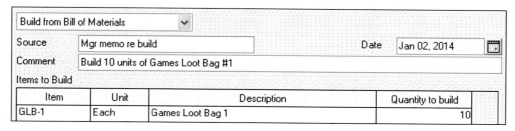

If you display the Journal, you will see:

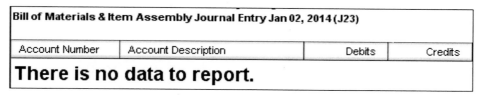

3 ➤ **Post** the entry when correct.

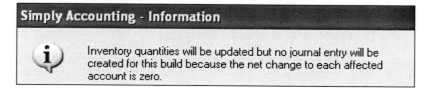

4 ➤ Click **OK** to continue. **Exit** to the Home window.

5 ➤ To confirm that the 10 units have been built, display the **Inventory Summary** or **Inventory Quantity report** to see the 10 units created.

6 ➤ **Print** Journal entries All (with corrections) for January 02, 2014.

Simply Accounting by Sage Premium 2009 Student Version B Software Installation Instructions

This Appendix assumes you are loading the *Simply Accounting by Sage Premium 2009 Student Version* software, which was included with this textbook, on a Standalone computer.

You do not need to have Internet access from the computer where you are installing the Student Edition software, but you will need Internet Access to register the software and receive the appropriate activation key code. See Exercise A-3, step 5.

Please read the following "Installing Simply Accounting" important information. The instructions in this Appendix assume that you are installing Simply Accounting, using a Full Install, on a standalone computer. *Simply Accounting Premium 2009 Student Edition* should not be installed on a server or network and the authors are not responsible for server or network installation problems.

Installing Simply Accounting

When you install Simply Accounting, you need to know how many computers must have access to your company data and how your company's computers are set up.

Is your company data stored on a file server?

If your company data is, or will be, stored on a Windows file server, perform a **Data-only** installation of Simply Accounting on your server. This option installs the MySQL Connector and the Simply Accounting Connection Manager service that manages all connections to your company data. It **does not** install the Simply Accounting program. To learn more, see Standard Network setup below.

Note that if you store your data on a Windows Server (2003, 2008, or Small Business Server 2003), you need to perform additional setup tasks so that other users can access your Simply Accounting data.

Additional setup tasks for Windows Server 2003
Additional setup tasks for Windows Server 2008
Additional setup tasks for Windows Small Business Server 2003

Using Linux?

You can also store your data on a number of supported Linux servers. To learn more about supported Linux distributions, and to download the Simply Accounting Connection Manager for Linux, visit www.simplyaccounting.com/install.

Standalone Computer

User PC

Full Install company data

This is the most common installation choice for small businesses.

Choose if:

You only need to use Simply Accounting on one computer.

You or your system administrator need to:

Perform a Full Installation of Simply Accounting on your computer.

A portion of the information available in Fig. A-6b "Installing Simply Accounting". Credit Sage Software, Inc.

Make sure your computer meets the system requirements below for optimal performance.

The System Requirements are:

- Pentium ® III [or equivalent], 1 GHz or higher (Pentium 4, 2GHz recommended).
- 512 MB RAM (1 GB recommended)
- 820 MB hard disk space [additional 100 MB of hard disk space needed for installation]
- Internet Explorer 5.5 SP2
- Microsoft® Windows® 2000, XP or Vista
- 256 colour or higher SVGA monitor optimized for 1024 x 768; supports 800 X 600 with small fonts
- ACT! By Sage integrations requires ACT! 2008 or ACT! 2009
- CD-ROM Drive
- Forms that can be sent via e-mail require MAPI compliant e-mail client, Internet connection, e-mail service and word processor
- Word and Excel integration requires Microsoft Word and Microsoft Excel 2003 or 2007
- Outlook© synchronization requires Microsoft Outlook® 2003 or 2007. (Simply Accounting Premium and higher)
- Mouse

If you do not have Word, Excel or Outlook as noted, you can still use Simply.

Restrictions and other information

The student edition of the 2009 Premium software has the following restrictions:

1. Can be used for a maximum of 14 months (425 days), after which the software will expire.

2. Can NOT open data created in previous versions.

3. You will NOT be able to convert data from this version into future student versions.

4. Technical support may be available from instructors, or for a fee from the Simply technical support number.

Exercise A-1: Modifying the Microsoft Windows Firewall

The Simply program installation works best with Microsoft Windows Firewall. The author's firewall was not compatible with Simply and had to be disabled. The following instructions are for setting up the Microsoft Windows firewall.

1 ➤ Click the **Start** icon, move to **Settings**, click **Control Panel**, double-click

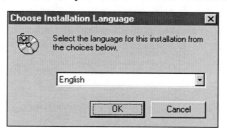

with a selection of **On (recommended)** as shown. Click **OK** to accept the setting and **X** to return to the Home Window.

Exercise A-2: Installing the Simply Student Release B Software

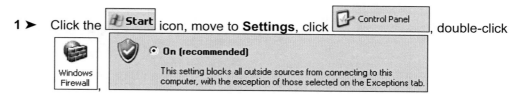

1 ➤ Insert the **Simply 2009** program into the CD-ROM drive. The CD should load automatically.

If you do not see Fig. A-1, the software did not load. Click **Start, Run, Browse**, locate your **CD-ROM drive** SA_2009BCP1 (E:) . *Note*: your drive letter may be different than (E). Double-click **Launch.exe**; click **OK** at the Run window. You may not see the exe in Launch. You should see Fig. A-1.

Fig. A-1: Choose Installation Language.

2 ➤ Select **OK**.

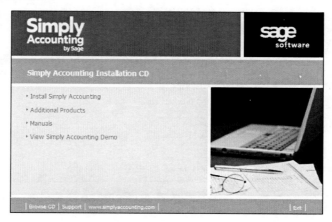

Fig. A-2: Install window.

3 ➤ Click on **Install Simply Accounting**. You may have to double-click depending on your computer. Please wait for the InstallShield Wizard to prepare the setup to guide you through the setup process.

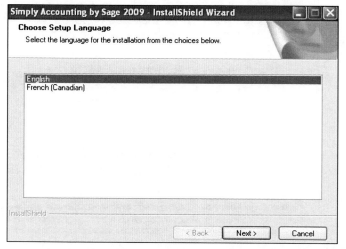

Fig. A-3a: InstallShield Wizard- Choose Setup Language.

4 ➤ Click Next > . Please wait for the InstallShield Wizard to prepare the setup to guide you through the setup process.

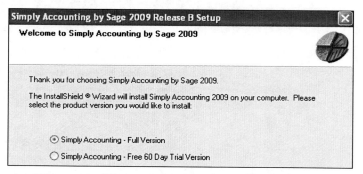

Fig. A-3b: InstallShield Wizard- Select Version.

5 ➤ Do NOT click Free 60 Day Trial Version, as you would only be able to use the software for 60 days. With a selection of **Simply Accounting - Full Version**, click Next > .

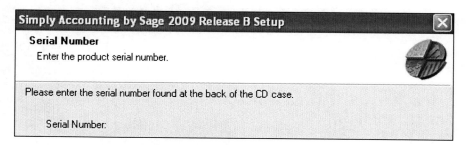

Fig. A-4: Release B Setup window

6 ➤ Serial Number **Type the information as shown**:

The serial number is also on the CD label. Click Next > .

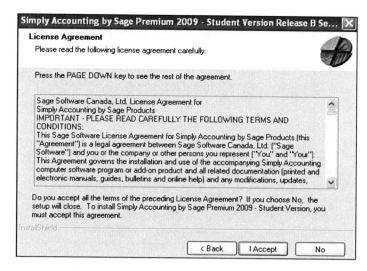

Fig. A-5: License Agreement.

7 ➤ Review the window information. If you choose No, the setup installation will close. To install the Student Version, you must accept this agreement. Click ⎮ **I Accept** ⎮.

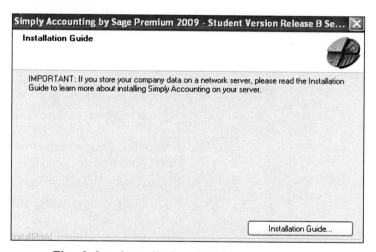

Fig. A-6a: Installation Guide.

8 ➤ Click on the ⎮**Installation Guide**⎮ button. You will see information about installing on a network. It is not recommended that you install the Student version on a network.

9 ➤ Click on the **Maximize** ☐ button. The window on the right side "Installing Simply Accounting" is the same as the information on page 1 of this Appendix.

10 ➤ At the top on the right side, if you click on ⎮ 🔲 Show All ⎮ the information in the middle of the page at Standard Network expands to display Networking information. As noted previously, this Appendix is using a Full Install on a standalone computer.

11 ➤ Click ⎮ 🔲 Hide All ⎮ to close the Networking information.

12 ➤   Move the vertical bar in the middle to the right until you see the following:

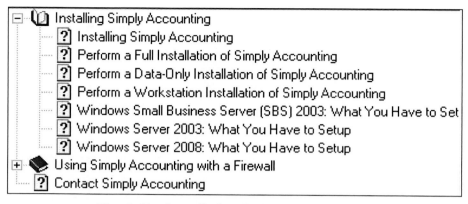

Fig. A-6b: Installation Guide details.

The first item; Installing Simply Accounting is the same as the form on page 1 of this Appendix.

The second item; Perform a Full Install of Simply Accounting is similar to this Appendix. This Appendix has a number of changes for students.

The third and fourth items; *The Data-Only* and *Workstation Install of Simply* will not be discussed in this Appendix. As noted on page 1, Simply Accounting 2009 Student Edition should not be installed on a network and the authors are not responsible for network installation problems.

You can also click the ⊞ at Using Simply Accounting with a Firewall to see:

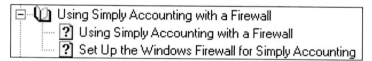

Fig. A-6c: Installation Guide Firewall details.

You may click these items to see what Simply exe files will be added to your system. See Fig. A-6d to see the exe files.

13 ➤   Click ☒ to close the Installation Guide information. Click ⌐**Next >**¬.

If you are not using the Windows Firewall, you will see the following window:

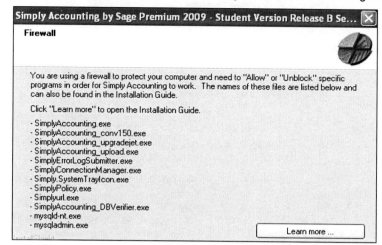

Fig. A-6d:　Installation Guide Firewall files to accept.

If you click Learn more..., you will see the information at Fig. A-6b.

If you are using the Windows firewall, you do not need to make any changes. You are not setting up a network.

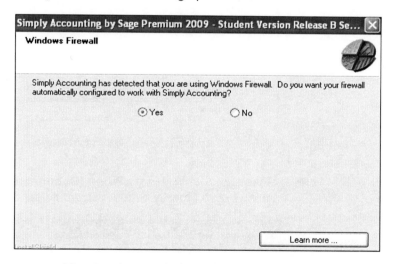

Fig. A-7:　Windows Firewall.

If you were to click on Learn More..., you would see the information in Fig. A-6c regarding *Using Simply Accounting with a Firewall*. Click X to return.

14 ➤　　Click Next >.

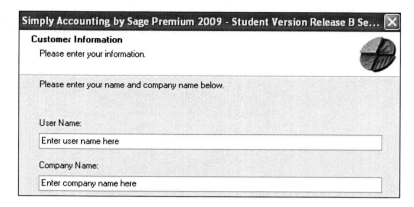

Fig. A-8: Customer Information

15 ➤ User Name   Type in your **actual student name**, `Tab`.

16 ➤ Company Name Type in your **actual student name**. Do **NOT** type a company name, as the registration will be rejected later. You must use your own name. `Tab`, click `Next >`.

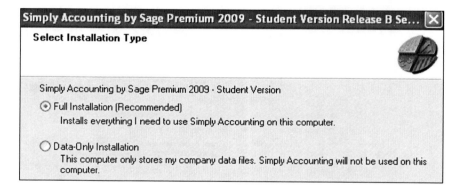

Fig. A-9: Select Installation Type.

17 ➤ Make sure that **Full Installation (Recommended)** is selected. If you clicked on the `Learn More...` button, you would see Fig. A-6b. Click `Next>`.

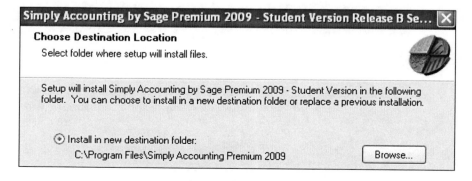

Fig. A-10a: Choose Destination Folder.

The author's suggested path (destination folder) should include the name Student Version for identification.

18 ➤ Click `Browse...`.

19 ➤ Type **Student Version** as shown. Click **OK**.

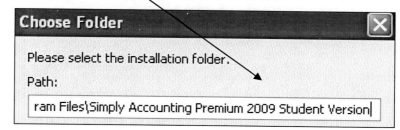

Fig. A-10b: Amended path with Student Version name.

 Note: Your path may have Student Version wording on two lines.

○ Install in new destination folder:

C:\Program Files\Simply Accounting Premium 2009 Student
Version   Browse...

20 ➤ Click Next >.

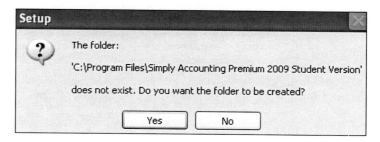

Fig. A-10c: Confirm Folder path.

21 ➤ Click **Yes** to create the folder.

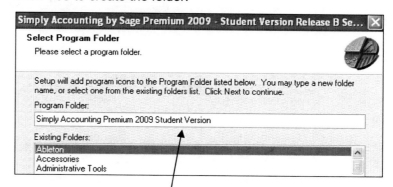

Fig. A-10d: Select Program Folder (after name change).

22 ➤ Program folder Type **Student Version** as shown. Minor bug in Simply that it does not carry the name Student Version forward. The *Existing Folder* names may be different on your computer. Click Next >.

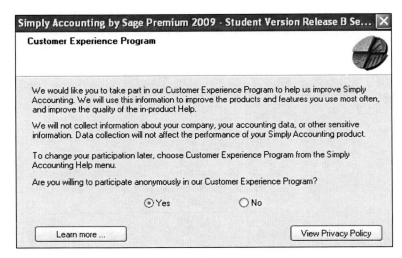

Fig. A-11: Customer Experience Program.

In 2009, the Customer Experience Program is available for students.

23 ➤ With a selection of Yes, I will participate or No, I will not participate, click Next > .

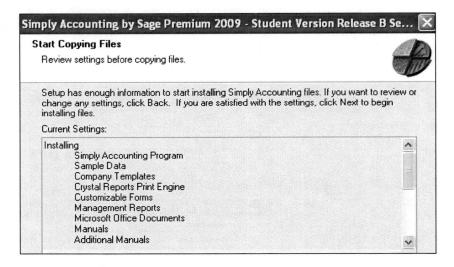

Fig. A-12: Start Copying Files (Installing files).

24 ➤ Click Next > .

Do NOT click Cancel or turn off the computer. Simply installs the program in the folder identified in Fig. A-10c. Depending on the speed of your computer, this may take a few minutes. **Wait** for Fig. A-13 to appear. You will see the following window.

 Simply by Sage announces that Simply CARE is not required and is not available for the student version, because the payroll function allowing them to perform automatic payroll calculations is included with the student edition.

When students purchase the full retail product (not student edition) they can purchase any of the Simply CARE Products.

 Simply by Sage announces that Simply CARE Elite Support is not available for the student version. When students purchase the full retail product (not student edition) they can purchase any of the Simply CARE Elite Support.

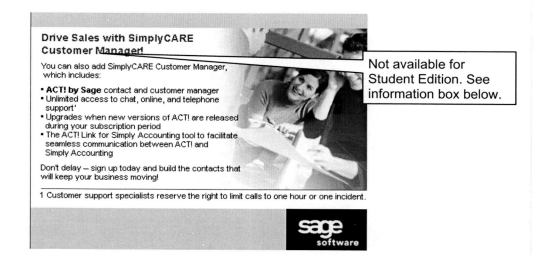

Not available for Student Edition. See information box below.

 Simply by Sage announces that Simply CARE Customer Manager is not available for the student version. When students purchase the full retail product (not student edition) they can purchase Customer Manager.

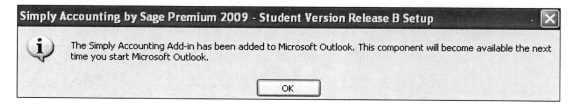

Fig. A-13: Microsoft Outlook.

25 ➤ Click **OK**. There is no exercise in the text to use Microsoft Outlook. Depending on the speed of your computer, this may take a few minutes. **Wait** for Fig. A-14 to appear.

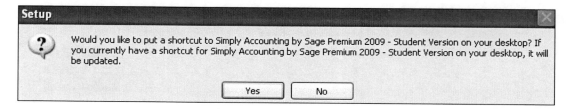

Fig. A-14: Shortcut.

26 ➤ Click **Yes** to create a shortcut on your desktop.

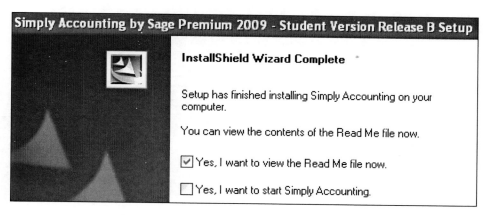

Fig. A-15: *Install Wizard Complete*

 Do NOT remove the Simply CD-ROM at this time or you will see a Blue Screen or a similar program error window,

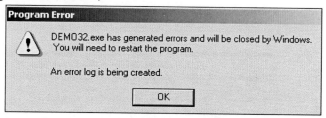

which indicates major errors and you will have to complete all the instructions again.

 If you leave the ☑ checked at Yes, I want to view the Read Me file now, you may see information about late changes to the Simply program. There are no changes to the Student version.

```
    Late Program Changes for Simply Accounting 2009

This file contains information that is not included
in the Simply Accounting manuals, or that has changed
since the manuals were published. We suggest that you
print this file and note all changes in the manuals.

Thank you for selecting this product from Sage Software
```

Fig. A-16: *Late Changes information.*

Click **X** to close the Notepad window.

27 ➤   Click to put a ✓ checkmark at **Yes, I want to start Simply Accounting.** Click **Finish,** and you will see windows similar to:

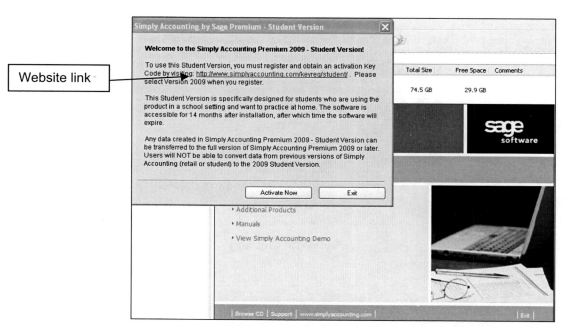

Website link

Fig. A-17: Register and Activation window and Installation window.

Exercise A-3: Student Registration and Activation

1 ➤   Click on the **website** link, and you are taken to the Simply Accounting by Sage, Student Version Registration window.

If you do not have Internet access from your own computer, write the website link address on a piece of paper, or type it in a word processing document. You can use the school Internet access by typing the website into the Internet Address window and link to the Simply website.

2 ➤   Click on **Version 2009 (Premium)**.

3 ➤   Complete the **Company Name** (your student name) and **Email Address** fields. As mentioned before, do **NOT** type a company name, as the registration will be rejected. You must use your own name. You may also fill the information in the lower section.

4 ➤   Click **Submit** (lower down in the window). You should receive an immediate response (Serial Number and Key Codes) as shown below as well as an e-mail response.

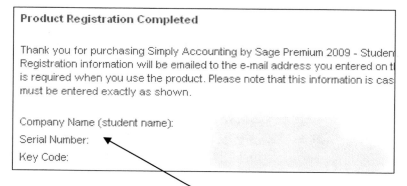

5 ➤   The author has removed the student name, Serial Number and Key Code from the above image. **Exit** from your Internet browser.

6 ➤   **Open** your e-mail program and you should have received the activation codes. **Print** the document. It will be easier to enter the codes if you can read them. Put the document in a safe place in case you need to reinstall the software.

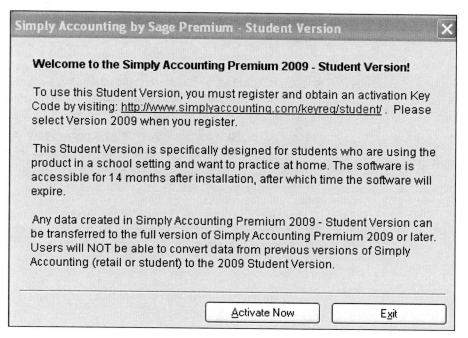

7 ➤   Click the **Activate Now** button.

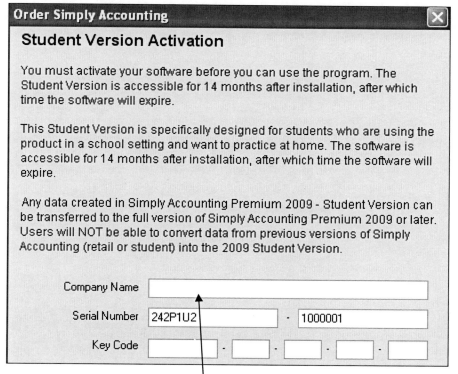

8 ➤ Company Name   Enter **your name** in the field exactly as it is spelled in the documents received.

9 ➤ Key Code   Enter the **Key Code** as indicated in the document. All letters must be entered in CAPITAL letters. Click **OK** when complete.

If you receive an error message, carefully double check the code again.

10 ➤   Click **OK**.

11 ➤   You will see the Simply Premium window similar to Fig. 1-1a in Chapter 1. Click **Exit** to return to the Installation window. It is assumed that you have not completed Chapter 1, Exercise 1-1: Unzipping the Master Data Files from the CD.

12 ➤   Click **Exit** to close the Installation window. After the Installation window is removed, you can remove the Simply CD-ROM.

Complete text Exercise 1-1 to unzip the Master Data Files and continue with the text exercises.

If you didn't get a chance to enter the Activation code at Exercise A-3, step 7, you can Activate later. When you open Simply Accounting to start the program, you will be prompted to enter the Activation code then.

Index

Work Logbook for Simply Accounting Premium 2009   *See Exercise 1-24, Maintaining a Logbook.*

Date	Backup #	Data Information (Where you get to each class)	Name of File in Storage Location
Sept 08	1	Finished Ex. 1-13, page 1-44	01_Photos_Sep_08_2009a